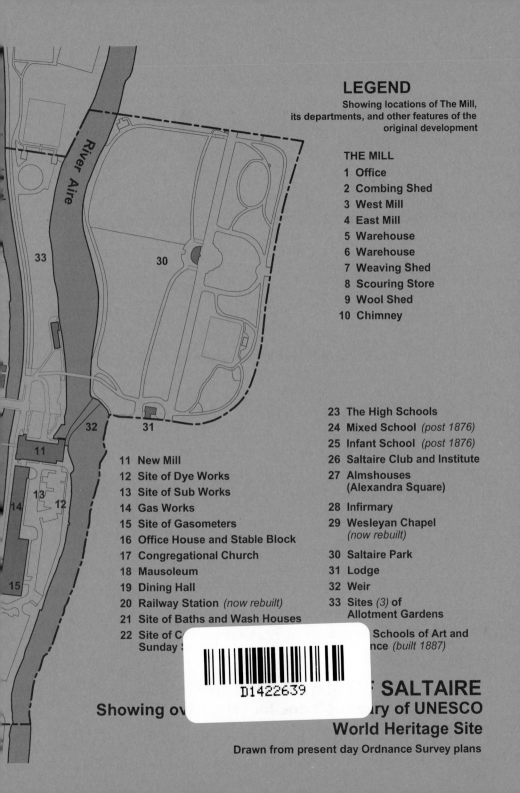

LEGEND

Showing locations of The Mill, its departments, and other features of the original development

THE MILL

1 Office
2 Combing Shed
3 West Mill
4 East Mill
5 Warehouse
6 Warehouse
7 Weaving Shed
8 Scouring Store
9 Wool Shed
10 Chimney

11 New Mill
12 Site of Dye Works
13 Site of Sub Works
14 Gas Works
15 Site of Gasometers
16 Office House and Stable Block
17 Congregational Church
18 Mausoleum
19 Dining Hall
20 Railway Station *(now rebuilt)*
21 Site of Baths and Wash Houses
22 Site of C͏.͏.͏.͏.͏
    Sunday S͏.͏.͏.͏

23 The High Schools
24 Mixed School *(post 1876)*
25 Infant School *(post 1876)*
26 Saltaire Club and Institute
27 Almshouses
    (Alexandra Square)
28 Infirmary
29 Wesleyan Chapel
    (now rebuilt)
30 Saltaire Park
31 Lodge
32 Weir
33 Sites *(3)* of
    Allotment Gardens
    ͏.͏.͏. Schools of Art and
    ͏.͏.͏.nce *(built 1887)*

͏.͏.͏.F SALTAIRE

Showing ov͏.͏.͏. ͏.͏.͏.ry of UNESCO
World Heritage Site

Drawn from present day Ordnance Survey plans

D1422639

BALGARNIE'S

SALT

BALGARNIE'S

SALT

With commentary and additions

by

Barlo and Shaw

Nemine Juvante (Saltaire) Publications
2003

Cover Design by David Weber

ISBN 0 9545840 0 7

Printed in Great Britain by Hart and Clough Ltd., Ezra House, West 26 Business Park, Cleckheaton, West Yorkshire, BD19 4TQ.

First published by Nemine Juvante (Saltaire) Publications 2003.

About the writers Barlo and Shaw

Barlo and Dave Shaw are amateur historians with a passion for Saltaire.

Barlo hails from 'a little town called Littletown,' within what was known as the heavy woollen district of the West Riding of Yorkshire. Born of Nonconformist, teetotal and conscientious-objector parents, he recognises the values of the religious community in which Salt and Balgarnie placed themselves. After attending a succession of schools in the area, Barlo chose not to follow his father into the mill, pursuing instead a career as a draughtsman in the building and construction industry. His work took him to the Netherlands for three years, and involved time in Saudi Arabia and North Africa. In the early 1970s, two years were spent as Assistant Resident Engineer on the Robin Hood's Bay sea wall project. For the last 20 years Barlo has worked freelance, discarding the drawing board and slide rule in favour of digital technology and computer-aided systems. Barlo retains an ability also to discard consonants at the start and end of many of his words - a feature that extends to his use of his surname - and regards Morecambe and Wise as our country's greatest statesmen.

Dave Shaw is a recently retired scientist whose previous publications were chiefly the results of meteorological research. Born and raised in Bradford, where he attended Hanson Grammar School, Dave graduated in mathematics at Manchester University before joining the Meteorological Office. Research occupied the first half of his career, following which he moved into operations and training. He spent a year working for the United Nations in Cairo, Egypt, and four years at the European Centre for Medium Range Weather Forecasts, Reading. His last post in the Meteorological Office was as its head of International Relations. He was for several years the Honorary General Secretary of the Royal Meteorological Society, and for ten years a local government councillor in Bracknell. An admirer of Bradford's several generations of textile workers, Dave worked briefly in the industry during student vacations at Bradford Corporation's Conditioning House – 'Happy days with good people.'

About this book

This book is an unusual publication insofar as part of it was written in the 19th century, and the remainder in the 21st century.

In the 10 months following the death of Sir Titus Salt in December 1876, Reverend Robert Balgarnie wrote a biography of Sir Titus, the founder of Saltaire, whose vision and industry continue to be recognized in the present day. This first biography of Sir Titus is now a collector's item – long out of print, difficult to find, and too expensive for many would-be purchasers. The original text of the biography is faithfully reproduced here, and that text forms the main part of this present book.

The author Balgarnie, writing the biography in 1877, was not addressing an audience of the 21st century. Whilst his words remain an invaluable and highly readable account of the life of Sir Titus, the present day reader will inevitably be less familiar with the circumstances and characters that Balgarnie refers to in his 19th century account than would have originally been the case. As present day writers, we have provided over 350 footnotes of commentary and additions to accompany Balgarnie's text, and augmented the six illustrations of the original with other plans and images. Helped by historian and writer Patricia McNaughton we have also added appendices which we hope bring further to life the story of Salt and Saltaire.

The motive for writing the first biography is clearly stated by the Congregational minister Balgarnie in his opening chapter: 'to stimulate young men at the outset of their career'. Such a motive reflects the times and values of the original writer. In bringing the biography back to life 126 years later, we too had equally clear objectives, which were perhaps equally reflective of our times and our values. Firstly we wanted to republish Balgarnie's biography of Sir Titus Salt in commemoration of the bicentenary of Sir Titus' birth and the 150th anniversary of the opening of his mill at Saltaire, so as to afford today's readers the opportunity of an appreciation of Salt's achievements. Secondly, we wanted to seek to recover the costs of republishing through sales. Thirdly we wanted to have fun doing it. The first and third objectives have been achieved, and if you the reader buy this book, you will be helping us achieve our second objective – for which we thank you!

In reproducing the text of Balgarnie's book, it has been electronically scanned and checked, with the intention of producing a faithful copy of the original words, punctuation, font, etc. During this process we encountered commendably few editing errors in the original text. Only in the very few cases where such an error was judged to be unquestionably accidental have we corrected it; in cases of any doubt we have been faithful to the original.

So as not to impede the flow of Balgarnie's account, the additional illustrations which have been introduced have been placed appropriately in relevant appendices, or specifically in Appendix 8, rather than within the author's original text.

There is much more that has been told, and remains to be told, of Salt and Saltaire than appears in these pages. We look forward to a future when access to information will be far better than it is today, and when the appreciation of our heritage is shared and celebrated by all. We hope you, in reading this book, are left with an increased pride in that heritage.

Finally we hope Rev. R. Balgarnie would have approved of our work.

Barlo   *Dave Shaw*

Saltaire, September, 2003

Foreword

Protestantism and the spirit of capitalism were closely linked – as Max Weber argued, against Karl Marx, in his classic study. Titus Salt provides a classic example of the protestant capitalist, as this volume illustrates. The drive to justify one's life through hard work and enterprise, the self-imposed obligation to share one's success through charitable giving, the reluctance to flaunt wealth through luxurious living: all these elements are evident throughout the book. At the age of fifty, he contemplated retirement from business. He could have bought himself a landed estate, with an impressive country house; he had already leased Methley Park from the Earl of Mexborough. From there he would have acquired a title, and his family would have been absorbed into the English aristocracy. Instead, he consolidated his five Bradford mills into a grand new enterprise, combining business with philanthropy and social improvement, and built Saltaire.

The nineteenth century represented the high period of non-conformity. Quakers, Congregationalists, Methodists and Unitarians, already well-represented in the towns and trades, rose to wealth through the industrial revolution, and to political influence through the Reform Acts. They were paternalistic towards their workers – as the young Titus's behaviour in the 1825-6 woolcombers' strike in Bradford indicates – but actively concerned about 'moral improvement' of workers' lives and conditions. They built chapels, schools and Sunday Schools, libraries and institutes. Their faith gave them a strong sense of moral certainty; and their success in business strengthened that sense. The Congregational Church in these years, the book makes clear, was an important political, social and economic network. Crossleys and Salts shared religious ties, as well as commercial and industrial interests; Titus Salt junior linked these two industrial families even more closely by marrying Catherine Crossley. Bradford's first mayors, after the town's incorporation, were drawn in succession from the congregation of Horton Lane Chapel.

This is a devotional biography, by a Congregationalist minister, intended 'to stimulate young men at the outset of their career, by such a rare example of sterling principle, of indomitable perseverance, of resolute will, of thoughtful and patient toil, that led up to fortune and honour', and to teach the moral that 'the resources were within himself...and a Hand higher than his developed and directed them.' This is a doctrine of justification by works, at least as much as by faith. Balgarnie portrays Titus Salt as deeply conscious of the limitations of his faith for much of his life, but of striving to justify his life through success on this earth and through sharing part of his success with the less fortunate. The confidence of Congregationalists that success in business reflected the quality of their lives as well as the development of the market is shown in Henry Forbes' reported remark: 'Titus, we seem to prosper in business in proportion as we give.' Titus gave a great deal for the erection of chapels, and also for churches within the Church of England; but he also supported education in the broadest sense, and became involved in a wide range of charities. The biography also makes clear, however, that he lived in increasingly grand style, both at Crow's Nest and at Methley Park. He generously entertained his workers on special occasions, but he also developed a taste for exotic plants and fruits, and must have depended upon a large household of servants (hardly mentioned in the volume).

He could alternatively have moved on to a career in national politics. His political platform, as a reformer, was radical for the time; one item in his platform, the removal of bishops from the House of Lords, has still not been reached. He had been a successful magistrate, and mayor of Bradford; but his established style as a man of few words did not fit Westminster. It is evident that he did not like the parliamentary game. He never spoke, and he resigned his seat to W. E. Forster, a friend and associate, who pursued much more effectively the reformist cause of extending education to the masses.

At the beginning of the 21st century, critics of corporate capitalism are pressing the agenda of 'corporate social responsibility' onto reluctant chief executives. For many companies, corporate social responsibility is a necessary peripheral activity, to have something positive to say in their Annual Report and to improve their corporate image. Titus Salt, on the contrary, believed that social responsibility and success in business were inextricably linked. His deep involvement in public service throughout his life, his record of charitable donations, above all the care he devoted to the social and educational facilities of Saltaire, mark him out as a conscientious capitalist of the first rank. He was, nevertheless, a capitalist businessman of his time, hesitant about the ten hour day, slow in introducing the Saturday half-holiday, deeply opposed to combinations of workers in unions. But by the standards of his time his willingness to devote a significant proportion of his wealth to public (as well as religious) causes, and to support the political movement for reform, educational and social improvement, justify the erection of statues and the honours that he received in his old age. And Saltaire is his most impressive monument.

William Wallace

Rev. Robert Balgarnie

Acknowledgements

We would like to thank the many friends and colleagues who have helped in the research and preparation of this book. Although drawn from a variety of backgrounds and in many cases unknown to each other, they have a common bond - they have given their help freely and kindly, which is cause in itself for celebration.

We are particularly indebted to Patricia M. McNaughton. Patricia is an Elder of St. Andrew's United Reformed Church, Ramshill, Scarborough (formerly South Cliff Congregational Church), where the author Balgarnie ministered and where Sir Titus Salt often worshipped. Patricia's knowledge of Balgarnie is both precious and unrivalled, and her writing of the appendix on Balgarnie is much appreciated.

Special thanks are due to Lord Wallace of Saltaire for writing the Foreword. More than that, Lord Wallace suggested improvements to an early draft of our commentary that led us to produce a more informed final version.

Denys Salt's outstanding role in preserving and promoting the heritage of Salt and Saltaire is recognized by all those actively involved in the subject. This book is just one project among many that he has aided over a great many years, and we thank Denys for his advice, his encouragement and his friendship.

Clive Woods was heavily involved in the early part of our project, and indeed it was through Clive that we came to know each other; we thank Clive for his help and advice.

We applaud the creative talents and enthusiasm of David Weber. His design of the cover of our book is but one example of how David has given his unreserved support to our project.

Writers of local history are inevitably drawn into largely unseen networks of local history groups, individual enthusiasts, professional librarians and archivists. It is from these ranks that one draws the bulk of new information and research, and we here pay tribute to the many members of that community. Alyson Wilson of the Clapham Society provided key information about the Salt family in Clapham. Shirley Oxenbridge and her colleagues in the Tunbridge Wells Family History Society helped greatly in tracing the whereabouts of Salt's daughters in their later lives. Gill Huggins (Bathampton Local History Society), Arthur Green and Denys Clarke provided invaluable help in tracing Edward Salt's time in Bathampton. Christopher Ketchell and June Bogie gave considerable help regarding the orphanage in Hull, to which Sir Titus gave financial support. Tish Lawson provided valuable and newly researched information on Edward Salt and Charles Stead.

Julie Woodward, Carol Greenwood and Andrew George are librarians and archivists whose advice is as appreciated as it is unstinted.

Hutchinson Whitlam Associates were both helpful and tolerant of our many calls on their facilities, which they provided freely. We benefited from the technical advice of Stuart Brown concerning the possible quarry sources of Saltaire's masonry. We have not addressed the subject greatly in our commentary, and are convinced that it is sufficiently novel and important to merit further attention in its own right.

Abney Park Trust and Dr. Williams's Library, of London, are invaluable sources of information on the Nonconformist movement, and their volunteers and staff are heartily thanked.

The previously unpublished photograph of Rev. Robert Balgarnie, which appears on both the cover of this book and within it, is reproduced by kind permission of the Minister and Elders of St. Andrew's United Reformed Church, Ramshill, Scarborough, formerly South Cliff Congregational Church.

Elaine Sutton has taken us to task in the most constructive way possible, and helped us eliminate the majority of errors in our draft versions of this book. We claim exclusive ownership of, and responsibility for, all remaining errors.

Most of our meetings to plan the book took place in the Boat House Inn, Saltaire, and we thank landlord Stephen Ashworth for his hospitality and good beer.

Finally, for their patience and understanding, we thank Ann & Liz........

Yours ever
Titus Salt

SIR TITUS SALT,
BARONET:

HIS LIFE AND ITS LESSONS.

BY

REV. R. BALGARNIE,

Minister of the South Cliff Church, Scarborough.

With Portrait and Photographic Illustrations.

LONDON:

HODDER AND STOUGHTON,
PATERNOSTER ROW.

MDCCCLXXVII.

S. W. THEAKSTON & CO., PRINTERS, SCARBOROUGH.

TO

DOWAGER LADY SALT,

Of Crow Nest,

THIS MEMOIR OF HIM WITH WHOM HER OWN

LIFE WAS UNITED FORTY-SEVEN YEARS,

IS RESPECTFULLY DEDICATED,

AS A HUMBLE OFFERING OF AFFECTION,

BOTH TO THE LIVING AND THE DEAD,

BY

THE AUTHOR.

PREFACE.

THIS work has been written during the summer season, and amid the pressing duties that a large sea-side congregation entails. We are fully aware of its many imperfections; but, such as it is, we send it forth. It has been, throughout, a labour of love, which we have gladly performed, in memory of one whose long friendship has been to us, both an honour and a privilege. Though the lack of material, especially in connection with his earlier years, has rendered our task more difficult than we anticipated, yet we have done our best. If the record of such a life shall furnish the reader with an example worthy of imitation,—if it shall stimulate him to lofty purpose, —above all, if it shall induce him to regulate his course by Christian principles, and "to seek those things which are above,"—the highest desires of the writer will be attained.

Scarborough, November, 1877.

CONTENTS.

CHAPTER I.

PAGE

CHAPTER II.

CHAPTER III.

CHAPTER IV.

CHAPTER V.

CHAPTER VI.

CHAPTER VII.

CHAPTER VIII.

CHAPTER IX.

CHAPTER X.

CHAPTER XI.

CHAPTER XII.

CHAPTER XIII.

CHAPTER XIV.

CHAPTER XV.

CHAPTER XVI.

CHAPTER XVII.

CHAPTER XVIII.

CHAPTER XIX.

CHAPTER XX.

ILLUSTRATIONS.

The above illustrations feature in the original book.
For further illustrations see Appendix 8.

SIR TITUS SALT, BARONET:

HIS LIFE AND ITS LESSONS.

"Friend of the suffering! helper of the weak!

Poor words are all that now we can afford,

Unless where tears of deeper homage speak

Or silent reverence hails the worth supreme

Which made thy life one good-diffusing beam."

—A.W.[1]

CHAPTER I.

INTRODUCTORY.

"Wherefore, I praise the dead, which are already dead, more than the living which are yet alive."—*Ecclesiastes.*[2]

WHEN the grave closed over the honoured remains of Sir Titus Salt, and his name and virtues were on many lips, a wish was expressed that a biography of him should be written. From the various sketches that had appeared in the London and provincial press, as well as from local publications, that had been widely circulated, the more remarkable facts of his history were already known; but it was naturally supposed that a public man, like Sir Titus, whose name was "a household word" in the neighbourhood where he lived, whose fame had

---

[1] Anna Letitia Waring (1823-1891) was a well known hymn writer and poet. A Quaker, she was a member of the Clapham Sect (Ref: DNB).

[2] Ecclesiastes Chapter 4 Verse 2.

spread far and wide, whose commercial and philanthropic enterprises were pre-eminent,—must have many other incidents in his life, which some biographer would bring to light, and which the public would be eager to know. Who the biographer should be, was a question the present writer would have answered by selecting an author well known to the public; but it had not once entered into his mind that to a hand so unskilled as his would be confided the work. The responsibility of the selection, therefore, rests not with himself, but with the Publishers, who thought that "a short memoir of Sir Titus Salt should be prepared which might be useful to place in the hands of young men." It is in compliance with their request, that this Memoir is written, and expressly with the object in view thus indicated—to stimulate young men at the outset of their career, by such a rare example of sterling principle, of indomitable perseverance, of resolute will, of thoughtful and patient toil, that led up to fortune and honour, for, as we shall afterwards see, it was not from any adventitious circumstance of birth or affluence, not from "good luck" or the patronage of others, that Sir Titus rose to greatness. No: the resources were within himself. The forces were innate, and a Hand higher than his own developed and directed them. It was surely the consciousness of this that led him to inscribe on his coat of arms the words *"Quid non Deo juvante?"* What not by the help of God? Would that every young man might adopt such a motto at the very beginning of his career, for it is but the substance of words in the Old Book, "In all thy ways acknowledge Him, and He shall direct thy paths."[3] "The blessing of the Lord it maketh rich, and He addeth no sorrow with it."[4]

In perusing this memoir it is possible the reader may be disappointed with the lack of striking incidents therein. For this the writer cannot be held accountable. Except for the things Sir Titus did, there is very little material for a biography to be found. Most biographies are made interesting by records of conversations and extracts from letters and speeches, but in this case such materials are scanty. His words were always few, often painfully few. His power of conversation was so small that among strangers he often sat as "the silent man." This arose not from lack of sympathy with the subject, or of thought in connection with it, but

---

[3] Proverbs Chapter 3 Verse 6.
[4] Proverbs Chapter 10 Verse 22.

from a constitutional reserve and nervousness which he could not help.[5] It was only in the quiet of his home and in the presence of intimate friends, that his views and feelings found utterance. As for his letters they were also few and brief, and, except on rare occasions, were written by another hand; not that his diction and penmanship were in any way defective, on the contrary, they were of a superior kind—terse, pointed, and legible. But he had no liking for the pen. It seemed too small an instrument for his large and practical mind to express itself by. His speeches delivered on two or three public occasions are preserved, and will be reproduced in these pages; but they "only half conceal and half reveal" the soul of the speaker. His library was large and well selected; but his knowledge of books was limited, and the range of his reading confined to religious publications, and the daily press. It will be evident, therefore, that the usual materials for a biography are in this case unobtainable. His deeds alone are his memoranda. Other men live in the books they wrote, or the words they spake, but he lives alone in what he did. And just as books have to be studied to know the mind of the author, so his deeds have to be studied likewise to know the principles and motives that gave them birth. Like a strong oak, he silently grew into the large space he filled in the eye of the world, and was apparently unconscious of the greatness that gathered around his name. Perhaps, when he lived those who were nearest saw not that greatness, but now—that the oak is laid low and the vacant space is left, and the great cable roots that moored him to the soil are bare,—not till now are his girth and proportions known.

What then, it may be asked, are the available sources from which the materials of this memoir are to be drawn? In the first place, we hereby acknowledge our obligations to the writers of various sketches in journals and newspapers; also to the interesting little work entitled "Saltaire and its Founder."[6] These sketches, though necessarily fragmentary, have suggested the lines on which this biography is constructed, and given directions to our own researches. We have corresponded and conversed with persons who were the contemporaries of his commercial life; who were associated with him in

[5] Examples of Salt's reticence for public speaking are provided later – e.g. in his parliamentary record, see Chapter XIII.
[6] The author was Abraham Holroyd (Ref: Hol1). Editions of the book published in 1871 and 1873 record that Holroyd was based at 36, Victoria Road, Saltaire.

municipal and parliamentary affairs; who were his counsellors and almoners in his philanthropic and religious projects. We have personally visited the scenes of his early days both at Morley and Wakefield, and have gleaned from the failing memories of old people the only incidents they can recall. But chiefly have we drawn from our own personal knowledge of the late Baronet, which an intimate and unbroken friendship of many years supplies. These are the materials which we attempt to weave into the fabric of a memoir: there may be little skill displayed in preparing the loom or arranging the threads, but the hand of affection guides the shuttle.

CHAPTER II.

"Go up and watch the new-born rill
Just trickling from its mossy bed,
Streaking the heath-clad hill with a bright emerald thread.
Cans't thou her bold career foretell,
What rocks she shall o'erleap or rend,
How far in ocean's swell
Her freshening billows send?"

TITUS SALT'S ANCESTRY—HIS GRANDPARENTS' CONNECTION WITH SHEFFIELD—
REMOVAL TO LEEDS—HIS FATHER AND MOTHER—BIRTH PLACE AT MANOR
HOUSE, MORLEY—HISTORICAL REMINISCENCES OF MORLEY AND ITS PEOPLE—
DESCRIPTION OF MANOR HOUSE—TITUS SALT TWICE BAPTISED—CHILDHOOD—
GOES TO A DAME SCHOOL—INCIDENTS OF SCHOOLBOY LIFE—HOME
EDUCATION—TITUS SALT'S BIBLE.

THE ancestors of Titus Salt (whose title may be dropped for the present) came originally from Staffordshire; but this information is derived from tradition, not from authentic documents. The family of Salt still holds an honourable position in that county. How it came to migrate northward we do not know. It has left a branch in Derbyshire, where it is also held in honour; but it is at Sheffield where this branch takes root in Yorkshire, and authentic information is obtained. It appears from old deeds that Titus Salt, of Sheffield, whitesmith[7], in 1763, married one Sarah Taylor, a widow, by whom he became entitled to some freehold property, described as "in a certain place near the new church in Sheffield commonly called Cherry Square." In 1755, there is a conveyance of property from the Rev. Christopher Alderson, of Aston, to Titus Salt, then described as of Hunslet Moor, in the parish of Leeds, whitesmith.

---

[7] A whitesmith was a worker of tin (Ref: OED).

In 1802 occurs his will, in which he is described as of Hunslet Moor, ironfounder; he devised his Hunslet property to his son Titus Salt, and his Sheffield property to his son Daniel Salt. This Daniel Salt is described in a deed of 1811, as of Morley, in the parish of Batley, yeoman. When Titus and Sarah Salt removed from Sheffield to Leeds is not recorded, but Hunslet was undoubtedly the place of their abode. There the ironfounding business was carried on, not, we fear, with uninterrupted success, for at one time it failed, and Titus Salt then lost a large portion of his property. There, too, they died; the husband in 1804, the wife in 1802: both were well stricken in years, and are buried in Hunslet churchyard.[8] These were the grandparents of the late Baronet. We remember once passing with him through that neighbourhood, when he pointed to a certain locality and said, "My grandfather lived there."

Mr. Daniel Salt succeeded to his father's ironfounding business which he carried on for a few years. On the 5th July, 1802, he married Grace Smithies, of the Old Manor House, Morley. Her father, Isaac Smithies, had recently died, leaving no one to succeed him in his business of drysalter.[9] In consequence of this, Daniel Salt came to reside, after his marriage, at the Old Manor House, and for a while carried on both his own business, at Hunslet, and that of his late father-in-law, at Morley. This arrangement, however, was of short duration; the Leeds business was given up, and he afterwards was known at Morley as "Daniel Salt, white cloth merchant and drysalter." These were the parents of the late Baronet, from whom he inherited those mental and physical qualities that made him what he became.

Mr. Daniel Salt, his father, was a plain, blunt Yorkshireman, both in manner and speech. He was tall in size, strong in bone and muscle, with an impediment in his utterance.[10] He is still remembered for his energy and industry in business,

---

[8] Although Hunslet church remains, and is still in use, the area is now heavily urbanized, and the graves were removed from the site in the second half of the 20th century. Our attempts to trace the gravestones relating to the burials referred to have been unsuccessful.

[9] A drysalter was a dealer in gums, dyes, drugs, and – sometimes – in oils, spices, pickles, etc. (Ref: OED).

[10] It is extremely unlikely that Balgarnie ever met Daniel Salt – the former was only 17 when the latter died – and so this description is judged to be based on accounts by others. However the reported impediment in Daniel Salt's speech is of note when seen in the context of Titus Salt's oft reported reticence in public speaking.

and for many quaint and original sayings that fell from his lips.

Mrs. Daniel Salt was a woman of delicate constitution, retiring in her disposition, sweet and gentle in her ways; sometimes subject to mental depression, an earnest Christian and a staunch Nonconformist.[11] Their portraits, taken in later years, now hang in the dining room at Crow Nest.[12]

Such were some of the characteristics of the parents, and which, with a few modifications, were reproduced in their son Titus, who was born at the Old Manor House, on the 20th September, 1803, and, according to the record in the Family Bible, "At four o'clock in the morning." The hour of his birth may be forgotten, but not the day. During his life, many public celebrations of the day were held; but now when he is gone, it will be celebrated as "The Founder's Day,"[13] in several institutions that his benevolence enriched.

Let us now visit Morley, the place of his birth and the scene of his childhood. Morley has an interesting history of its own, going back to Saxon, if not Roman periods.[14] At the time Titus Salt was born, it was a village of 2,100 inhabitants. At the time we write it has grown into a town with nearly 13,000 people. It is situated in the parish of Batley, from which it is distant three miles, about four miles from Leeds, five from Dewsbury, and seven from Bradford and Wakefield. It probably took its name from the words *moor* and *ley,* which together mean literally, moorfields, and would describe the physical aspect of the district when it was named. The highest point in the neighbourhood is the site where the church of Saint Mary-in-the-Wood stood for centuries, around which many generations of the inhabitants are buried, and where the new

---

[11] For an account of the Nonconformist movement, see Appendix 4.

[12] Crow Nest was to be the main family home of Salt. For further accounts, see Chapters IX, XVI. The property has since been demolished. In the present day, portraits of Daniel and Grace Salt are on view in the Saltaire Studies Centre, Shipley College.

[13] The occasion is still recognised in Saltaire in the present day. BALG makes further reference to the term in Chapter XIV.

[14] In Saxon times Morley was selected as the head of the wapentake - a district within which a rudimentary form of local government prevailed. The term wapentake derives from the term 'weapon-touch' - a ceremony whereby the appointed governor of the district would hold up his spear and each person in the gathered assembly would then approach him and touch his spear with theirs (Ref: MAM, p26).

Congregational Church[15] now stands. The view from this position, minus the sea, reminds one of Burial Hill at Plymouth, Massachussetts, the spot where the Pilgrim Fathers sleep, and in sight of Plymouth Rock, where they landed.[16] From this commanding position, at Morley, the eye takes in the entire village or town nestling around it, with its straggling streets, commodious places of worship, busy manufactories, and old mansions surrounded by ancient trees, where colonies of rooks long have settled. There are several coal mines and stone quarries in the neighbourhood, which are a source of considerable wealth. But this is the Morley of to-day. At the time we refer to there were only four places of worship in it; now there are fourteen. There was only one mill for the manufacture of cloth; each house had a manufactory of its own, where the sound of the weaver's shuttle was constantly heard.

But it is the moral and religious aspects of the place, at the beginning of this century, in which we are most interested. As the vintage of a district takes its character from the soil that produces it, so the surroundings of one's birth-place often colour and give character to the whole life. It was so with Titus Salt at Morley. He there received those moral and religious impressions which remained with him through life. The people of Morley had much of the old Puritan spirit among them. The Sabbath was strictly observed. Family worship was common in many a home. The Bible and Bunyan's "Pilgrim's Progress" were the books most frequently read. Good Friday was not in their calendar, and the many fast days which human authority originated they did not recognise. Nor need we wonder at this. Apart from the Puritan memories that clustered round the place, there was no Established Church in it till 1830, so that Nonconformity then occupied the unique position of having no National Church in the town.[17] Was not the church of St. Mary-in-the-Wood connected with the

---

[15] The church being described still stands. It is now St. Mary's in the Wood United Reformed Church. It is the only instance in England and Wales of an ancient Episcopal place of worship which did not return to the Established Church at the restoration of the Stuart monarchy in 1660.

[16] Balgarnie is speaking from direct knowledge of the scene at Plymouth, which he had visited in 1867 (see Appendix 1).

[17] Morley at the time in question, although having a population of a mere 2,100, was nevertheless an important centre in the area, and the concentration of Nonconformist activity is particularly noteworthy. Indeed, the very house in which Titus Salt was born has some significance in Nonconformist heritage. The origins of the strong tradition of

Church of England? It originally belonged to the Roman Catholics, and remained in their hands till the Reformation in 1534. Since then it has been alternately in the hands of Episcopalians, Presbyterians, and Independents. It has had different names in its time, St. Mary and St. Nicholas being two of them. In later years it was known as Morley Old Chapel, and occupied by the Independents till 1873, when the structure became unsafe and was pulled down. It must have been a source of bitter regret to the inhabitants when this ancient historical edifice vanished from their sight. What hallowed associations were connected therewith! Here many of the ejected ministers of 1662 sought refuge when silenced by the Act of Uniformity.[18] In the chapelyard their tombstones still stand, under which their precious dust is hidden till Christ shall bid it rise. John Wesley often visited Morley and preached the Gospel to the people. By these visits of this eminent man a spirit of religious earnestness was awakened which continues until now.

Such is a brief survey of Morley and its people when Titus Salt was born. Let us enter the Old Manor House[19] and look at the place where he first saw the light. It is well designated "old," for it was built about three hundred years ago, and was evidently not "built to sell," but to last. The walls are in some places three feet thick; the roof is low and covered with slabs instead of slates. In front, the ivy throws its green mantle over the old walls; behind, a contemporary pear-

---

Nonconformity in the area can be traced back to the events in the 1660s which gave rise to the movement. The occupant of the Manor House at that time was a Captain Oates (Ref: MAM, p205). It was the Presbyterian Oates who led the Farnley Wood Plot of 12th October, 1663, in which an insurrection was mounted against the Restoration government with the immediate intent of capturing Leeds (Farnley Wood being three miles SW of Leeds and a similar distance north of Morley). Coming in the year following the Act of Uniformity, the event was part of the wider scale Northern Risings of 1663. The insurrection failed, the Farnley Wood plotters were tried, and on 16th January, 1664 Captain Oates and 15 other rebels were executed in York (Ref: Hopp).

[18] See Appendix 4.

[19] The Old Manor House no longer exists. A plaque on the present day building at the corner of Queens Street and Albion Street reads "SITE OF THE OLD MANOR HOUSE. BIRTHPLACE, IN 1803, OF SIR TITUS SALT, PIONEER OF THE ALPACA WOOL TRADE FAMOUS FOR THE BUILDING OF SALTAIRE, THE MOST FAMOUS MODEL VILLAGE OF THE 19TH CENTURY". The illustration in BALG (and reproduced on page 12) is from a photograph presumably taken many years after Salt's birth. As one can see, the house appears to be a very modest building. For further illustrations, see Appendix 8.

tree stands, still bringing forth "fruit in its season." If a "Manor" was attached to the house in olden times it is not so now, for it is surrounded by dwelling-houses and warehouses. In Daniel Salt's time there were two or three fields of pasture connected with the house, which belonged to the Earl of Dartmouth, by whom it was sold to Dr. Ellis, and is now occupied by a medical practitioner. But the Old Manor House has been subject to various changes, both within and without, since Titus Salt lived in it. When he afterwards paid a visit to it, with his children, he could hardly identify the old place. The front entrance had been removed to the south end. Old windows had been built up, and new ones made. The rooms on the ground floor, which were originally about six feet high, had been sunk a couple of feet, and were now entered by steps downwards. That part of the premises where his father's drysalting stores were kept, was transformed into a drawing room. The kitchen, with its stone flags, the ceiling, with its bare wooden beams, where the oat cakes were suspended to harden and the hams to dry; the wide stone staircase leading to the floor above; many of these remained much the same, but all other marks of identity were effaced. No, not all. One object alone was left which vividly recalled the period of boyhood, and that was the pear-tree at the back of the house. "Ah," said he, "I remember that tree well, for I often climbed it to gather its fruit."

It is in this old-fashioned house we are introduced to Titus Salt. He was the first of a large family, consisting of three sons and four[20] daughters, all of whom are gone—save one. It is not a little singular that he was twice baptized: the first time on the 9th November, 1803, by the Rev. Thomas Clough, of Morley Old New Chapel; the second time on the 27th February, 1805, at Batley Church, by the Rev. J. Sedgwick. The reason for this double baptism was, not because there was any doubt about the validity of the first, but probably for the sake of an entry in the parish register, which was then the only legal record of births, deaths, and marriages. To some readers it may thus appear doubtful whether Titus Salt was a child of Nonconformity or of the Established Church.

---

[20] A transcript of the Salt family bible records that there were in fact five daughters, there being not one but two daughters named Hannah, both dying before their first birthday – see the Family Tree in Appendix 8.

OLD MANOR HOUSE, MORLEY.

THE BIRTHPLACE OF SIR TITUS SALT, BART.

His parents at this time were connected with the Old New Chapel above referred to: this congregation was an offshoot from the Old Chapel, hence the double name given it. The separation took place on doctrinal grounds, many of the hearers being dissatisfied with their minister's views, which had a strong flavour of Socinianism.[21] They met in a licensed dwelling-house at first, until a site for a chapel was obtained from the Earl of Dartmouth, which was erected in 1765. It was the chapel of which the Rev. T. Clough was the pastor in 1804, but owing to a notice from Lord Dartmouth to quit the premises, a new one was erected in 1835, called "Rehoboth Chapel," of which the Rev. J. P. James is the present pastor. We can therefore satisfactorily answer the question as to whether Titus Salt belonged to Nonconformity or the Establishment. In a certain sense he belonged to both, legally to the latter; hereditarily, and afterwards conscientiously, to the former.[22] To those who have been taught to lay much stress on the rite of baptism, as affecting the moral nature and influencing the future destiny of the recipient, we can only say, be Sir Titus Salt's first baptism valid or invalid, he at least received the rite in two communions, and in this respect he differed from many.

The other children born at Old Manor House were Sarah, Hannah, and Isaac Smithies; the two last named died in infancy and were buried at the Old New Chapel, Morley. The state of Mrs. Salt's health being so delicate, she was unable to nurse the children born to her, but a valuable substitute was found in Mrs. Ellis, who tended them as if they were her own during their infancy. Happily Titus did not inherit the feeble constitution of his mother, but the strong and vigorous constitution of his father. As soon as he was able to run alone he mingled with the children of the village. A cousin, still living, who was his playmate says "he was a bright boy for his years; full of fun when with those whom he knew well, but shy with strangers." This testimony is true, for the same characteristic was manifested in his riper years. Another playmate, still living, remembers that Titus had a wooden horse which his father bought him. In possession of such a toy he was an object of envy to the other children around

---

[21] Socinianism was a religious perspective which denied the divinity of Christ. The sect was formed by Loelius and Faustus Socinus, Italian theologians of the 16th century (Ref: OED).
[22] Several examples are quoted in BALG's later chapters which serve to emphasise Salt's willingness to support religious denominations other than Congregationalism.

him. Seated upon it, he spent many an hour riding up and down the flagstones. But he seldom enjoyed his pastime alone, as his playmates were permitted to share it. Amongst them was Joe Ellis, who says "I was one who took turns with him."

When Titus arrived at the usual age he was sent to a dame school[23] in Morley, kept by Mrs. Nichols, under whose care he was taught to read. It must have been this school he once referred to in after years. Happening one day to meet a gentleman from Morley in a railway carriage, the conversation turned on Morley, which recalled old memories. As soon as the gentleman mentioned his name he exclaimed "I remember your mother; we went to school together."

Of course, this dame school was only preparatory to another, but whether it was the Morley Town School, kept by Mr. Trenam[24], is uncertain; if so, he came under the influence of a man held in high esteem in the village. Be that as it may, there is credible evidence that when eight or nine years old he went to a school at Batley, then under the care of the Rev. J. Sedgwick, curate of the Parish Church. It was a long distance for a boy of his years to walk every day. How few boys now-a-days would do it! Six miles to school and back! Yet he was only one of a group to whom the journey was a healthy and bracing exercise. They started each morning at half-past eight o'clock, and reached Batley in time for school at half-past nine. A happy group of boys that was, and cheerily their voices rang as they passed along Scotchman-lane together.[25] This lane was noted for the number of gipsies who encamped there and often succeeded in purloining property from the neighbouring villages. But these school-boys kept each other's courage up by keeping together. They were

---

[23] Dame schools were common in the 18th and 19th centuries. Run by elderly women in their own homes, they would, for a small weekly fee, provide young children with rudimentary introductions to reading, writing and perhaps arithmetic (Ref: DicEd).

[24] An alternative spelling of this name is "Trenholme" (Ref: MAM, p207).

[25] Scotchman Lane still exists, and for an appreciation of the journey being described, readers are encouraged to retrace Titus' steps down the hill from Morley to Batley and then back – quite a journey for a nine year old in mid winter. Along the lane is an interesting pub that readers (but alas, not the young Salt) can avail themselves of - the Needless. A suggestion that two taverns on the land owned by Lord Cardigan in Morley be renamed in honour of his heroism in the fatal Charge of the Light Brigade was described by a local woollen manufacturer as 'Arbitrary and Needless'. The names stuck, and the latter pub still stands (Ref: EPub, p38).

accustomed to meet at a rendezvous in the lane. Those who were in time wrote their names on a piece of slate, which was deposited in a well-known hole in the wall, for the perusal and encouragement of the boys who were late. The curriculum at Batley school was both classical and commercial, but Titus' attention was confined to the ordinary branches of instruction. As for dinner, he carried it with him. It consisted of oat cake, and milk fresh from the cow. To this latter circumstance he once incidentally alluded a few years before his death. Some children happened to be visiting at Crow Nest; on their return from the dairy, where they had tried their hand at milking the cows, great was their amusement and surprise when their kind-hearted host told them that in his school-boy days, he had to go in the dark mornings, to draw his own supply for the day before setting out for school.

But what was Titus Salt's education at home? It need not be told that the character and habits generally take the permanent shape and form that the plastic hand of a parent gives them. To his father he was indebted for many wise counsels, and for instructions in practical mechanics with which his former occupation made him familiar. But his higher home education was imparted by his mother. It was from her he acquired that respect for religion, that regard for the Sabbath, that reverence on entering the house of God, that personal attachment to Christian ministers and their work, which were retained as long as he lived. It was by her alone his youthful lips were taught to pray, to read the Bible both morning and evening, and to make it "the man of his counsel in the house of his pilgrimage."[26] Among many relics of the deceased baronet at Crow Nest, not the least precious is the well-worn pocket Bible, the gift of the parent to the son, with the following inscription

---

[26] The matriarchal role in matters of religion is noteworthy. BALG is presumably reporting information imparted by Titus Salt himself. Whilst there is no reference in BALG to any similar role being played by Caroline Salt in the upbringing of the next generation, the adherence of the daughters of Titus and Caroline to the Congregational faith is more evident than that of some of the sons (see Appendix 3).

TO TITUS SALT.

"May this blest volume ever lie
Close to thy heart and near thine eye;
Till life's last hour thy soul engage,
And be thy chosen heritage."

It is worthy of notice that to each of his own children he presented a pocket Bible in which was written, with his own hand, the above lines. May the prayer therein expressed be realized!

CHAPTER III.

Let us know,

Our indiscretion sometimes serves us well,

When our deep plots do pall: and that should teach us,

There's a divinity that shapes our ends,

Rough-hew them how we will.

—SHAKESPEARE.[27]

REMOVAL FROM MORLEY—CROFTON FARM—HISTORICAL ASSOCIATIONS—
FARMHOUSE LICENSED FOR PREACHING—TITUS SALT'S SCHOOL LIFE AT
WAKEFIELD—TESTIMONY OF COMPANIONS—HIS SCHOOLMASTER—TITUS
SALT'S PERSONAL APPEARANCE—HOME LIFE AT CROFTON—HIS FATHER'S
DIFFICULTIES IN FARMING—WHAT TITUS IS TO BE—NOT A DOCTOR—THE
ACCIDENT THAT DECIDED HIS FUTURE—THE HAND OF GOD RECOGNISED—GOES
INTO A WOOLSTAPLER'S WAREHOUSE AT WAKEFIELD—LEAVES WAKEFIELD FOR
BRADFORD—"STOCK-IN-TRADE" TO BEGIN LIFE WITH.

MR. Daniel Salt removed from Morley about the year 1813. Titus was then
nearly ten years of age. To the son, this removal was only a pleasant episode in
a boy's history; but it was not so to the parents. To them it was a severe trial
indeed; for were they not leaving the Old Manor House, where their wedded life
began, and their children had been born? And then, in the Old New Chapel
burying-ground there were those little graves, in which their hearts were left.[28]

---

[27] Hamlet, Act 5, Scene 2.
[28] The burial ground to which BALG refers is the one on the south side of Chapel Hill,
Morley. In the present day the burial ground still exists, but in a very poor state and with
redevelopment of the area possibly threatening its future. Inspection of the site in early
2002 did not reveal any graves of the Salt family, but some of the graves were hidden by
vegetation. Although BALG speaks of "little graves" in the plural, there is reason to believe
that only one of the children had died by the time the family left Morley around 1813. Titus'
sister Hannah Maria Salt was born 13th July, 1806 and died 26th April, 1807; his brother

The cause of this removal from Morley is not precisely known. It might be that Mr. Daniel Salt preferred the country life of a farmer to that of a drysalter, or that his present occupation was unremunerative, and the cultivation of a farm might possibly increase his resources. In this latter expectation, however, he was certainly disappointed. No doubt at that time farming was a profitable occupation to many. The wars with Napoleon Bonaparte then raged, during which, prices were high, and fortunes, among large farmers, were rapidly made; but when peace was proclaimed, prices went down. It was therefore at a time of farming prosperity that Mr. Daniel Salt removed from Morley, and entered upon the farm of Crofton.

Crofton is an old-fashioned village situated about three miles from Wakefield, on the Doncaster road, then belonging to Sir Henry W. Wilson, Bart. The farm consisted of about one hundred acres of arable land, with a comfortable dwelling-house and farm-offices contiguous. The parish church stands in the immediate neighbourhood, of which the Rev. Edward Hill was vicar for many years, and from which he was ejected by the Act of Uniformity,[29] for conscience' sake. The death of this saintly man was a very affecting one. "He had attained a prolonged age, and was confined to his room. In the same chamber was his wife, who had been bedridden for two years, and was near her end. Mr. Hill left his bed with difficulty to take leave of her, and as he kissed her for the last time, he said, 'Ah, my dear wife, thou hast followed me for forty years, tarry a little and let me go before thee.' He was with some difficulty carried back to his couch, and immediately expired, his wife dying within two hours. They were buried at Halifax in the same grave."[*] Titus Salt was thus brought again into a locality around which the memories of good men still lingered, and which at his time of life were likely to leave a deep and lasting impression upon his heart.

Isaac Smithies Salt was born 11th July, 1810, and died 19th September, 1819. One would therefore expect that only Hannah Maria Salt was buried in the graveyard.
[29] The Act of Uniformity of 1662 was fundamental in establishing the Dissenters movement, of which the Congregational order was part. The Act led to the ejection of those 2,000 ministers of the Anglican Church who could not accept the services and rubrics of the latter's Book of Common Prayer. See also Appendix 4.
[*] See "Nonconformity in Yorkshire," by Rev. J. G. Miall, p. 86.

Crofton was also celebrated for a young ladies' boarding school, kept by Miss Mangnall,[30] who was then widely known, not only for the efficiency of her training, but for the popular book on education entitled "Mangnall's Questions." In the homestead of Crofton other children were born.[31]

The nearest Congregational place of worship to Crofton, was Salem Chapel,[32] Wakefield, of which the Rev. B. Rayson was the minister—a man highly esteemed both for his learning and piety. With Mr. Rayson's congregation and ministry Mr. and Mrs. Salt were connected, but as the distance was great, and the health of the latter feeble, she was unable to attend Divine Service regularly; yet the loss of public worship was made up to her by services conducted in her own house. For this a license had to be obtained from the civil authorities, to escape the penalties then imposed on those who dissented from the forms of the Established Church. The Old Manor House, Morley, had been licensed for a similar purpose. The following copy of an old form of license is given in Smith's History of Morley[33] :—

"A congregation or assembly of Protestant subjects dissenting from the Church of England doe hold their meetings for religious worship on the Lord's Dayes, in Topliffe Hall, Woodkirk, and they hold other occasional meetings at J. Pickering's house at Tingley.

Jo PICKERING.

Thos. ATKINSON.'

It was under a license similar to the above that religious services were occasionally conducted in the farmhouse at Crofton, without the use of "The Book of Common Prayer." Many hallowed gatherings took place there. The people in the village were free to come, and some who hungered for the bread of

---

[30] Richmal Mangnall (1769–1820) was educated at Mrs. Wilson's school at Crofton Hall, and worked there as a teacher, eventually taking over the school until her death on 1st May, 1820. Her *Historical and Miscellaneous Questions for the Use of Young People* became a standard work. She also wrote a *Compendium of Geography* in 1815. Her school was widely regarded (Ref: DNB).

[31] The children in question are judged to be Edward (b 1814) and Hannah (b 1821), but the record is not as clear as it could be.

[32] Maps of the period show that Salem Chapel was in George Street, Wakefield. The site is now occupied by 'The Ridings Centre', a shopping mall.

[33] An 1876 publication, not to be confused with Ref: MAM.

life felt it "good to be here." The Rev. Mr. Bruce, of Zion Chapel,[34] Wakefield, frequently officiated on these occasions. By him, and other good men, the lamp of divine truth was kept alive in this and neighbouring places, which, but for such ministrations, had well nigh gone out.

Such were the religious surroundings of Titus Salt at Crofton, between 1814 and 1818, and those who, in after years, were struck with the simplicity of his faith, his preference for inornate worship, his attachment to Nonconformity, will now see where his principles were planted, and how they were nurtured.

But his secular education had yet to be acquired. He had now arrived at the age of eleven, and was sent by his father to the day school connected with Salem Chapel, Wakefield; the Rev. B. Rayson, along with the duties of his pastorate, uniting those of a schoolmaster. The school was held in a building adjoining the chapel in George-street, now used as a printing-office. In a letter from a gentleman, still living, who was at school with Titus, the following extract is given :—

Mr. Rayson gave up the school at Christmas, 1815, from which time it was conducted by Mr. Enoch Harrison, who had for several years been Mr. Rayson's principal assistant, and with whom young Salt remained some time. His father's residence being upwards of three miles from the school, Titus generally rode on a donkey, which was left until the afternoon at "The Nag's Head," a small inn near to the school, bringing with him in a little basket, his dinner. In person he was tall and proportionately stout, and of somewhat heavy appearance. His dress was usually that of a country farmer's son, viz., a cloth or fustian[35] coat, corduroy breeches, with long gaiters, or, as they were generally called, "spats," or leggings, buttoned up the side, with strong boots laced in front. He was generally of a thoughtful, studious turn of mind, rarely mixing with his school-fellows in their sports and play, and rather looked upon by them as the quiet, dull boy of the school. His words were generally so few that I cannot call to mind any particular thing that he either said or did. The school was a mixed school for both sexes, the boys occupying the ground floor and the girls the room above, and it was considered the best private day school in the town.

---

[34] Zion Chapel was also in George Street, west of Salem Chapel. The building still exists, as a United Reformed Church.
[35] Fustian is a thick twilled cotton cloth with a short nap (Ref: OED).

At this school his sister Sarah[36] also attended. They rode on a donkey together, and it was probably more for her benefit than his that its help was required; for at Morley, even when he was younger, and the distance much the same, the journey to and from school was performed on foot. But the teacher to whom Titus Salt was most indebted for his education was the Mr. Enoch Harrison above referred to, and this memoir of the pupil would be incomplete were it not to contain a brief sketch of one who did much to equip him for his future career. From Mr. Harrison's own lips we gathered the particulars of Titus' school-life at Wakefield. When we saw the former he was in declining health, yet clear in intellect and retentive in memory; but, alas! since that interview, which we had hoped to renew, he has passed away at the ripe age of eighty-one years. From the obituary which appeared after his decease, the following extract is taken :—

It would be no flight of imagination to say that this announcement is calculated to arrest the attention and awaken the sympathies of men and women scattered throughout the entire kingdom, and of others also, who long ago left the town to seek and find their fortunes in distant lands; it would, in fact, be difficult to place any limit to the number of those who owed, in great part, their chief and lasting possessions, to an early association with Mr. Harrison. Some of our most distinguished townsmen, of past and present times, have been proud to tell that when boys they attended his school, and to that circumstance attribute hardly less than to their own personal virtues, their ability to rise in the world of business, politics, or religion, and their safeguard from the manifold influences which, yielded to, have made wrecks of others. Mr. Harrison made the training of youth his one great life-work; it was the sphere from which he never departed. All the resources of a capacious mind, a retentive memory, and a calm judgment, were devoted to the duties of the desk and the class-room, and were never suffered to be dissipated by any foreign considerations. The result was what it could only be—certain and ample success. His teaching was eminently substantial; his pupils were grounded in the several branches of learning to which their attention was directed, and all that was undertaken was thoroughly done and severely tested. Among those who passed through Mr. Harrison's school we may mention the late Sir Titus Salt, Baronet.— *Wakefield Express* of 26th May, 1877.

---

[36] Sarah, being 15 months younger than Titus, would have been approx. 10 years old at the time.

Such is the merited tribute paid to this remarkable schoolmaster under whose care Titus Salt spent four years of his life at Wakefield. The instruction imparted was what was recognized as "a plain commercial education," including history, geography, and drawing. If any of the pupils wished to study the classics they were permitted to attend the Grammar School, of which Dr. Naylor and Dr. Sissons were the masters. Mr. Harrison had a vivid remembrance of Titus Salt, of whose career he was justly proud, and whom he occasionally visited, both at Methley[37] and Crow Nest, in after years. It may also be said that the pupil was proud of his teacher, of whom he often spoke with respect, and sometimes exhibited to his friends those specimens of drawing and penmanship which, under this tutor's instruction he had, as a boy, prepared.[38] When Saltaire was opened, in 1853, Mr. Harrison was among the guests invited to the banquet.

But it may be asked, What was Mr. Harrison's opinion of his pupil? "He was," says he, "never a bright pupil. He was very steady, very attentive,— especially to any particular study into which he put his heart. Drawing was his chief delight. He was a fine, pure boy; stout and tall for his age, with a remarkably intelligent eye. So much did his eye impress me that I have often, when alone, drawn it from memory, simply for my own gratification. I have sketches of him somewhere among my papers, with crimped frill round his neck, just as he appeared then; but though naturally very quiet, he was sometimes given to random tricks."

From the foregoing particulars we can form some idea of Titus Salt at the age of fifteen. It is a well-known saying, "The child is father of the man," which in this case was abundantly verified, for the traits of character observable in his youth were not less conspicuous in his manhood. "A very steady boy" he was, and the germs of a great future were hidden in him. Steadily he jogs along the Doncaster road every day to school on his donkey, with his sister behind on the

---

[37] Methley was to be the Salt family home for several years. For further account, see Chapter XIII.

[38] Three drawings by Titus Salt, executed at Mr. Harrison's academy can be found in the Saltaire Studies Centre, Shipley College. Their titles are Group of Cottages; Dismasted Grenlander; House near Tunbridge Wells, Kent. (Tunbridge Wells features in the lives of some of Salt's family some 80 years later - see Appendix 3 - and it is interesting to speculate why this subject was used by Salt at such an early age).

pillion. We may be sure he was always in time, for punctuality was the rule of his life. What though he might be regarded as "the dull boy" of the school? Thus it was with Isaac Newton and Thomas Chalmers in their schoolboy days. Of the former it is said that when at the Grammar School of Grantham, he was always at the bottom of the class until he received a kick from another boy, whom he punished by getting above him. There were latent powers in the mind of young Titus that some day would be evoked, but he gave no signs of precocity or genius such as mark the early life of some distinguished men. It was not at a leap that he was to outstrip other men, but by hard work and resolute perseverance. Is not this an encouragement to young men who hesitate to start in the race for wealth and honour, among so many brilliant competitors? Know this from Titus Salt's character and career: that "the race is not always to the swift, nor the battle to the strong"; but that nothing is lost to well-directed and steady effort: nothing is to be obtained without it.

Note also, that he was successful in those studies "into which he put his heart." Thus it was with him in after life. It was by concentrating his mind and heart on one object that he excelled other men, and made for himself a name amongst them. One thing he did at a time, and because of this he did it well. Were his "words always few"? It was not by these he was to become great. Of mere talkers the world has always enough. Words are breath, but thoughts have life that endures. Was his attire plain and neat in boyhood? He had no affectation of dress in manhood: he wore nothing for mere show, and what suited his taste once was not superseded by something more attractive afterwards. Was he a "pure" boy at fifteen, in speech, in feeling, and in sentiment? Those who knew him best, in after years, can testify that anything in the way of untruthfulness, indelicacy, or dishonourableness, his soul abhorred. As for "the remarkably intelligent eye" that the schoolmaster was struck with in his pupil, it was not less so in manhood and old age. It was an eye large, clear, and searching, which when calm, beamed benevolence, but when troubled, was equally capable of inflicting its ire on those who excited it.

Titus Salt was now seventeen years of age, and the question must be settled, "What is he to be?" He had no fortune to fall back upon, and if one was to be acquired it must be by his own efforts. His father's circumstances, though not straitened, were not affluent. Indeed, the farm at Crofton did not pay, but brought loss to the tenant. An old acquaintance, still living, at the age of 92, remembers Mr. Salt complaining of the badness of the times since the close of the war :— "Yes," he said, in his own peculiar way, "a man might have bread and milk to breakfast and supper, but that is not a living." While, therefore, it was evident that his son Titus must do something for his livelihood, it was not so easy to decide what. Had he no predilection of his own? Yes; it appears he had for some time cherished the purpose of being a doctor, in which case his education was only now at an incipient stage, and a considerable outlay of money must yet be incurred. One cannot help speculating as to what position Titus Salt would have occupied in the medical profession had his first intentions been carried out. His keen insight, calm judgment, and decision of character, were qualifications most likely to insure success in such a profession. Indeed, whatever occupation in life he had chosen, and put his heart into, would have led to distinction. But the question so important both to father and son was to be taken out of their hands. "The lot is cast into the lap, but the whole disposing thereof is of the Lord." An accident, apparently trifling, determined his future course. One day, he happened to be cutting a piece of wood with a sharp knife, which slipped, and inflicted a deep wound in his hand; blood flowed profusely, the sight of which made him faint. His father, coming in at the time, exclaimed, "Titus, my lad, thou wilt never be a doctor!" In this opinion the son acquiesced, and henceforth the idea of entering the medical profession was abandoned.

To what occupation was he then to turn his attention? Wakefield had long been celebrated for its wool market, while the trade of the district was in a flourishing condition; but as hand-loom weaving then prevailed, the business of woolstapling[39] was, of course, much restricted. When, however, steam power was introduced and manufacturing processes assumed gigantic proportions, the trade generally migrated into larger centres, and that of Wakefield gradually slipped away. Still it had not entirely removed in the year 1820, when Titus Salt was placed with Mr. Jackson, of Wakefield, to learn the woolstapling business. It was in Mr. Jackson's warehouse that his first knowledge of wool was obtained, and in connection with which his fortune was to be made. This

---

[39] Woolstapling is the buying and selling of wool.

knowledge, however, was of a limited kind. Woolsorting formed no part of his duty, so that his chief occupation consisted in supplying small customers with wool, and in the keeping of accounts.

The farm at Crofton continued to decrease in value, and nothing remained for Mr. Salt but either to go on farming at a loss or give up the lease. The latter course he resolved to take; but the landlord interposed objections to it, so that the tenant was obliged to remain on the farm till the lease expired. Then came the question as to what his own future occupation was to be.

After the experience acquired and the losses sustained, at Crofton, he had no heart to take another farm. He could not return to Morley, for his brother-in-law, Robert Smithies, had succeeded to the business, and now occupied the Old Manor House. There seemed little opening in Wakefield, whither his son had gone to learn woolstapling; and where trade was rapidly declining. But while these doors were apparently shut, another and a wider was opening, which invited him to enter. Bradford was just entering upon that wonderful career of commercial prosperity which is almost unparalleled in the history of English towns: the tide of population, capital, and enterprise, seemed flowing thither from many quarters. Mr. Salt resolved "to take it at the flood," and to migrate with his family to this important centre of industry. Thus, his son's connection with Wakefield was brought to a close, and Bradford was henceforth to become the scene of his remarkable course in life.

But before proceeding to trace his Bradford career, we cannot close this chapter without directing the attention of young men to the "stock-in-trade" he was to begin with. It is said of a distinguished artist that, when asked how he mixed his colours, his prompt reply was, " *With brains, sir.*" Titus Salt had brains which gave shape to his lofty forehead, and force to his massive power of will. He had also a sound constitution, robust health, and a cheerful countenance. But along with these he possessed fixed principles of right and honour; moral qualities of dutifulness, amiability, and kindness; religious qualities of reverence and benevolence; business qualities of thoroughness, punctuality, perseverance, and energy; educational qualities of method and precision. With these,—and by the help of God,—he entered upon the business of life.

Boast not the titles of your ancestors, brave youth!

They're their possessions, none of yours.

When your own virtues equalled have their names

T'will be fair to lean upon their fames,

For they are strong supporters! But till then

The greatest are but growing gentlemen.

—BEN JONSON[40]

---

[40] Ben Jonson (1573?–1637), playwright and poet.

CHAPTER IV.

"I am one

Who feels within me a nobility

That spurns the pratings of the great.

And their mean boast of what their fathers were,

While they themselves are fools effeminate,

The scorn of all who know the worth of mind

And virtue."

—PERCIVAL.[41]

TITUS SALT ENTERS BRADFORD—PROBABLE ORIGIN OF THE WORD "BRADFORD"— ITS EARLY HISTORY AND TRADE—TITUS GOES TO MESSRS. ROUSE'S—LEARNS WOOLSTAPLING UNDER JOHN HAMMOND—CHARACTERISTICS OF THE FIRM— TITUS AT HIS WORK—THOROUGH KNOWLEDGE OF BUSINESS–JOINS HIS FATHER IN WOOLSTAPLING—CONNECTS HIMSELF WITH HORTON LANE SUNDAY SCHOOL—REV. T. TAYLOR—TITUS SALT AS LIBRARIAN, TEACHER, AND SUPERINTENDENT—CIVIL OUTBREAK IN BRADFORD—TITUS SALT'S COURAGE— MILITARY CALLED OUT—HIS INFLUENCE WITH THE WORKING CLASSES EXEMPLIFIED.

In the year 1822, Titus Salt came with his parents to Bradford, he being then about nineteen years of age. To himself this was an eventful period of his life. Little did he know the future that lay before him in the town he now entered as a stranger, and that he was to become an important factor in the development of its trade, in the growth of its civic and political life, in the multiplication of those physical, moral, and religious agencies that were to make it distinguished

---

[41] James Gates Percival (1795–1856) was born in Berlin, Connecticut, the son of a doctor, and was educated at Yale. He was regarded as the leading American poet of his day, but his poetry has not stood the test of time (Ref: DicLB).

among other towns of the kingdom. As little could he foresee that in this place he was to reap fortune and fame, to have a colossal statue erected in its midst while living, and when dead, to be borne to his grave with the mournful respect of the whole community.

As Titus Salt's business life and the growth of Bradford are somewhat contemporaneous, touching each other at many points, it will be necessary to give the reader some idea of the town, as it was, and as it is. Its name is of Saxon origin, which is supposed to be Bradenford, or Broadford.[42] There is a town in Wilts of the same name, with which, in postal communication, it has been sometimes confounded. The propriety of the name in Wilts is obvious, for it stands on the banks of the Avon, where a "broad ford" is visible; but this is not the case in the present instance. There is no river nearer it than the Aire, at Shipley, a distance of three miles. There is not even a stream of such dimensions in the neighbourhood that would justify the designation "broad" to any "ford" across it. Whence, then, has the name "Bradford" arisen? The town itself is situated at the junction of four valleys, which, in the olden time were well watered from the surrounding hills. Now-a-days, the water among those hills is collected into reservoirs, and transmitted to the town through artificial pipes; the old channels have, therefore, become almost dry, and the erection of buildings has well nigh effaced them. It is supposed, however, that the small stream at the bottom of Church Bank was once of considerable size, and that the "ford" once "broad" near this spot, gave the name to the town.

From the commencement of the present century, the growth and prosperity of Bradford are intimately connected with improvements in its worsted manufacture. Previous to this, its trade had been carried on in the slow and unproductive methods of olden times, but the introduction of the inventions of Arkwright and others brought about an entire revolution. While other towns adhered to the antiquated system of domestic spinning, Bradford began to erect mills and warehouses. In its proximity to rich fields of coal, iron, and stone, it had ample scope for enterprise; while, later on, the introduction of the railway

---

[42] This account by BALG of the origins of the name "Bradford" is not the most comprehensive. A fuller, probably more authoritative, account (and one which offers alternative origins) exists (Ref: Jam1, p413).

system gave fresh impulse to its commercial life. In such circumstances it was no marvel that Bradford drew towards itself the trade of other towns, and that its population rapidly increased. From 1801 to 1821 it had more than doubled itself. When Titus Salt became a resident its population was about 10,000, now it is about 170,000, and its splendid manufactories, warehouses, and public buildings dedicated to art, science, philanthropy, and religion, are the true indices of its great prosperity.

Such is the town to which Titus Salt came in 1822, and with which his life was to be closely identified for the next fifty years.

Mr. Daniel Salt commenced the business of wool-stapling in a small warehouse in Bermondsey.[43] It was the intention of the father that his son should be associated with him in that business, but it was deemed advisable for the youth first to acquire a practical knowledge of it in some Bradford establishment. The manufactory of Messrs. Rouse and Son had commenced in 1815, and was rapidly rising into prosperity. It was fortunate for Titus Salt that he obtained employment there, for not only did he acquire a knowledge of wool-sorting, but also of the various processes of combing, slivering, spinning, and weaving,—all of which were to become conducive to his own commercial success. For his practical knowledge of wool-sorting he was chiefly indebted to John and James Hammond, two brothers, in the employment of the firm. He once acknowledged this in our hearing, when the name of Hammond was mentioned. "It was John Hammond," he said, "who taught me to sort wool." As an evidence of the value attached to the services of these two brothers, by the firm, they were both remembered in Mr. John Rouse's will, and one became afterwards a partner in the business. It was a maxim with the Rouses,—"Those who have helped us to get money, shall help us to enjoy it,"—one worthy of the highest commendation, and which Titus Salt adopted as his own when he became an employer of labour,—

---

[43] Bermondsey was a short street immediately to the east of the better known Cheapside in Bradford. It can be seen on maps as late as 1876 (Ref: Map1). With the development of the Midland Hotel in the latter part of the 19th century the street ceased to exist.

"For in making his thousands he never forgot
The thousands who helped him to make them."

Let us enter the establishment of Messrs. Rouse and Son, and see Titus Salt at his daily employment His work there was real, not nominal; thorough, not superficial. Had he shrunk from the drudgery and soil of business at the first, he could not have reached that point of eminence in it which he gained at last. Imagine him introduced to the sorting-board; he is a tall young man with a "brat," or loose blouse, worn over his clothes to keep them clean; the fleece of wool is unrolled and spread out on the board. Being impregnated with natural grease, it holds entangled in its fibre a variety of substances with which the sheep, while living, had come into contact; these must be carefully removed. All the wool of the fleece is not of the same quality, but varies in length, fineness, and softness of fibre. It is the business of the sorter to separate these different qualities and to put each into a basket. It is evident such occupation requires long and careful education, both of the eye and the hand. Had Titus Salt confined his attention exclusively to this one department of the business, and then at once joined his father, he might, perhaps, have been a successful woolstapler, but not a manufacturer; but, as we have said, he resolved to know every process, from the fleece to the fabric, and into each he put his heart. The next process was washing with alkali or soap and water, and his knowledge of this served him in after years when his first experiments in alpaca began, and which he performed with his own hands. The next process was combing. It is necessary in the production of yarn that all the fibres should be drawn out and laid down smooth and distinct, and that all extraneous matters should be extracted. When Titus Salt was with the Rouses, this operation was done by hand: now, the combing machine, with its ingenious improvements, has superseded it, and become the glory of the trade. The wool thus combed is prepared for spinning. This process consists in passing the "slivers" of combed wool between a series of rollers, which produce "rovings." It is immediately from these "rovings" that yarn is produced by spinning, which is then woven into the fabric.

Such was the occupation of Titus Salt at the Rouse's establishment during two years. There was no department of their business of which he had not some practical knowledge. Thus thoroughly equipped, he joined his father in the wool-stapling trade, which was henceforth carried on under the name of "Daniel Salt and Son." It soon became evident that there was ample scope for the energies of the young partner in this line of business, which was rapidly increasing. He threw his whole soul into it, with the ardour and enthusiasm of youth. No difficulties were insurmountable; no fluctuations were allowed to damp his courage or thwart his purposes. To him was entrusted the duty of attending the public wool sales in London and Liverpool, and effecting purchases from farmers in Norfolk and Lincolnshire, after the season of sheep-clipping. John Hammond, who travelled on behalf of the Rouse's, was frequently his companion in these journeys, and his judgment was sought in any emergency. A more forcible illustration of the expansion of trade in Bradford cannot be given than that in 1825, there were twenty-eight stage coaches, plying in and out of the town. Ten years before, the number was only four. The spinners had made great improvements in their spinning machinery to meet the increasing demand for fine yarns. The increase of inhabitants produced a want of market accommodation, to supply which a market-house, in Hall Ings, was opened, which was superseded by a larger one adjoining Darley Street, in 1824. Now, the commodious Exchange Buildings, standing in Market Street, are the latest architectural sign of its trade prosperity.

But Mr. Titus Salt's time and energy were not wholly devoted to business. On coming to Bradford, his family connected themselves with Horton Lane Chapel,[44] then under the pastorate of the Rev. Thomas Taylor, a man whose memory is still revered by the older inhabitants. This chapel was, at that time, the only one in Bradford belonging to the Congregational body, and may be regarded as the mother of those that have sprung up since. A Sunday school had been recently formed in connection with it, of which Mr. James Garnett[45] was

---

[44] Horton Lane Chapel was a major focal point in both the life of Salt and the development of Bradford, see Appendix 4.

[45] For a fuller account of James Garnett, see Appendix 4.

one of the superintendents. Being an earnest worker himself, he was always on the look-out for young men in the congregation likely to be of service in the Sunday school. Mr. Titus Salt was not long without an invitation to take part, which he readily accepted. He was first appointed librarian, then teacher, then superintendent, and to these circumstances may be traced the deep sympathy with Sunday schools which he manifested throughout his subsequent life. It may not be out of place here to mention that the last act of his life was to erect a Sunday school at Saltaire, the cost of which was £10,000. There are old Sunday scholars still living who remember him in each of the above offices. One says "he was a capital librarian, and always recommended the book best adapted to the reader." Another says, "the class consisted of ten scholars, and he taught us 'The Assembly's Shorter Catechism.' " Another says, "we liked him as the superintendent, but the only drawback was, he would never offer public prayer in the school" Another says, "he was very simple and quiet in his manner, not given to much speech, but a deep-thinking young man."

Why do we record these simple facts? Because in such occupations Mr. Titus Salt presents to young men an example worthy of being followed. His connection with Horton Lane Sunday school was of great benefit to himself. Would that he had then been fully decided for God, and had exercised his "vocal" gifts in public! Perhaps he would then have been free from those nervous restraints that hampered him in after life. But the Sunday school work diverted his thoughts and sympathies once a week into other channels, leading away from self and business, Godwards. In trying to teach others, he was himself taught, and in becoming associated with a band of Christian workers, he formed friendships that conduced to the growth of his true manhood. In such circumstances the Sunday was not a day of idleness or of weariness to him, but one of pleasant and profitable occupation, and if any young man shall be constrained to follow such an example, we doubt not, he will personally reap the advantage of it.

But it was not on the Sunday only that Mr. Titus Salt devoted time and energy to the benefit of others; he early began to manifest that sympathy with the working classes which took so many practical forms afterwards. By the power of such sympathy he acquired an influence over men which increased as he grew in years, and won the esteem of the community. His first appearance on any public occasion was one long to be remembered in Bradford. In the year 1825, there was a strike among the woolcombers[46] which lasted six months, and produced great distress and alarm. In fact, it was a civil rebellion, in which blood was shed and life sacrificed.[47] All business was stopped, and the operatives being liberally supplied with money from a distance, were emboldened in their reckless course.[48] Added to the stoppage of trade, a large banking firm with which the tradesmen of Bradford had extensive dealings, now suspended payment, by which many were seriously affected, and a public panic thus ensued. But it was not until May, 1826, that matters reached a crisis. The operatives, thinking that the introduction of weaving machinery was the cause of all these disasters, and inflamed by popular demagogues, proceeded to attack Horsfall's mill.[49] But what had Mr. Titus Salt to do with this? "I remember" (says a living eye-witness) "Titus Salt took an active part in trying to bring the malcontents to reason; he went into the very thick of the mob, and was not frightened a bit; he remonstrated and reasoned with them, but all in vain." When, however, they refused to listen to reason, and proceeded to violence, the case was altered, he stood up for law and order in spite of all consequences;

---

[46] Woolcombing is the process of straightening wool fibres, and of their separation into short and long fibres (Ref: WorW, p10).

[47] BALG's claim that the strike had associated with it the shedding of blood and the loss of life is difficult to support. Indeed, in a strike that was to run from June until November, and involve approx. 28,000 combers and weavers in the Bradford area, the only recorded breach of the peace in Bradford was an attack by four unionists on a non-striker, for which they were sentenced to two weeks' imprisonment (Ref: Ward, p126). The shedding of blood and the loss of life was to come later, in the riots of 1826.

[48] BALG's description of the strikers' action as reckless is contentious. The dispute was a fundamental one, concerning rates of pay and union recognition, and took place against a looming threat to the workers' livelihoods from mechanization. The employers for their part acted largely in concert, resorting to such tactics as the dismissal of not only union members but also their children (Ref: Ward, p121).

[49] Horsfall's mill stood approx. 250 yards NE of St. Peter's Church (the present day cathedral) (Ref: Map2). The incident at the mill was a major one, involving loss of life. The attacks started on Monday 1st May, the first being mounted in the late afternoon, the second, with a greater number of approx. 450 men, occurring 8–9 p.m. that same day. In these attacks windows were smashed, but following the reading of the Riot Act during the second attack, the mob dispersed. On the Wednesday a larger group of men – approx. 1,000 strong – marched in the afternoon from where they had assembled on Fairweather Green, and the mill (now fortified) was attacked for a third time. It was during this attack on 3rd May that loss of life occurred (Ref: AHofL, pp324-325, SofB, pp219–221, Scr2, Ward).

special constables were required to protect both life and property. The same eye-witness says, "I remember seeing William Rand[50] and Titus Salt hurrying up and down, trying to induce their fellow-townsmen to come forward as special constables.[51] When the military were called out, one of them dashed along the streets warning the inhabitants to keep within doors, as their lives were in danger."[52] The result was, the mob was dispersed, but not until the Riot Act had been read, and several persons killed[53] or wounded. We narrate these incidents as supplying interesting proof of the public spirit of Mr. Titus Salt at the age of twenty-three.[54] Few young men would have ventured to face a mob of excited workmen, and to calm them by moral suasion, and this step was the more remarkable from his naturally quiet disposition. But it is worthy of notice that the strong sense of duty that actuated him on this occasion was a prominent feature of his whole life. When his mind was convinced of the rectitude of any

[50] William Rand was about 30 years old when this incident occurred. He and his elder brother John were working in the family business of his father, trading under the name of John Rand and Sons, of Horton Lane. The business was at the centre of the development of the worsted trade in Bradford. Furthermore, John and William Rand were the main owners of *The Bradford Courier and West Riding Advertiser*, a newspaper that had opposed the strike of 1825; and the strikers' leader John Tester had been employed by them prior to the strike. A life long Anglican and originally conservative, William Rand was later to take a more Liberal stance, becoming an active member of the Anti Corn Law League, a supporter of free trade, and an advocate of the Ten Hour Act. William Rand was to be among the first group of Bradford aldermen to be appointed in 1847, and went on to become Bradford's fourth mayor in 1850 – the first mayor of Bradford to lack any religious affiliation to Horton Lane Chapel. His year in office coincided with the Great Exhibition of 1851, at which Bradford manufacturers were very much in evidence. The town by this time had grown to over 103,000, and expansion was still occurring at a great pace, as can be testified by the large number of new streets, houses, mills, shops, churches etc. His later years were spent in comparative seclusion, and he died in December, 1868 at his home in Kirklands, Baildon, aged 72 (Refs: Bain, Rob4, Cud3, pp125–130, Ward, p121).
[51] Salt's alignment with Rand is noteworthy, mindful of the latter's circumstances in the 1825 strike. It would be interesting to research Salt's role in the events of 1825 – for example to establish whether he played any part in the regular meetings of the employers that were held at the Sun inn to co-ordinate their actions before and during the strike (Ref: Ward, p121). What is clear is that Salt, from a very early stage in his career, determined to involve himself in the industrial affairs of Bradford.
[52] The military was called out on the Wednesday (Ref: Ward, p127), which seems to fix the actions of Rand and Salt to that day; perhaps they were also present on the Monday.
[53] The persons killed were Jonas Barstow, an 18 year old youth, and Edward Fearnley, a 13 year old boy, a consequence of twenty to thirty shots being fired into the mob (Ref: AHofL, p325, Ward, p128).
[54] Salt was only 22 - not 23 - at the time of the Horsfall's mill riots.

cause that demanded his support, no obstacle deterred him, his natural timidity forsook him, and he became bold and self-reliant in dealing with masses of men.

Another instance of a similar kind occurred many years after, when he was a large employer of labour. A strike had taken place among his workpeople, which created great anxiety in the district, and the country generally.[55] The *Times* newspaper devoted a leading article to the subject; how the breach between master and workmen was to be healed, whether capital or labour would win the day, were the anxious questions to be solved. But Mr. Titus Salt was equal to the occasion. When a deputation of the workpeople waited upon him to discuss the point in dispute, what was their surprise when he calmly, yet firmly, answered them thus!—"You are not in my service now. You have, of your own accord, left me; return to your work, and then I shall consider your proposals." The request was reasonable, the argument unanswerable; and such was their confidence in the rectitude of their master that they at once resumed work, and the point in dispute was, very soon afterwards, satisfactorily settled.

---

[55] Two strikes occurred at Saltaire during Salt's lifetime. The strike which BALG goes on to describe is judged to be that of 1868, which started on a Thursday and was resolved by the following Monday. The other strike occurred in 1876. Longer lasting and more serious, this strike by the mill's weavers, spinners and combers led management to lock out the entire labour force (Ref: GtPat, pp317-320).

CHAPTER V.

"True love's the gift which God has given

To man alone beneath the heaven;

It is not fantasy's hot fire,

Whose wishes, soon as granted, fly;

It liveth not in fierce desire,

With dead desire it doth not die;

It is the secret sympathy,

The silver link, the silken tie,

Which heart to heart and mind to mind,

In body and in soul can bind."

—SCOTT.[56]

THE FIRM OF "DANIEL SALT AND SON"—THE JUNIOR PARTNER—HIS BUSINESS HABITS—TRANSACTION AT DEWSBURY—INCREASE OF TRADE—DEFERENCE TO HIS FATHER—FRUGAL HABITS—BUYS A GOLD WATCH WITH HIS FIRST EARNINGS—HIS FRIEND, MR. HENRY FORBES—RESOLVES TO GIVE PART OF HIS INCOME TO GOD—A BLESSING UPON IT—END OF THE BISHOP BLAIZE FESTIVAL— MECHANICS' INSTITUTE TAKES ITS PLACE—BRADFORD BECOMES THE METROPOLIS OF THE WORSTED TRADE—DISTINCTION BETWEEN WORSTED AND WOOLLEN YARNS—MR. TITUS SALT FALLS IN LOVE—WORKS HARD AND WAITS— ENTERPRISE IN UTILISING DONSKOI WOOL—SPINS FOR HIMSELF—MARRIAGE— "OUR TITUS."

THE firm of "Daniel Salt and Son" soon became established in Bradford, and

---

[56] From *The Lay of the Last Minstrel* (canto 5, st.13), written in 1805 by Sir Walter Scott (1771-1832). The Scottish novelist and poet, although of an earlier age than Balgarnie, spent time in the Border counties of Balgarnie's own youth, and drew on the area for inspiration in his writings, which even after his death retained a great influence on Victorian Britain, characterizing for many the entity of Scotland.

well known in the surrounding district; their knowledge of the trade, the class of wools they sold, and the spirit of enterprise they manifested, could not fail to be appreciated in such a thriving community. Much of the success of the firm was undoubtedly owing to the practical knowledge of the junior partner, whose manly form and open countenance had become familiar to the frequenters of the wool sales and markets. Both buyers and sellers liked to do business with him. It was not that he had much to say in commendation of the article he sold, but what he said was always to the point. The rule which he began business with, and adhered to, throughout his life, was to let the quality of the goods speak for itself,—a good rule, which every young man commencing business should adopt as his own. It was the rule given by the mother of the Crossleys[57] at the outset of their remarkable career, and which the Wise Man long before inculcated upon his Son: "Let another praise thee, and not thine own mouth; a stranger and not thine own lips."—(Proverbs, xxvii. 2,) Were such a rule more observed in trade generally, how quickly many exaggerated advertisements would disappear!

As the business of the firm increased locally, it also ramified into the neighbouring towns, such as Halifax, Huddersfield, and Dewsbury. The senior partner confined himself chiefly to the local trade, while the enterprising junior found scope for his energies far and near. A gentleman still living, remembers him as a young man, coming to Dewsbury. We give his own words :—" Mr. Titus Salt came to my warehouse one day, and wanted to sell wool. I was greatly pleased with the quiet power of the young man, and his aptitude for business, but most of all was I struck with the resolute way he expressed his

---

[57] The Crossley family of Halifax was an important West Riding family in its own right, whose fortunes and standing in society ran alongside those of the Salt family. As with Salt, the themes of textiles, public service, Congregationalism and philanthropy permeate the family's life in the 19th century. The 'mother of the Crossleys' referred to was Martha Crossley (nee Turner), who despite being a generation older than Salt was certainly known to him – there is a report of his calling on her during a visit to the family's Dean Clough Mills (Ref: Bret3, Part I, p7). Three of her sons – John, Joseph and Francis - were major figures, each of who made major impacts on Halifax's 19th century development. Furthermore there was a link through marriage of the two families. Salt's sister Anne married John Smith of Jersey, whose sister Hannah married Joseph Crossley. The two families were to be brought into closer union with the later marriage in 1866 of Titus Salt Jr. to Catherine Crossley, second daughter of Joseph Crossley (see Appendix 3). For a fuller account of the Crossleys, see Bret3.

intention of taking away with him that day, £1000 out of Dewsbury." Nor was this a mere empty boast, for the same informant says, "Before he left Dewsbury, I myself gave him a bill for that amount." Does not this incident afford an insight into his business habits at an early period of his career? When out on business, he meant business. He did with his might whatsoever he put his hand to, and it was not with fussiness or manoeuvre he did it; but his straightforwardness, and quiet yet resolute manner, were enough to secure the respect and confidence of discerning men.

Thus he steadily advanced, step by step, in business. Though nominally the junior partner in the firm, he was in reality its head. The father looked up to the son for the practical knowledge he possessed; while the son paid that deference to the father's judgment which his experience of the world supplied, and that respect to a parent's wishes which filial love dictated. This was undoubtedly a critical position for a young man to occupy, and one that might have inflated him with vanity or led him early to assert his freedom from parental restraint. But, no; his father's house was still his home; the spell of a mother's presence and love was upon him; and the influence of the domestic circle served to keep his heart warm, and his tastes simple and pure. Of course, living at home with his parents, his personal expenses were small, so that he was able to save a portion of his income, and to open a private banking account for himself.[58] It is said he was "very careful of his means;" he early acquired the habit of "taking care of the pence," knowing full well "that the pounds would" more readily "take care of themselves." And this good habit was not abandoned in after life, for even in the plenitude of his wealth and the munificence of his gifts, he was always careful, not only of his money, but of such trifling things as blank leaves of letters, pamphlets, and scraps of paper, which were not thrown into the waste-basket, but laid aside for use. In order that he might husband his finances he scrupulously avoided any expenditure upon himself, unless for things of utility; no extravagance in attire or ornament, no outlay for the gratification of personal vanity would he ever allow.

It is true that about this period he indulged himself in the purchase of a gold

---

[58] It is worth noting in passing that ultimately, in 1871, Salt was to become one of the vice-presidents of the Yorkshire Penny Bank. (Ref: YPBnk, p63).

watch; but the way he proceeded in obtaining it, was so characteristic, that it is worthy of being recorded, as an example to young men in similar circumstances. Many young men commencing business would have regarded a handsome gold watch, with massive appendages, as almost a *sine qua non* among their associates, but Mr. Titus Salt inwardly resolved that he would not permit his wish to be gratified until he had worked hard to merit it. He therefore bargained with himself that when his accumulated savings amounted to £1000, a gold watch should be his reward. The goal set before him was, in course of time, reached, and the prize was fairly won. It was no flimsy foreign article he bought, but a watch, like himself solid in quality, thoroughly English in make, with face open and honest, the true index of right movements within. How proud he was of that watch in after-life! For it was a memento of his early toils, and the first fruits of his own industry. It was worn by him till the close of his life, and when his own hand became too feeble to wind it, he handed it to others to be wound in his presence.[59]

Among the associates of Mr. Titus Salt one individual deserves especial mention, who was his attached friend through life, and, perhaps, more than any other, helped to strengthen and develop his character. His name was Mr. Henry Forbes.[60] This gentleman had but recently come to Bradford, as a commercial traveller; but his vast energy and remarkable talent for business soon lifted him into a higher position, and marked him as a rising man. Mr. Robert Milligan,[61] with the characteristic shrewdness of a Scotchman, soon appraised the commercial traveller's abilities, and offered him a partnership in his business. The firm of Milligan and Forbes has long occupied a foremost place among the merchants of Bradford, and is one of many whose enterprise and wealth have done much to consolidate the trade of the town, and promote its social and architectural improvement. But it is with Mr. Forbes, as the early friend of Mr. Titus Salt, we have now to do. At Horton Lane Chapel, they were often thrown together, not only in Christian worship, but in work. Mr. Forbes found in his friend a mind congenial with his own, and a heart susceptible of generous

---

[59] In his will, Salt was to bequeath his watches to his widow Caroline.
[60] For a fuller account of Forbes, see Appendix 4.
[61] For a fuller account of Milligan, see Appendix 4.

impulses. One rule they adopted together, and observed during their lives, is worthy of imitation, and that was, to give a portion of their income to God, through the channels of religion or benevolence. It was well for these business men that they adopted such a rule early in their career, for it is more easily observed by one just rising into wealth, than by one who has attained it. The former begins when the heart is uncorroded by the love of money; the latter (if he ever begins at all) when his finer sympathies are often shrivelled or dead. To the one, "giving" yields pleasure, and becomes a luxury; to the other, it inflicts pain, and is avoided as a nauseous drug. Mr. Titus Salt early began to tread the path of active benevolence. Few men have given more generously of their substance in their lifetime, of which we shall have abundant proof in another chapter. Mr. Forbes was wont to say to his friend, "Titus, we seem to prosper in business in proportion as we give." To some persons this may appear incongruous or untrue, but have they not read the following distich?

> "There was a man whom many counted mad;
> The more he gave away, the more he had."

And what is this second line but another form of putting the text of scripture? "There is that scattereth, and yet increaseth; and there is that withholdeth more than is meet, but it tendeth to poverty. The liberal soul shall be made fat; and he that watereth shall be watered also himself." (Proverbs xi. 24, 25.) How strikingly this truth was confirmed in the history of Mr. Titus Salt! His hand and heart were ever open to the claims of religion and benevolence, and yet, "the more he gave away, the more he had"; like the patriarch of old, "the Lord blessed his latter end more than his beginning."

In the previous chapter we noticed the spirited position taken by Mr. Titus Salt in connection with the woolcombers' strike, in 1825-26. We refer to it again as commencing an important epoch in the moral improvement of Bradford, with which he and Mr. Forbes were identified. The disastrous strike was an unfortunate sequel to the Septennial Festival of Bishop Blaize, the patron saint of the woolcombers. In 1825,[62] this festival was celebrated with greater pomp

---

[62] The exact date was 3rd February, 1825 (Ref: AHofL, p316).

than ever, and the streets had never before presented such a scene of dissipation and frivolity. The description of it, as given by a contemporary, reads like a romance, so far as the pageant was concerned, but the influence it exerted upon the minds of the people must have been most demoralizing indeed.[63] It was a relic of semi-barbarous times, and strangely out of character with the present. It was an anachronism which evidently ought to be brought to an end. So thought the intelligent part of the community; but how was it to be accomplished? It was like destroying a tree that had stood for centuries in their midst, and many voices were loud in the cry of "Woodman, spare that tree." To this question the efforts of Mr. Forbes, Mr. Titus Salt, and others, were directed. Public meetings were held at which methods for the moral and intellectual improvement of the people were discussed. Lectures to the working classes themselves were commenced to promote this end. What was the result? The Blaize festival was never celebrated again. Before the next Septennial a new order of things was inaugurated.[64] A building was hired, where educational classes, library, and reading-room were established. Several years elapsed before a permanent building was erected, but this was the nucleus of the present Mechanics' Institute,[65] which has since increased in usefulness, and is one of the most prosperous of the kind in the country. A school of design in connection with this institute was commenced in 1848, for instruction in the fine arts, and especially in relation to the manufactures of the district. May we not, in the formation of this institution, recognise the foreshadow of that splendid building afterwards erected at Saltaire, the cost of which was £25,000, the object of its erection

---

[63] BALG is writing of the event more than fifty years later, and of course he had no direct experience of the prevailing scenes. Another account (Ref: AHofL, pp316–317) of the 1825 festival paints a different picture to BALG. It may be the same account that BALG refers to as a "romance", but it does not read as such. This other account describes a perfectly orderly, well organized event with a procession which started at 10 a.m. and which dispersed at 5 p.m.

[64] Perhaps this "new order" is an early example of social engineering by the young Salt, Forbes and others. Seen in conjunction with his actions at Horsfall's mill, it seems that Salt even as a very young man had a will to bring about a social order that he deemed appropriate for the newly developing Bradford.

[65] The Mechanics' Institute movement sought to provide part-time courses (usually in the evenings) in the crafts and sciences, to improve the education and prospects of workers. By 1851 there were approx. 700 institutes, mainly in London and the other major industrial cities. They were the forerunners of technical colleges and civic universities (Ref: DicEd).

being the moral, physical, and intellectual improvement of the workpeople?[66]

As for the Bradford trade, after the memorable strike of the woolcombers, it not only recovered its briskness, but received new impulse. Power-looms and combing machines gradually came into general use. New mills were being continually erected, which, of course, meant business to the woolstapler, and especially to the firm of "Daniel Salt and Son," whose prosperity ran parallel with that of the community. From the period when machinery was introduced, the worsted industry of Bradford increased till the last trace of the ancient woollen manufacture began to disappear, and the town became the metropolis of the worsted trade.

As it is chiefly with the worsted trade Mr. Titus Salt's name is more intimately connected, the uninitiated reader may wish to know the difference between the woollen and the worsted trades. The term "worsted" is said to have derived its origin from a village of that name in Norfolk where this kind of manufacture was first carried on. Worsted goods used to be the staple trade of the city of Norwich, but, owing to neglect of the factory system, it was transferred, like the trade of various other places, to Bradford. The difference between woollen and worsted manufacture is due, in great part to the way the yarn for each is spun. Yarn for woollen cloth is very slightly twisted, so as to leave the fibre as free as possible for the felting or milling process. Worsted yarn, on the contrary, is hard spun and made with a much stronger thread. When worsted goods leave the loom they require only a superficial dressing, and in this respect they differ much from woollen cloths, which require elaborate finishing processes. In a word, woollen fabrics are designed for the attire of men, worsted fabrics for that of women. Worsted yarn was, therefore, capable of being spun into light fabrics of various quality and form, thus affording greater scope for skill and enterprise, both on the part of the manufacturer and the woolstapler. The brain of the latter was sometimes taxed to supply the necessary raw material for the production of worsted fabrics. The wools of Lincolnshire and Norfolk were in great request, and many were the journeys Mr. Titus Salt

---

[66] BALG is referring to the Saltaire Club and Institute, the erection of which is described in Chapter XV. In the present day the establishment is known as the Victoria Hall and Institute, or simply Victoria Hall.

took to obtain them for his busy customers.

It was in one of those journeys into Lincolnshire that he met with her who afterwards became his wife. Mr. Whitlam, her father, was a large farmer, who resided at Manor House, Grimsby. Rich though he was in flocks and herds, he was still richer in a large family of eighteen sons and daughters, of whom only eight survived the period of childhood. Caroline was the youngest of all, and is now the last survivor. We have read in Grecian mythology of a certain adventurer who set sail for Colchis in quest of the golden fleece, and there fell in love with Medea, whom he brought back as his wife. The young woolstapler of Bradford was the Jason on this occasion; the fleece he was in quest of was wool; but in her who won his heart and became his wife, he acquired a treasure more precious than the fleece of gold. Nor was he the first adventurer or the last, who sailed towards the port of Grimsby, on the same errand, and returned with a similar prize. Another Bradford woolstapler[67] had previously married Amelia Whitlam. It may be that he had brought back a good report of the land, and of the fair treasures still left in the Manor House of Grimsby. Be that as it may, Mr. Titus Salt had somehow received such a glowing description of Mr. Whitlam's daughters that he ventured on this expedition for himself. We once heard him narrate the story of his love adventure. In doing so, he smilingly looked at his wife, and then, as if speaking in confidence to his friends who were near, playfully added, "You know, when I went courting I made a mistake. It was another sister I was in quest of, but this one first met my eye, and captivated my heart at once." Well he knew it was no mistake, but that a Divine hand had guided him in his choice, as the experience of above forty years had already proved. Another Bradford woolstapler[68] was the third successful adventurer to Grimsby, and became the husband of Lucy Whitlam, so that three sisters came to reside in the same town.[69]

---

[67] The person in question was George Haigh, who married Amelia in 1820 (Ref: GtPat, p47).
[68] The person in question was Charles Timothy Turner, who married Lucy in 1833 (Ref: GtPat, p47).
[69] The three married couples lived very close to each other in Bradford: Titus Salt had a house on North Parade (a continuation of Manor Row), quite close to that of his father; and the Haighs and the Turners lived next door to each other in Manor Row. Furthermore

But it must not be supposed that Mr. Titus Salt hastily rushed into matrimony. It was not his habit to do anything in a hurry, much less in taking an important step like this. There was a delay of a year or two. Perhaps one reason was the extreme youth of the selected lady,[70] but another was, that his means were insufficient to justify the immediate fulfilment of his engagement. Love was, therefore, placed under the restraint of prudence. But nothing was lost by this delay; on the contrary, much was gained to himself. A new impulse was given him in the prosecution of business, which was sustained by a high and noble motive. As his personal skill and industry had previously won an inferior prize, why might he not now redouble his efforts to reach a higher goal and possess the prize that Love had already won? This he resolutely determined to do. We therefore find him henceforward devoting his time and energy to business with an enthusiasm unknown before. He seemed burning with an ambition to strike out new paths for himself, and to become a leader in commercial enterprise. The father was quite satisfied to work on the old lines, but he was unable to restrain the ambition of his son, who seemed to him like the Athenians of old, always delighting "in some new thing." This was a striking feature in Mr. Titus Salt's character, which subsequent events illustrate. He possessed what might be regarded as the inventive faculty, which, had it been directed to mechanics, would perhaps have led to eminence like that of George Stephenson. Indeed, the construction of his mind had considerable resemblance to that of the famous engineer whose practical sense, honesty of purpose, and determination in carrying it out, are well known. His quiet, yet searching eye, seemed always gathering materials for his busy brain to work into something practical.

The first attempt outside the lines of his ordinary business was in the utilising of raw material, heretofore unappreciated in the worsted trade. With the increasing demand for long wools, the idea suggested itself to Mr. Titus Salt, "Why should not the Donskoi wool be used in the worsted as well as the woollen manufacture?" This wool, as its name indicates, is grown on the banks of the river Don, in the south-eastern parts of Russia. It is a coarse and tangled

---

Edward Salt (uncle of Titus) lived in Manor Row after his marriage in the late 1830s (Ref: GtPat, p47).
[70] Titus' future wife must have been 16 or 17 years old when they first met, being 18 years old when they married on 21st August, 1830.

material, apparently unadapted to the production of a fine fabric, but to his eye, it had possibilities of lustre and fineness in it, which were well worthy of a trial. Having invested in a large stock of this Russian wool, Mr. Titus Salt was naturally anxious to dispose of it to his customers, but they declined to become purchasers. This was rather a trying time for the woolstapling firm of "Daniel Salt and Son," and especially for the junior partner, whose speculative tendencies had involved them in this seemingly unprofitable investment. What was to be done with the article on hand, was the problem that perplexed the firm, and which Mr. Titus set himself to solve. He resolved that instead of asking the manufacturers to purchase it, he would utilise it himself. For this purpose he took "Thompson's Mill," Silsbridge Lane, Bradford, and having fitted it with suitable machinery, he proceeded to spin the Donskoi wool into yarn, and weave it into fabric. The result of the experiment was entirely successful; the fabric produced was such as to astonish and convince the most sceptical of its commercial value, and to place him in an enviable position before his fellow-townsmen. Successful in this first experiment, he added a larger factory in Union Street. Trade grew so rapidly under his hands that in a few years he was carrying on, not only the two mills above mentioned, but also Hollings' Mill, Brick Lane Mill, and one in Fawcett Court.[71] His intention when he commenced the manufacturing business, was to confine himself to spinning. This course he pursued for some time, and disposed of his yarns to the Messrs. Fison;[72] but some misunderstanding having arisen with that firm, he, with his characteristic decision, resolved "to spin and weave for himself." Thus his first experiment in manufacture was crowned with success: not only was the practical knowledge he acquired with the Rouses utilized, but a new staple in the Bradford worsted trade was introduced. But this was not the only reward of

---

[71] Each of the five sites referred to by BALG can be located by reference to the relevant map of Bradford (Ref: Map3). Silsbridge Lane was approx. half a mile west of St. Peter's church. Union Street and Fawcett Court were closely adjacent to each other, approx. one quarter of a mile SW of St. Peter's church. The Hollings' Mill site is judged to be that of the present day Hollings' Mill, in what is now Lower Grattan Road, which in Salt's time could have been described as being near the western end of Silsbridge Lane. Brick Lane was less central, being approx. 1 mile west of St. Peter's church.

[72] Messrs Fison and Company were spinners and manufacturers of Bradford and Burley, near Otley. The company employed over 600 people (Ref: AofY2, p46). William Fison features later in the Salt story, see Chapter VII.

his skill and perseverance. The higher goal, on which his heart was set, was at last reached, and Caroline Whitlam became his wife. They were married in the Parish Church of Grimsby,[73] on the 21st August, 1830, the bridegroom being twenty-seven years of age,[74] and the bride only eighteen. The home they first occupied was situated at the bottom of Manningham Lane, not far from the residence of Mr. Salt senior, to whom the remarkable success of his son was a matter of paternal pride. How proud he was to speak of "Our Titus," and of the position he had attained! Little did he know that his son was only at the threshold of his commercial success, and that the homely phrase "Our Titus" would come to be adopted by the community, as familiarly expressive of their affection for one who had become their adopted son, and of whose noble and distinguished career they were all justly proud.

---

[73] One should not infer the Whitlam family's religious affiliation from its use of a parish church for the marriage. It was only after the 1836 Registration Act that Nonconformist congregations could apply to have their meeting houses licensed for marriages.
[74] Titus Salt was only 26 years old – not 27 – on the date in question.

CHAPTER VI.

"All my life long
I have upheld with most respect the man
Who knew himself, and knew the ways before him,
And from amongst them chose considerately.
With a clear foresight, not a blinded courage;
And, having chosen, with a steadfast mind
Pursued his purpose."

—PHILIP VAN ARTEVELDE.[75]

MR. TITUS SALT'S PERSONAL APPEARANCE—UTILISING OF ALPACA, NOT AN ACCIDENT—COTTON FAMINE—INSPECTION OF SEA-WEED—ALPACAS AT CROW NEST—FORM AND HABITS OF THE ANIMALS—DISCOVERY OF NEW STAPLE—MR. SALT VISITS LIVERPOOL AND SEES THE NONDESCRIPT WOOL—EXAMINATION AND EXPERIMENTS—BUYS THE WHOLE CARGO—ADAPTATION OF MACHINERY FOR SPINNING IT—DIFFICULTIES OVERCOME—OVERTURES TO JOHN HAMMOND—"A MAN OR A MOUSE"—MATERIAL IN USE BEFORE—INCREASE OF ALPACA TRADE—INTRODUCTION OF COTTON WARPS—ERECTION OF SALEM CHAPEL—MR. AND MRS. D. SALT'S CONNECTION WITH IT—THEIR DEATH—MR. TITUS SALT AT BUSINESS—CHILDREN BORN AT BRADFORD.

Mr. Titus Salt had now reached the prime of manhood. He was tall in stature, measuring about six feet; robust in health, and florid in complexion; he had large intelligent eyes; a lofty forehead, crowned with long black hair. The portrait of him at the beginning of this book was taken in his advanced years, and, therefore, conveys but a faint impression of what he was at the period to

---

[75] *PHILIP VAN ARTEVELDE* was a well known Victorian play by Sir Henry Taylor. Philip van Artevelde (1340–1382) had been a popular Flemish leader who supported the workers, and in particular the weavers, in a struggle between the Goods (propertied classes) and the Bads (workers).

which we now refer; but those who knew him then speak of him as "a tall, thin, good looking man"; or, to take the testimony of an admiring friend, "he was every inch a man."[76]

He was now busily occupied in manufacturing Donskoi wool into worsted fabrics. His success in this enterprise, and that, too, in the face of local prejudice and opposition, had not only astonished the community, but it had enabled him to guage his own abilities and gain confidence in himself. To one like Mr. Titus Salt, who was constitutionally nervous and diffident, the gain was great indeed. It evoked other mental powers that had hitherto lain dormant, and made his present success a starting point for higher achievements. The utilising of the fibre called alpaca in the worsted trade was, in reality, the *magnum opus* of his life, and the basis of his fame and fortune. It was, in fact, the discovery of a new staple[77] in worsted manufacture, by which the trade and commerce of the world were enriched, and mankind at large, benefited.

Perhaps some persons would regard this discovery as an accident, with which mental ability had little to do. Strange that such accidents generally happen to men of genius and energy, not to the simpleton or the sluggard! Did it not look like an accident when an apple was seen falling from a tree at Woolsthorpe; or water boiling in a tea-kettle at Glasgow? Yet the former suggested to Newton the law of gravitation, and the latter to Watt the condensing steam engine. But what then? It required mental power in either case to deal with the facts, and follow them up to their issues. It also involved long and persevering toil, such as no other men had previously exercised in the same direction. Thus it was with Mr. Titus Salt in the utilising of alpaca in a way hitherto unknown. He had the eye to see what other men saw not, the mind to think what other minds thought not, the patience and perseverance in making experiments which others had not made, and he thereby reached a point of eminence in the manufacturing world which few have reached; and the same idiosyncrasy was manifested on other

---

[76] We know of no portraits or other representations of Salt as a young man. The youngest looking representation of Salt as an adult is perhaps the bust of him which was presented to him by his workers (see Chapter XII), which in the present day stands in the vestibule of Saltaire United Reformed Church (previously the Congregational Church).

[77] The staple is the fibre of a piece of wool, typically a term used in the context of quality (Ref: OED).

occasions, as well as this. One of these may be here mentioned. It happened during the cotton famine in Lancashire, when the mills were silent, and the staple supply was all but cut off by the American civil war. An interesting letter had just appeared in the London *Times,* in which it was alleged that along the seaboard of England ample materials existed capable of being utilised as a substitute for cotton. Mr. Titus Salt was visiting Scarborough at the time. One day, we found him quite alone, far from the town, on the southern beach. The tide was very low, and the rocks uncovered. We observed him busily engaged picking up pieces of sea-weed, which he very carefully examined. Some were twisted and thrown away; others were rubbed, and their fibres spread out in the palm of his hand. When asked what he was in quest of in such an out-of-the-way place, he quietly said, "I have been trying whether this stuff could be manufactured; but it won't do!"

Though the result of this investigation amounted to nothing practical, it certainly shewed the natural bent of his mind, and that the discovery of alpaca, as a new staple of industry, was not likely to be an accident, but the product of a mental force and habit peculiarly his own.

We now proceed to describe the circumstances connected with this valuable discovery, but first it may interest the reader to know something of the animal that bears the name "alpaca." Mr. Salt had once a considerable flock of alpacas in his possession, which originally belonged to the late Earl of Derby, and were sold at Knowsley with the zoological collection in which his lordship took delight; but the animals never took kindly to the country of their adoption. They wanted the drier and steep mountain regions of their native Peru. Part of this flock was sent out to Australia and the Cape of Good Hope to be naturalized in those wool-growing countries but at home they were difficult to keep alive. Indeed, one by one they died, so that now, one solitary representative alone is left at Crow Nest,—the last of all the flock!

The existence of the animal called the paca or alpaca was known nearly three hundred years before, and its long fleece was a matter of boasting by the Spanish governors of Peru in the sixteenth century. The word "alpaca" is the general name for that form of the "Camelidae" which is to be found only in the New World. It is so closely allied to the llama that many naturalists regard it as a variety of the same genus rather than a distinct species. Its wool is straighter than that of the sheep. It is silken in its texture, uncommonly lustrous, very strong in proportion to its thickness, and breaks very little in combing. In appearance the alpaca somewhat resembles the sheep, but it has a longer neck, and a more elegant head, which it holds proudly erect. Its eyes are large and beautiful. Its motions are free and active, the ordinary pace being a rapid, bounding canter. If regularly shorn, the wool will grow about six inches a year, but if allowed to remain upon the animal several years, it will then attain a length of twenty or even thirty inches. It frequents the highest mountains of Peru and Chili, in flocks of one or two hundred. In a wild condition it is shy and vigilant; but when brought very young to the huts of the Indians it can be easily domesticated, and made useful in carrying burdens from the mountains to the coast, the peculiar conformation of its feet enabling it to walk securely on slopes too rough and steep for any other animal. In this, do we not see the wisdom of the Creator of all things, who has adapted one kind of camel for the soft sands of Eastern deserts and another for the rough paths of the Western mountains?[78]

It was in the year 1836 that the wool of the alpaca first came under the notice of Mr. Titus Salt. He happened to be in Liverpool on matters connected with his business, when, in passing through one of the dock warehouses, his eye fell upon a huge pile of dirty-looking bales of alpaca, with here and there a rent in them that disclosed their contents. It is well known that the late Charles Dickens made this incident the subject of an amusing article in *Household Words,* and though the greater part of his description may be regarded as imaginary, yet the basis of it is undoubtedly fact, as we can personally verify by statements from Mr. Titus Salt's own lips.[79] The Liverpool brokers, with whom this memorable transaction took place, were fictitiously designated "C. W. & F. Foozle and Co."; but their real names were Messrs. Hegan and Co. It appears that to this firm had been consigned above three hundred bales of alpaca wool, in the hope

---

[78] These words of BALG were written a full 18 years after the publication of Darwin's *Origins of Species*. BALG's words are probably reflecting the Congregational thinking of the day.

[79] *Household Words* was a weekly journal which included articles on politics, science and history. In this particular article, written under the title "The Great Yorkshire Llama", Dickens goes on to describe a visit that he himself made to Saltaire, at a time when the mill was under construction (Ref: Dick).

that some English manufacturer might be inclined to buy it. It had lain long in their ware-house unnoticed, and become such a nuisance that if a purchaser did not soon turn up, they had determined to re-ship it to Peru, whence it came. It was at this juncture that Mr. Titus Salt happened to see the new material, of which he had no previous knowledge. Having pulled out a handful from one of the bales, he examined it, as a woolstapler would, but said nothing, and, quietly went his way. Some time after, business again brought him to Liverpool, when he took occasion to visit a second time the warehouse containing the nondescript wool, and spent some time minutely examining it. It was evident that during the interval a new idea had taken possession of his mind, and he was now, in his own quiet way, seriously revolving it; but in this instance he not only examined the material, but took away a small quantity in his handkerchief and brought it to Bradford, with a view to ascertain if anything could be made of it. In furtherance of this inquiry he shut himself up in a room, saying nothing to anyone. His first act was thoroughly to scour the material he had brought, then to comb it, which operations he performed with his own hands. He then carefully examined the fibre, testing its strength and measuring its length. Whether he spun any of it into thread we do not know, but the result of his experiments thus far was a surprise to himself. He saw before him a long glossy wool, which he believed was admirably adapted for those light fancy fabrics in the Bradford trade which were then in great demand.

It was about this time he happened to meet his friend John Hammond, whom he tried to interest in this new staple. He said to him, "John, I have been to Liverpool and seen some alpaca wool; I think it might be brought into use." But John Hammond did not encourage him in such a speculation. As for Mr. Salt, senior, he strongly advised his son "to have nothing to do with the nasty stuff." But the advice of neither friend nor father availed to shake his opinion that the staple in question was highly valuable and capable of being used in the worsted trade. Indeed, the more others disparaged it, the more tenaciously he held to the opinion, which had been formed after much thought and experiment; and if no one could be found to approve or encourage, why should he not have the courage in this matter, to act for himself?

Judge, then, the surprise of the Liverpool brokers when the Bradford manufacturer returned soon after, and made an offer for the whole consignment of alpaca, at eightpence a pound. To quote from the amusing article in *Household Words,* "At first the head of the firm fancied our friend had come for the express purpose of quizzing him, and then that he was an escaped lunatic, and thought seriously of calling for the police; but eventually it ended in his making it over in consideration of the price offered."

Such is the unvarnished story of the discovery of alpaca by Mr. Titus Salt. But he was only now at the beginning of his difficulties, for this material, which was easily purchased, had yet to be spun into yarn and woven into fabric, ere the public could be convinced of the soundness of his judgment in reference to it. How was this to be done? There was no likelihood that the Bradford manufacturers would look more favourably on this new staple than they had done on the Donskoi wool. To attempt the sale of it among the manufacturers was entirely out of the question, and therefore to manufacture it himself seemed the only alternative. But there was still a practical difficulty. His machinery at present in use was not adapted to the new material. But a mind like his knew of difficulties only as "things to be overcome." When once an idea took possession of him, and his plans were matured, and his course clear, then his imperious will seemed to lay everything under arrest for the accomplishment of his purpose. Circumstances must bend to him; not he to circumstances. To young men who are always expecting something to turn up, and who, like the traveller wanting to cross the stream, waited for all the water to run past,—to such we would say, learn from Mr. Titus Salt not to lean on artificial props at all, but on your own manly selves; not to be "hangers-on" upon Providence, but to remember that Providence helps the man who puts an honest heart into all the work of his hands.

After many anxious months the necessary machinery was made, and the alpaca wool passed through the various processes preliminary to its being spun and woven. It was now his turn to wonder. Imagine, then, his extreme delight when, out of the unsightly material which first met his eye in Liverpool, he saw that beautiful fabric, which has since carried his name far and wide, and is now prized and worn by rich and poor, in all parts of the civilised world.

In entering upon this new branch of business, Mr. Titus Salt made overtures to John Hammond to join him in partnership, for he evidently felt the need of some one to share with him the burden of the undertaking, which had now become heavy. But these overtures were respectfully declined on the ground that the Rouses having always treated him with kindness and liberality, he must remain in their employment as long as he lived. It was in Garraway's[80] coffee rooms, London, that these two early friends had the interview for the consideration of the above proposal, which ended by Mr. Titus Salt saying "Well, John, I am going into this alpaca affair right and left, and I'll either make myself a man or a mouse."

But in this account of the discovery and utilising of the alpaca wool it is but right to state that the material had been known in this country long before. In the year 1811, Mr. William Walton, in a published work, had described the wool of the llama tribe as possessing "a fibre of extraordinary length and of a fine glossy texture." In 1830, Mr. Outram,[81] of Greetland, near Halifax, had produced a fabric, from alpaca wool, which was sold as a curiosity at a high price. The Indians of Peru had also, from time immemorial, made blankets and cloaks of the same material, but this does not, in the least, detract from the merit of Mr. Titus Salt, whose investigations and experiments were conducted on a perfectly independent basis, and to whom undoubtedly belongs the honour of having added this new staple to the industry of the country, and adapted it to purposes hitherto unknown.

It will thus be seen how the practical experience he acquired at the Rouses was brought into use at this important period of his life: but for this he would have had to depend upon others to supply the knowledge requisite in each department of the business. But, like the skilled master of a ship, who had risen from the lowest to the highest position in her, he knew every detail himself, and was therefore competent to direct his numerous subordinates with judgment and precision. The life of Mr. Titus Salt was henceforth one of intense devotedness

---

[80] Garraway's was a fashionable 19th century coffee house in Change Alley (off Cornhill) in the City of London. Although now demolished, a plaque on the modern day building marks the site of the coffee house. An engraving and a water colour illustration of the coffee house, executed in 1853 and 1873 respectively, are held in the Guildhall Library and Art Gallery, London.

[81] Benjamin Outram, woollen cloth manufacturer (Ref: Pig1).

to business: his brain was ever busy and his hands ever occupied in the management of the various manufactories now in full working order. The demand for alpaca goods increased with remarkable rapidity, so that within the short space of three years the import of the staple had risen to 2,186,480lbs., and now the yearly consumption, with other kindred fibres, in the Bradford trade alone, amounts to about 4,000,000lbs.; the price which at first was only eightpence, had risen to two shillings and sixpence per pound. Alpaca and mohair (to which we shall afterwards refer,) together constitute an important item in our national trade; these two articles alone standing at about £1,600,000 in the annual imports of raw materials. Of themselves they would not, of course, give to the worsted trade its present proud position in the country; but it is not too much to say, that the skill and enterprise of Mr. Titus Salt, amongst spinners and manufacturers, preeminently contributed to the attainment of that high position. Each branch of the industry has been a source of strength to the other, and of the multitude of mills in Bradford and the neighbourhood, now engaged upon these articles, the origin of many of them might be traced indirectly to him whose busy life we are endeavouring to sketch.

But it was not so much the immediate profit that accrued to himself that rendered his present achievements so remarkable, but the stimulus it gave to trade generally. A new mine, as it were, was opened in Bradford, which invited many toilers to work it, for the treasures it possessed. Employment was thus created for thousands of workpeople, who were attracted from all parts of the country by the high remuneration offered. Whole streets of dwellings soon sprung up in the vicinity of the mills. Merchants, who had hitherto transacted business through local agents, found it necessary to remove their residence from the metropolis and other places, to this thriving centre of industry. Even foreigners regarded it their interest to leave their fatherland, to become naturalised citizens of this country and dwellers in this community. Of these foreigners, Germany has supplied a large quota, who form an important element in the local prosperity. Indeed, the indirect results of Mr. Titus Salt's achievements are so interwoven with the growth of Bradford, in population, in building, in trade and commerce, in moral and intellectual improvement, that it is impossible to separate the one from the other.

The introduction of cotton warps[82] in weaving was a fortunate circumstance for the district. This took place about the year 1837. It essentially changed the character of the worsted stuffs, and gave to the manufacture an extension unknown before. In former years the chief consideration with most purchasers was the durability of the fabric; but when a taste for light, elegant, and cheap articles of dress was formed, the question arose, how this taste was to be met, and what cheaper thread, other than worsted, could be introduced? But for this departure from the old lines, the worsted manufacture by itself could never have produced that endless variety of fancy fabrics, with which we are now familiar. But what had Mr. Titus Salt to do with this important step? Perhaps nothing, directly, but there was a singular coincidence of time in the introduction of cotton warps and the utilising of alpaca. In fact, they were contemporary, the one was the complement of the other, and both gave a mighty impulse to the trade of the district, and secured for it the pre-eminence that it still retains.

Mr. D. Salt carried on the woolstapling business at Cheapside, until about the year 1833, when, his means being amply sufficient for the remainder of his days, he relinquished it. He had built a house in Manningham Lane to which at this time he removed. Mrs. D. Salt is still remembered for her Christian character and consistency; she was much attached to Horton Lane Chapel, and took a lively interest in its various organizations. Ministers of religion were frequent guests at the house, and the ministerial visits of her pastor, the Rev. T. Taylor, helped her on her heavenly way. When the movement for the erection of Salem Chapel began in 1833, both Mr. and Mrs. D. Salt took much interest in it. The increase of the congregation at Horton Lane was considerable, and the consequent lack of accommodation had long been felt. Mr. D. Salt was a member of the building committee of Salem Chapel, also Mr. R. Milligan and Mr. Henry Forbes. The last mentioned gentleman brought into this undertaking that amazing energy for which he was remarkable, and, like many earnest impulsive men, he found it difficult to co-operate harmoniously with others more cautious than himself. The difficulty, however, was equally great on the other side, for on one occasion, Mr. Daniel Salt's patience was well nigh exhausted, and in his homely Yorkshire speech, he said, "I'll tell thee what,

---

[82] The warp is the thread which runs the length of a piece of woven fabric (Ref: OED).

Forbes, if thou art not the first horse, thou wont pull a pund."

The chapel[83] was opened in 1836, by the Rev. Dr. Winter Hamilton, Rev. T. Lessey, and Rev. Dr. Raffles, and in it the Rev. J. G. Miall has successfully ministered for forty years. Thirty-eight members were transferred from the mother church as the nucleous of the new one. Mrs. D. Salt was received into communion soon after, but Mr. D. Salt never became a communicant, although he was always a regular worshipper. Like many other men, he allowed the early part of life to pass away without making an open profession of his faith by coming to the communion table, and as he advanced in years he found the difficulties that hindered him not diminished; so that, while endeavouring faithfully to fulfil the other duties of religion, this one remained unfulfilled to the last. The course he adopted was not only a loss to himself but to others whom his good example might have benefited. Perhaps it was the want of this religious decision on the part of the father, that influenced his son in the same direction, for as we shall afterwards see, it was not until a later period of his life that he avowed his faith in Christ, and became a communicant. To all young men we would earnestly say,—before setting out in the business of this world, let the greater business relating to the soul and God be settled. It is more easy to attend to it in youth than in manhood. It is more reasonable to give to God the firstlings of life than the leavings. It is more safe to commit the keeping of the heart to Christ in youth, than run the risk of finding afterwards a more convenient season for doing so. It is more wise to "seek *first* the kingdom of God and his righteousness, and all other things shall be added unto you."

Mr. Salt died[84] at Bradford, on the 28th December, 1843, aged sixty-two years, after which Mrs. Salt went to live with her daughter, (Mrs. Atkinson,) at Mirfield, where she died 10th November, 1854, aged seventy-six. They were both interred in the burying-ground attached to Salem Chapel.

Some persons may be surprised that, in the work of erecting Salem Chapel,

---

[83] The Salem Chapel in question was situated on Manor Row, between Salem Street and Stone Street. It was opened on 29th January, 1836. The proposal to build Salem Chapel emanated from the vigorous mother church of Horton Lane Chapel at a meeting on 7th December, 1832. This chapel is not to be confused with the Salem Chapel at the junction of Oak Lane and St. Mary's Road, which was opened in November, 1888. (Ref: Cud4, pp48–53).

[84] The death followed "a long and painful illness" (Ref: BO, 4th January, 1844).

which enlisted the sympathies of his parents and of his attached friend, Mr. Forbes, the name of Mr. Titus Salt does not appear.[85] It may be that his energies and time were absorbed in the multifarious and responsible business to which he had put his hands. That declaration of his to make of himself "either a man or a mouse," though a homely one, was most expressive, for it indicated the weighty sense of responsibility which now pressed upon him, that he had staked everything on this business enterprise,—that if successful the reward would be ample, but if he failed, the downfall would be crushing. We may, therefore, excuse him if his sympathies and efforts did not at this time commingle with those of his kindred and friends in the work of chapel building. In after years he gave abundant proof that this kind of enterprise had a warm place in his heart. Many were the places of worship he helped to build both by his purse and suggestion, and one out of many may here be mentioned, namely, that of Saltaire, which alone cost him £15,000.

It was, indeed, a matter of thankfulness that, amid a multiplicity of duties, sufficient to overwhelm any other man, his health was vigorous, his spirits buoyant, and his anticipations hopeful. Happily, he now possessed a home,[86] which was to him a peaceful haven that he put into at night, to renew his mental and physical outfit for the coming day. There, too, a young and loving wife greeted his return, whose gentleness was a pillow for his weary brain; and when little ones came into the home, their presence brought sunshine, and their voices music, which chased the cares of life into happy oblivion. The children born in Bradford were William Henry, (now Sir William,) George, Amelia, (now Mrs. Wright,) Edward, Fanny, (deceased), Herbert, and Titus.[87]

---

[85] Salt is in fact listed as one of the original trustees in a later publication (Ref: Cud4, p50).
[86] Salt had a house in North Parade prior to 1836; between 1836 and 1843 he lived at a house at the junction of Thornton Road and Little Horton Lane (Ref: GtPat, p47).
[87] It appears to have been BALG's intention here to provide a chronological listing of the children born in Bradford. In fact Herbert was born before Fanny – see Appendix 3.

CHAPTER VII.

"To business that we love we rise betimes,

And go to it with delight."

—SHAKESPEARE.[88]

"He does allot for every exercise

A several hour; for sloth, the nurse of vices,

And rust of action, is a stranger to him."

—MASSINGER.[89]

"If little labour, little are our gains:

Man's fortunes are according to his pains."

—HERRICK.[90]

MR. SALT'S BUSY LIFE—HABIT OF EARLY RISING—EXAMPLE TO YOUNG MEN—ATTACHMENT OF HIS WORKPEOPLE—ANECDOTE—INSTANCES OF PUNCTUALITY—METHODICAL EXACTNESS—"HAVE YOU DONE, SIR?"—WHOLE-HEARTEDNESS NECESSARY TO SUCCESS—WORKS OUT HIS LIFE'S PLAN—TURNS HIS ATTENTION TO POLITICS—SUPPERS IN WAREHOUSE—BRADFORD ENFRANCHISED—HIS POLITICAL VIEWS—FIRST PARLIAMENTARY ELECTION—ELECTED CHIEF CONSTABLE—BRADFORD INCORPORATED—MADE ALDERMAN—APPOINTED MAGISTRATE AND DEPUTY LIEUTENANT.

THE next ten years that followed the commencement of the alpaca manufacture, were perhaps the most arduous period of Mr. Titus Salt's life.[91] We have seen what marvellous energy and perseverance he displayed in setting up the machinery in the various mills, but the same qualities were equally necessary to keep it going. These mills, being situated in different parts of the town, and the burden of their management resting solely upon himself, the strain upon his

---

[88] Antony and Cleopatra, Act 4, Scene 4.
[89] Philip Massinger (1583-1640), English dramatist and poet.
[90] Robert Herrick (1591-1674), poet. From the poem "No Pains, No Gains".
[91] The period being referred to is approx. 1839–1848.

mind must have been very great. Had he relaxed his diligence, after the initial stage of operations was passed, then assuredly the complicated system he had originated would soon have stopped. The same hand that had built and launched the vessel must now be at the helm, to steer her. Indeed, we may say he lashed himself to the helm, for he seemed always at his post; and, because one master-mind presided over the various works, everything in connection with them went on smoothly. How he was able to do all this, singlehanded, is a question that has puzzled many, and which young men might find it beneficial to consider. Know, then, that he was a very *early riser,* and his unvarying rule was to be at the works before the engine was started. Is it not written, "the hand of the diligent maketh rich"? and here is a signal illustration of it. It used to be said in Bradford, "Titus Salt makes a thousand pounds before other people are out of bed." Whether the sum thus specified was actually realised by him we cannot say, but it is the habit of early rising we wish to point out, and inculcate on those whose business career is about to begin. In these times of artificiality and self-indulgence, when the laws of nature are often wantonly violated, the chances of success are dead against those who follow such a course. Let young men especially avoid it; yea, let them take Mr. Titus Salt as an example of early rising. That this was his constant habit is confirmed by the testimony of an old workman, who says, "I was only once in my life late at the mill, and Mr. Salt was there, as he always was, in time." Of course, this habit was somewhat relaxed in after years, though it often continued to assert itself. For example, he was usually the first of his family circle who came downstairs in the morning. Once, the writer was leaving the hospitable mansion of Crow Nest at five o'clock a.m., and to his surprise he found his host in the hall waiting to say, "good-bye."

It is almost superfluous to mention that his early presence at "the works" exercised a high moral influence over his workpeople. Well they knew they had not merely to do with delegated authority, but with that which was supreme. If any of them were late, it was the master's rebuke they feared. If any were conspicuous above the rest for regularity and skill in their duties, it was the master's approval they expected, and this approval was shewn by the promotion of those who served him best. Some who entered his employment in the humblest capacity have been raised to the highest positions in it. There was thus a personal acquaintance formed, and a mutual sympathy established, that greatly helped to bridge the gulf which too often has separated master and workpeople, and sometimes placed them in an attitude of antagonism to each other. Throughout his manufacturing career he had great moral power in attaching the workpeople to himself; they all looked up to him as a friend rather than a master, and they obeyed and served him with all the devotion of a Highland clan to their noble chieftain. The following letter from an old workman, now a manufacturer, will speak for itself:—

Mr. Salt engaged me in his service in the year 1840. His mill and warehouse were then in Union Street, Bradford. I was with him nearly twenty-seven years, and when he came from Bradford to Saltaire, I came with him. He was a man of few words, but when he did speak, it was to the point, and pointed; he meant what he said, and said what he meant. If I asked him for an advance of wages, he always said "I'll see," and it was done. He was a fair-dealing master between man and man. When he heard tell of a man trying to injure another man, that man had to go through the small sieve. If a man did his duty, he was always ready to give him a lift over the right. This I have myself proved. One day, Mr. Salt was coming down Manchester Road, Bradford, in his carriage, when he saw one of his workpeople, who had been ill for some time; he stopped his carriage, and gave him a five-pound note. Whenever he saw true distress, he was always ready with his heart and hands to help them. He was a persevering, plodding man. He had a very strong struggle with the alpaca wool. It was, in some instances, thirty-six inches long; but he was determined to master it, which he did.

Another striking feature of his character, and one which enabled him to accomplish so much work, was his *punctuality*. Never was military despot more rigid than he in the observance of this rule: when he made an engagement he was punctual to the minute, and he expected the same in others who had dealings with him. Once at a church-building committee meeting, of which he was chairman, the secretary arrived a few minutes late: it happened that on his way thither, he had met a friend upon whom he levied a subscription. But how could he meet the chairman's frown? He entered the room holding up a bank note, saying, "I have been detained by this." "All right," said the chairman, "I thought you must be after something of the kind. I shall be glad to excuse you again on the same terms." Such was his punctuality that he was hardly ever known to miss a train, or to be in a hurry for one. It was the same at home as in business; the hour of meals was observed with precision, and all other domestic arrangements were conducted on the same principle of order. With watch in hand he would await the time for evening prayers, and then the bell was instantly rung for the household to assemble. When the usual hour arrived for his family and household to retire to rest, the signal was at once given and observed. When guests were staying at his house, he was the timekeeper of their movements, and in regulating themselves accordingly they were seldom mistaken. When a journey was to be taken with his wife and family, say to the metropolis or the seaside, nothing was left to chance; but the day and hour of starting, together with other minor arrangements, were written down some time beforehand.[92]

Another marked characteristic in the prosecution of his immense business was his *methodical exactness;* but for this habit, which was natural to him, he never could have personally controlled the various departments in connection with "the works." He was scrupulously exact in the arrangement of his papers, and knew where to lay his hand on any document when required. His letters were always promptly answered. He was exact in his accounts, exact in the

---

[92] There is an occasion reported when a lack of punctuality cost Salt the opportunity to purchase property in Burley, the eventual purchasers being Wm. Fison and W. E. Forster. There is reference to the incident being related, in the words of Fison, to the *Yorkshire Post*:

"We applied to the solicitor to the estate, and received a letter stating the property was on offer to the late Sir Titus Salt, who had not then founded his great works at Saltaire and received his title. The solicitor said that he could not negotiate until after one o'clock in the day, and that if the estate was not then sold he would be prepared to negotiate. We went at one o'clock, Forster and I, and the estate was not sold. We accordingly made an offer. It was not accepted, but ultimately we came to terms, signed the agreement for the purchase, and were just leaving the solicitors office when who should we meet but Mr. Titus Salt coming up the stairs prepared to increase his offer and buy the property. Vexed enough he was, too, at his being too late. Had he kept the appointment before one o'clock Saltaire works would have been here instead of where they are. That is how we bought Greenholme. Some may say it would have been better for Burley had Mr. Salt and not ourselves been the purchaser. Be that as it may. I think every one will agree that the beauties of the Wharfe and the purity of its streams have not suffered at our hands". (Ref: Spei1, pp152–153).

words he spoke—which never had the colour of exaggeration about them—exact in his purchases and sales. When he had fixed his price he stood by it, so that no one ever thought of arguing with him to take a farthing less. A gentleman in the trade, still living, says, "I once received a quiet rebuke from Mr. Salt, which was most valuable to me in my future career. It happened at his warehouse in Union Street, Bradford. I was a young man then, and spent a long time in trying to make a bargain with him. He heard me out to the last, and then said quietly, 'Have you done, sir?' I took the hint, and it taught me to talk less, and, when enough had been said, to go about my business, that others might attend to their own."

But if we were to sum up all the qualities that conduced to his success at this period, all those mental characteristics that enabled him to prosecute his immense business single-handed, it would be expressed in the word *whole-heartedness*. It will be remembered that in his boyhood the testimony of his schoolmaster was to the same effect. Has not the heart a wonderful power to draw every other faculty after it? How many men drag out a miserable existence, owing to the very consciousness that they have been mistaken in their occupation? As a consequence of this, they have never followed it with their whole heart, they have always hankered after something else, and that to which they have originally put their hands, has, of course, turned out a failure. Better for a young man carefully to watch the bias of his mind, and the particular taste evinced; then in that direction his future course ought to be steered. This is just nature giving a broad hint, and what she thus indicates is likely to prosper; then let him determine to succeed, and succeed he must. It was thus with Mr. Salt; his early proclivities found their true sphere in the occupation he now pursued.

It was a noble sight to see one like him toiling early and late, adding stone to stone in the edifice of which he was the architect and builder. Many, doubtless, looked coldly on, and doubted whereunto this thing would grow; but quietly this "plodding" man continued his unwearied labours; resolutely he held to his purpose that he would "make himself a man;" thoughtfully he constructed the plan of his future career, and diligently he worked it out. "Seest thou a man diligent in business; he shall stand before kings: he shall not stand before mean men."—Proverbs, xxii., 29.

But lest it should be thought that Mr. Salt was so much absorbed in purposes of self-aggrandisement, that he had no time left to promote the welfare of the public, we shall endeavour to supply evidence to the contrary. In the year 1832, three important projects excited great attention among the inhabitants of Bradford, in the furtherance of which Mr. Salt took an active part; these were,— railway communication with Leeds, the formation of works to supply the town with water, and the first parliamentary election for the borough. It is to the last of these, however, we would more especially refer, as throwing some light on Mr. Salt's political opinions, which ultimately led up to his becoming a member of Parliament himself. It was owing to the passing of the first Reform Bill that Bradford obtained the franchise, and was thereby entitled to return two representatives to the House of Commons. The inhabitants had fully shared in the political agitation which preceded and necessitated the passing of that measure; but Mr. Salt's share in it did not stand out prominently before the public eye in the way of speech-making; he was, however, an ardent reformer, and had his own way of shewing it. In his warehouse when business was over for the day, he gathered round him a number of earnest and thoughtful men— men of business like himself. There, political questions were discussed, and methods devised for their practical solution. At these meetings Mr. Salt acted the part of host, and provided a sumptuous supper for his political friends; among whom Mr. Forbes may be specially mentioned. It was not only at the time of the reform agitation that such gatherings were held, but also when other questions, such as—the abolition of slavery, the repeal of the corn laws,[93] or church rates, were engaging public attention; there, in his warehouse, was this band of earnest men doing their best to mould popular opinion, and their sympathies were ever on the side of liberty at home and abroad, both personal, commercial, and religious.

The first candidates for the representation of Bradford were Mr. E. C. Lister[94]

---

[93] The Corn Laws forbade the import of foreign corn without the payment of a heavy duty on such import. At this time insufficient corn was being grown in England to meet demand and so the price of bread – a basic commodity – fluctuated greatly. As a consequence the Anti-Corn Law League had been formed, under the leadership of Richard Cobden, with the aim of gaining a repeal of the Corn Laws (Ref: SofB, pp236-237).
[94] Ellis Cunliffe Lister had settled in 1819 in the Manningham area, on land which had been in the family for some centuries (Ref: Park). He established Lilycroft Mill there in 1838 (Ref:

and Mr. John Hardy;[95] both these gentlemen were intimately connected with the town by many personal ties, and both came forward as reformers; the third candidate was Mr. George Banks,[96] who professed semi-Whig principles. As an evidence of the growth of political liberty since that day, it is worthy of notice, that, while some of the above candidates were opposed to vote by ballot as un-English, to the extension of the suffrage as unnecessary, to the total abolition of the corn laws as impolitic, to the immediate emancipation of the slaves as impracticable, to the separation of the Church from the State as dangerous— four of these measures have been fully carried out, and the fifth partially. What will be accomplished in the next forty years, who can tell? On this occasion the two Liberal candidates were returned, but two years after, the first reformed Parliament was dissolved, and the political agitation of 1832 was renewed in Bradford; there was no Conservative candidate on this occasion; but in addition to the two old members, another was brought forward in the person of Mr. George Hadfield, whose political creed had the full sympathy of Mr. Salt, and those associated with him. From these circumstances Mr. Salt's political opinions at this time may be gathered and summarised, thus—he was in favour of the extension of the suffrage, vote by ballot, the general education of the people, the abolition of capital punishment, the repeal of the corn laws, the abolition of taxes on knowledge,[97] economy in the public expenditure, the abolition of flogging and impressment of seamen, and the removal of bishops from Parliament. No doubt, at that time, these opinions were considered too

---

GtPat, p67). Lister was too ill to take part in electioneering in 1832, so his position on specific issues is not known (Ref: GtPat, p40). He was the father of the more famous son, Samuel Cunliffe Lister.
[95] John Hardy was the Recorder of Leeds, and a partner in the Low Moor Iron Works. He lived in the old Manor Hall in Kirkgate (Refs: Cud3, pp39-40; GtPat, p39).
[96] George Banks was a Leeds businessman who had the support of an interesting cross section of people, including Samuel Hailstone, the Anglican Minister Henry Heap, the Baptist B. Godwin, and the Dissenters Robert Milligan, Henry Forbes and James Garnett (Ref: GtPat, p40).
[97] The so-called taxes on knowledge had three elements, each of which increased the cost of published material such as newspapers, putting them beyond the means of most people. The first was a stamp duty tax of 4d per paper; the second a tax of 3s 6d per advertisement; the third a duty on the actual paper on which the news was printed (the amounts quoted are those current in 1825). Although the amounts were reduced somewhat in later years, the actual taxes were not abolished until 1853, 1855 and 1861 respectively (Ref: VicBd, p116); also see Chapter XII.

5

pronounced, but as he had been far in advance of other men in his commercial views, it was not to be wondered that his political views were in advance also. Although the two old members were returned at the second election, Mr. Salt had the satisfaction, during his life-time, of seeing most of the above measures placed on the British Statute Book.[98]

Until we come to the period when he became a candidate for parliamentary honours it is unnecessary to refer to the other political principles, which he firmly held and conscientiously endeavoured to promote. We therefore pass on to notice those local matters which were contemporary with this period of his life. Amongst these the incorporation of the town claims special attention. Up to the year 1845, all local affairs had been managed by commissioners appointed under "the Improvement Act," who were a self-elected body, the majority of whom took very little interest in its administration. The head constable was appointed annually by the Court Leet of the manor, but strange to say, over the police force and other local functionaries he had no official control. To the post of head constable Mr. Salt was elected,[99] but it was with great reluctance he accepted it. Indeed long before this the inhabitants had urged him to accept the appointment; but this, as well as other public offices, he had persistently declined, both from his natural aversion to it, and the pressure of business engagements. He therefore accepted the office of head constable more as a concession to public opinion than to gratify his own desires, and though entering upon it reluctantly, he performed its duties with remarkable efficiency. From what we have already seen of the character of the man, and the energy he threw into every undertaking, we may be well assured that it would be also the same in this. As the chief of the town, he convened all public meetings, and presided

---

[98] This account of Salt's politics is a reasonable record of his position on several key issues of the day (Salt's voting record during his time as an M.P. is covered in Appendix 6). He was a liberal dissenter, and it was appropriate that in 1835 he became a founding member of the Bradford Reform Society, along with his close allies Robert Milligan, Henry Forbes, William Byles and Henry Brown (Ref: VicBd, p125) – all five were Congregationalists, four of them being destined to become mayors of Bradford (the fifth - Byles - was the editor of the *Bradford Observer*, see Appendix 4).
[99] This appointment by election occurred around 1843 (Ref: Bret2, p36).

over them;[100] but his authority was limited, and his power to effect local improvements almost nominal. The whole system belonged to a by-gone age, when Bradford was little more than a village, but it was utterly out of harmony with its position now as the metropolis of the worsted trade, and containing about 80,000 inhabitants. Mr. Salt was among the last of its chief constables.[101] To his strongly-expressed views on the subject, the change that took place shortly after is largely due; he was convinced that the time had arrived when the community had a right to demand a charter of incorporation. Yet, strange to say, there was great opposition at first to the proposal, and when brought to the test of a vote the opponents of it had a majority of above two thousand ratepayers. Two years after, the application to Her Majesty's Privy Council was renewed, and supported in a more powerful manner, so that a charter of incorporation was ultimately granted.

From this period may be dated another era in the history of Bradford. The new charter having placed the power of government in their own hands, the inhabitants determined that no efforts should be wanting to make the town worthy of its commercial position.[102] Up to this time it had obtained the unenviable distinction of being the dirtiest in the kingdom, and the seat of the greatest mortality. It wanted drainage, lighting, paving, water, police; in fact, everything necessary to lift it from chaos into cosmos. The first mayor chosen

---

[100] It is clear that even in the early 1840s Salt was seen as a suitable spokesman for Bradford. This is relevant when one sees Salt later that decade being proposed as the first mayor of Bradford.

[101] With the subsequent granting of a charter of incorporation to Bradford in 1847, a new office of Chief Constable, with responsibility for managing the police force, was to be required. This appointment was duly made at the first meeting of the newly formed Watch Committee under the chairmanship of William Rand on 13th November, 1847, only for this appointment to be rescinded and the post advertised on 18th November, 1847 in the *Bradford Observer*. This led to the appointment of William Leverett of the Liverpool Police as the first "modern day" Chief Constable of Bradford, with an annual salary of £200 (Ref: Polc, pp13-14). The post was to survive until 1974, when Bradford City Police was replaced by the West Yorkshire Metropolitan Police Force.

[102] The power of government was not literally in the hands of the inhabitants of the town. The criteria for enfranchisement were such that in a borough population of 66,718 persons, only 5,457 men had the vote (Refs: GtPat, p119; Cud3, p107).

was Mr. R. Milligan,[103] and amongst the list of aldermen were the names of Mr. Salt and Mr. Forbes.[104] This was a well-merited tribute to men who had done much to promote the trade of the town. No act of the community could be more expressive of the high esteem in which they were held. The first municipal honours the electors had it in their power to bestow, were conferred on their fellow-townsmen who most deserved them. In July, 1848, Mr. Salt's name was included in a list of eleven[105] gentlemen selected by the Town Council, and recommended to the Queen, as the first bench of magistrates for the borough. His appointment as a deputy-lieutenant of the county followed shortly afterwards.

---

[103] Three candidates were initially proposed for the office of mayor – Robert Milligan, William Rand and Titus Salt. The "feeling of Council preponderating in favour of Milligan," Rand and Salt retired and Milligan was elected unanimously (Ref: Cud3, p106).

[104] The other aldermen elected (on 18th August, 1847) were Henry Brown, James Garnett, Thomas Beaumont, Joshua Lupton, Christopher Waud, William Cheesebrough, Edward Ripley, William Rand, Samuel Smith, Joseph Smith and George Rogers (Ref: Cud3, pp105-106). The qualification for the office of alderman was the possession of property to the amount of £1,000, or a rating of £30 per annum, not being a parson, but being a resident householder within 7 miles of the borough, and occupying house, warehouse, counting house, or shop within the borough (Ref: Cud3, p103). That several of the elected aldermen were attached to Horton Lane Congregational Chapel is particularly notable, as discussed further in Appendix 4.

[105] The number may be wrong. Another source, probably more authoritative, identifies 16 names which were put forward (after some acrimony), by the Town Council, 12 of which were subsequently approved by the Lord Chancellor (Ref: Cud3, pp109-110). The approved list included several of the aldermen, and again had a notable number from the Horton Lane Chapel, including Salt, Milligan and Forbes.

CHAPTER VIII.

"The fame that a man wins himself, is best.

That he may call his own. Honours put on him

Make him no more a man than his clothes do,

Which are so soon ta'en off"

—MIDDLETON.[106]

"To hide true worth from public view

Is burying diamonds in the mine;

All is not gold that shines, 'tis true;

But all that is gold, ought to shine.

—S. BISHOP.

MR. SALT ELECTED MAYOR OF BRADFORD—ADDRESS OF MR. H. FORBES ON THE OCCASION—FREE TRADE BANQUET—MR. SALT A FREE TRADER—ALARMING CONDITION OF OPERATIVES—DISTRESS—SOUP-KITCHENS NEEDED—RELIGIOUS AND MORAL WANTS—ORIGIN OF ST. GEORGE'S HALL—SINGING BEFORE THE QUEEN—VISITATION OF CHOLERA—THE MAYOR'S PHILANTHROPY—RETURNING TIDE—OPERATIVES FEASTED—"BRADFORD OBSERVER."

IN the month of November, 1848, Mr. Salt[107] was elected Mayor, he being the second burgess of Bradford called to fill that office. In proposing his name to the Council, Mr. Alderman Forbes[108] said :—

---

[106] From *Hengist, King of Kent*, written 1619-1620 by Thomas Middleton, playwright (1580-1627).

[107] At this time, Salt was 45 years old, and he and his wife had eight children – see Appendix 3.

[108] The influence on the Town Council of the leading members of Horton Lane Chapel could not be seen more starkly than we see it here. The first mayor (Milligan) is being replaced by the second mayor (Salt), with the nominating alderman (Forbes) destined in due course to become the third mayor – all three being active members of the one chapel. For further discussion, see Appendix 4.

You are all, gentlemen, familiar with Mr. Salt's character and position. The founder of his own fortune, he has raised himself to an eminence in the manufacturing interest of this town, surpassed by none; and he now finds himself, as a reward for his industry, intelligence, and energy, at the head of a vast establishment, and affording employment to some thousands of workpeople. As we all know, Mr. Salt was the means of introducing a most important branch of trade into this town, I mean the alpaca trade, and thus rescuing that trade from comparative obscurity. Bringing to bear upon it his capital and skill, he not only realized great advantage for himself, but produced new fabrics in the manufactures of this district, thus developing a branch of business most important and beneficial to the working population. I believe, gentlemen, the same sagacity, practical good sense, cool judgment, and vigorous energy which have hitherto distinguished Mr. Salt, will be brought to bear upon the public business of this borough. You need not be told of his princely benefactions to our various local charities, nor of that magnificent generosity which is always open to the appeal of distress, and the claims of public institutions, having for their object the improvement of our population. With a warm heart, a sound head, a knowledge of our local interests conferred by long experience, and a disposition manifested on every occasion to do all that lies in his power to promote the prosperity of the borough, I do not think we could select a gentleman better qualified to succeed our late worthy Mayor Robert Milligan, Esq.

We have given the above speech in full, for the two-fold reason that it presents a miniature portrait of Mr. Salt, sketched by an intimate friend, and shews the high position he had attained in the eyes of his fellow-townsmen, who, on this occasion, unanimously elected him their chief magistrate. As an evidence of the attachment of Mr. Forbes to Mr. Salt, the former had the above speech engraved on a massive silver pedestal, surmounted by a figure of Justice holding the scales. This he presented to the newly-elected mayor, as a memorial of their long friendship.[109]

One of Mr. Salt's duties soon after his election was to acknowledge the toast of "The Corporation," at a banquet held to celebrate the abolition of the corn laws. In no part of the West Riding of Yorkshire were the friends of free trade more energetic than at Bradford, and none more so there than Mr. Salt. It was

---

[109] Our attempts to trace the present day whereabouts of the silver pedestal have been unsuccessful.

likely that an enterprising community like this, and a bold innovator on traditional methods of manufacture like himself, would be foremost in favour of free trade all over the world. Mr. Salt was a liberal subscriber to the Corn Law League, and an ardent admirer of Cobden, Bright,[110] and General Thompson. The latter gentleman had, by the publication of his "Corn Law Catechism," and other great services rendered to the free trade cause, gained a title to public gratitude; that title the Bradford electors promptly endorsed at the election of 1848, when they returned him to Parliament. The nomination on this occasion was moved and seconded by Mr. R. Milligan and Mr. W. E. Forster,[111] who afterwards became the representatives of the borough. It was, therefore, a happy circumstance that at the great banquet referred to, the chief magistrate should have been in hearty sympathy with that movement, the consummation of which was now being celebrated in the town. Well might Bradford keep high festival

---

[110] Cobden, Bright and Salt were to become contemporary members of parliament eleven years later – see Chapter XIII.

[111] William Edward Forster (1818–1886) was to become Bradford's most successful statesman of the 19th century. An extensive, two-volume biography of Forster's life is available (Ref: Forst). Born of Quaker parents in Bradpole, Dorsetshire, Forster had arrived in Bradford in 1841 to partner T. S. Fison in a wool stapling business. The following year he extended his business interests by going into partnership with William Fison as woollen manufacturers, a partnership that endured to the end of Forster's life. A highly energetic and well read man, Forster took an interest in the mid 1840s in the consequences of the potato famine in Ireland, and came to public attention through his campaigning on behalf of the Irish. His marriage in 1850 to the daughter of a clergyman of the Church of England led to his separation from the Society of Friends. His political aspirations were national rather than local, and he was to succeed Salt as the M.P. for Bradford in 1861. His parliamentary career was markedly more successful than that of Salt, and he quickly established himself in parliament as an effective speaker and campaigner. He was appointed Minister of Education in Gladstone's Liberal Government of 1868, an appointment that was for a few months threatened by the petitioning against Forster's election by supporters of H. W. Ripley. Ripley, also elected to parliament, had been petitioned against. The case against Ripley was upheld and he was unseated; Forster was exonerated. BALG refers to these events in Chapter XVII, but fuller accounts are available (Refs: GtPat, pp329–333; Forst, pp447–456). Forster's greatest achievement was the drafting and passage into law of the 1870 Education Act, which sought to provide education for all children. Although a Liberal, some of Forster's policies were not to the liking of Bradford's leading Nonconformists. He failed to meet their expectations, firstly to end the special status of the established Church in the education system; and secondly to support the moves for the disestablishment of the Church. The 1880 election saw Gladstone appoint Forster as Chief Secretary for Ireland but the appointment ended in disagreement in 1882 when Forster resigned. Forster was to die four years later after some months of illness, and was buried in the graveyard at Burley, close to his family home of many years.

now, for it owed much of its subsequent prosperity to the mighty impulse which the inauguration of free trade gave. As an evidence of this, when the Exchange Buildings were erected, a number of carved figures were inserted around the outside, among which are to be recognised Cobden, Salt, Gladstone, and Palmerston.[112] In the principal hall of the Exchange a beautiful statue of Cobden, in white marble, has been recently unveiled by the Right Hon. John Bright.

And yet, the year 1848 was, in one sense, a disastrous one for Bradford and the immediate neighbourhood. The Chartist agitation in the spring of that year had occasioned great excitement and consternation.[113] The "Six Points of the Charter, or nothing!"[114] was the motto which the Chartists inscribed on their banner, and in support of which they were ready to employ physical force. What with their riotous assemblages, drilling by moonlight, the manufacture of pikes, and long processions through the town, the aspect of matters at this time was most threatening. Nor was this the only cause of alarm to the community. The number of unemployed operatives, principally woolcombers, was very large. It was not that trade at this period was really bad, but the introduction of woolcombing machinery had rendered manual labour almost obsolete.[115] Fortunately, in Mr. Salt a gentleman was found equal to the crisis, as far as human aid could meet it. It was not the first time it had fallen to his lot to deal with masses of men inflamed by passion. But here was "hunger", added to political discontent and idleness. What was to be done? Immediate relief was given by opening soup kitchens in various parts of the town. In one week, 17,680 lbs. of bread and 2954 quarts of soup were distributed; 1200 families, large and small, participated in this especial form of bounty. So numerous were

---

[112] Lord Palmerston in fact laid the foundation stone of the Exchange, and – during the same visit to Bradford in 1864 – toured the mill at Saltaire - see Chapter XVII.

[113] For an account of the Chartist risings in Bradford, see Ref: Char.

[114] The six points of the Charter were universal male suffrage; equal electoral districts; removal of property qualification for M.P.s; payment of M.P.s; secret balloting; and annual general elections (Ref: E19c, p84).

[115] The key figure in the mechanisation of woolcombing was Samuel Cunliffe Lister. Very active in the acquisition of patents, he finally developed in the mid 1840s the Lister Nip Comb, a machine capable of doing the work of 100 hand combers. Within five years half the estimated 10,000 hand combers in Bradford had disappeared from the trade (Ref: MaMis, p10).

the applications for relief, at the Board of Guardians, that steps were taken to transfer to their own parishes all families who had not a legal settlement in the town. Hundreds of men were employed in test labour. A scheme for promoting emigration was devised; and at the meeting held in furtherance of it, Mr. Salt expressed his deep sorrow in witnessing so much distress. Previous to the French Revolution, in January, he said, he had been able to keep the greater number of his hands in full work; but since that event his sales of goods to merchants had fallen off £10,000 a month. Nevertheless, he was willing to engage one hundred of the unemployed woolcombers, and lay their produce by. At this dark time in the history of Bradford, Mr. Salt was the leader in all these schemes of practical benevolence, and the foremost subscriber to their funds.

Amongst many general movements, in which Mr. Salt took part at this period, was one for establishing the Saturday half holiday.[116] It was first commenced by the stuff warehousemen of the town, and afterwards taken up by the *employés* in shops. At his instance an influential meeting was held in the Exchange Rooms, to devise means for the repression of profligacy and the promotion of morality. At that meeting[117] Mr. Salt said he had become acquainted with scenes of wickedness in the town, of which he could not possibly have conceived; and, acting with a few friends, he had called them together, in the hope that some means might be adopted to improve the religious and moral condition of the borough. In his opinion, there was a want of adequate religious instruction, and also of means of innocent recreation for the working classes, and he should be glad to see the idea of Alderman Samuel Smith[118] carried out, and a public music hall established. He firmly believed that by some such means, beer shops and similar places would be far less patronised than they were.

No one can read these statements without discerning beneath them the noble spirit of benevolence that animated the speaker. The same whole-heartedness he had put into schemes for his own aggrandisement, was also displayed for the benefit of his fellow-men. It is this characteristic that makes him so worthy an

---

[116] It was not until 10th June, 1870 that Messrs Titus Salt, Sons and Co. began to close their premises at 1 p.m. on Saturday (Ref: AofY3, p325).
[117] The meeting was convened on 25th June, 1849, following its announcement by Salt on 21st June, 1849 (Ref: BO, 21st June, p5).
[118] For a fuller account of Smith, see Appendix 4.

example for young men to follow. There are men living now whose only ambition has been to acquire wealth, which they have either hoarded or expended on their own personal gratification. What are the appeals of benevolence or philanthropy to them, but mere sentimental whining? Pity them! They live to themselves. They die unregretted. They have no mourners to follow them to the grave, except such as duty compels. True, they are decently put away into darkness, but "while the memory of the just is blessed, the name of the wicked shall rot." It was not so with Mr. Salt. Abundant evidence was afforded during this year of his mayoralty, that the moral and religious condition of the town made a deep impression on his heart. At the meeting referred to, many of the views expressed, and the measures suggested, were but the sowing of seed that was to yield a harvest afterwards, not only in the town where he dwelt, but in the new town of Saltaire which he founded. As we shall see, when that part of his life comes before us, he made ample provision for the wants of his workpeople in the direction indicated at the aforesaid meeting.

But what was the present result, locally?[119] It is not improbable that his hearty commendation of Alderman Smith's suggestion gave birth to the movement which led to the erection of St. George's Hall, as a place suitable for concerts and other public entertainments. The Exchange Buildings and the Mechanics' Institute had become totally insufficient to accommodate the increasing population; but in the erection of this new hall provision was made for 3328 persons. It was built at a large cost, by a company of shareholders, of which Mr. Salt was one, and though the dividends arising therefrom have often been small, yet the moral benefit to the community has been inestimable. Within its walls religion, science, politics, philanthropy, and music have gathered crowds of eager listeners, and thus it has become the centre of moral influence for elevating the minds of the whole community. To the existence of this beautiful and most commodious building the well-known musical taste of the inhabitants is largely due. Its festivals have frequently brought together the highest talent of

---

[119] The meeting of June 1849 led to the preparation of a report on the moral condition of the town. The report was received and discussed at a meeting held on Friday, 1st March, 1850 (Ref: BO, 7th March, 1850, p14).

the country; and the Bradford Choral Society,[120] which was formed soon after St. George's Hall was opened, has become justly famous for the general musical proficiency of its performing members; and as an evidence of this, it may be here mentioned that in 1858, this society, under the able leadership of Mr. William Jackson, sang at the Crystal Palace, when such was the enthusiasm with which they were received on that occasion, that they were immediately summoned by the Queen to sing at Buckingham Palace. Alderman Smith had the honour to accompany them, and to him Her Majesty personally expressed her high appreciation of the Yorkshire vocalists. We record at length these incidents, as supplying proof that Mr. Salt's words at the meeting referred to, were not lost, but that they brought forth fruit not many days after.

In the latter part of Mr. Salt's mayoralty, the cholera, which had for months ravaged the island, committed fearful havoc amongst the poorer districts of the town. Between the months of June and October above 400 deaths occurred. Many families were thereby plunged into mourning, and their sad lot evoked the deep sympathy of the wealthier classes. Mr. Salt not only liberally contributed money, but he personally visited the scenes of distress,—speaking words of hope to the smitten, of comfort to the bereaved, of practical advice to the yet unscathed, how they might personally avert the impending calamity. Happily, the malady abated, and finally disappeared, when thanksgiving services to Almighty God were recommended by the mayor, and simultaneously held throughout the whole community.

It will thus be seen that the official post Mr. Salt filled during these twelve months was not a sinecure. Seldom during a similar period have so many events occurred to tax the energies of the chief magistrate. What with the enforced idleness of many operatives, the want of bread, the danger of civil rebellion, the visitation of cholera,—there were anxieties enough to overwhelm him; and all this public work had to be done while his own immense private business required his personal superintendence. It was certainly a school where his knowledge of human nature was increased; where he obtained an insight into the social condition of the people such as he did not before possess; where the

---

[120] The Society is elsewhere referred to as the Bradford Festival Choral Society (Ref: Cud3, p136).

moral sympathies of his nature were moved to their depths, and the channels of his practical benevolence were widened and deepened.

But let us turn the picture; for although the mayoralty of Mr. Salt was rendered remarkable by these depressing events, there were others of a brighter kind to relieve the gloom.

Before the year closed, a vast improvement had taken place in the commercial prospects of the town. Like the tide which had reached its ebb, the flow soon set in, bringing prosperity with it, and re-filling with gladness, hearts that had been recently filled with gloom. We have seen how, a short time previously, employers were subscribing their money to feed the distressed operatives; now they were giving large sums to feast them. Mr. Salt was the first to take advantage of the newly-acquired railway facilities to give 2,000 of his "hands" an excursion to the country. Having taken up his own summer residence at Malham, amid the glorious scenery of Craven, he wished that those toilers who had so few opportunities of healthy enjoyment, should breathe for a day the mountain air, and ramble in the woods and fields to their hearts' content.[121] It is said that Sir Francis Crossley's resolution to present a park to the people of Halifax, was made in America, when revelling amid the grand scenery of the White Mountains.[122] "Why," thought he, "should I not help to give healthy out-door recreation to those who are unable to obtain it?" Perhaps such a thought

---

[121] There is an informative account available of the trip (Ref: BO, 23rd August, 1849, p5). BALG asserts that Salt had in fact set up a summer residence at Malham, but there is no sense of this in the newspaper account. Salt travelled from Bradford with his workers, in the company of his eldest son William Henry and other private guests. At this time, of course, his workers were still deployed in his various mills in Bradford. The 2,000 travelled by train to Bell Busk station, built that same year (1849) on the line established by the Midland Railway Company to carry Victorian tourists from the West Riding of Yorkshire to the seaside resort of Morecambe. (The line was later extended to become the world famous Settle to Carlisle line). There was little at Bell Busk, other than the countryside. The majority of the workers relaxed in the immediate vicinity of the station, but two or three hundred of them set off for Malham (five mile distant) and succeeded in getting to Gordale Scar, the local beauty spot. Here the band took up position, and there was a well received musical interlude before they returned to Bell Busk to catch the train. On the way back Salt and his friends tarried at the Roebuck Inn, Malham where they had a "sumptuous tea given by the landlord, with a suit from Crow Nest." It may be that the "summer residence" was in fact one of the hotels in the area.

[122] Corroboration of Crossley's North American inspiration is provided by Bretton in his account of the 1855 tour by Crossley and his wife (Ref: Bret3, Part VI, p17).

may have passed through the mind of Mr. Salt, on that day when he saw his 2,000 workpeople enjoying themselves in Craven; but many excursions of a similar kind, and t"The People's Park," which he afterwards gave to Saltaire, afforded ample proof that he was heartily and emphatically "the friend of the people."

At the close of this eventful year, the *Bradford Observer*[123] wrote—"Our worthy mayor, Titus Salt, Esq., has long enjoyed wide-spread and well-merited popularity throughout this district. His kindness and consideration as an extensive employer, and his munificence and public spirit as an influential citizen, had long ago won for him 'golden opinions from all sorts of men.' He has lost none of his fame by the manner in which he has discharged the onerous duties of first magistrate of this borough, but has rather gained additional lustre to a good name".

The above testimony may be regarded as that of the community, and appearing as it did, in a journal so competent to judge of true merit, so fearless to censure and generous to praise when deserved, it was one highly gratifying to him concerning whom it was written.

---

[123] The *Bradford Observer* is used by both BALG and us as a source of information. It should be noted that both Salt and his father had shares in the venture which founded the newspaper in 1834. A comprehensive account of the newspaper's history and of its printer and manager, William Byles, can be found in an account by James, who points out that "the consortium which founded the *Observer* reads like a roll call of Bradford radical Liberalism" (Ref: VicBd, pp115–136). William Byles was a member of Horton Lane Chapel (see Appendix 4).

CHAPTER IX.

"The true ambition there alone resides,

Where justice vindicates and wisdom guides;

Where inward dignity joins outward state,

Our purpose good, as our achievement great;

Where public blessings, public praise attend,

Where glory is our motive, not our end;

Wouldst thou be famed? have those high acts in view;

Brave men would act, though scandal would ensue."

—YOUNG.[124]

HOSPITALITIES AT CROW NEST—ACTS OF KINDNESS—DEATH OF TWO CHILDREN—£1,000 GIVEN TOWARDS PEEL PARK—ELECTION OF MR. R. MILLIGAN AS M.P.—MR. SALT'S PURPOSE TO RETIRE FROM BUSINESS—RECONSIDERS HIS PURPOSE—RESOLVES TO REMOVE HIS "WORKS" FROM BRADFORD—SELECTION OF A SITE NEAR SHIPLEY—MR W. FAIRBAIRN'S OPINION OF IT—FIRST INTERVIEW WITH ARCHITECTS—CONVERSATION ABOUT PLANS AND COST—SELECTION OF ENGINEER—INQUIRIES ABOUT THE EXHIBITION BUILDING IN HYDE PARK—ORIGIN OF NAME "SALTAIRE"—PREPARATIONS FOR OPENING—CONVERSATION WITH LORD HAREWOOD.

IN the summer of 1844,[125] Mr. Salt removed his residence to Crow Nest, a large

---

[124] *Love of Fame*, by Edward Young (1683-1765), English poet and dramatist.

[125] The events described in this chapter relate to the period 1844 to mid-1853 (the chapters of BALG are not, and presumably were not intended to be, precisely consecutive). The period is noteworthy because of the events not only in Salt's life but also in the life of the author Balgarnie. In 1851 Balgarnie, at the age of 25, took up his ministry in Scarborough, which was to lead to his meeting with Salt – see Appendix 1. The reader needs to be aware that the previous chapters of BALG are informed by Balgarnie's derived knowledge; subsequent chapters, which cover approximately the final 25 years of Salt's life, are informed by Balgarnie's closer, often immediate, knowledge.

and commodious mansion, about seven miles west[126] from Bradford, and situated near the village of Lightcliffe. His removal thither was occasioned by the want of accommodation for his increasing family,[127] and the benefit likely to be derived from the purer air of a country home. As his occupancy of Crow Nest until 1858, (when he removed to Methley Park), was in the capacity of tenant,[128] a description of the mansion is postponed until the period when he returned as its sole proprietor and permanent resident.

During the year of his mayoralty the hospitalities connected with his office were here dispensed with great liberality; the members of the corporation and other public bodies gathered around his bountiful table. Men of opposite views in politics, of different positions in society, of various pursuits in life, all were brought together in social fellowship; while deputations from numerous societies, both as ministers and missionaries, often found at Crow Nest a home. Amongst those ministers who were intimate friends of Mr. Salt, and to whom he was much attached, were the Rev. J. Paul,[129] of Wibsey, and the Rev. Jonathan Glyde, of Bradford. The latter had succeeded the Rev. T. Taylor, at Horton Lane Chapel, and by his mental culture and earnest piety, exerted an influence over all with whom he came into contact.[130] Mr. Salt was one who felt this influence.

But during the first period of his residence at Crow Nest, it was little more than a resting-place for the night. Early and late, his immense business in

---

[126] BALG's directions are inaccurate. Crow Nest was approx. 6 miles SSW of the centre of Bradford.

[127] On setting up home at Crow Nest in 1844, Salt was 40, his wife 32, and seven of their 11 children had by this time been born – the eldest being William Henry, aged 12, and the youngest being Titus Jr. who would have been approaching his first birthday – see Appendix 3.

[128] Salt rented the estate from Miss Ann Walker, one of the daughters of John Walker, the last male heir of the Crow Nest estate (Ref: HtoT, p476).

[129] John Paul (1797–1860) was a native of Glasgow, where as a youth he came under the influence of Greville Ewing. The latter was a popular preacher who had broke with the Church of Scotland in 1798 and who in 1812, as a Congregational minister, had helped form the Congregational Union of Scotland. After several years of preaching in Glasgow, Paul was recommended by the Glasgow Congregationalists to the Horton Lane Christian Instruction Society, and came to Bradford in 1834. He was assigned Wibsey and Little Horton, where he worked for the remainder of his life. When Paul died in 1860, Salt, Milligan and Forbes were pall bearers at his funeral – a measure of esteem in which he was held in Bradford (Refs: DNB; BO, 31st May, 1860, p5).

[130] For fuller accounts of Revs. Jonathan Glyde, T.Taylor, see Appendix 4.

Bradford demanded his constant presence and undivided attention. To be early at "the works," not only necessitated his rising and breakfasting betimes, but driving in a conveyance all the way thither; for it must be remembered railway communication was then in its infancy, and between Lightcliffe and Bradford it had not yet been opened.[131] Yet, such was the vigour of his constitution, the buoyancy of his spirits, and the heart he put into all his duties, that he seemed to carry his burdens lightly. Nor did the success in business already attained, or the honourable position in life he had reached, spoil the simplicity of his character. There are persons living who remember that in driving between Crow Nest and Bradford, he would not unfrequently give "a lift" to a poor woman with a child in her arms, or stop to take up a dusty pedestrian who seemed fatigued with travel; and this was done with a kindness of look and tone that made the recipients of the favour feel that it came from one not above them, but on a level with themselves. This circumstance, though trifling in itself, is, as George Herbert[132] says, "A window through which we look into the soul." As Mr. Salt, in his own personal career, had always an instinctive dislike to mere patronage from others, so he now sensitively shrunk from manifesting it towards his fellow-men. When he lent a helping hand to anyone, he conveyed the impression that he was receiving, rather than conferring, a favour. Often, in ministering to persons in reduced circumstances, he first consulted those who had personal knowledge, as to what was the most delicate method of conveying his bounty. Sometimes his benefactions were sent indirectly, through the hand of a friend; at other times, directly and anonymously, by means of the post. Thus a large proportion of his generous deeds can never be known on earth, but their "record is on high."

Crow Nest was the birthplace of four of his children, viz., Whitlam, Mary, Helen, and Ada; but the first two did not abide long with their parents; they came only to claim citizenship with earth, and then God took them.[133] Their

---

[131] A railway station was opened at Lightcliffe on 7th August, 1851. (Ref: DirRS). The station was adjacent to the entrance of the Crow Nest driveway.
[132] George Herbert (1593-1633), clergyman and poet. Considered to have written some of the best sacred poetry in English (Ref: DicLB).
[133] The children Whitlam and Mary died in the spring of 1851 – see Appendix 3.

bodies were laid in the burying-ground of the Congregational Church,[134] Lightcliffe, until the family mausoleum was built at Saltaire, to which they were afterwards transferred by permission of the Home Secretary. The death of these two children was the first shadow that fell on his domestic circle. He had lived most of his life in the sunshine of prosperity, so that when it was overcast by bereavement, his sorrow indeed was great; but it came not by chance or accident, but from a Father's hand, and surely at the right time also; for it reminded him how soon human hopes may be blighted, and man's fondest treasures snatched away.[135] Could his heart have given full expression to its grief, as the forms of his children were laid in the grave, these lines would probably have embodied it :—

> "Holy earth, to thee I trust
> Two bonnie heaps of precious dust;
> Keep them safely, sacred tomb,
> Till their father asks for room."[136]

The loss of these children seemed to endear to him those who were left. On his return from business in the evening, the first inquiry was, "Where are the children?" Some of them would climb his knee, dishevel his hair, or induce him to become a "quadruped," to their intense delight. When they were sufficiently advanced in years to be sent to boarding schools, the letters that he occasionally sent them were full of paternal love, interspersed with wise counsel, in the prosecution of their studies, and ardent desires for their future happiness. Some of these letters are treasured still by those to whom they were addressed.

Prior to the year 1850, Bradford did not possess any public park or open space adapted to the purposes of healthy recreation. We have seen in the last

---

[134] The church is not the one which stands today, but rather the one sometimes referred to as Bramley Lane Chapel (Ref: HtoT, p498).

[135] It gives some insight into Salt's commitments (and perhaps strength of character) that the year in which he saw the deaths of Whitlam and Mary also saw him planning and commencing the building of Saltaire; exhibiting at the Great Exhibition; and continuing to run his five mills in Bradford.

[136] The origins of this verse are not known to us. It is possible that the words are Balgarnie's own.

chapter, that during Mr. Salt's mayoralty, the necessity of making such provision for the working classes was by him strenuously advocated. One step in this direction had already been taken in the opening of St. George's Hall, but something more was needed, and the time for it had now come. The abolition of the corn laws had been celebrated with great enthusiasm in the borough. Sir Robert Peel[137] had brought forth the top stone, and crowned the edifice which Cobden and Bright had reared, and his sudden death in the zenith of his fame had thrilled the heart of the nation. What memorial of this eminent statesman, whose closing act brought such a boon to the people, could be more appropriate than a park for their benefit, bearing his honoured name? Whether this project originated with Mr. Salt, or some one else, we are unable to say, but certainly, it had his warmest sympathy, and not only sympathy, but substantial help. He offered to subscribe £1,000 in furtherance of it; and at his personal solicitation, his friends, Messrs. Milligan and Forbes, promised a similar sum. The subscription list having thus been auspiciously commenced, steps were at once taken to procure a suitable site, which, after certain negociations, was obtained. The greater portion of "The Bolton House Estate," consisting of forty-six acres, was purchased for the sum of £12,000. Subsequently, that purchase was augmented by the acquisition of an adjoining property, making the total area about sixty-one acres. After it came into the hands of the Park Trustees, £6,000 were spent in planting it with shrubs, and in constructing beautiful walks, artificial terraces, and sheets of water, so that the Peel Park[138] of Bradford is

---

[137] Sir Robert Peel (1788–1850) had two periods in office as Prime Minister: 1834-1835 and 1841-1846. Peel's administrations brought about changes which met with the approval of Bradford's industrial leaders – not only the repeal of the Corn Laws, but improved provisions for the maintenance of public order, and the lowering of import duties on raw materials (Ref: DNB).

[138] Further words concerning Peel Park are merited. The park's funding was planned to be by public subscription, which started in 1850 with donations of £1,000 each from Salt, Milligan and Forbes. Unfortunately, the Park Committee ran into debt during its construction and it was not until 1863 that the debt was cleared and the park presented to the Corporation. The design of the park has been attributed to a number of people including Thomas Dixon (a Bradford land agent and surveyor), and Lockwood and Mawson; and of the Grand Terrace to William Gay, who designed Saltaire Park. There are interesting similarities between the two parks in the designs of the parks' lodges, and the bridge railings on Peel Park's Grand Terrace are similar in design to those in Saltaire (Refs: PeelP; Dir56; BO, 9th March, 1893, p7).

now one of the finest, for its extent, in the United Kingdom; the only drawback being its remote situation from the town; but this has been recently counterbalanced by the opening of Lister Park, so called after a distinguished local manufacturer, and situated nearer the centre of population. The Peel Park is, however, not the only local memorial of the eminent statesman whose name it bears. In an open space, surrounded by splendid warehouses, the Peel Statue was inaugurated in 1855.[139] Bradford thus enjoys the unique honour of having two costly memorials of the same individual, one as a park for the recreation of the people, the other as a work of art, to recall the form and features of the statesman who repealed the corn laws. The next statue erected in Bradford was in honour of him whose career we are now tracing, but with this difference, the former was erected to a public benefactor, when dead, the latter, to one while living.

In the return of his friend, Mr. Robert Milligan, to Parliament, Mr. Salt took an active part. His first election took place in 1851, and was unopposed; but the second, which was in 1852, was the result of a severe contest. On that occasion Mr. Salt was the seconder of Mr. Milligan's nomination, who was returned, along with Mr. Wickham,[140] the latter having a majority of only two votes over General Thompson, the third candidate.[141]

Mr. Salt was now approaching the period of life when he hoped to relinquish business, and enjoy in retirement the ample fortune he had made. If any one had ever earned a just title to *otium cum dignitate,*[142] it was he. His life, from the age of twenty, had been an excessively busy one; the term "working-man," so commonly applied to manual labour, might, with special emphasis, have been

---

[139] Sir Robert Peel's statue, by the sculptor William Behnes (1795-1864), was unveiled on Tuesday, 6th November, 1855 by the Mayor of Bradford, William Murgatroyd. The statue stood in Spice Cake Corner (approx. 300 yards SW of St. Peter's Church (the present day cathedral), see Map2), which had been in Salt's ownership. The area was renamed Peel Place following the inauguration, Salt giving the land for the purpose (Ref: Cud3, p133). In 1957, with the reconstruction of Bradford city centre, the statue was removed to Peel Park, where it stands in the present day on the Grand Terrace (Ref: Rob1).

[140] Henry Wickham Wickham (1800-1867) was a partner in the Low Moor Iron Works, and M. P. for Bradford from 1852 to 1867. Salt's own, shorter parliamentary career was included in this latter period, and the two members voted in similar, but not identical ways (see Appendix 6).

[141] One report gives Wickham a majority of 6 votes over Thompson (Ref: BfdE1).

[142] Trans: Leisure with dignity.

applied to him. Much he needed rest, and the time he had fixed, in his own mind, for acquiring it was his fiftieth birthday. Then, as he imagined, he would dispose of his various mills, and on a landed estate of his own, spend the remainder of life in rural occupations. One cannot help asking the question— What if this purpose of his heart had been then carried out? An active mind like his, thus withdrawn in its prime from the activities of business, might have fallen into premature decay, just as the digestive organs when deprived of their accustomed food become self-consuming. For, be it remembered, his life of commercial activity had left him but little time for reading and mental culture, so that to have been released from business would have taken him completely out of the element in which his habits had been formed and his tastes exercised, and probably shortened his days.

However, happily for himself and for others, this purpose was not carried out, and surely another mind than his own controlled him in this matter, and guided his steps aright. Instead of retiring into comparative obscurity and inactivity, he was yet to give "a local habitation and a name" to the new branch of trade he had inaugurated; to become the founder of a model town which strangers from afar would come to visit; to embody on a splendid scale those plans for the religious, social, physical, and intellectual improvement of the people that had long been cherished; to enter upon a career of noble and disinterested benevolence to which the past was only the prelude; to receive honours from men such as few have been privileged to enjoy; and to bequeath to his family a name which is their richest heritage.

How long a time was spent by Mr. Salt in reconsidering his cherished resolution, and in resolving other plans for the future, it is impossible to say; this much we venture to affirm, that it cost him many anxious hours by day, and sleepless hours by night. It was the habit of his mind to look at a question calmly from all sides, to weigh its various contingencies, and patiently to solve the difficulties that apparently surrounded it; then, when all these mental processes were completed, to communicate the result to others. The chief friend to whom he confided his great future project was Mr. Forbes. There is no evidence to shew that his plans for the future were intended to be on the gigantic scale which they ultimately assumed:[143] they were, no doubt, conceived in that spirit of originality and enterprise that had hitherto characterised all his undertakings; but we question whether his imagination had ever pictured to itself the colossal establishment that was to spring up on the banks of the Aire; it was rather a *growth,* than a cut-and-dried plan thrown off from his brain in all its completeness. This, however, is certain, he was resolved that, in bringing into one centre the various manufactories he had hitherto carried on, he would not be a party to any further increase of the working population of Bradford, which was already overcrowded; indeed, with its smoky atmosphere and sanitary defects, polluted streams and canal, there was everything to militate against the moral and physical improvement of the people. If his new plans and purposes were to take shape and embodiment, it must be in a locality where ample space, pure air, and an abundance of water were primary considerations.[144] Where was such a locality to be found? was a question he had first to answer. It has been alleged that his original purpose was to purchase a site near Wakefield, where the latter part of his schooldays was spent; but this is apocryphal. It is not likely that his practical sagacity could have overlooked the great advantage to be derived from proximity to the metropolis of the worsted trade. It was after various surveys of the neighbourhood, that his eye, at last, fell on the site where Saltaire now stands; and just as the skill of a military commander is displayed in the selection of a field where his army is to be drawn up to win a victory, so this great captain of industry manifested equal skill, in selecting a spot where his civil forces were to be concentrated and where peaceful victories were to be won.

The locality selected was one of the most beautiful and picturesque to be found in the neighbourhood of Bradford, from which it is distant about three

---

[143] There is in fact evidence that Salt envisaged a comprehensive development from an early date. An 1853 account of the inauguration of the mill records plans for "wide streets, spacious squares, ground for recreation,......baths and wash-houses, a covered market, schools, a place of worship...." (Ref: BO, 22nd September, 1853, p5). Reynolds also cites 1854 correspondence between Lockwood and the General Board of Health as indicating that "the original scheme was if anything slightly more grandiose than the completed village" (Ref: GtPat, p265).

[144] In his planning of a new, centralized manufacturing base, Salt was not to entirely abandon his interests in Bradford premises. A warehouse in Bradford was owned by the firm in the 1850s, and on into the 1870s (Ref: Part).

miles. It is charmingly situated on the banks of the Aire, and in the middle of the valley through which that river flows. Surveying the region from the higher ground at Shipley, the eye takes in an extensive landscape of hill and dale, of wood and water, such as is seldom seen in proximity to a manufacturing town. The famed Shipley Glen is in the immediate neighbourhood, which excursionists, in quest of beautiful scenery, love to frequent, while beyond the hills there is a heathy moorland, stretching away towards Wharfedale. To the right, the river winds round the village of Baildon, not far from which, on the height above, stands Ferniehurst, the picturesque residence of Mr. Edward Salt. Almost in front, rising abruptly from the valley, and completely covered from base to summit with trees, stands "The Knoll," the residence of Mr. C. Stead,[145]

---

[145] Charles Stead (1823–1902) had a long and eventful association with the firm. Born in Wortley near Leeds, Stead had been a fellow pupil of Henry William Ripley at an academy in Little Horton. After first working in the textile trade with Messrs. Billingsley, Tankard and Co., Stead joined Salt when the latter appointed him manager of the manufacturing department at the Hollings' Mill site (probably in the 1840s). Stead must have been very capable; in 1854, with the company now at the Saltaire site, he was made a partner in Titus Salt Sons and Co. For the next 38 years, Stead remained with the company, building, in the late 1850s (on land bought from Salt) a rather grand family home at the Knoll, on the northern side of the River Aire, approx. 1,000 yards ENE of the mill. He lived there in some style, with several servants and a Swiss governess for the several daughters of the family. Stead continued as a partner throughout the 1860s and 1870s (a William Stead, perhaps his elder brother, also became a partner of the company in 1873). Stead, as the company's representative at the Bradford Chamber of Commerce, led the opposition in that forum to Disraeli's 1874 Factory Act, which finally conceded the true ten-hour day. In the Saltaire mill strike of 1876, it was Stead, now as managing director, who met with the strikers to resolve the dispute. His public life was focused on Shipley rather than Bradford. Chairman of Shipley Local Board for 17 years, an alderman of West Riding County Council and a J.P., Stead was a prime mover for civic improvements in Shipley. Late in life he was chairman of Shipley Liberal Executive, but stood down from this post in 1892 after backing an unsuccessful campaign to select A. E. Hutton in preference to William Byles as the official candidate for the Northern Division of the West Riding constituency. Through the deaths first of Sir Titus in 1876, and then of Titus Jr. in 1887 (see Appendix 3) Stead remained at the centre of the company's operations. Following the death of Titus Jr., Stead was elected chairman of the board of directors (at which time a C. F. Stead became a director). In the 1880s the company suffered financial setbacks (see Appendix 3) and in 1882 Stead mortgaged his house and grounds as security for the firm. With the eventual failure of the company in 1892 the bank foreclosed on the mortgage, and Stead lost the Knoll. By now in his late 60s, Stead moved to Southport where he died in 1902. His body was brought back to Nab Wood Cemetery (half a mile west of Saltaire) for burial (Refs: BDA, 15th February, 1902, p3; GtPat, p68, p74, p316, p319, p323; Ibbet; YDO, 14th February, 1902, p5; YDO, 17th February, 1902; S. A. Lawson, pers. comm.).

a member of the Saltaire firm. To the left, looking towards Bingley, the valley is still more beautiful; while overlooking it may be seen the extensive domain of Milner Field, on which his son, Mr. Titus Salt, has erected a costly mansion.[146] It was a spot in the valley nearly equi-distant from Ferniehurst and Milner Field, that Mr. Salt fixed as the site where his proposed "works" were to be erected. The following is the opinion of Sir William Fairbairn[147] in reference to it :—

It has been selected with uncommon judgment as regards its fitness for the economical working of a great manufacturing establishment. The estate is bounded by highways and railways which penetrate to the very centre of the buildings, and is intersected both by canal and river. Abundance of water is obtained for the use of the steam-engines, and for the different processes of manufacture. By the distance of the mills from the smoke and cloudy atmosphere of a large town, unobstructed and good light may be secured, whilst, both by land and water, direct communication is gained for the importation of coal and all other raw produce on the one hand, and for the exportation and delivery of manufactured goods on the other. Both porterage and carterage are entirely superseded, and every other circumstance which would tend to economise production, has been carefully considered.

But the whole of the property now known as the Saltaire Estate did not originally belong to one proprietor. That in which the mill now stands belonged to W. C. Stansfield,[148] Esq., of Esholt, and was purchased by Mr. Salt for

---

[146] BALG has here described the three most relevant residences in the immediate environs of Saltaire, each occupying attractive positions to the north of the river, and together amounting to a total of perhaps 350 acres of the land on the river's northern side. Lying outside the boundary of the village, the three residences would no doubt have been regarded as part of the community, with each of their three owners setting out each day to play his part in the management of the mill. If the reader has the opportunity, it is worth finding a vantage point on the high ground of Shipley, as in the account of BALG, to imagine the scene at the time. Sadly none of the buildings remain.

[147] Fairbairn was to be the engineer who designed and commissioned the power plant in the mill at Saltaire. For a fuller account, see Appendix 7.

[148] We judge this to be William Rookes Crompton, who took the name Stansfield when he became owner of the Esholt estate, an estate which adjoined the land which became Saltaire. The first Stansfield to buy the Esholt estate was Robert Stansfield in 1755. He died without issue and the estate passed first to his sister Anne, wife of William Rookes, and then to a daughter Anna Maria, who married Joshua Crompton of Derby; the latter pair were the parents of William Rookes Crompton. The area of land purchased by Salt from W.R.C. Stansfield included a corn mill, a worsted and fulling mill, together with goit, dam

£12,000. The land adjacent belonged to different proprietors, amongst whom may be named Lady Rosse.[149] The acquisition of the estate of Saltaire was thus a growth as well as the erection of the town itself.

It was in November, 1850, when Mr. Salt first called at the chambers of Messrs. Lockwood and Mawson,[150] Bradford. Mr. Forbes, who had been in his friend's confidence, had previously given a hint to these architects that Mr. Salt would be calling to have an interview with them. Towards evening, he made his appearance, and, having taken a seat by the fire, he said, "I'm going to build a mill near Shipley, and I want you to help me; but you must not expect to get all the work to do, for I have already bought the ground through Mr. George Knowles,[151] another local architect." Mr. Lockwood expressed his thanks, and his readiness to carry out Mr. Salt's wishes. "May I ask," he said, "what sum you purpose laying out on the works?" Mr. Salt replied, "probably £30,000 or £40,000." He then unfolded to Mr. Lockwood the plans he had thought out, mentioning many special features, which need not here be enumerated. "But," said he, with considerable emphasis, "I want the mill first; when can you have a pencil sketch ready?" Mr. Lockwood replied, "It shall be ready on the following Wednesday." On the day appointed, Mr. Salt came to the office, when a sketch of the mill was submitted for his inspection. Having very carefully examined it, he quietly shook his head, and the following conversation took place

Mr. SALT :—" This won't do at all."

Mr. LOCKWOOD, (rather surprised and chagrined at this abrupt judgment)

---

and island, known collectively as Dixon's Mill (to which BALG refers in Chapter X). The Wakefield Deeds Registry (Vol. QX/306/345 dated 31st December, 1850) shows the sale/ purchase was between W.R.C. Stansfield, of Esholt Hall, Esq (1), Titus Salt, of Crow Nest, Esq (2), and John Rawson, of Bradford, Gent (3) (Ref: WMofS, p22). W.R.C. Stansfield was for a time M.P. for Huddersfield. He died aged 81 on 5th December, 1871(Ref: AofY3, p441). Esholt estate was eventually sold by Stansfield's descendants to Bradford Corporation, becoming the site of the present day effluent treatment works (Ref: WofSD, p90).

[149] The Earl of Rosse's estate included land in the Bradford area stretching from Heaton and Manningham to Shipley (Ref: BfdMp). The Lady Rosse to whom BALG refers is presumed to be Countess Dowager Mary Rosse, who died in 1885 (Ref: Cud4, p203).

[150] For fuller accounts of Lockwood and Mawson, see Appendix 7.

[151] Mr. George Knowles FRIBA, was an architect and estate agent of Leeds Road, Shipley (Ref: Dir56). He lived at Moorhead House, Shipley, and died on 26th July, 1895. He is buried at Bingley (Ref: BO, 29th July, 1895).

:— " Pray, then, what are your objections to the sketch?"

Mr. SALT :—" Oh, it is not half large enough."

Mr. LOCKWOOD :—" If that is the only objection, I can easily get over it; but do you know, Mr. Salt, what this mill, which I have sketched, will cost?"

Mr. SALT :—" No: how much?"

Mr. LOCKWOOD :—" It will cost £100,000."

Mr. SALT :—" Oh, very likely."

From this conversation Mr. Lockwood perceived that expense was not a consideration, provided the work was efficiently done. The detailed plans were immediately proceeded with, and carefully drawn, into which Mr. Salt's own suggestions were incorporated, and which had special reference to ventilation, convenience, and general comfort. Hitherto, manufactories had been built with little regard to such conditions, and as for the buildings themselves, there was a decided lack of architectural taste in them. But the manufactory now proposed was to be, externally, a symmetrical building, beautiful to look at, and, internally, complete with all the appliances that science and wealth could command. When the detailed drawings were submitted to Mr. Salt, there were very few exceptions taken to them; the only questions, touching cost, were the following

Mr. SALT :—" How much?"

Mr. LOCKWOOD :—" About the sum I named before".

Mr. SALT :—" Can't it be done for less?"

Mr. LOCKWOOD :—" No, not in the way you want it to be done."

Mr. SALT :—" Then let it be done as soon as possible."

The erection of the mill was immediately proceeded with, but no contracts were issued. Mr. Salt was in great haste to have the work done speedily, so that it was let to various contractors, under a schedule of fixed prices, and not by tender;[152] thus different sets of workmen were simultaneously engaged at various points, and gradually "The Palace of Industry" rose to view.

The next point that demanded attention was the choice of a suitable engineer for the construction of the complicated machinery to be introduced. Mr. Salt hesitated between a well-known engineering firm at Bolton, and the Messrs.

---

[152] For further information on the building of Saltaire, see Appendix 7.

Fairbairn, of Manchester; the engines in the mills of Messrs. Marshall, Leeds, were the workmanship of the Bolton firm, and Mr. Salt went over to Leeds to inspect them; thence he proceeded to Bolton and had an interview with the engineers themselves; thence to Manchester to see Mr. Fairbairn. When he had calmly weighed the merits of each, he selected the latter for the engineering work which he himself required.

At the end of 1851, the Great Exhibition in London was closed, and the building in Hyde Park was advertised for sale. Mr. Salt thought that a part of that building might be utilised as a weaving-shed in his new works; he accordingly, in company with Mr. Lockwood, went to London to examine the structure, with a view to purchase what portion of it might be required. The result of the examination was, however, unsatisfactory. So far as space, light, and ventilation were concerned nothing could have been better; but it was not sufficiently substantial to bear the strain of machinery: the idea was therefore abandoned, and a weaving-shed, two acres in area, was constructed of stone and covered with glass.

The building was now covered in, and the question was to be settled, What shall the name be? One evening Mr. Fairbairn and Mr. Lockwood were dining at Crow Nest, when the above question was put by the host to his guests. It was suggested that each should write down a name by himself, and that the most appropriate one should be selected out of the list. One wrote the word "Salttown," another "Saltburn"; but these names did not seem to express all that was needed. At last, Mr. Salt suggested that the name of the river on which the mill stands should be considered. All at once they each exclaimed, "Saltaire! Saltaire! That's it"! And one playfully added, with wineglass[153] in hand, "I now propose success to Saltaire." Thus the name of "the works" had its origin.

In the spring of 1853, the building was hastening towards completion, and the vast machinery was nearly set up. The question of inauguration had next to be

---

[153] It is sometimes assumed that Salt was teetotal, but this suggests otherwise. His holdings of wine and liquor were sufficiently large that they are addressed in his will, in which Salt bequeaths them to his wife Caroline. Another example of Salt providing alcohol to his guests (including his workers) is found in Chapter X, where it records that the banquet to mark the opening of the mill included the provision of wine to the thousands of guests.

considered. The approaching twentieth of September was Mr. Salt's fiftieth birthday, and as that was the time when he had intended to relinquish business, it was the day which his friends thought most appropriate for the opening of "the works" that bore his name, and which were to commence a new era in his commercial life. It had been suggested to Mr. Salt that this was an event of sufficient importance to justify an invitation being sent to the Lord Lieutenant of the county; but instead of forwarding it, Mr. Salt and Mr. Lockwood went over to Harewood, and had a personal interview with his lordship. Lord Harewood cordially accepted the invitation, and made many inquiries as to the alpaca trade, and the gigantic establishment about to be opened. During luncheon, Lord Harewood, addressing Mr. Salt, said, "How is it, Mr. Salt, that you do not invest your capital in landed property and enjoy the remainder of your life free from the strain of business?" Mr. Salt replied, "My Lord, I had made up my mind to do this very thing, but on reflection I determined otherwise. In the first place, I thought that by the concentration of my works in one locality I might provide occupation for my sons. Moreover, as a landed proprietor I felt I should be out of my element. You are a nobleman, with all the influence that rank and large estates can bring, consequently you have power and influence in the country; but outside of my business I am nothing,—in it, I have considerable influence. By the opening of Saltaire, I also hope to do good to my fellowmen."[154]

Such is a brief account of the conception of, and preliminary steps leading up to, Saltaire. In the next chapter, the opening ceremony, together with a description of the establishment, will engage the attention of the reader.

---

[154] Salt's words here are important, in that it is here that we first find Salt stating his motives in building Saltaire. He returns to this subject at the formal opening of the mill (see Chapter X) and again at the workers' presentation to him of a bust in 1856 (see Chapter XII).

SALTAIRE.

From the North Side.

CHAPTER X.

"Rear high thy towers and mansions fair,

Thou gem of towns—renowned Saltaire.

Long may thy graceful spires arise

In beauty pointing to the skies,—

For labour dwells ennobled here,

Our homes to bless, our hearts to cheer.

From morn to eve the sun, I ween,

Shines not upon a fairer scene.

—ANON.

OPENING OF SALTAIRE—GREAT BANQUET—BILL OF FARE—SPEECHES ON THE OCCASION—"THE PEERAGE OF INDUSTRY"—CONCERT IN ST. GEORGE'S HALL— DESCRIPTION OF "THE WORKS" —MACHINERY—ERECTION OF TOWN—INTERIOR OF DWELLINGS—DAY SCHOOLS.

THE opening of Saltaire was an event, memorable, not only in the personal history of its founder, but in that of the commercial trade of the district and the country generally. Never before had the enterprise of one man ventured on a scheme so magnificent. Other manufacturers had erected large works, but the plan of Saltaire was so bold in its conception, so extensive in its design, so complete in its execution, that it placed the owner on a pinnacle of fame, without rival. But before entering the mill proper, we would first survey the scene which the inauguration banquet presents. As we have said, the 20th September, 1853, was the fiftieth anniversary of Mr. Salt's birthday; it was also the period when his eldest son, now Sir William Salt, Bart., came of age. There were, therefore, three events to be celebrated, either of which by itself might have evoked the sympathy of the community; but this triple combination was enough to call forth enthusiastic expressions of admiration and respect for the father, and good wishes for the son. The banquet was held in the great combing-shed of the building, which was elaborately decorated for the occasion, and had sitting accommodation for 3,500 guests. The weaving-shed would have held a company twice as numerous, but the other was deemed preferable. In length, the combing-shed is 210 feet, and in breadth, 112 feet; the roof is supported by 50 light cast iron columns, which, for the festival, were wreathed with laurels. On one side was placed a long table, occupied by Mr. Salt and the principal guests; the seven centre tables traversed the hall, and at them 644 ladies and gentlemen were seated; right and left of the centre ones were twenty tables for the workpeople, who, to the number of 2,440, were brought from Bradford by special train. As an evidence of the large-hearted hospitality of Mr. Salt, the order given to the purveyors was for 3,750 guests; and as a further proof of it, let us glance at the actual provision[155] for such a company. The following is the bill of fare:— Four hind-quarters of beef, 40 chines of beef, 120 legs of mutton, 100 dishes of lamb, 40 hams, 40 tongues, 50 pigeon pies, 50 dishes of roast chickens, 20 dishes of roast ducks, 30 brace of grouse, 30 brace of partridges, 50 dishes of potted meat of various kinds, 320 plum puddings, 100 dishes of tartlets, 100 dishes of jellies, etc.; altogether there were two tons weight of meat, and a half ton of potatoes. The dessert consisted of pines, grapes, melons, peaches, nectarines, apricots, filberts, walnuts, apples, pears, biscuits, sponge cakes, etc.; there were 7,000 knives and forks, 4,000 tumblers, 4,200 wine glasses, and 750 champagne glasses.

Such was the provision Mr. Salt made for his guests, with almost oriental profusion, and we give the above detailed account, as illustrating one of those deeds that reveal the man. His hospitality was in keeping with the generosity of his heart: whatever he did he must do it well; meanness was foreign to his nature, and in affording pleasure to others his soul delighted. But who were the special guests on this auspicious occasion? In the *Illustrated News* of 1st October, 1853, sketches are given of "The Principal Table," "The Model Mill," and "The Evening Concert in St. George's Hall." At the table, with Mr. and

---

[155] The catering was contracted to C. M. Wilks of the White Horse, Boar Lane, Leeds, who had a farm at Allerton Bywater, near Methley, from where some of the meat was supplied. A comprehensive account of the proceedings is available (Ref: BO, 22nd September, 1853, p8).

Mrs. Salt as the central figures, appear the Lord Lieutenant,[156] Mrs. Smith, (the Mayoress of Bradford,) and Mrs. Frank (now Lady) Crossley, while in close proximity were members of Parliament, the Mayor and Corporation of Bradford, magistrates, mayors of various towns, and private friends of Mr. Salt

It would be inconsistent with the design of this volume to reproduce the various speeches delivered at the banquet, except such parts as throw light on the character and enterprise of him whose life we seek to pourtray. The Earl of Harewood said he should go back with a high notion of the manufacturing classes; he wished the shades of the late Sir Robert Peel were there to see the happiness and prosperity that reigned amongst them. When he saw the enormous structure which Mr. Salt had erected, and the good architectural taste displayed in the building, he could not but say, that the whole was greatly to Mr. Salt's credit; but he would specially draw attention to what he was doing for the good of the working classes by building them commodious, well ventilated cottages, perfect in a sanitary point of view, so that his work-people might be conveniently and comfortably lodged. This was an example of building good mills, and providing well at the same time for those who worked in them. After a passing allusion to the fearful ravages of the cholera in other towns, arising from bad drainage and overcrowding, he said, no such source of disease would exist at Saltaire.

The Mayor of Bradford, (Mr. Samuel Smith,) said the man was still living, and present in the room, who carried the first gross of machine-spun yarn to the Bradford market. What progress since then! They had built palaces of industry almost equal to the palaces of the Caesars! Instead of manual labour they had availed themselves of the wonderful resources of mechanical science; instead of a master manufacturer carrying a week's production on his back, he harnessed the iron horse to the railway train, and daily conveyed away his goods by the ton; instead of being content with old English wool only, they now ransacked the globe for materials to work up.[157]

---

[156] The Lord Lieutenant was Henry Lascelles (1797–1857), 3rd Earl of Harewood. He was to die "from the effects of an accident whilst hunting", aged 59 on 22nd February, 1857 (Ref: BO, 26th February, 1857, p5).
[157] Very similar words are recorded in the BO's account of the Mayor's speech (Ref: BO, 22nd September, 1853, p8).

Mr. Salt's words were, as usual, few and appropriate; but surely little was needed from his lips in the presence of deeds which so eloquently spoke for him. Still, in expressing his gratitude for the kind allusions made to himself, he said he had still further pleasure in seeing that vast assemblage of his own workpeople around him. Ten or twelve years ago, he had looked forward to this day, on which he completed his fiftieth year, when he thought to retire from business and to enjoy himself in agricultural pursuits; but as the time drew near, and looking to his large family, five of them being sons, he reversed his decision, and determined to proceed a little longer and to remain at the head of the firm. Having thus determined, he at once made up his mind to leave Bradford; he did not like to be a party to increasing that already overcrowded borough, but he looked around him for a site suitable for a large manufacturing establishment, and he pitched upon that whereon they were then assembled. He would do all in his power to avoid evils so great as those resulting from polluted air and water, and he hoped to draw around him a population that would enjoy the beauties of the neighbourhood, and who would be a well fed, contented, and happy body of operatives. He had given instructions to his architects that nothing should be spared to render the dwellings of the operatives a pattern to the country. If his life should be spared by Providence, he hoped to see satisfaction, happiness, and comfort around him.[158]

Such words have the true ring in them. No proud vaunting of what his own skill had accomplished; no purposes of self-aggrandisement obtrude to indicate a sordid spirit; no fair visions of unfolded wealth yet to be acquired by the erection of this colossal structure; but underneath all we discern the praiseworthy motives that actuated him, namely, to benefit his family and his fellow-men.

Among the many tributes paid on this occasion to Mr. Salt, not the least interesting was one from Mr. French,[159] on the part of the operatives, who said he looked with pride and satisfaction on the mass of working people assembled

---

[158] BALG does not quote fully the precise words spoken by Salt, which are reported in the newspaper of the time (Ref: BO, 22nd September, 1853, p8) but his précis is a very close and accurate record, and its contents are important in that we find Salt for a second time stating his motives in building Saltaire.

[159] Our attempts to discover more about Mr. French have been unsuccessful.

in a place which might perhaps one day become a city; and he concluded by reading a poem, composed by Mr. Robert Storey,[160] the "Craven Poet." It is entitled

THE PEERAGE OF INDUSTRY.

To the praise of the peerage high harps have been strung
    By minstrels of note and of fame;
But a peerage we have to this moment unsung,
    And why should they not have their name?

CHORUS.

    For this is his praise—and who merit it not
    Deserve no good luck should o'ertake them—
    That while making his thousands he never forgot
    The thousands that helped him to make them!

'Tis the Peerage of Industry! Nobles who hold
    Their patent from Nature alone,
More genuine far than if purchased with gold
    Or won, by mean arts, from a throne!

And of Industry's Nobles, what name should be fair,
    If not his whose proud banquet we share?
For whom should our cheers simultaneously burst,
    If not for the Lord of Saltaire?

The Peer who inherits an ancient estate,

---

[160] We judge this to be Robert Story (1795–1860). Story (to use the spelling found in the *DNB*) was born at Wark in Northumberland, the son of a "border peasant". In 1820 he moved to Yorkshire and started a flourishing school in South Street, Gargrave. His *Songs and Lyrical Poems* were very popular and some of his poems were set to music (Ref: DNB).

And cheers many hearts with his pelf.

We honour and love; but is that man less great

   Who founds his own fortune himself?

Who builds a town round him; sends joy to each hearth;

   Makes the workman exult 'mid his toil;

And who, while supplying the markets of earth,

   Enriches his own beloved soil?

Such a man is a noble, whose name should be first

   In our heart, in our song, in our prayer!

For such should our cheers simultaneously burst;

   And such is the Lord of Saltaire.

But this inauguration banquet did not close the festivities. A concert was given by Mr. Salt in the evening, which took place in St. George's Hall, Bradford, and to which the guests of the day were invited. The hall was crowded in every part: the stalls were occupied by the principal guests, and the area and galleries by the workpeople. The appearance of Mr. Salt was hailed with several rounds of cheering; the entrance of Mr. Forbes, as well as that of the mayor, was also the signal for loud applause. The solo vocalists—consisting chiefly of native talent[161]—were accompanied by an efficient choir and an instrumental band; and the occasion, being one in which their hearts were in fullest sympathy, called forth their warmest efforts. The enthusiasm of the audience was unbounded, and, as the proceedings terminated by repeated cheers for their distinguished host, he was overcome with emotion, and could only acknowledge the compliment by a low bow. As an evidence of the character of the workpeople, not a single instance of intoxication or misconduct occurred throughout the day.

Such were the great opening festivities of Saltaire. Let us now take a brief survey of "the works," on which so much thought and money had been

---

[161] It was around this time that the Bradford Festival Choral Society was being formed, under the Mayoralty (1851–1854) of Samuel Smith (Ref: Cud3, p136).

expended, and about which so many eulogiums had been uttered.[162]

The great building itself is of light coloured stone,[163] in the Italian style of architecture, and, though a quarter of a century has elapsed since its erection, it still retains all the freshness of a recent structure; smoke has not soiled it, nor has the hand of time left its mark upon it. The south front of the mill is 545 feet in length, exactly that of St. Paul's. Its height is 72 feet above the level of the Midland Railway, which passes within a few yards. It has six storeys, and when seen from the southern approaches the whole front has a commanding appearance. The railway passenger, travelling along that route, northwards, must have been arrested by the glass-covered engines, which are visible in their movements, from the carriage window. These engines are placed in the centre of the building, and are themselves the central power by which the vast machinery is kept in motion. The first four floors are divided by the intervening engine-houses, but the top room runs the whole length of the building. The total area of the flooring is upwards of 55,000 square yards. The ground floor is 16 feet high, and the floor above, 14 feet, each being fire-proof. The roof is of iron, and the windows are formed of large squares of plate-glass opening on pivots. The warehouses, 330 feet in length, run northwards from the front building in the form of the letter "**T**," only lengthened in its perpendicular limb. On either side of the warehouse the ground is occupied by extensive sheds; that on the eastern side of the weaving-shed covering two acres, and holding 1200 looms; that on the western side is used for combing machines, etc. It was in this building the inaugural banquet was held. On the same side are also rooms for sorting, washing, and drying wools, and for reeling and packing. Beneath is a tank capable of holding 500,000 gallons of rain water collected from the roofs, and which, when filtered, is used in the processes of manufacture. On the top of the warehouse a large iron tank is placed, containing 70,000 gallons, drawn by engine pumps from the river, and available in case of fire. The two chief entrances to the works are by the western side: one for the workpeople and heavy traffic; the other for members of the firm, clerks, and people on business.

---

[162] We judge that the account which BALG gives of "the works" is taken from an earlier, fuller account (Ref: Hol1, pp21-26).

[163] For an account of the fabric of the buildings, see Appendix 7.

The offices face the main road, which crosses the canal and river by an immense iron bridge leading to the Park and other places. In front are the beautiful church, dining-hall, and the commodious town, to which we shall afterwards refer.

But if any part of "the works" demands special notice, it is the steam engines. These, as the work of Mr. Fairbairn, were considered a marvel of ingenuity and skill; yet, such has been the progress since in mechanical science, that the original engines have been superseded by four beam engines on the Corliss principle, an American invention, and indicating 1,800 horse power. In the construction of the engine beds alone, 2,400 tons of solid stone were used. There are fourteen boilers; the chimney is 250 feet high, *i.e.* about one-fourth higher than the "Monument," and is twenty-six feet square at the base. Green and Twibill's economisers are used; yet the consumption of coal is about fifty tons a day, or 15,000 tons a year. The weight of the shafting which the engines have to set in motion is between 600 and 700 tons. The calculations for the weaving-shed were that it should hold 1,200 looms, producing each day 30,000 yards of alpaca cloth or mixed goods, equal to nearly eighteen miles of fabric; this would give a length of 5,688 miles in one year, which, in the graphic words of Mr. W. Fairbairn, would, "as the crow flies, reach over land and sea to Peru, the native mountains of the alpaca." The gas-works, at the north-east side, are of great magnitude. There are two gasometers which supply the works and the town with light. As the Midland railway, and the Leeds and Liverpool canal almost touch the premises at opposite sides, the facilities for traffic could not well be surpassed.

But, as we have said before, Saltaire has been a growth: and since the opening day many additions have been made to "the works". At a later period,[164] a new spinning-mill and dye-works were erected on the site of Dixon's mill. One object Mr. Salt had in view, in this new undertaking, was to utilize the water-power which was running to waste. A horizontal wheel, known as a "turbine," was introduced at the time, but as the water supply was irregular, it was

---

[164] Up to this point in the chapter BALG has been describing circumstances and events of 1853; the remainder of the chapter relates to appreciably later periods of development, through to 1871.

afterwards superseded by a horizontal engine, eight feet stroke, direct acting, making 45 revolutions or 720 feet speed of piston per minute. The erection of a new chimney was objected to as detracting from the view on that side of the premises. Mr. Salt's reply was, "I'll make it an ornament to the place." To this end he built it in the form of a lofty tower, with elaborate masonry at the top, and it has more the appearance of an Italian campanile than a mill chimney.[165] In 1871, a shed was built on the east side of the original mill, with a stowage capacity for 12,000 bales of wool. The whole area covered by "the works" alone is about ten acres. The buildings are supplied with warm air in winter, and cool air in summer; long lines of ventilators worked by levers are inserted, and all effluvia are carried by pipes into the chimney flue. Thus the sanitary condition of the workpeople has in every way been considered.

But Mr. Salt's great conception did not end with the erection of the mill. It also embraced what was still more dear to him,—the provision of comfortable dwellings, church, schools,—in fact, every institution which could improve the moral, mental, and religious condition of the workpeople. The number of "hands" employed at "the works" was, at that time, between 3,000 and 4,000, who had, for the most part, to be housed at Saltaire.

With a lithographed plan of the town before us, let us notice a few points about it which serve to illustrate some features of Mr. Salt's personal character. His loyalty is to be recognised, for the three chief thoroughfares of the town are Victoria Road, Albert Road, and Albert Terrace. His affection for his family comes out, for Caroline Street bears the Christian name of his wife, and the other streets are named after his children, grand-children, and other members of his family. Again, his esteem for his architects is expressed in the names Lockwood Street and Mawson Street.[166] In all, there are twenty-two streets, besides places, terraces, and roads, which contain 850 houses, and forty-five almshouses, making a total of 895 dwellings, covering an area of twenty-five acres.

---

[165] BALG is here describing the chimney of the spinning-mill and dye-works – the mill which has come to be known as the New Mill, on the north side of the canal. Its architectural style follows that of the campanile of the Church of Santa Maria Gloriosa, Venice (Ref: Trl2, p19).
[166] The naming of the streets in Saltaire merits a fuller account – see Appendix 7.

Let us enter one of the dwellings, and examine its internal arrangements. From the sample the whole bulk may be judged. It is built of the same stone as the mill, and lined with brickwork. It contains parlour, kitchen, pantry, and three bedrooms. Some of the houses are designed for larger families, and others for boarding-houses. These dwellings are fitted up with all the modern appliances necessary to comfort and health; they are well ventilated, and have each a back garden, walled in, and flagged; the rents are moderate, and the houses are in much request. Part of Victoria Road is occupied by tradesmen's shops, the post-office, the savings bank, and the office of *The Shipley and Saltaire Times*. The whole cost of these dwellings, in 1867, amounted to £106,562, exclusive of the land.[167]

With so much consideration for the welfare of the workpeople, it was not likely that the educational wants of the children would be forgotten. In laying out the town, a central and most convenient site was set apart, on which elementary schools were to be built. From the first, provisional accommodation had been made elsewhere, but it was not till 1868 that the site was occupied. The report of the Government Inspector, after their erection, was "That the school buildings, for beauty, size, and equipment, had no rivals in the district." The cost of their erection was £7,000. They are situated on the west side of Victoria Road, and provide accommodation for 750 children. The style adopted is Italian, which is uniform with the other buildings of Saltaire. The boys' and girls' schoolrooms are placed at opposite ends of the building, each being 80 feet long by 20 feet broad. Between the wings in the front is a double colonnade; to the back are extensive open playgrounds, laid with asphalte, also covered playgrounds for wet weather; in front the ground is tastefully laid out with walks and shrubs. Two sculptured lions are placed at the corners of the garden palisades, emblematical of "Vigilance" and "Determination"; these are works of art, superior, in the estimation of many, to those at the base of the Nelson monument in Trafalgar Square; indeed, they were originally designed for that monument by Mr. Milnes, the sculptor; but a misunderstanding having

---

[167] It is recorded that "In the Times and Daily News, the expense of this gigantic undertaking is set down at half-a-million of money, but we believe every expense connected with it will be more than met by less than half of the money sum named" (Ref: BO, 30th September, 1852, p5).

arisen between him and Sir E. Landseer, they were not exhibited in London, but transferred to Saltaire.[168] Mr. Salt, from the first, had the schools placed under Government inspection, for though many of his Nonconformist friends were then unfavourable to State interference in education, he strongly advocated it, not for the sake of the grants, but for the benefit resulting from the inspector's visits. When the Education Act of 1870 came into force, Board schools were erected for the district in the neighbourhood of Saltaire; Mr. Salt therefore resolved to give up his elementary schools, and turn the building into middle-class schools, for which purpose they are admirably adapted. These, with the Institute, which we shall afterwards mention, bid fair to make Saltaire renowned, not only for its manufactures but also for its educational advantages.

---

[168] In addition to this account in BALG, we know of two other contemporary accounts with the same assertion that the lion sculptures were originally destined for Trafalgar Square (Cud1, p316; Hol1, p41 - each written in the few years prior to BALG). Cud1, written in 1876, gives the fullest account: "They (the lions) were first designed by the sculptor, Mr. Thomas Milnes of London, for the base of the Nelson Column in Trafalgar Square, but for some unexplained reason the commission was transferred to Sir Edwin Landseer. Meanwhile the models attracted the notice of Sir Titus Salt, who had them removed to Saltaire....They have all been carefully modeled from animals in the Regent's Park Zoological Gardens....the weight of each is nearly three tons". That the models should have attracted Salt's attention is likely to be linked to the fact that Salt knew Milnes. The bust of Salt which was presented to him by his workpeople on 20th September, 1856 (see Chapter XII) was sculpted by Milnes, who attended the presentation ceremony in St. George's Hall (Ref: BO, 25th September, 1856, p6). Milnes was a guest at the laying of the foundation stone of Saltaire Congregational Church on 27th September, 1856 (Ref: BO, 1st October, 1856, p6). The two female figures, six feet high, above the doorway of the Club and Institute are by the same sculptor (Ref: Hol1, p55), and were presumably made around the time of that building's construction in 1869. Thus it seems likely that Salt, over a period of at least 14 years, had been aware of Milnes' work. It is also possible, but not yet substantiated, that the two alpaca sculptures outside the chapel of the Tradesmen's Homes (see Appendix 5) are by Milnes; these latter sculptures are thought to have originally adorned Salt's estate at Methley Park (pers. comm., current manager of Tradesmen's Homes). A further account of the lion sculptures is available (Ref: Rob2).

CHAPTER XI.

His faith and works, like streams that intermingle,
In the same channel ran;
The crystal clearness of an eye kept single.
Shamed all the frauds of man.

—ANON.

He that's liberal
To all alike, may do a good by chance,
But never out of judgment.

—BEAUMONT AND FLETCHER.[169]

ERECTION OF SALTAIRE CHURCH—DESCRIPTION OF IT—MR. SALT A CONGREGATIONALIST—CHARITY TOWARDS OTHER COMMUNIONS—ERECTION OF BATHS AND WASH-HOUSES— ERECTION OF ALMSHOUSES—THE MILLS IN FULL OPERATION—A WORKMAN AT FAULT—VISITORS TO SALTAIRE—FAIRBAIRN AND DARGAN—HEILMANN'S COMBING MACHINE—UTILISING OF MOHAIR—THE ANGORA GOAT—VISIT TO CONSTANTINOPLE OF HIS SON—THE NAME OF "SALT" POTENT IN THE EAST.

WHEN Mr. Salt was Mayor of Bradford in 1848, he gave abundant proof of his solicitude for the religious wants of the population, and for which no adequate provision had been made. In the flush of commercial prosperity, it is to be feared that many who shared in it failed to realise the moral obligations that wealth entails, especially in providing places of worship for the working classes. Happily at a later period, the hearts of Christian men were quickened in this direction, and the various religious communions put forth great efforts to supply the deficiency, so that now Bradford is a town second to none in the number and

---

[169] The Spanish Curate, Act 1, Scene 1. Francis Beaumont (1584–1616) and John Fletcher (1579–1625) were playwrights who worked together in the early years of the 17th century.

excellence of its churches and Sunday schools. To the erection of many of these Mr. Salt had been a generous contributor; but now that the weighty responsibility of bringing some thousands of workpeople to reside at Saltaire devolved upon him, there was good reason to expect that their spiritual necessities would enlist his sympathy, even as their physical wants had done. Nor was this expectation disappointed. In arranging the plan of the town, from the first, a superior site had been selected for a church, but previous to its erection, a temporary one had been provided. In the year 1858,[170] the church was commenced, and was opened the following year. It is situated between the railway and the canal, and in front of the offices connected with "the works". The approach to it, from the main road, is by a long asphalted avenue, bordered on either side with grass and shrubs, neatly kept. The architectural style of the edifice is, of course, Italian, but carried out with a richness of detail, that makes it surpass all other buildings in the neighbourhood.[171] It seems Mr. Salt had purposely designed that God's House should have the very best of everything it was in his power to give, and, surrounded as it is by his vast manufacturing establishment, it

"Stands like a palace built for God."

---

[170] We are not convinced that this date is accurate; we suspect that work may have started earlier. The same date is quoted elsewhere (Ref: Hol1, p34) but it may be that BALG is simply relying on that source. Our doubt stems from the fact that the foundation stone of Saltaire Church was laid, by Mrs. Salt, on 27th September, 1856 (Ref: BO, 1st October, 1856, p6). It seems unlikely that, having laid the foundation stone in 1856, work did not get underway until 1858.

[171] It is important to place the building of Saltaire Church in the context of other similar developments around this time. In 1855 Frank Crossley had laid the foundation stone for the Square Congregational Church in Halifax; in 1856 Edward Akroyd laid the foundation stone for All Souls Church at Akroydon (Ref: Bret1, p82). Subsequent to the building of Saltaire Church – and almost before the cement was dry – Salt was appointed, in November 1859, to the Building Committee for a new Congregational Church in Victoria Road, Harrogate. Built to the design of Lockwood and Mawson, with the corner stone being laid by Frank Crossley on 14th August, 1861, the opening of the Harrogate church fell almost to the day on the two hundredth anniversary of the Great Ejection of 1662 (Ref: HisCH, p15). The church still stands in the present day, beautifully well kept in the hands of the West Park United Reformed Church. Akroyd went on to also fund the building of St. Stephen's Church at his Copley works (Ref: Bret1, p91). All five of these churches are truly imposing examples of church architecture of the time; their main benefactors were close associates. It is fully fitting that Salt provided such a magnificent focal point for religious devotion in Saltaire.

The porch consists of a series of Corinthian columns, raised above the ground, by six circular steps. These columns support eight smaller ones, which terminate in a dome, beneath which is the chamber where the clock, with its chime of six bells, is placed, the musical notes of which sound sweetly over the neighbourhood. On the south side is the family mausoleum, which is entered from the interior of the church. Let us enter within the latter and see its harmony and simple elegance. It is in the form of a parallelogram, ninety-five feet by forty-five feet. A continuous base runs round the building, supporting, at intervals, massive Corinthian columns, curiously formed, and which seem to the eye like polished malachite.[172] The spaces between the columns are occupied by windows, filled with delicately tinted glass. A broad aisle runs up the centre of the church, and the seats are of solid oak, polished and carved. A massive balustrade encloses the communion table and the pulpit, which, with the organ, occupies a domed recess. Two large circular chandeliers hang from the ceiling, formed of ormolu, with discs of cut and ground glass. The family pew is placed in a gallery over the entrance, facing the communion table; but it has never been occupied by them.[173] Mr. Salt, when worshipping there, preferring to be seated among the people. The whole cost of the edifice was about £16,000.

It is well known that Mr. Salt was, both from education and conviction, a Nonconformist. To the Congregational or Independent form he had been accustomed from childhood. In this communion divine worship, is as a rule, simple; the doctrines are not formulated into a creed, but the Holy Scriptures are regarded as the only supreme standard. The form of church government is avowedly based on the model of the Apostolic Churches, which they believe

---

[172] The columns are not in fact of malachite. The present day Guide Notes (available to visitors to the church) record that their appearance is the result of the application of the Scagliola decorative technique.

[173] It is interesting that the family did not use the pew. Access to the gallery is gained via an external door of the church, to the left of the main entrance. The stairway to the gallery is very narrow, which would have made it difficult for ladies in dresses of the day to reach the gallery. Furthermore, the chandeliers are hung in a position that obstructs much of the view from the gallery. It is local folklore that Mrs. Salt wanted a family gallery but that Mr. Salt did not, and that it appealed to his sense of humour to have the facilities provided in a way that met the letter but not the spirit of his wife's wishes.

were "Congregational," *i.e.,* the members of the congregation managed their own affairs; "Independent," *i.e.,* there was no governing body outside the congregation. The choice of the ministry in Congregational Churches, as well as its support, is, therefore, left in the hands of Christian worshippers; and the patronage either of individuals or of the State, is entirely inadmissible. It was in harmony with these principles that the church at Saltaire was begun. The selection of the first pastor was handed over to the congregation; the voluntary contributions of the people towards his stipend were encouraged; and the whole material fabric conveyed to trustees, that it might be held as a Congregational Church in perpetuity.

But, though warmly attached to Congregationalism, he was no narrow-minded sectarian. The liberty he claimed in the exercise of his own religious convictions, he fully accorded to others: none of his employés were compelled to attend the church he had built; on the contrary, he afforded every facility to other denominations to erect places of worship on his estate. To the Wesleyans he granted a site comprising 1300 square yards, and laid the foundation-stone of their chapel; he was also present at one of the opening services. The Primitive Methodists were presented with the site on which their chapel stands. The Baptists have two chapels on the confines of the town. The Episcopalians having a church so near as Shipley, (in which parish Saltaire is situated,) the erection of another was not deemed necessary. The Roman Catholics have also a church in the immediate neighbourhood. The Swedenborgians[174] have a room for their meetings. Thus, the religious wants of the people are met, and the spirit of Christian liberality and charity exhibited by Mr. Salt is a worthy example for others to follow.

In a large establishment like Saltaire, the workpeople are necessarily exposed to various accidents from machinery. To meet such cases an infirmary is erected, with every convenience for surgical operations and medical treatment.

---

[174] Swedenborgians are adherents of the views of the Swedish scientist and mystic Emanuel Swedenborg (1688–1772). They tended to work within existing churches, believing that "the aim of life is to develop one's inner spiritual world by repentance, good living, inner awareness and loving God, this leading to a life in heaven as an angel among a series of grades of angels" (Ref: DicBR). The group to which BALG refers was about 150 strong, and met at 13, Victoria Road on Sunday and Monday evenings, where they had a flourishing Sunday School (Ref: Hol1, p85).

If a person is maimed for life he receives a pension, or such light employment is provided for him as he may be able to follow.

The baths and wash-houses afford further evidence of Mr. Salt's interest in the health and comfort of his workpeople. They are situated in Amelia Street, and were built at a cost of £7,000. There are twenty-four baths, twelve on either side of the building, for men and women respectively, each having a separate entrance. A Turkish bath is also provided. The wash-houses are the result of Mr. Salt's perception of the need of them for the comfort of the work-people. In passing along the streets of Saltaire, his eye was sometimes offended by the lines of clothes, which, on washing-days, were hung out-of-doors. In visiting the dwellings he had ocular proof of the inconvenience connected with a domestic laundry. He therefore resolved to erect public wash-houses for the people, and to furnish them with all the newest appliances. These consist of three steam engines and six washing-machines. Each person bringing clothes to be washed is provided with a rubbing and boiling tub, into which steam, hot and cold water are conveyed by pipes. When the washing process is finished, the clothes are put into a wringing-machine, contrived on the centrifugal principle, by which a strong current of air is driven through them and the moisture expelled; they are next put, in frames which run on wheels, into the drying-closet, heated with hot air, after which they are ready for the mangling and folding rooms; so that clothes carried to the wash-houses, in a soiled condition, can be, in the course of an hour, washed, dried, mangled, and folded.

The almshouses are another proof of his thoughtful provision for the aged and infirm, and were erected "In grateful remembrance of God's undeserved goodness, and in the hope of promoting the comfort of some, who, in feebleness and necessity, may need a home." They are situated in the upper part of Victoria Road, on one side of which 20 of them are placed, and on the other side 25, making 45 in all capable of receiving 75 occupants. In passing along Victoria Road, these almshouses attract the notice of every visitor, and have the appearance of Italian villas, with walks and flower gardens in front, and creeping plants by the windows. Internally, they are provided with everything requisite to the comfort of the inmates, such as ovens, boilers, pantries, water, and gas,—all free. The inmates may be either men or women; single, married, or widowed. Each married almsman, residing with his wife, receives a weekly allowance of ten shillings; and each single almsman or woman, seven shillings and sixpence; which allowance is paid weekly.[175] The qualifications for admission are good moral character, and incapacity for labour, by reason of age, disease, or infirmity. Although preference is given to persons who have been in the service of the firm, it is not restricted to such, but others who stand in need and are personally known to the trustees, are also eligible.

There is no distinction of religious creed in considering applications, but all are placed on an equal footing, and, when accepted, are free to attend the place of worship they prefer; but, as many of them are aged and infirm, and thereby unable to go far from their homes, a neat little chapel has been provided for their special benefit. On the day it was opened, Mr. Salt, who was present, said that "his sole desire was that they should be all happy, and he hoped they were so, and that nothing would give him greater pleasure than to know that this was the case." The chapel is well lighted and ventilated; its walls are adorned with appropriate texts of Scripture, and services are held in it every Sunday morning and Wednesday night. One event of the year is the annual tea given to the inmates, at which Mr. Salt and his family have been accustomed to attend. It was a sight worthy of the artist's pencil, when, on such an occasion, their benefactor appeared in their midst. At one of these celebrations they presented him with a pair of gold spectacles and a silver-mounted walking-stick, as an expression of their warmest gratitude. Truly, to him might be applied the language of Scripture—"When the ear heard him, then it blessed him; and when the eye saw him it gave witness to him. Because he delivered the poor that cried, and the fatherless, and him that had none to help him. The blessing of him that was ready to perish came upon him, and he caused the widow's heart to sing for joy."[176]

But as some of the institutions above described were erected sometime after Saltaire was opened, let us go back in thought to 1853, and see the machinery of "the works" ready for starting. How different the aspect which meets the eye

---

[175] BALG's words are based on the regulations governing the almshouses. A full record of the regulations, and further account of the almshouses, is available (Ref: Hol1, p43).
[176] Job Chapter 29 Verses 11–13.

from that which was visible on that 20th September, when Mr. Salt gathered his numerous friends around him to keep high festival! Everything now has the appearance of business. The combing-shed, where the sumptuous banquet had been spread, is now filled with machinery of the most recent invention; the weaving-shed is covered with its acres of looms, where many hands stand ready for work; the warehouses are stored with wools, soon to pass through the necessary processes prior to becoming fabric. At last, the great steam-engines begin to move, sending their motive power into every part of the vast system, which, as if touched by a mysterious hand, wakes up into life; the complicated wheels begin to revolve, the ponderous frames to quiver, the spindles to whirl, and the shuttles to glide. Now, the silence of the place is broken by the din of machinery, in which the human voice is quite inaudible, and then comes forth the product of it all, the beautiful texture known as alpaca. How animated the scene! But it is not one soon to vanish away, like the inaugural festivity, but to continue long after the cunning hand of its originator has crumbled into dust.

Here, then, we behold this enterprising manufacturer, at the age of fifty, commencing a new career; but the accumulated experience of the past thirty years was now of immense advantage to him. It seemed as if he had been all along preparing himself for the wider field of enterprise, in which still greater wealth and fame were to be reaped. His faculty for organization was exhibited on a scale untried before; but such was his knowledge of men, that out of the thousands of workpeople he was able to select those who were competent to fill the various posts of duty. May we not say that whatever administrative abilities are considered necessary to the governor of a colony, were equally necessary to the governor of this colony of industrious workers? And it was not with despotic power he governed them, for although dependent upon him for the means of support, they had unlimited confidence in the uprightness of his character and the kindness of his heart.

On entering his "works" one day, he discovered some of the yarn had been spoiled in the spinning process. He immediately inquired who had done the mischief. A workman stepped forward and said "It is of no use, sir, accusing anybody else, I am the man who did it." Of course, he expected nothing but summary dismissal for his negligence, and anxiously waited the verdict "What do you mean to do?" asked Mr. Salt. "Do better, sir," was the reply. "Then," said his master, with a smile, *"Go and do it."* This workman is still living, and his opinion of his master is given in the following words :—" When his mind was made up, nothing could move him. He never *flinched* from hard work. Never talked about a thing, but did it. Never used an unnecessary word. He was a kind master to me."

The opening of "the works" of Saltaire soon became known throughout the country, and awakened much interest among various ranks and classes. The Press had not only given an account of the inaugural banquet, but of the gigantic establishment, with all its interior arrangements and outward surroundings. The consequence was that not only men of business, but of science and philanthropy, came from all parts of the kingdom to Saltaire, and expressed themselves both astonished and delighted with what they witnessed. At first, every facility was afforded to strangers in gratifying their curiosity or satisfying their inquiries; but in course of time it became necessary to adopt certain regulations in the mode of admission. Beside the interruption to work, the expert eye of the visitor easily gathered a harvest of new ideas while inspecting various costly inventions. It was afterwards found that these ideas were not only purloined, but reproduced, to the injury of the patentee, as well as the proprietor. This led to the adoption of the rule at present in force, which restricts admission to those who are personally known to the firm, one of whom generally accompanies the visitor over "the works."

Shortly after Saltaire was opened, several carriages filled with gentlemen, drove up to the gates, under the leadership of the late Dr. McLeod,[177] of Benrhydding. Mr. Salt received them with much cordiality, for among them were two well-known names, around which much interest gathered. These were Mr. Wm. Fairbairn, (the late Sir William[178]), and Mr. Dargan, the well-known Irish contractor. After an inspection of the establishment, Mr. Salt invited the

---

[177] Dr. W. McLeod (or Macleod in Ref) was from Scotland. He came to Ben Rhydding (again, a variation in spelling to that used by BALG) in 1847. The proprietor of the Ben Rhydding Hydropathic Establishment, he took an interest in local affairs. He died aged 57 in 1875 (Ref: BO, 27th January, 1875, p3).
[178] Fairbairn died three years prior to the writing of BALG, on 18th August, 1874 (Ref: AofY3, p638).

whole party to dinner, and Mr. Lockwood, who was also present, was commissioned to proceed to Bradford, to make the necessary arrangements. That dinner party is well remembered by at least one of the guests, for the sparkling sallies of wit that were made on the occasion, and of which the Irishmen present were the chief contributors, and also for a memorable incident that took place at the close. Mr. Fairbairn, Mr. Dargan, and Mr. Lockwood remained for an hour, after the other guests had left. Turning to the host, Mr. Dargan said, "Now, Mr. Salt, I want to know your history." But there was no answer. "Come," he said, "I must have it." "My history," said Mr. Salt, very modestly, "has nothing particular about it;" and, in a few words, he mentioned those salient facts with which the reader is already familiar. "Now," said he, "I should like to know the history of you three gentlemen." Mr. Dargan's life was certainly a very eventful one, and worthy of a brief record here. He said, "My father was a farmer in Ireland, and my mother an exceedingly clever woman, who brought up her children in a most judicious manner, but suddenly she died, and my father became an altered man for the worse. Everything on the farm went to wreck and ruin, and two years after my mother's death, he died also. The little property that fell to my share, I gave up to my sisters, and I made up my mind to seek my fortune elsewhere. I went to Dublin and crossed to Holyhead, where workmen were blasting the rocks for the breakwater. I went into the quarries and worked for 12S. a week. Thinking I could myself work better than they, I sought and obtained other employment at £2 a week. After awhile I thought I could yet better myself, and gave notice to leave; but the contractor offered me a situation with a salary of £200 a year. I accepted it, and got married. Then came the railway mania, when every man who had a knowledge of land-surveying was sure of finding employment. I went back to Ireland and learned what I wanted. My newly-acquired knowledge was soon called into requisition. I undertook to survey part of a line of railway, and in the first year I made £2,000. Afterwards I took a contract for some of the works, one of which was a bridge. It was there," he said, turning to Mr. Fairbairn, "Fairbairn, you and I first met. Since then, I have made millions, but have not kept them." Such is the story of Dargan's life, as given by himself on the occasion referred to. As a supplement to it, it may be interesting to know that he planned the Industrial Exhibition of Dublin, in 1853, with a view of developing the resources of his native country, and as a help towards its realisation, he placed £20,000 in the hands of the working committee, which sum was lost, for, in a monetary point of view, the Exhibition was a failure. At the opening ceremony the offer of knighthood was offered to him, which he declined.

Mr. Salt then called on Mr. Fairbairn to relate his history, which has recently been published at length in "Pole's Life of Sir William Fairbairn." It affords a striking illustration, along with those of Mr. Salt and Mr. Dargan, of what men with moderate education and limited means may accomplish. They were all self-made men, who entered upon the business of life with a determination to succeed; into every undertaking they put their undivided energies, and each success became a stepping-stone to still higher attainments.

Mr. Lockwood's "Life" was also given on this occasion, but as it is happily not completed it would be out of place to record it in part. Suffice it to say that he, too, is an example to young men, how the cultivation of talent, devotedness to professional duties, combined with tact and courtesy, can lead to eminence.

One of the most remarkable machines in "the works" of Saltaire is that used in the combing of wools, and which is worthy of notice, not only from its own intrinsic value, but from other circumstances, to which we shall briefly refer. The original inventor of this machine was Heilmann, a Frenchman, who took out a patent for it in England about the year 1849. The principle of his invention is what is called the "nip," which means the mode of taking firm hold of the ends of the wool, and holding them as firmly as the hair of the head is fixed in the scalp. For the perfecting of this machine the trade is mainly indebted to Mr. Samuel Cunliffe Lister, of Bradford, whose name is perpetuated both by the park at Manningham and the statue erected there. From the interesting history of the firm of "James Akroyd and Son, Limited," we give the following extract :—

" An essential part of Mr. Lister's completed machine is what is called 'Heilmann's Patent.' This patent was purchased conjointly by the firm of James Akroyd and Son, and Titus (now Sir Titus) Salt, Sons, and Co., about the year 1852, and re-sold to Mr. Lister for about £40,000, the amount of the original purchase, money, reserving the right of use to the vendors."

It will thus be seen that in the works of Saltaire no expense was spared to make the machinery perfect, a principle on which the firm has continued to act, and which enables them to maintain that high position in the trade to which they are so justly entitled.

From the reputation of Mr. Salt in connection with alpaca, it might be supposed that this was the only staple manufacture at Saltaire; but it is not so. His success in the utilizing of Donskoi wool and alpaca, led him to try other experiments of a similar kind. His eye was ever quick to perceive the demands of the trade, and his patience and perseverance enabled him to continue his experiments with any new material submitted, until its properties and capabilities were ascertained. The material to which reference will now be made is "mohair"—the wool or hair of the Angora goat. Unlike the alpaca, this animal is indigenous to the Eastern world, as the former is to the Western. Its home is the mountainous interior of Asia Minor, the centre of which is Angora, a town situate about 220 miles east of Constantinople. Angora has long been celebrated for its breed of goats with beautiful silky hair, eight inches in length. Of this goat-hair, commonly called "mohair," a yarn is made, from which is manufactured the beautiful fabric called Utrecht velvet, which is used most extensively for upholstering purposes, curtains, &c., and with which many of the Continental railway carriages are lined. Of the skin of the Angora goat the fine oriental leather is made. But the wool or hair of this animal is not, like that of the alpaca, a new material in the production of textile fabrics. It is perhaps one of the most ancient in the world. There is reason to believe that it is to this material reference is made in Exodus XXV., 4 verse. Speaking of the covering of the Jewish Tabernacle in the Wilderness, God says—"And blue and purple and scarlet, and fine linen and *goats' hair.* It is perhaps also to the beautiful and silky appearance of this material that Solomon refers in Songs, IV., I,—"Thy hair is as a flock of goats that appear from Mount Gilead." It would thus appear from the above quotations that the goats' hair, in ancient times, was utilized, and was peculiarly soft and beautiful.

But whatever be the origin or antiquity of mohair, it became, shortly after Saltaire was opened, one of the staple articles in use, and, along with alpaca, is manufactured into an endless variety of the worsted goods which are to be found on every draper's counter in the kingdom, and worn in various forms by the inhabitants of countries beyond the seas. In order that regular supplies of mohair may be obtained for manufacturing purposes, an agent of the Saltaire firm permanently resides at Constantinople, through whom all business negociations are conducted. The name of "Titus Salt" is well known in various parts of Turkey, and has long been synonymous with all that is honourable in connection with British commerce. As an evidence of this, the youngest son[179] of Mr. Salt happened to be visiting Constantinople in the year 1865. This visit was not for purposes of business, but simply as a tourist in Eastern parts. But one day he presented a draft at a banking-house, bearing the honoured name of his father, which was also his own. It was soon noised abroad that "Titus Salt, from England," had arrived in the capital, and on 'Change[180] it was conjectured that commercial pursuits must have brought him; the consequence was that prices took a sudden rise, and extensive purchases were anticipated. These hopes, however, were raised only to be dashed to the ground, for the English tourist soon took his departure without making any particular investment, except in articles of curiosity.

The business negociations with the East were sometimes conducted with the quiet dispatch peculiar to diplomacy. We once happened to meet the firm at luncheon, when a telegram arrived, which was handed to Sir Titus, and passed to the other partners. It was, last of all, handed to us; but, lo! it was written in cypher, which no one knew save the sender and they to whom it was sent. Thus, between Saltaire and Constantinople, business was being transacted at this moment, and, for aught we know, wealth thereby acquired. May not young men learn from this incident, how unostentatiously business may be carried on? It is not by bustle or "great swelling words" but "in quietness and confidence shall be their strength." And may not the same remark be applicable to spiritual as well as to temporal things? They who maintain secret traffic with Heaven grow rich in treasures that shall remain their possession for ever.

---

[179] BALG is referring to Salt's youngest living son Titus, then aged approx. 21.

[180] It is difficult to be categorical as to which Exchange BALG is referring, but we believe it is the Wool Exchange in Bradford. (An exchange existed prior to the 1867 opening of the purpose built facility in Market Street). The term "Change" was used colloquially in reference to the Wool Exchange (see e.g. Ref: AofY2, p283).

CHAPTER XII.

"From lowest place when virtuous things proceed,
The place is dignify'd by the doer's deed:
When great additions swell, and virtue none,
It is a dropsied honour."[181]

"The purest treasure mortal times afford,
Is—spotless reputation; that away,
Men are but gilded loam, or painted clay."[182]

—SHAKESPEARE.

THE WORKPEOPLE AT CROW NEST—THE FEAST IN THE GROUNDS—BILL OF FARE—
PRESENTATION OF HIS BUST—ADDRESS ON THE OCCASION—MR. SALT'S REPLY—
A SOIREE MUSICALE—SPARE TIME DEVOTED TO THE PUBLIC GOOD—WELCOME
TO JOHN BRIGHT—MR. SALT AS CHAIRMAN OF REFORM CONFERENCE—
CANDIDATE FOR PARLIAMENTARY HONOURS—HIS SPEECHES ON THE
OCCASION—LETTER TO ELECTORS—ELECTED AS M.P.—SOCIAL SCIENCE
MEETINGS AT BRADFORD—LORD BROUGHAM AT SALTAIRE—CONGREGATIONAL
UNION MEETINGS.

THE first part of this chapter will be devoted to a description of two scenes in which Mr. Salt appears, first, as the entertainer of his workpeople; and second, as the recipient, in a tangible form, of their gratitude and love. It would have augured ill for the inhabitants of Saltaire, had they beheld the marvellous sympathy of their noble master for their temporal and spiritual welfare, without reciprocating it in some way. It is said "love cannot be all on one side," and the same aphorism may be applied to kindness and goodwill, which also require

---

[181] All's Well that Ends Well Act 2, Scene 3.
[182] Richard II Act 1, Scene 1.

reciprocity for their healthy growth. In the case of an employer of labour like Mr. Salt, his moral nature would not have suffered loss had his kindness met with no response on the part of his workpeople; the consciousness of having done his duty would have brought its own reward, but the consequence to the morals of the people themselves would have been disastrous. To them the master would have been merely as a benevolent individual, and they but the objects of his compassion and the recipients of his bounty. But when genuine sympathy on one side has evoked the same quality on the other, the relation of capital and labour rests on a substantial basis.

At Saltaire we have a splendid example of the hearty sympathy subsisting between master and work-people. The latter resolved to present Mr. Salt with a colossal bust of himself, and on the 20th September, 1856, the ceremony took place. It will be remembered that this was his birthday, and also the day on which Saltaire was opened in 1853. Only three years had elapsed since the sumptuous banquet had been held on that occasion, at which the workpeople sat among other invited guests; but instead of resting under the shadow of that bygone act, Mr. Salt was ready to repeat it, and invite them again to another festivity. The ceremony of presenting the testimonial was therefore united with the birthday festival, in which this mutual sympathy between master and workmen was beautifully exemplified; for, as already indicated, in the first part of the proceedings Mr. Salt appeared as the generous host, in the second part he was the honoured guest.[183]

Work was suspended at Saltaire on that memorable day, for the festival was to be held at Crow Nest, the residence of Mr. Salt, and a general invitation was given to all "the hands" in the establishment to visit him at his home. The number who accepted it was 3,000, and they were conveyed thither at his expense, by railway. As they passed in procession through the streets of Bradford, on their way, they presented to the inhabitants unmistakable evidence of being what Mr. Salt, three years before, hoped they would be, "well paid, contented, and happy operatives." The procession consisted of spinners, combing-shed hands, warehousemen, and handloom weavers. The women and

---

[183] An exhaustive account of the day's events is available (Ref: BO, 25th September, 1856, p6).

girls led the way, four a-breast, preceded by the Saltaire drum and fife band. Many flags and union jacks were carried in the procession, while two banners of blue silk, bearing the arms of Mr. Salt, with the motto, *Quid non Deo juvante,* beneath, were conspicuous above all. An eye-witness of the procession wrote:— "In that moving mass of humanity—honest and industrious men and women— we beheld a sight which could not fail to awaken the best emotions of the human heart, and to inspire the philanthropist with joy and gladness."

On arriving at the entrance to Crow Nest grounds, they passed down a pathway, lined on either side by overhanging trees. On approaching the house, they beheld a herd of llamas, alpacas, and Angora goats, collected on the green sward on the right, which excited much interest on the part of the workpeople. Though many of them had daily been handling the fibre derived from such animals, most of them had never before beheld a living specimen. The mansion lies embosomed in a beautiful dell, and on the front door steps stood Mr. Salt, surrounded by his family, to bid them welcome. The procession continued its course through the conservatories and greenhouses, issuing thence into the gardens, and ultimately emerging into the park, in which were preparations on every side for the enjoyment of the people. And now the sports of the day began, which consisted of various innocent amusements, such as running, leaping, climbing, dancing. No intoxicating liquor was needed to exhilarate them; nor was any provided. The fresh air and scenery around were sufficient; while the noonday sun poured down its rays and filled every heart with joy. And then came the feast itself. How can pen describe it! On an elevated part of the park, a "monster" marquee[184] was erected, the superficial area of which was 3,000 yards, capable of accommodating comfortably 5,000 persons. There were thirty-two tables, equal to 870 yards in length, and covered from end to end with white glazed calico. The seating was double that length, or nearly a mile. The interior of this immense-dining hall was decorated with flowers and evergreens, while outside, flags and banners were hung in profusion.

---

[184] The account of the day's events in BO, 25th September, 1856, p6 makes reference to the shape of the marquee being that of a letter "T". References to the use of the letter "T" in this and other activities of Titus Salt – e.g. the design of the mill – leads to speculation by some that this was a deliberate motif used by him, or by others acting on his behalf.

To show the extent of provision[185] made for this extraordinary feast, the following is the bill of fare, namely:—" Beef, 1,380lbs., ham, 1,300lbs.; tongues and pies, 520lbs.; plum, bread, 1,080lbs.; currant bread, 600lbs.; butter, 200lbs.; tea, 50lbs.; sugar, 700lbs.; cream, 42 gallons; and a great quantity of celery." The weight of the earthenware used was four tons and a quarter; of the glass, three quarters of a ton; and of the knives, forks, and spoons, one ton and a quarter. Before grace was sung, Mr. and Mrs. Salt passed round the tables, amid the enthusiastic applause of their guests. It was a scene that must have filled the heart of the generous host with gladness, that he could thus help to make his fellow-creatures happy; that he could be the means of sending new life into every fibre of their physical being, and of offering them a draught of the purest pleasure, that would bring no regrets on the morrow, except that the scene itself had vanished away.

But the second part of the proceedings was yet to come. The former was only the background, to bring out in relief the picture itself. Now the scene is shifted from Crow Nest to St. George's Hall, Bradford, where the presentation of the bust took place in the evening. The stalls were filled with the personal friends of Mr. Salt, who appeared in full dress; while the area and galleries were crowded with workpeople. The chairman,[186] on this occasion, stated that the idea of presenting Mr. Salt with some token of esteem originated three years since, but circumstances had prevented the accomplishment of the purpose. At first, the opinion prevailed that Mrs. Salt should also be presented with some expression of their appreciation of her kindness; but, believing that in honouring her husband, she herself would feel honoured, they had resolved to unite their

---

[185] The sources of the provisions merit comment. Tables and seats were provided by Mr. John Ives, a joiner and builder of Shipley. The cutlery, glassware etc. were provided by Mr. C. Rhodes of Bradford. Beef was provided by Messrs. T. Watkins and Shaw of Bradford, and Mr. Sagar of Bradford and Saltaire. Other edibles were provided by Mrs. Greenhough of Wakefield Road, Bradford (Ref: BO, 25th September, 1856, p6). In contrast to arrangements already noted for the celebrations in 1853, more local traders were being used to supply the provisions. This may well have been a conscious act designed to assuage critics of Salt who felt he had, in moving to Saltaire, abandoned Bradford. Such criticism is known to have been voiced later in the same decade; a remark to that effect is reported in the debates that accompanied Salt's 1859 parliamentary campaign, as BALG shortly describes.
[186] Mr. Mowbray, C.E. (Ref: BO, 25th September, 1856, p6).

contributions in the purchase of a work of art, which would remain an heirloom in the family for ever. The sculptor selected was Mr. T. Milnes,[187] who also executed the lions that adorn Saltaire. The bust is of the purest Carrara marble, standing on a shaft or pedestal of Sicilian marble. At the base of the shaft various symbolised figures represent the sources of Mr. Salt's wealth. The shaft on which the base rests is supported by an alpaca and an Angora goat, — the animals which supply the new material for manufacture. At their feet lies a fleece enwrapping a cornucopia, from which is pouring forth a profusion of rich and luscious fruit, and falling as it were on to the works and dwellings of Saltaire, which are brought out in relief on the base of the pedestal. The artist has made one foot of the alpaca to rest on a wreath of olives,—thus indicating Peace; and one foot of the goat upon the fleece, from which is springing out abundance for employer and employed—thus indicating Plenty. The whole is six feet six inches in height, from the base of the pedestal to the crown of the head, and weighs within a fraction of two tons.[188] The address presented on the occasion was the following

TITUS SALT, ESQ.

SIR,—We, the workpeople in your employment, in presenting to you the marble bust of which we now ask your acceptance, would briefly refer to the motives that have induced us to take this step—one which may be considered almost unprecedented in the history of manufacturers. Your workpeople have for some time back felt a strong desire to present to you, in a tangible form, some token of their affection and regard, not only as a tribute to the genius and enterprise which have called forth the admiration of all well-wishers of their country, but to the high and noble spirit of philanthropy which you have always manifested, and which has been actively at work, not only in

---

[187] Milnes was not the first choice of sculptor. A Bust Committee had been formed and "...the Committee entrusted the work to an artist in the neighbourhood, being desirous of encouraging and raising native talent." Before completion of the work the artist abandoned the project leaving the committee with a deficit. In seeking alternative means of completing the work a flaw was found in the bust's marble and this initial scheme was then abandoned. Only then was Milnes appointed (Ref: BO, 25th September, 1856, p6).

[188] The rear of the bust carries the inscription "Presented to Titus Salt Esquire by the workpeople in his employment as a token of their respect and esteem. Saltaire September 20th, 1856". While Milnes was the sculptor, the actual designer of the piece was Mr. Lobley of Bradford (Ref: AHof L, p683).

securing the happiness and prosperity of your workpeople, but in the undeviating support which you have rendered to those public institutions which are calculated to promote the present and lasting benefit of the public at large. And when we consider that this day is the anniversary of the inauguration of the works at Saltaire, we are reminded of the results of that genius and enterprise, as manifested in the gigantic establishment you have raised. Not only has its adaptation for manufacturing purposes been considered, but you have been equally careful to secure the health and comfort of your workpeople. Well does it deserve the appellation of the "Palace of Industry." And, Sir, your attention has not been entirely absorbed in providing for the physical wants of your workpeople, but a higher and nobler purpose has had a share of your attention, viz., the cultivation of the mind; and though Saltaire has been so recently built, we have had a library and reading-room in operation more than twelve months; the library[189] containing more than 1,200 volumes of well-selected works, which are enjoyed and appreciated by a great number of workpeople. Sir, if we look back at the seasons of commercial depression which have from time to time visited the West Riding, entailing heavy losses upon the manufacturers, and distress upon a great portion of the working population, we are not unmindful that you, Sir, have nearly counteracted the effect of such seasons of distress upon your own workpeople, by keeping them fully employed; for however long the storm may have lasted, a diminution in the hours of work, and a consequent loss to the operatives in wages, have never yet taken place in your establishment. We think, Sir, these are circumstances characteristic of your efforts which you may look back upon with pride and satisfaction, and which we remember with feelings of gratitude; and the benevolent spirit which has been manifested to those who have been unfortunate, and the efforts that have been made to render at all times your workpeople happy and contented, have given rise to feelings of affection and love, which will be lasting as our lives, and have laid upon us a debt of gratitude which cannot be repaid. But, Sir, we beg that you will accept the testimonial we offer, not for its pecuniary worth or artistic merit, but as a tribute of our love. In conclusion, we would say that it is our sincere desire that you may live long to look with pleasure and satisfaction upon the testimonial we offer; that your future course, and that of your sons, may be characterised by the same prosperity which has hitherto marked your career, and that, when age compels you to retire from active life, it may be a source of happiness to you to recollect that you have lived in the affections of your work-people. September, 20, 1856.

---

[189] At the time of this address in 1856, the Saltaire Club and Institute had yet to be built, and so the library being referred to was located elsewhere. In the 1861 census No. 4 Albert Terrace is recorded as being not a family residence but a library, and is probably the library being referred to in this address. It is noteworthy that from the outset Salt was providing facilities in Saltaire, albeit interim, for his workers to improve themselves.

The above address was handed to Mr. Salt by Mr. S. Wilson,[190] in the name and on behalf of the work-people,[191] who said, in presenting the bust,—"It is out of my power to lift the ponderous weight: were it sovereigns, I would gladly count the enormous weight and place it in the hands of one of whom I believe it will ultimately be said, 'Well done, thou good and faithful servant: thou hast been faithful over a few things, I will make thee ruler over many things: enter thou into the joy of thy Lord.'"[192]

Mr. Salt's acceptance of the testimonial was made in the following words :—

My Friends,—In accepting this beautiful work of art at your hands as a tribute of your affection and esteem, I assure you it is most gratifying to my feelings, and I consider this as the proudest day of my life. Three years ago, when I had the pleasure of meeting you at the opening of the works of Saltaire, I then stated my motives and objects in erecting them. So far, I have reason to hope that my wishes will be fulfilled, and that I shall be there surrounded by an industrious, a happy, and a moral people; and, so long as I am supported by you as heretofore, with God's blessing, I have no doubt of success. I am sure, therefore, that you will take it in good part, if I remind you that you must be co-workers with me, for it is only as *you,* each one of you—young and old, great and small—do *your*

---

[190] We judge S. Wilson to be Samuel Wilson, who for more than 20 years was Salt's cashier. He died on 28th September, 1867 at his home in Blackpool (Ref: BO, 3rd October, 1867).
[191] There is regrettably little known about the key, individual members of Salt's workforce at this time. BALG names a few workers in this account, and BO, 25th September, 1856 names six others: Messrs. Cawthra, J. Farrar, Holdsworth, M. Marshall, John Pool, and Taylor. William Cawthra was a foreman, who died, aged 54, on 2nd April, 1866 (Ref: BO, 12th April, 1866). There is a Joseph Farrar who died in 1878, aged 72, interred in Undercliffe Cemetery, in a plot adjacent to those of Robert Milligan and Henry Brown (see Appendix 4), but we do not know if it is the same individual. Millar Marshall (1813–1883) was born in Yeadon and had first worked in the late 1830s as a spinning overlooker for Salt at the latter's Union Street mill. At the opening of the Saltaire mill, Marshall held the post of manager of the drawing and spinning department, living for a time at 50, George Street. He left Salt's employ in 1865 and set up a small mill at Windhill, a business he kept until his death. Marshall was a committed Methodist, being a member of the Wesleyan Society for over 60 years. He was instrumental in the establishing of Saltaire's Wesleyan Chapel, the foundation stone of which was laid by Salt on 6th October, 1866 (Salt having contributed to the funding of the project). In 1881 Marshall was living at 19, Cross Banks, Shipley; he died with a "malignant disease of the liver" in 1883 (Refs: ShST, 12th May, 1883; PRO 1861, 1881 censuses; SMCH). We have no knowledge of Messrs. Holdsworth, Pool and Taylor.
[192] Mathew Chapter 25 Verse 21.

part, that I can succeed in promoting the object I have in view. This is my most earnest wish for Saltaire. I thank you for the kind reference you have made to my sons, in your address. I can only say, in regard to this, that they know my highest ambition for them is, that they should conscientiously employ the property and position which they may inherit from me, in carrying on whatever undertaking I have had the honour of commencing, for the benefit of the working-classes, and that this beautiful bust and pedestal will be to them a constant incentive. Ladies and Gentlemen who occupy the stalls, let me thank you for the cordial sympathy which you have manifested. What has just taken place I am sure must convince you that the task of improving the condition of the working-classes, however difficult and laborious it may be, is not thankless or unprofitable.[193]

In acknowledging the resolution of thanks for the hospitalities at Crow Nest, Mr. Salt said,—

I beg to assure you, that the pleasure you have felt this day has been reciprocal. Myself and family have been greatly delighted to see you, I assure you. I cannot but plead guilty to a little pride. I did feel proud of my workmen to-day, when assembled in the park. I am very glad the weather has been so favourable, and that everything has gone off so well. But I will not detain you by any remarks. I feel no doubt but the talented artistes who are to occupy the remainder of the evening, will add to the proceedings of to-day 'the end which crowns the whole.' I cannot sit down, however, without bearing in mind, that there are some among you, who have worked hard in making the arrangements for this day. To them I take the opportunity of offering my most heartfelt thanks.

A workman, in seconding a vote of thanks to the chairman, said, in his own provincial dialect, "Ah've wrout for sixteen yeear for Mister Salt, an' ah can saya that ah ham weel pleeased and weel satisfied wi' him; an' ah am weel pleeased wi' aar chairman; an' ah second 't moation wi all my hart, an' sit ma daan."[194]

---

[193] The foregoing record of Salt's actual words makes explicit his motives and objectives in building Saltaire, as he earlier expounded in 1853 (see Chapters IX and X). Key to his stated aspirations are his concept of his workforce co-working with him; and the ambition that his sons should continue his undertakings so as to better the working classes. The aspiration that his sons would continue his undertakings (as distinct to simply continuing their employment) is stated here more explicitly than in 1853.
[194] BALG's brevity here does not fully capture the purpose of the workman's contribution. From a reading of the full account (Ref: BO, 25th September, 1856, p6) it is clear that the

A soirée musicale filled up the day's programme, which afforded a rich feast to the lovers of music. Between the parts, coffee and other refreshments were served in the saloon. The bust presented on this occasion was considered a striking representation, in marble, of Mr. Salt's features at the age of fifty-three; but the later productions of the artist are those by which his personal appearance will be known by posterity. To these and other works of art, of which he was the subject, reference will afterwards be made. The bust in question, for many years has occupied a position in the entrance hall at Crow Nest; and by directions in the will of the deceased baronet, it will be removed to the Club and Institute, at Saltaire, where it will permanently remain in the midst of the people he loved so well.[195]

We thus obtain an insight into the sympathetic relationship that then subsisted between Mr. Salt and his workmen, and which continued until the end of his life. Nor was this, happily, an isolated case of the kind, in Yorkshire. The workpeople, for instance, at Haley Hill, Halifax, were animated by similar sentiments towards their employers. That this spirit of goodwill was reciprocal, is abundantly verified by many noble institutions, for the moral and religious improvement of their workmen, erected by Messrs. Akroyd.[196] Surely, such instances of mutual respect between masters and workpeople, may be taken as a proof that fair, honest, and honourable treatment will always insure loyal hearts

---

vote of thanks, by "Mr. Marchall" (sic – it was probably the aforementioned Marshall), was spoken in this way not through real linguistic limitations, but as a joke, showing that - grandness and formality of the occasion notwithstanding - there was still a place for humour at the common expense.

[195] In his will Salt directed that his executors were to deposit the bust in "a Public Institution, or other similar place, as they may think most suitable, unless I shall myself have deposited the same during my lifetime." In the present day the bust stands in the vestibule of Saltaire United Reformed Church (previously the Congregational Church). We know of no record that the bust was ever placed in Saltaire Club and Institute.

[196] The pre-eminent figure in the developments of Messrs. Akroyd at Haley Hill was Edward Akroyd, who had acquired sole ownership of the company in December 1853 on the retirement of his brother Henry (Ref: Bret1). Edward Akroyd (1810–1877) had similar paternalist concerns to Salt, and as contemporaries there were no doubt many occasions when the men found themselves in each other's company. An Anglican rather than a Congregationalist, Akroyd was both a successful worsted manufacturer and an M.P. Concern for his workers' welfare is evidenced by the developments of housing and social institutions around his mill sites. Akroyd's family home, Bankfield, stands on the hill at Akroydon, approx. one mile north west of Halifax, and is today a museum. The distance between Crow Nest and Bankfield is approx. three miles.

as well as industrious hands.

From the opening of "the works" Mr. Salt had devoted his time and energy to the organization of the various departments in connection with them. In this complex duty he was heartily seconded by his sons and the other members of the firm, but, as might be supposed, Mr. Salt continued his grasp of the helm, and his judgment and will were still the ruling power in the business. After the lapse of a few years, however, he felt he might somewhat relax his energies, and leave to others many details that had hitherto been managed by himself. But this was not that he might take rest from toil. No; his active mind seemed never at rest,—at least, it was like the rest of the spinning-top when "sleeping," as boys call it, *i.e.,* the rest of imperceptible motion. Still, with his marvellous constitution and energy, work did not tell upon his frame, as it often does upon others; so that the time and effort now withdrawn from Saltaire were devoted to the public. The removal of his manufacturing business to Saltaire did not in any way affect his relation to the town of Bradford. In its municipal, political, and commercial affairs, he continued to take a prominent part. In the beginning of 1859, Mr. Salt had the honour to move the resolution of welcome to Mr. John Bright,[197] in the presence of one of the largest audiences ever assembled in St. George's Hall. For this eminent man Mr. Salt had long cherished the highest admiration and esteem. Once, on paying a passing visit to Crow Nest, we found him unusually depressed in spirits. On enquiring the cause, we ascertained that in the morning papers a premature announcement of the death of Mr. Bright had been given. When we assured him that a contradiction of it had appeared in a later edition, the shadows on his countenance disappeared, and with a warm grasp of our hand, he said, "Thank you for bringing the good news."

At the Reform Conference, held on the day following the above meeting, when representatives from many parts of Yorkshire met, Mr. Salt was elected to preside. These facts may be regarded as indicative of the high place he occupied

---

[197] John Bright (1811–1889) was a Quaker and politician. Like Salt, he had from an early age opposed, and sought an end to, compulsory tax support of the established church. Bright also campaigned against the privileged position of the landed aristocracy, and advocated free trade, cheaper food and repeal of the Corn Laws. He was first elected to parliament in 1843, and throughout a long parliamentary career supported universal suffrage and the secret ballot. These latter issues were very live issues in the late 1850s, around the time of his appearance at St. George's Hall.

in the esteem of the community, and of his attachment to the Reform movement. He was a Reformer of the noblest type—not hostile to customs or laws because of their antiquity. In this he was rather conservative; but all legislative enactments not based on sound moral principles of right and justice, and which appealed not to common sense for their maintenance, had in him a strenuous opponent. As for mere expediency, either in politics or religion, his soul abhorred it. This accounts for his consistency throughout his life. There was no trimming of sails to catch the popular breeze; no deviation from the straight course which duty prescribed or conscience approved, even if he had to stand alone. And the reason is obvious: he thought for himself; calmly he felt his way, amid conflicting opinions, until he found the rock of principle, and on this his foot was planted. At a great meeting held about this time in Bradford, to condemn the Reform Bill brought in by Mr. Disraeli[198] (now Lord Beaconsfield), Mr. Salt gave utterance to sentiments which he firmly held to the close of his life. On that occasion he said he hoped the Reformers of England would never rest satisfied with any Reform Bill proposed by any party which did not admit the working classes to their due share of the franchise. He considered it quite a misnomer to call the Bill then before the country a Reform Bill. He hoped the middle and working classes would unite as one man, and insist upon a real, true, and efficient Reform Bill. Such political sentiments, expressed with that manliness so conspicuous in him, made a deep impression on the minds of the Liberal party of Bradford, and marked him out, in their opinion, as one of their future representatives. The opportunity for acting on such an opinion was not far off.

Lord Derby's Government being defeated on the second reading of the Reform Bill, a dissolution of Parliament took place in the Spring of 1859. The candidates for Bradford were Mr. Wickham, who presented himself for re-election; Mr. Harris, and Mr. Salt. The first was already known in his political

---

[198] Disraeli at the time in question (1859) was serving as Chancellor of the Exchequer in the Government of Lord Derby. By the time BALG was written (1877), Disraeli had assumed the title of Lord Beaconsfield and was in the middle of his second term of office as Prime Minister. This second term of office was later to end in defeat in the election of 1880, an event that was marked by a celebratory dinner at the home of Titus Salt Jr., see Appendix 3.

capacity; the second was a Churchman, of moderate Conservative opinions, and a local banker; the third was a liberal-minded Nonconformist, and at the head of the largest worsted manufactory in the world. All three candidates were locally known for their deeds of active benevolence, and were regarded by all classes with the greatest respect. The question of politics was, therefore, the only one that was at stake on this occasion.

Let us, then, see Mr. Salt in the novel position as a candidate for the borough. But this position was not one which he, himself, sought. It was pressed upon him at a large meeting of electors and non-electors, held in St. George's Hall, at which a hearty resolution was passed, in acknowledgment of the services of their late member, Major-General Thompson.

The following speech was delivered by Mr. Salt :—

Mr. Chairman and Gentlemen,—In the first place, you will allow me to express my heartfelt and sincere appreciation of the resolution you have passed. I think that the resolution in acknowledgment of the services of Major General Thompson is most proper and fitting on the present occasion. If we remember his great exertions for the repeal of the Corn Laws, which can never be forgotten by his country, we cannot do him too much honour. Passing to the object of the meeting,—we have been called upon, Gentlemen, by the present Government, to give our verdict upon the question of Parliamentary Reform; and Lord Derby has brought in a bill, which he calls a Reform Bill, but it is for you to decide whether or no it is such. In my opinion, it is not. It is an evasion; and, therefore, the country is now called upon to speak out upon the question. For the representation of the borough, we have three candidates. There is myself, called into the field by yourselves. We have Mr. Wickham, who has long been your representative, and who has worked well for the borough. I have never had cause to find fault with him, nor have I ever found anyone else find fault with him. Then we have another candidate, whose address is just brought upon the platform,—Alfred Harris, Esq.,—a more respectable gentleman there is not in this borough, and as a magistrate and a citizen, we all wish to honour him; but if he represents the feelings of the majority of the electors of this borough, I am very much mistaken. I repeat that the present Government of Lord Derby has called upon us to decide the question, whether you want Reform or not. The bill which they have proposed I consider quite a sham and an evasion of the question, and it will rest with you to say whether you concur in that view or not. I have been called upon by the Reform Registration Society to come forward as a candidate for this town. I assure you it is not from any ambition on my part that I have acceded to this request, but if you do elect me to represent you, I shall consider it a very great honour, and all my exertions shall be directed to the cause of reform. I have been ardently devoted to this all my life. It is forty years since I came to this borough. I came as a boy. I have been educated in commercial affairs in this borough, and you all know my political principles. I have always advocated the principles of Reform. For the last thirty years I have never flinched from them, and they are the principles I now profess. I advocated the Reform Bill of 1832, and I also supported the successful efforts to repeal the Corn Laws, and for the extension of education amongst the working-classes. Since that time I am quite satisfied we ought to make still further progress in the extension of the franchise. Lord John Russell has advocated a measure by which it is proposed to give the franchise to £10 occupiers in counties, and to £6 occupiers in boroughs. Of course, I shall advocate this, and, if the opportunity occurs, I shall go further. But I think the best way is to take as much as we can get. I shall also support the vote by ballot; I think it is quite essential to give independence to voters, and whether they are shopkeepers or the working-classes. I would have them all independent by giving them the ballot. And, as a commercial man, you may be sure I shall advocate all possible economy in the expenditure of the public money. I am sorry to say that the public money has been greatly wasted. I am also a great advocate for peace, but still I would have us to be prepared for any emergency. We must keep the command of the seas; but that may be done at a great deal less expense than has been incurred. I will say, in conclusion, that I shall be glad to answer any questions which any electors present may think proper to submit to me. If I am sent by you as the representative of this borough, I assure you it will be regarded by me one of the greatest honours you can confer; and I hope that my opinions on all great questions, and upon all occasions, will be in unison with the majority of the electors of this borough.

The resolution in support of Mr. Salt as a candidate was moved by Mr. Robert Milligan, one of the retiring members for the borough, who said—

They all knew Mr. Salt. He had been nearly all his life amongst them. He might say that, in his opinion, Bradford was more indebted to that gentleman than to any other then residing in the borough. He had established and conducted a manufacturing and mercantile business not surpassed in any other town in England. Mr. Salt had been the means of introducing into the borough an entirely new business, by which he had employed thousands of hands for many years, and by that means he had increased the trade of Bradford and enriched a great many of the inhabitants. He had not only done this, but he had enabled the working classes to earn a livelihood, which, had not the business been introduced, they might have had to seek elsewhere.

During the course of the meeting several questions were put to Mr. Salt, and answered in a straightforward way; but a remark having been made that though he had been instrumental in effecting the incorporation of the borough, he had subsequently removed his establishment to Saltaire, in order to avoid the heavy taxation entailed as the result of that incorporation,—this remark was answered by Mr. H. F. Lockwood, the architect of Saltaire, and as his speech throws some additional light on Mr. Salt's character and worth, the following extract from it will be perused with pleasure. He said—

He would answer the remark that had been made, because he knew Mr. Salt was too modest to do so. There was no one of whose acts he could speak more worthily than he could of his. Besides, the question raised—which was highly important— should be set at rest. There had been some tradesmen throwing it in their teeth that Mr. Salt took his works down to Saltaire, and deserted Bradford. Mr. Salt worked at a disadvantage in Bradford. He had, as they knew, five or six mills[199] in different parts of the town, difficult of access, and still more difficult of surveillance. He felt the necessity of concentrating these works, but when he determined in his own mind to do so, he resolved, that while he increased his power of production, those who assisted him should share all the benefits and blessings which it was in his power to obtain by such concentration; and instead of it being a disgrace to Mr. Salt, in taking such a course, he thought that every man present ought at once to rise and say it was an honour to him. It was his own (Mr. Lockwood's) good fortune to be entrusted with the direction of these works, and, in that capacity, he might tell them that Mr. Salt gave him instructions upon all occasions to study the health, comfort, and happiness of his people, expense in no case being a consideration. He desired him to give them plenty of space, plenty of fresh air, plenty of pure water. Would any man say that Mr. Salt deserted Bradford? He could only tell them that in the enormous contracts for his works, Mr. Salt always gave the preference to Bradford men,[200] and the amount of these contracts executed in the town was £250,000. Did they

[199] We have no knowledge of a sixth mill, but it may be that Lockwood is including the warehouse which was retained by Salt in Bradford long after the opening of the mill at Saltaire – see earlier footnote in Chapter IX.
[200] As previously noted, Salt had used Bradford and Shipley caterers and tradesmen for his 1856 anniversary celebrations. In 1859 when the celebrations were held at his new residence of Methley Park – nearer to Leeds than Bradford – Salt continued to use some Bradford and Shipley suppliers: Mr. Wormald of Wakefield Road, Mr. Charles Rhodes and

call that deserting Bradford? At one time there were no fewer than 3,000 men employed belonging to Bradford. Mr. Salt was always doing great good in other ways. Let them look at his beneficent acts. The other week he knew that he gave instructions to his solicitors to alienate a mass of property which cost £11,000 for the benefit of those around him. His motto might be written—"Deeds, not words !" Mr. Salt's unostentatious deeds of beneficence were not confined to persons connected with one church or denomination, but extended to all. He had known him, for instance, go to a clergyman of the Church of England in feeble health, with a handful of notes, and say, "There, take that; every shilling of it is to be spent at the seaside."

The resolution in support of Mr. Salt was enthusiastically passed, in acknowledging which he said he could assure them, that he felt they had placed him under very deep obligations, by this expression of kindness and confidence. He had always been attached to the borough of Bradford; all he possessed was from it; and this mark of their great confidence would rivet him to it more closely. If he were sent to Parliament, he hoped he should remain firm to the principles which he had ever professed.

The following letter from General Thompson was sent to the Chairman of Mr. Salt's Committee :—

Elliot Vale, Blackheath, 9th April,1859.

My dear Sir,—Tell Mr. Salt that my success at the last election was entirely owing to his leaving the field open; and if he will come out for the Ballot, (which he will see is essential to enabling me to do it without rebuke from my friends and supporters,) I will do the same for him on the present occasion; and consider that the appearance of a man of his eminence, in support of the great question of the day, as doing much more for the popular cause than could result from any effort of my own.

Yours very truly,

PERRONET THOMPSON.

From the speeches delivered on this eventful occasion, both by Mr. Salt and his friends, it will be seen what were his political convictions. At that time considerable anxiety prevailed, in some quarters, lest the lowering of the

---

Messrs. J. and W. Sagar of Saltaire and Bradford. However, Leeds and Methley suppliers provided the tenting and joinery work. Joseph Dawson of Saltaire superintended the overall arrangements (Ref: BO, 22nd September, 1859).

franchise would admit the working-classes, in such large numbers that it would seriously affect the British Constitution. It was, therefore, all the more assuring to those who entertained such fears to find a large employer like Mr. Salt so heartily advocating the measure. But perhaps his political views could not have been more clearly put than in the following comprehensive address :—

TO THE ELECTORS AND NON-ELECTORS.

Gentlemen,—Having been invited by a large meeting of electors, convened under the auspices of the Reform Registration Society, I have consented to ask at your hands the honour of representing your important borough in the ensuing Parliament. A life spent in the trade of the district, and the humble part I have taken in all our local movements, will, I trust, be accepted as a guarantee of my acquaintance with your interests and an earnest of my desire to promote them. My political principles are well known to all of you, and even those who in some respects differ from them, will, I hope, do me the justice to admit that they have been as consistent as they have been sincere. For Peace, Reform, and Economy, I have worked with you for more than thirty years, and these great objects I am not now likely to desert. To the question which Lord Derby has put to the country, I trust the answer will be clear and decisive, and that the representation may be settled, so that a happy and united people at home may strengthen our Government in seeking to preserve peace abroad.

The issue of the impending election is, I take it, Reform or No Reform; Advancement or Retrogression. I am, and always have been, for Reform, and I believe the advancement of the country is indissolubly connected with that principle.

When I speak of Reform, I mean an extension of the suffrage to the industrial classes of the community; the lowering of the occupation franchise in counties, by which many intelligent men now excluded may be introduced into the electoral body; the adoption of the ballot, as the only feasible method yet proposed for insuring freedom of election; and such a re-distribution of seats as shall destroy nomination boroughs, and confer the franchise upon large and important communities. A Reform Bill embodying these principles, I believe the country is prepared to carry, and less than that I hope it will not accept.

Believing that these views are held by a large majority of the electors of Bradford, I am encouraged to offer myself as a candidate. I will only add, that, as no personal feelings were allowed to create division at our last election, so I trust at this important crisis our union will insure success. And should you place me in so honourable and responsible a post, my best efforts shall be devoted to fulfil its obligations to your entire satisfaction.

I have the honour to be,

Gentlemen,

Your obliged and obedient Servant,

Bradford, 9th April, 1859.   TITUS
SALT.

In reference to the "Ten Hours Bill," which restricted the hours of labour in manufactories, Mr. Salt said he would not interfere with that measure, which had already passed into law; he was quite satisfied with its beneficial operations; he rejoiced to say that he had always been an advocate for it; in fact, for nearly twelve months before that enactment came into force he had adopted it in his own case, by reducing the hours of his workpeople. With regard to the taxes on knowledge, he had always approved of Mr. Milner Gibson's efforts to obtain the repeal of those taxes.[201] With regard to the grant to Maynooth,[202] he was opposed to all grants for religious purposes, but he would not single out any one in particular for his opposition.

Such was the political creed which Mr. Salt avowed in view of the day of election. When the nomination of candidates took place, which was then conducted in public, Mr. Wickham and Mr. Salt had the show of hands, and at the declaration of the poll they were both returned as the Members for the borough. When he reached home on the same evening, the whole neighbourhood turned out to meet him; the horses were taken from his carriage, which was drawn by the people; while the ringing of bells and enthusiastic cheers of the crowd testified to their joy at the successful issue of the contest. Mr. Salt had now reached a position of honour in the community that he little

---

[201] See Chapter VII for footnote on taxes on knowledge. In the 1840s two pressure groups emerged, the Newspaper Stamp Abolition Committee and the Association for the Repeal of Taxes on Knowledge. Thomas Milner Gibson M.P. (1806–1884) was a prominent leader of these groups; their campaigns were eventually successful.

[202] Maynooth College was a Roman Catholic training college in Ireland. The annual government grant to the College was substantially increased by Peel in 1843, an action which met with strong opposition from various quarters. Indeed, Gladstone, whilst voting for the grant, nevertheless felt the need to resign on the grounds that the measure was incompatible with his previous writings on the subject of Church and State (Ref: AgeR, pp350-351).

dreamed of when, as a youth, he came into its midst. Bradford had no higher post to which it could raise him; and let it not be forgotten, that whether we contemplate his marvellous career in its commercial, municipal, or political relations, it was by dint of his own manly efforts that he succeeded; and this fact places him on a pinnacle before the eyes of every young man, not merely as an object to be admired, but an example to be followed.

In the autumn of the same year the annual Congress of the British Association for the Promotion of Social Science[203] was held at Bradford, under the presidency of the Earl of Shaftesbury. Among many illustrious men gathered together on that occasion, the late Lord Brougham occupied a prominent place, and delivered the annual address, in which he took a comprehensive view of many leading social questions of the day. Not the least interesting part of this annual congress, wherever it is held, is the hospitality shewn to its members; but on this occasion it was exhibited on that scale of unbounded liberality for which Bradford is famous. Among the sights in the town and neighbourhood that visitors were eager to see was, of course, Saltaire, to which they were specially invited, and were conducted over the establishment by Mr. Salt himself. Among the visitors was the venerable Lord Brougham and other *savans,* including a party of rising barristers. When the highest floor in the building was reached, Lord Brougham sat down to rest himself upon a large woolsack: pointing to his seat, and turning to one of the barristers, he facetiously remarked, "This is where you would like to be!"

Another meeting, of an ecclesiastical kind, took place at Bradford prior to this, and in which Mr. Salt was deeply interested, viz., the annual assembly of the Congregational Union of England and Wales.[204] The late Rev. Dr. Harris

---

[203] The National Association for the Promotion of Social Science had been formed in the autumn of 1856, following an inaugural meeting at Lord Henry Brougham's home. The work of the Association focused on five issues: Jurisprudence and the amendment of law; education; punishment and reform; public health; and social economy. Between 1857 and 1885 the Association became one of the most important fora in Victorian Britain. Its Annual Congresses became major civic events and when Bradford was chosen as the venue in 1859 the *Bradford Observer* gave much publicity to the choice (Ref: BO, 13th January, 1859).

[204] The Union was a significant feature of the Congregational Church's national and regional organization (Refs: HCon, HYCon), and several of the individuals referred to in BALG were active in its affairs. Balgarnie himself was particularly active, having been

was chairman on that occasion, and among those who were present may be mentioned the Revs. John Angell James, Dr. Halley, Dr. George Smith, Walter Scott, and Jonathan Glyde. Mr. Frank (afterwards Sir Francis) Crossley presided at the public meeting, and Mr. Salt at the public breakfast. In the autumn of 1876, the same assembly met in Bradford; but, alas, what changes had occurred during the interval! All those honoured men had passed away, except the last, who was then so feeble in health that a resolution was cordially carried, expressive of the sympathy of the Congregational body with him in his affliction, their grateful acknowledgments of the services he had rendered to philanthropy and religion, also their earnest prayers that he might be graciously supported to the end of life. The end was not then far off.

---

elected President of the Yorkshire Congregational Union in 1873 (see Appendix 1). Concerning Balgarnie's election, and judging by the various records in our possession, the Union seems to have used the titles of "President" and "Secretary" to describe one and the same post.

CHAPTER XIII.

"Here finds my heart its rest,

Repose that knows no shock;

The strength of love that keeps it blest

In Thee, the riven Rock:

My soul, as girt around,

Her citadel hath found,

I would love thee as thou lov'st me,

O Jesus most desired."

—RAY PALMER[205]

REMOVAL TO METHLEY PARK—DESCRIPTION OF MANSION AND ESTATE—FAREWELL ADDRESS ON LEAVING CROW NEST—"A CARRIAGE OR A CASTLE"—HE RESIGNS AS MEMBER FOR BRADFORD—PARLIAMENTARY LIFE—FAILING HEALTH—VISITS SCARBOROUGH—"A WEARY MAN"—"A WORD TO THE WEARY"—EXTRACT OF A SERMON—LETTER TO AUTHOR—DEATH OF SECOND DAUGHTER—FIRST COMMUNION—SERVICE IN THE HALL AT METHLEY.

THE first residence of Mr. Salt at Crow Nest extended over a period of seventeen years.[206] In the year 1858, he received notice from the proprietor, that the house would be required for his own occupation.[207] This was an unexpected

---

[205] Ray Palmer (1808–1887), American hymn writer and preacher. In 1866 he became secretary of the American Congregational Union, based in New York. It is possible that Balgarnie met Palmer during the former's visit to the USA in 1867.

[206] BALG's dating of Salt's time at Crow Nest, and of the subsequent move to Methley Park is confused. In Chapter IX BALG records that Salt moved to Crow Nest in 1844. In this chapter BALG relates the notification to quit Crow Nest as being given in 1858, but then goes on to identify the date of occupancy of Methley Hall as "about the end of 1856"; and here he speaks of Salt's occupancy of Crow Nest having a duration of 17 years. We believe Salt's departure from Crow Nest occurred in 1858, and that the duration of occupancy was 14, not 17, years. That the departure occurred in 1858 is confirmed by Bret2, p42; and further corroboration that Salt was still at Crow Nest in November, 1857, is given by Rob3, p92.

[207] The circumstances that seem to have brought about this unexpected notice from the owner are both interesting and complicated. As previously footnoted in Chapter IX, the

announcement to the family, who had been so long settled there, that the thought of leaving had not once entered their minds. It was the home, where the elder children had grown into maturity, and the younger ones had been born, and which had become specially dear to the parents, since the shadow of death had twice fallen upon it. Mr. Salt would have bought the property from the owner, to secure it as a permanent residence for himself, but the latter declined, at *that* time, to sell it, so that no alternative was left but to seek a home elsewhere. In laying out the Saltaire estate, a site had been selected by the owner, on which he had proposed, some day, to build a house. That site is, perhaps, the most beautiful in the neighbourhood, commanding, as it does, an extensive, view of "the works" of Saltaire, and the valley of the Aire beyond Bingley. It is now called "The Knoll," (from its physical conformation,) on the summit of which stands the residence of Mr. Charles Stead. Had Mr. Salt proceeded at that time to carry out his primary intention of building a family mansion there, considerable time must have elapsed before its completion; but as Crow Nest was so soon to be vacated, it was necessary to procure a house which might at once be made ready for his occupation. Among many eligible mansions that came under his notice, Methley Park was the one selected, and it is here that he resided for the next nine years, and where various circumstances occurred in his history to which we shall refer in this chapter. Methley Park had been the seat of the Earls of Mexborough for many generations. It is situated six miles from Leeds on the road to Wakefield, from which it is distant about five miles. At the time to which we refer, the mansion of Methley had remained untenanted for several years; the roof had become dilapidated, the corridors were damp, and the various apartments musty and cob-webbed; while outside, the courtyard and terrace gardens were over grown with grass and weeds. The beautiful park, with its ancient oaks, the herd of deer, the gardens and plantations, had become objects of attraction to excursionists, who roamed whither they listed,

---

owner in 1844 was a Miss Ann Walker. Having no descendants of her own, she had proposed to her sister Elizabeth, who had married George Mackey Sutherland of Aberader, Inverness, that if their son – Charles Evan Sutherland – were to adopt the name Walker and take up the Walker family coat of arms, then she would leave her estates at Lightcliffe to him. The parties agreed; Miss Ann Walker died in 1854; Charles Evan Sutherland Walker came of age in 1856, and presumably laid claim to his estate (Ref: HtoT, pp475–476).

sometimes surreptitiously carrying off shrubs and flowers, or leaving names cut on the leaden roof of the mansion, as their only claim to immortality.

It was painfully evident that everything was out of gear on the estate, and that some enterprising tenant was needed, whose capital and energy might restore it to its former condition. Mr. Salt was offered a lease of the place, at an almost nominal rent, which offer, after much deliberation, was accepted, and he at once instructed his architects to make the necessary preparations for his occupancy. This was a herculean task to be accomplished in a limited time, but in the execution of it, no expense was spared to render the lordly mansion worthy of its antecedent history. As we[208] accompanied Mr. Salt in one of his visits to Methley Park while these preparations were going forward, it is as an eye-witness we refer to them, and to the striking contrast which their completion afterwards afforded. The mansion was then in the hands of a little army of joiners, bricklayers, painters, gilders, and cleaners, all under the supervision of Mr. Lockwood. The terraces and gardens were in course of transformation from the aspect of a wilderness to that of a paradise. The park was being thoroughly drained and surrounded by iron fences to keep the deer from straying, while throughout the whole estate there were manifest signs that the reign of desolation was drawing to a close. In a few months all was ready for the migration of the family thither, which event took place about the end of 1856.[209]

When it became known in the neighbourhood of Crow Nest that Mr. Salt was about to remove, the regret of the inhabitants was wide spread. As an evidence of it, a meeting was held, at which it was resolved to present him with an Imperial Bible, bound in the most elaborate style, with massive gold clasps. The following is a copy of the address inscribed in it

TO TITUS SALT, ESQUIRE.

---

[208] This is the first occasion in BALG where a direct statement is made indicating that the author was by this time (which we believe to be 1858) known to Salt. At this time Salt was approx. 55 and Balgarnie was 32, and the two had clearly established sufficient rapport that Balgarnie was accompanying Salt on a visit to the future Salt family home. Balgarnie records (Ref: Balg1) that, shortly after his settlement in Scarborough (which occurred in November 1851, see Appendix 1), he was introduced to Salt at the house of Sir Wm. Lowthrop. The latter was a Nonconformist with an interest in Scarborough's Bar Church.

[209] As discussed at the start of this Chapter, we believe the year was actually 1858.

In name of your friends and neighbours at Lightcliffe, we request your acceptance of this volume as a token of our high esteem for your character, and of our deep regret at your removal from amongst us.

The warm and practical interest which, during seventeen years' residence in the district, you have ever manifested in the promotion and extension of education, and everything pertaining to the material, moral, and spiritual well-being of the inhabitants, has endeared you to the community; and your departure leaves in many hearts and homes a blank which cannot easily be filled.

Into the scene of your future residence you are followed by the ardent desire of all classes, for the happiness of yourself and family. It is our earnest prayer that you may long be spared to diffuse around the place of your new abode those kind and genial influences which this neighbourhood has so long enjoyed, and that in the last remove you may inherit the reward which this sacred volume promises to those who have served their generation according to the will of God.

December, 1858.

(Signed by the principal inhabitants of the district.)

Let us follow Mr. Salt and his family to Methley Park, and enter the house where they have taken up their new abode. The reader who has travelled from Leeds to Normanton by the Midland Railway will have observed the beautiful village of Methley, through which he must pass, with the noble mansion and park situated about a mile to the right. It is built in a castellated style, of light stone, and adorned with towers and battlements. A remark, made by Mr. Salt many years before this period, is worth recording now. It was in connection with one of his early commercial adventures, and when many persons doubted his success, or prognosticated failure, that he said to a friend, *"I am in for a carriage or a castle."* What he meant by the remark was that in the event of failure in his new enterprise, he might, perhaps, be compelled to take up his abode in York Castle. Happily, the castle which he now entered was not in York, though in Yorkshire; nor was it as a debtor, but as a successful and affluent man of business. The entrance-hall is of more ancient date than the other parts of the building, and with its old oak panelling, mullioned windows, stained glass, and organ-loft, gives the impression, at first sight, of an ecclesiastical edifice; but a glance at the walls dispels that impression, for they are hung with old armour and trophies of the chase. It is needless to say that the new abode was furnished with all the elegance and luxurious taste that wealth could command. One circumstance may here be mentioned as illustrative of Mr. Salt's personal character; he said "I want my house made as attractive to my sons as possible, that they may not have to seek amusement from home." Hence, every provision was made for in-door and out-door amusement and recreation,—such as workshop and billiard room; shooting, riding, fishing, &c.[210]

By this change of abode he was now further removed from his "works," the distance being about twenty miles. Still, when business required his presence, this was no obstacle, and the time of his appearance there was always known. Those of his sons who resided with him, and were partners in the business, generally preceded their father thither. Thus relieved of many duties, he was enabled to attend more to matters of a public kind, amongst which, those connected with parliamentary life claimed his attention. In the previous chapter reference was made to his election as one of the representatives of Bradford. Though the honour conferred upon him on that occasion was really the highest his fellow-townsmen could offer; yet, whether he was wise in accepting it is open to question. In the opinion of many, he was not fitted for the post, either by his habits or previous training, but this seems one of those rare occasions in his life, when he allowed his judgment to be swayed by the wishes of others, and he paid the penalty for it afterwards. During the session of Parliament, his seat in the house was always occupied, and his name found on every division list.[211] But within the walls of St. Stephen's[212] his voice was never heard, except on some formal occasion, such as the presentation of a petition. To him, it was a scene widely different from that with which he had been long familiar. Speaking

---

[210] Notwithstanding the improvements made by Salt, Methley Hall has not survived, being demolished in 1963. Records state the main periods of work and restoration occurred in earlier times – 1590, 1620, and 1830-1836 (Ref: PEVSN). A short history, with good illustrations (but again without mention of Salt) is available (Ref: LHWR). In the present day a private hospital occupies part of the site. Parts of the estate are accessible via public footpaths.

[211] A detailed account of his time in parliament is given in Appendix 6.

[212] Parliament had met in St. Stephen's Chapel from 1547 to 1834. Following a fire in 1834, the Palace of Westminster (more commonly called the Houses of Parliament) was rebuilt in the 1840s, becoming the familiar landmark of the present day. St. Stephen's Hall, a replica of the original chapel, is contained within the present structure.

had always been his weak point; but here it was the chief business. Early rising and retiring had been the rule of his life, now the long sittings, the heated atmosphere, irregular hours, both of diet and sleep, the exciting debates and divisions, were enough to exhaust any man's energies, much more his, so unaccustomed to such an experience. In the House of Commons at that time, several of his personal friends had seats, such as Cobden, Bright, Crossley, and Baines.[213] Palmerston, Russell, Gladstone, and Disraeli, were then conspicuous as statesmen. To be associated with such men was, doubtless, a great honour, but it could not compensate for the broken sleep, the shattered nerves and gouty twinges, from which he so frequently suffered. Whether he intended remaining in Parliament till its dissolution we cannot say; at all events, he never took up his residence[214] in London, but with his wife and family occupied apartments at Fenton's Hotel,[215] Saint James's Street. On Sundays he attended Westminster Chapel,[216] and enjoyed the ministry of the Rev. Samuel Martin,[217] who, in addition to his ordinary services, had a devotional meeting every week for

---

[213] Frank (later Sir Francis) Crossley was at this time M.P. for the West Riding (Ref: Bret3, Part VI); Edward Baines was M.P. for Leeds.

[214] There is a tantalizing ambiguity in BALG's words. One interpretation is that Salt had a residence in London, but that he never occupied it. Although we know of no evidence that confirms such a circumstance, there is a very specific but unsubstantiated newspaper reference to Salt living in Clapham, which in the mid 19th century was a fashionable rural idyll beyond the bounds of the metropolis: "Living in the Atkins Road, surrounded by all that money could purchase, he was at peace with all men" (Ref: ClapO, 2nd June, 1883). The article was written some years after Salt's death, and is unspecific about the period being referred to. Extensive scrutiny of directories etc has failed to substantiate the account. The possible link with Clapham is important since, as we shall see, the Dowager Lady Salt moved there following Salt's death, to a mansion a few hundred yards from Atkins Road (see Appendix 3).

[215] Fenton's Hotel, now demolished, stood on the west side of St. James's Street.

[216] Westminster Chapel stands at the junction of Little James Street and Castle Lane, a few minutes walk from St. James's Street. The present day building was erected shortly after Salt's time in parliament, but he continued to use the chapel in later years during visits to London (see Chapter XVII), and would therefore have sat in the atmospheric surrounds of today's chapel. That earlier atmosphere is perhaps best sensed at a quiet time, away from the present day minister's use of a video projector and computer-generated graphics.

[217] Rev. Martin (1817-1878) was minister of Westminster Chapel from 1842 until his death in 1878. His congregations were so large that the Chapel was rebuilt during this period to accommodate almost 3,000 people, and he was elected chairman of the Congregational Union of England and Wales in 1862 (Ref: Peel, p111). Rev. Martin was well known to Balgarnie; on 15th August, 1860 he baptized Balgarnie's third daughter Jessie Marion in Scarborough (P. McNaughton, pers. comm.).

members of Parliament. Mr. Salt was one of many to whom such a meeting was a spiritual boon. But how thankful he was, when an opportunity occurred, to escape from the excitement of parliamentary life to Yorkshire! to see how business proceeded at Saltaire, or to rest amid the quiet scenes of Methley! On one occasion, he came to Scarborough for its bracing air. We were then struck with his altered appearance; his countenance was haggard, his spirits depressed, and his walking powers considerably impaired. When asked as to the state of his health, the answer given was "I'm a weary man." Thus it was apparent that his short parliamentary career had seriously affected his health. So low was he brought, that his thoughts dwelt on his latter end, which, to him, seemed approaching, and he began to make some necessary arrangements in anticipation of that solemn event. Mr. Lockwood was summoned to Scarborough, and instructions were given for the erection of a family mausoleum at Saltaire. Thank God! it was not to be required for him until seventeen years had elapsed, and many great and noble purposes of benevolence had been accomplished.

The present state of Mr. Salt's health seemed to the writer a suitable occasion for pressing upon his attention those momentous matters relating to his personal salvation and a future state of existence. It seemed hardly compatible with the mutual friendship that had existed so long to maintain utter silence on such subjects. Accordingly, on the following Sunday the topic of discourse was chosen with a view to comfort the weary and direct such to the only true source of rest. The text selected was from Isaiah 1. 4, "The Lord God hath given me the tongue of the learned, that I should know how to speak a word in season to him that is weary." With the manuscript of the sermon before us, a short extract may be taken, just to show "the word in season" that was made a blessing to his soul. The preacher first described the weary efforts of a caterpillar to reach the top of a painted pole in quest of foliage, but there was nothing for it there but the bare piece of wood, and it groped all round in vacant space as if disappointed :—

Thus it is with men! You may see them striving to reach some worldly object in quest of that which can satisfy their spiritual nature. *There* is a weary soul! and wealth says, "Come up to me!" Is not this a "word in season" to the weary? But when he climbs the pole to the top and looks around, the tree of life is not there. *There* is a weary soul! and honour says, "Come up to me!" Is not this a "word in season"? But when he reaches the top there is nothing that can satisfy. *There* is another weary one! and ambition says, "Come up to me!" Is not this a word in season? To be accounted great, learned, and wise! He climbs to the highest pinnacle of science. Perhaps he can count the stars and weigh them by a powerful calculus; yet after all there is a void in his heart, unfilled, for God is not there. *There* is another weary one! and superstition says, "Come up to me!" For that word "come" is always welcome to the weary, and she takes the veil, as it is called, and renounces the world! Farewell for ever to its pomps and vanities! Now for a life devoted to religion. Nothing but vespers, vigils, fasts, the counting of beads, and the repetition of collects. Is the soul satisfied with these? Has the heart found rest? I travelled once from London with two Sisters of Mercy. Beautiful name! They were clad in serge, which is the garb of mourning. They were thickly veiled like those bereft. Nevertheless, their half-concealed features were sometimes visible. The lines of sorrow were written there, with all the tracery of melancholy. They neither spoke, nor looked up, nor smiled. Ah! they had climbed the pole of superstition, and yet they were not happy. They had devoted their lives to the outward ceremonies of religion, but there was still an aching void which these things could not fill—they were seeking the living among the dead.

Such, brethren, is a specimen of the weariness of men. What does it all prove? It proves that man needs rest; but from the nature of those objects pursued—from the disappointment that ensues when the objects are reached—it is evident rest cannot be found in them; yea, the very effort to climb wearies the soul all the more. I tell you, until the soul comes to live in God himself, it can never be satisfied. Suppose that, in watching the movements of that poor caterpillar, you pitied it, and carried it to some leafy tree, and put it up among the branches, it would live there. And what is the Cross of Jesus but a tree of life which God has planted here, and by which fallen creatures may climb back to God? But man is blind, as well as fallen, and the Holy Spirit comes to open blind eyes and to lead weary souls to the Cross. Is not Christ the Living Vine? Oh! when the soul begins to feed on Him it begins to live. Weary souls! behold the Saviour on the Cross! He says, "Come unto Me." Words in season, indeed! You have climbed other poles in quest of good; let your affections be entwined round the Cross, and by this you will climb to the skies! You have sought it in wealth, now seek it in Christ; you have sought it in honour—why not now aspire to become "heirs of God and joint heirs with Christ"? You have climbed the heights of knowledge, —acquaint yourself with "Him whom to know is life eternal." You have gazed, perhaps, on a crucifix; let the eye of faith be turned to the living Christ; let the hand of faith grasp Him,—the arms of faith embrace Him, as all your salvation and desire, and, verily, you shall find rest.

We offer no apology for the insertion of the above extract. There were doubtless many strangers in church that Sunday morning, to whom the message was specially applicable. Mr. Salt was one of them; for when we met him the following day, he said, "That was a word in season to me yesterday; I am one of the weary in want of rest." Thus the door was opened for unreserved conversation on spiritual subjects.

Surely the Spirit of God was to be recognized in this! It is His work to quicken the conscience, to break the false peace of the heart, discovering to a man his own true character in the light of eternity, and thus impelling him to put the momentous question —"What must I do to be saved?" We do not say this anxious inquirer had no difficulties to be overcome, or doubts to be met, or fallacious conceptions of the method of salvation to be removed. Of these he had many, but he was willing to become as a little child, that he might enter the kingdom of Heaven. In short, it was evident that such an earnest seeker after rest and truth would ere long be a happy finder; for, as we have somewhere read,— "When a soul seeketh after salvation, there is another seeker, even the 'Good Shepherd,' who goeth after the lost sheep and never gives up until he finds it, and carries it home on his shoulders, rejoicing." Still, the light did not burst upon his mind at once: it came upon him gradually, like the dawn; perfect rest did not at once take possession of the troubled breast, but at occasional intervals he had some experience of it. After this interview we had no difficulty in freely conversing with him on religious themes. He seemed always ready to be instructed in the Way of Life. Several letters are now in our possession which indicate the state of his mind at this time. One of these is as follows

Methley Park, 21st April.[218]

MY DEAR MR. BALGARNIE,

I hope you will forgive me for not writing to thank you for the kind letter I received a fortnight ago. I have had plenty of time both to read and think about it, not having been to Bradford or

---

[218] It is difficult to deduce the year of this letter. BALG's forgoing words suggest a date following the decline of Salt's health while in parliament, which would suggest a date after 1860; however BALG's following words, relating to the years of illness of Fanny and her eventual death, suggest a date in the late 1850s. We suspect the year date was 1860.

Saltaire since the 3rd instant, which was the last day I was able to leave home. I was obliged to give up the Leicester [219]journey, but I hope to be able to go to Bradford tomorrow. I hope I have been enabled to believe that these our trials are for our good, and that our Heavenly Father intends them as such. I assure you I often peruse your kind note, and shall endeavour to profit by your kind advice and counsel.

I feel great responsibility to the Giver of all good, and pray to be directed aright, and to put my whole trust in Christ, which is the only sure foundation.

You will have all the news from dear Amelia.

I am, dear Sir, yours ever,

TITUS SALT.[220]

By-and-bye, God sent another affliction, which, though grievous at the time, was a means of great spiritual good. His second daughter, Fanny, fell into declining health. The first cause of anxiety in reference to her state, occurred at Scarborough, where she was seized with slight hemorrhage from the lungs. From this period it was evident that great care would be needed to prolong her life, and every means that skill and love could devise for that purpose, was brought into requisition. Amongst these was a sojourn at Pau and St. Leonard's, during two successive winters, with several members of her family.[221] Sometimes the fond hope was cherished that the insidious disease was arrested; at other times, the hectic flush and diminished strength dashed that hope to the ground. Methley Park was especially attractive to her. Its secluded walks she loved to frequent; but much as she enjoyed the beauty around, it seemed rather to point her thoughts and affections upwards, than bind them to earth. We had

---

[219] The planned visit may well have been to the home of Salt's eldest son William Henry, who had moved to Maplewell, Leicestershire (see Chapter XIX and Appendix 3).

[220] The content and tone of this private letter are telling. With all his worldly success and recognition, Salt's professed endeavour to profit from the words of a minister some 22 years younger than himself, and the expression of his religious faith, carry a strong sincerity.

[221] A journey to Pau by several members of the family would have been quite an undertaking. We know of no more distant journey undertaken by the family group. The French Pyrenean spa resort became very popular with the English in the 19th century, being referred to as the "Ville Anglaise" and "La Colonie Britannique" (Ref: LADLP, p195). St. Leonard's as a destination for the family is of note insofar as it was the resort where the Dowager Lady Salt was destined to die while on vacation there in 1893 (see Appendix 3).

frequent interviews with her then, and received several letters, which revealed such a spirit of gentleness, calm resignation, and simple reliance on the merits of Christ, that it seemed to those who knew her well, she was fast ripening for the better land. When the time of her departure came, it was very sudden, but she was ready. On a summer evening, in August, 1861, when the family were about to retire, she was seized with alarming symptoms in the library, from which she was unable to be removed. There on a couch she lingered, till her gentle spirit returned "unto God who gave it."[222] Her remains were laid in a temporary vault in the church of Saltaire, until the family mausoleum was completed. We stood with the father that day at the grave of his daughter, and drove back with him to Methley, when the funeral service was over. On our way, his thoughts seemed to linger by the tomb he had left, for once he said, with much emotion, " I could have lain down beside her." In response to the remark that this visit to Saltaire had been a very sad one, "Yes," he said, "the only sad one there I ever had."

Sometime after this painful visit, we came back with him to Saltaire; and this was not an occasion of sorrow but of joy. He had long been in the twilight as it were; hesitating and halting between Christ and the world. Blessed trouble, that had brought him to see, that full decision for God is the only way of peace and safety! It was, therefore, as a declaration of his faith in Christ that he went to Saltaire, that, with other communicants, he might partake of the Lord's Supper for the first time. It was a day never to be forgotten. Early on Sunday morning we set out from Methley in the family omnibus, his wife and daughters being with him. On the way thither, hundreds of tracts were given away or dropped for the villagers to gather. The church at Saltaire was then undergoing alterations, so that Divine service had to be conducted in the school-room. The visit, of course, awakened much interest among the worshippers, who had rarely before seen the family among them on the Sunday; but to himself the occasion was invested with greater interest than it could be to any one else. There was to them nothing outwardly to distinguish it from other Sundays, save that Mr. Salt remained with the members of the church, and took his place at the table of the Lord. How he seemed to enjoy that service! "The sermon preached," he said, "was worthy of being written in letters of gold." The theme of it was "Soul

---

[222] Fanny died on 4th August, 1861 – see Appendix 3.

winning," and seemed to affect him deeply. It may be here mentioned that no discourse was ever effective, in his judgment, however eloquent and argumentative it might be, unless it grappled with the conscience and struck the chords of the heart. His thankfulness, simplicity, and tenderness on this occasion were most touching. Surrounded as he was by the colossal buildings which his own hand had reared, it was truly beautiful to behold him now, as a little child, at the feet of Jesus. That hallowed scene stands vividly before our imagination, and we still seem to hear him say, "This is the day I have long desired to see, when I should come and meet my people at the Communion Table."

Shall we not describe another service that took place in the evening, after we returned to Methley? In the entrance-hall of the mansion all the people of the estate, together with those of the household, were gathered. It was an unusual sight, in that ancient hall often familiar with scenes of another kind. There, gardeners, and grooms, gamekeepers, and footmen, gatekeepers, and domestics of various grades, were met to worship God. Those who could not be accommodated in the centre of the hall occupied the steps of the great staircase; while on the oak dais, where in olden times the lord of the manor had feasted, with his retainers seated below him, sat a Christian family to mingle their voices in thanksgiving with their servants.[223] And when the story of redeeming love was preached, it seemed as if many eyes were eager to gaze upon the Divine Sufferer, and willing hearts ready to crown Him as their King.

> *   *   *   * Know,
>
> Without star or angel for their guide,
>
> Who worship God shall find him. Humble love,
>
> And not proud reason, keeps the door of heaven!
>
> Love finds admission, where proud science fails.
>
> Religion crowns the statesman and the man,
>
> Sole source of public and of private peace.

---

[223] BALG's account of the scene conveys the sense of changing social order in Victorian England. The old landed aristocracy was being replaced - in part at least - by a new industrial aristocracy. In the case of those West Riding industrialists epitomized by Salt, the new aristocracy was a paternalistic, radical body of textile magnates who had led society into an industrial revolution that had brought about the largest and most rapid demographic change the region had ever experienced, and in just a few decades.

CHAPTER XIV.

" To comfort and to bless.

To find a balm for woe,

To tend the lone and fatherless

Is angels' work below;

The captive to release,

To God the lost to bring.

To teach the way of life and peace,

Is a most Christ-like thing."

—HOW.[224]

RESIGNS HIS SEAT IN PARLIAMENT—LIFE AT METHLEY—ERECTION OF A NEW CHURCH AT CASTLEFORD—ATTENDS METHLEY PARISH CHURCH—A NONCONFORMIST, NOT A SECTARIAN—GIFT OF £5,000 TO THE SAILORS' ORPHANAGE—£5,000 TO THE BI-CENTENARY MEMORIAL—£2,500 TO A NEW CHURCH AT SCARBOROUGH—HOME ENGAGEMENTS—A DINNER PARTY—GIVES UP SMOKING—"RANDOM TRICKS" IN ADVANCED YEARS.

THE state of Mr. Salt's health in Parliament became so enfeebled, that on the eve of the Session of 1861 he resigned his seat. In a letter which he addressed to his constituents, the reason for taking this step was given in the following words :—" I find, after two years of experience, that I have not sufficient stamina to bear up under the fatigues and late hours incident to parliamentary life." The electors had, therefore, no option but to receive back the trust they had committed to his hands. Mr. W. E. Forster succeeded to the seat, which he has since retained, and has become distinguished as a statesman by several

---

[224] William Walsham How, D.D. (1823–1897). Born in Shrewsbury on 13th December, 1823, How attended Shrewsbury school and subsequently Wadham College, Oxford. Ordained in 1846, he became curator of St. George's, Kidderminster. In 1888 he was made Bishop of Wakefield. How was also the author of the still well known hymn "For All the Saints." With his friend Sir Arthur Sullivan, of operetta fame, he was joint editor of a popular Anglican hymnal of his day (Ref: FavHC).

important measures which, under his auspices, have passed into law.

We have, therefore, in this chapter, to consider him in his home at Methley. From this period may be dated many of those acts of benevolence that have made his name conspicuous amongst his fellow-men. It would be out of place, were it possible, to reveal to the world his various gifts to religion and philanthropy during his lifetime. It is believed they amounted to about a quarter of a million sterling.[225] But who can trace the various channels through which his bounty flowed; the hearts that it gladdened; the institutions which it enriched; the various schools and churches it benefited? "Every man's work shall be made manifest; for the day shall declare it." Just to illustrate the generosity of his heart and hand, a few facts which came under our personal cognizance may be here recorded. Had Mr. Salt not been a Christian he would doubtless have been benevolent; this was natural to him. But the great spiritual change already referred to, touched the deeper springs of his being, and gave an impulse to his generosity not heretofore manifest. The letter given in the previous chapter clearly indicates that he felt the responsibility of his wealth, and cherished the conviction that a portion of it ought to be consecrated to the glory of God, and the good of his fellow-men,—a conviction which seemed to become stronger as he advanced in years.

The Congregational Church nearest to his residence was at Castleford, a town situated about four miles from Methley, and noted for its glass bottle manufacture. The congregation there consisted chiefly of workpeople, who met for worship in a public hall. Mr. Salt felt it his duty from the first to identify himself with this little Christian community, and to aid them in every possible way. From the time of his coming amongst them their strength increased, their hearts were cheered, so that steps were soon taken to erect in the town a suitable church, towards which he and his family largely contributed. The foundation stone was laid by Mr. Salt,[226] on which occasion many guests were invited to Methley. We well remember how sensitively he shrunk from the duty imposed upon him at the public ceremony, and the apparent relief he experienced when it

---

[225] An account of Salt's benevolences known to us is given in Appendix 5.
[226] The ceremony took place on 8th July, 1862 (Ref: ConYk, p247).

was over. The church was opened by the Rev. James Parsons,[227] then of York, whose fame as a preacher stood pre-eminent. Of the congregation at Castleford, the Rev. Henry Simon was the respected pastor until he received a call to a larger sphere of work in London.[228]

Mr. Salt was no sectarian bigot, who could see nothing good outside the pale of his own communion. He was ever ready to encourage other Christian denominations in their "work of faith and labour of love"; and the liberality of his heart was not only manifested in gifts of money, but in other Christian acts, that indicated a spirit of charity towards those who, though differing from him in forms of government, were one in Christ. As an instance of this spirit, he very regularly, on Sunday evenings, attended Methley Parish Church, which was within walking distance of his residence. With the rector, the Hon. and Rev. P. Y. Saville,[229] (son of the late Lord Mexborough,) he was on intimate terms of friendship, and was a liberal contributor to the parochial charities. Perhaps it was from this circumstance, that some persons at the time concluded that Mr. Salt's principles as a Nonconformist were changed. But it was not so. It was rather that the higher principles of religion were exemplified, especially that of Christian love, without which all mere forms of worship and ecclesiastical polity are vain. That he held his convictions firmly at this time, was strikingly manifested in a letter which he wrote to the bishop of the diocese, who had applied to him for aid in a church-building scheme. Thinking that the bishop might have imagined he had become a member of the Establishment, Mr. Salt courteously replied, "I am a Nonconformist from conviction, and attached to the Congregational body. Nevertheless, I regard it as a duty and a privilege to co-

---

[227] The ceremony took place on 29th July, 1863 (Ref: ConYk, p247). James Parsons was destined to be the first president of the Yorkshire Congregational Union in 1873 (Ref: HYCon, frontpiece), a position in which he was succeeded by Balgarnie (Ref: HYCon, p36).

[228] The higher calling referred to was the ministry at Westminster Chapel. Rev. Simon went there in 1876, working in support of Rev. Martin before taking over fully in 1878. He remained at Westminster Chapel until 1887.

[229] The friendship of Rev. Saville with the family seems to have endured. At the Methley Hall feast hosted by Salt on 20th September, 1859, Salt danced with Rev. Saville's daughter (Ref: BO, 22nd September, 1859); 12 years later, and some years after the Salt family had left Methley Hall, Rev. Saville assisted at the second marriage of Edward Salt in Burley-in-Wharfedale (see Appendix 3).

operate with Christians of all evangelical denominations, in furtherance of Christian work." Would that such a spirit might universally prevail! Whether, in this particular instance, he forwarded a subscription or not, we do not know; but to the fund for renovating York Minster, he sent a handsome contribution through Mr. Leeman, M.P.;[230] and when the new Episcopalian Church at Lightcliffe was erected, he presented an elaborately carved stone pulpit, as an expression of his catholicity.[231]

Another instance of his liberality about this time, was the gift of £5,000 to the Sailors' Orphanage,[232] at Hull, which, on his part, was quite spontaneous. It happened that one evening, at Methley, we were conversing together about a recent visit of these orphans to Scarborough, of the importance of the institution, the necessity for its enlargement, and the claims which sailors' orphans had on the sympathy of manufacturers generally, whose goods are exported to foreign lands. He said nothing at the time in reference to these observations, but evidently he had laid them to heart, for some time after he said, "I should like to know more about that orphanage you were telling me of." As he then purposed being in Scarborough in the following week, it was agreed that the treasurer and secretary should be invited to meet him there, and submit to him the plans for the enlargement of the building. On the day appointed, these gentlemen waited on Mr. Salt, with their plans, which, after careful examination, he quietly returned, simply remarking, "I'll come over and see the place." As they retired somewhat disappointed with the result of their interview, we followed them to

---

[230] George Leeman (1809-1882), solicitor and Lord Mayor of York. (In the present day, Leeman Road, York is the home of the National Railway Museum, outside which a statue of Leeman can be found).
[231] Further examples of Salt's support of Christian denominations other than Congregationalism can be found in Saltaire. He gave land for the building of the Wesleyan Methodist Chapel, together with £100 to its building fund (Ref: ShCam, p35). In support of the Primitive Methodist Church in Saltaire Road, building of which began in 1872, Salt gave the land, and £100 to its building fund, and for a number of years a further £25 for every £75 raised by its congregation (Ref: ShCam, p30, p35).
[232] The Sailors' Orphanage was to be one of Salt's more significant benevolences, and has a strong heritage in its own right. Operated by the Sailors' Children's Society, the orphanage had earlier beginnings in Hull, and was in need of larger premises when Salt became involved. The premises to which BALG refers were in Park Street, approx. 300 yards west of the present day town centre of Hull. Occupying the Park Street site (Thanet House) in 1867, the orphanage was able to increase its earlier capacity, initially to accommodate 50 children, and with further expansion later in the decade (Ref: LongW).

the door, and ventured to hint that all would be right. But it may be preferable to give an extract from the minutes of the institution :—

The secretary, Mr. John Wright, met Mr. Salt at the railway station at Hull, and thence proceeded to the Orphan House, where they were joined by the deputy-chairman. Having shewn Mr. Salt over the whole establishment, they visited the Sailors' Institution, and then adjourned to the Station Hotel. Before leaving for Scarborough, Mr. Salt offered to place a cheque of £5,000 at the disposal of the committee, on condition that the present premises be enlarged so as to provide accommodation for 100 sailors' orphans, and that a suitable school for 200 children be erected, 100 of whom should be clothed and educated gratuitously. Whereupon it was resolved unanimously :— "That the munificent offer of Titus Salt, Esq., to place at the disposal of the committee the sum of £5,000 for the enlargement of the Orphanage Home and general extension of the society's operations, upon the conditions mentioned in the foregoing minutes, be and is hereby most thankfully accepted."

Thus the institution was lifted into a higher position of importance in the eyes of business men, and has since reached a point of prosperity not at first anticipated; for at the present date the sum of £21,258[233] has been expended on the premises, which have accommodation for 220 orphans. At the inauguration[234] of this orphanage Mr. Salt presided, when the Mayor and Sheriff of Hull were present, together with the laity and clergy of the town. The chairman's words were, of course, few, and in them no allusion was made to himself. The treasurer said, "This was a new building for them, but the institution had existed for many years, and they had been doing something in the way of benevolence, but he was sorry to say it was on a limited scale. They had now thrown off this limited liability, and were determined to go to the unlimited. The Company had taken into partnership a junior. He was a gentleman of great credit, and if his means were half as large as his heart, there

---

[233] Readers may wonder how BALG was able to quote such an accurate and updated (1877) figure. The orphanage's records show that Balgarnie had a long involvement with it over many years. Balgarnie no doubt played a significant role in securing Salt's support of the orphanage.

[234] The inauguration took place on 7th August, 1867 (Refs: HullT, 10th August, 1867, p6; AofY3, p125).

would not be many orphans in Hull uncared for." Another speaker[235] said, "Mr. Salt was very much grieved when he saw the announcement of his liberality in the newspapers, but he (the speaker) had told him that it was a very difficult matter to keep it a secret, for the donor was like one of those men whom the poet described when he spoke of 'doing good by stealth, and blushing to find it fame.' "

Nor was this the only instance of his liberality towards that institution. In 1869, he wrote to the secretary, saying, "there must be a great effort made to increase the annual subscriptions, so that you may fill the building. I shall increase mine to £50 per annum."[236] He also contributed £250, to provide some carved work to ornament the front of the building. It consists of a group of five figures, the centre one being "Charity," with two orphan children on either side; while the accessories of the group associate it with the maritime interests of the town. The sculptor was Mr. Keyworth, Junr., of London (a native of Hull).[237] With a view to promote the proficiency of boys in swimming, a silver medal, to be annually awarded to the best swimmer, was also given. As an evidence of the gratitude of the committee in Hull for all these generous gifts, a beautiful bust[238] of Mr. Salt stands in the entrance hall of the building; his full length portrait has been placed in the committee room,[239] and every year his birthday is kept by the

---

[235] The "other speaker" to whom BALG refers was none other than Balgarnie himself! (Ref: HullT, 10th August, 1867, p6).

[236] In fact 1869 was the year in which Salt's support for the orphanage really came to full fruition, with the official opening, on 3rd July, of the extended building, giving the orphanage a capability to accommodate 150 children (Ref: LongW, p50).

[237] The carvings by William Day Keyworth Jr. (1843-1902), can still be seen on the building in the present day. (Other examples of his work exist in Hull (Ref: Cred, p49)). In addition to the features described by BALG, Salt's coat of arms, surmounted by the alpaca, is prominent within the pediment. The four sculptured lions which adorn the frontage of Leeds Town Hall are further examples of the sculptor's work – Keyworth never visited Africa but studied the animals at Regent's Park zoo. Installed in 1867, the lion sculptures cost £550 compared with the £11,000 paid for their counterparts in Trafalgar Square (Ref: Hall, p9).

[238] The bust was also the work of William Day Keyworth Jr. (Ref: HullT, 3rd July, 1869, p5).

[239] The two artefacts referred to appear to have been lost or destroyed. Our searches and enquiries established that they are not in the present day in the Park Street building, nor are they at the Newland site, to which the orphanage relocated in the 1890s. They may at some stage have been transferred to a museum or archive for safekeeping, but if so, records of such transfer are not known to us.

orphan children as "The Founder's Day."[240]

In 1862 was celebrated the bi-centenary of English Nonconformity, which commemorates the memorable event of 1662, when 2,000 learned and godly ministers of the Established Church gave up their living and social status for conscience' sake. As the Congregationalists in this country regard those noble men as their ecclesiastical forefathers, the celebration assumed many practical forms, such as the erection of churches and schools in various parts of the kingdom; but it was thought, by many, that a public hall should be erected in some central part of the metropolis. In such a hall, the different societies affiliated with the Congregational denomination might be localised, the portraits of its eminent men preserved, ecclesiastical records kept, a library of Puritan literature opened, and the annual assembly of the Congregational Union held. This "Memorial Hall" was erected at a cost of £75,000 and is situated in Farringdon Street,[241] on the site of the ancient Fleet Prison, where many godly

---

[240] The Park Street site continued in use for approx. 25 years, with the children living in large dormitories. It was during the first ten years of this period that the orphanage was to have its close association with Salt; the children of the orphanage became quite celebrated (see Appendix 5). By 1893 the Society saw the needs for further expansion, and for a better environment for the children than could be achieved with large dormitories. A six-acre site was acquired at Newland, in Hull's Cottingham Road. Based upon a concept of "Cottage Homes" for the children, the Society began a building programme on the new site which saw several substantial villas being provided to replace the older style of accommodation in Park Street. One of the villas, opened on 1st May, 1896, was named after Sir Titus Salt in recognition of the role that BALG here describes. The migration was completed in 1897, at which stage the Park Street site was sold to Hull Technical Instruction Committee (Ref: LongW). The building remains, in the present day, a part of the city's educational facilities, and a tour of the premises reveals that appreciable parts of the 19th century structure are still intact. A comprehensive description of the building is available (Ref: ParkS). The involvement of the Salt family with the orphanage seems to have died with Sir Titus; we have found no later evidence (e.g. in the commemoration of the new building in the 1890s) of any involvement of the family.

[241] The building of the Memorial Hall, which stood on the corner of Farringdon Street and Fleet Lane, was a very significant milestone in the history of the Congregational church. BALG goes on to correctly identify the contributions made by several leading Congregational laymen. The author had good grounds for accuracy – he himself was deeply involved in the administration of the project for many years both during the planning and then in the actual management. On more than one occasion Balgarnie led prayers at the start of the project's committee meetings. Salt's future son-in-law, Henry Wright, a leading layman, was equally involved. The attendances of Balgarnie and Wright at committee meetings held in London are recorded over at least two decades. Balgarnie was still attending meetings in 1898, 32 years after contributing three guineas to the original fund. (Ref: MemH). Long after the passing of Salt (and indeed Balgarnie and Wright) the

men were incarcerated for their adhesion to Nonconformity. And now, what had Mr. Salt to do with this?

The reader will have seen, how his own early life had been passed amid scenes sacred to the memory of some of these ejected ministers. No wonder, then, that at this bi-centenary commemoration his warm sympathy was excited. Towards the building fund he contributed £5,000. Similar sums were given by other noble men, such as Mr. S. Morley and Mr. J. Crossley whose example in many good works, Mr. Salt, when not the leader himself, was always ready to follow. Two years before his death he visited the " Memorial Hall," and expressed himself highly pleased with the undertaking, which, after years of unavoidable delay, had recently been brought to a most successful consummation.[242]

Scarborough had long been a favourite place of resort to Mr. Salt and his family. His parents had brought him there as a boy, and seldom had a year passed since then, without the accustomed visit being paid. We have heard him describe the long journey in those coaching days, with his parents, and their sojourn in Merchants Row, which was then considered the most attractive part of the town. They attended divine worship in the Old Meeting House, now Eastborough Church, and enjoyed the ministry of the venerable Samuel Bottomley.[243] This sanctuary was of Presbyterian origin, and has an interesting

---

Memorial Hall was to be the venue of two historic gatherings – the meeting of 27th February, 1900 which saw the creation of the Labour Party; and the Trades Union Congress meeting of 1st May, 1926 at which the vote to hold a General Strike was carried. Sadly the Memorial Hall no longer exists. Having suffered bomb damage in the Second World War, the site was subsequently redeveloped and disposed of by the Congregational Union.

[242] The building of the Hall did indeed take a long time to realize. The Congregational Union of England and Wales had, at its 1861 Autumnal meeting, resolved that it would be a most suitable opportunity, in anticipation of 24th August, 1862, for commemorating "the great self denial and consistency of the two thousand ministers ejected from the Church of England following the 1662 Act of Uniformity". The meeting went on to look forward to a time when "the Congregationalists of 1962 will hold the Tercentenary Celebrations in London in their own Memorial Hall." Records show that the building was not completed until 1875 (Ref: MemH).

[243] Rev. Bottomley was minister of Eastborough Church for 58 years, dying in 1831. He had succeeded Rev. W. Whitaker, who himself was pastor for 50 years, and who died on 22nd October, 1776, aged 81. A monument to Rev. Bottomley can be seen in the present day in St. Andrew's Church, Scarborough, on the wall at the foot of the stairs.

history, going back to the dark days of persecution. An old family bible is still preserved by the present minister, the Rev. E. L. Adams, which bears the mark of a sword-thrust. It is said that the owner, having concealed himself in a barn, owed his life to the circumstance, that a dragoon, in probing the straw, imagined he had pierced a concealed fugitive. Mr. Salt's early visits to Scarborough were, therefore, associated with the "Old Meeting House" in that place. But when the town outgrew its ancient boundaries, this building became difficult of access to summer visitors. It is said, the late Dr. Winter Hamilton, on one occasion, had some difficulty in finding St. Sepulchre Street, in which locality the "Meeting House" was situated. On coming out of it one morning after service, he observed to a friend, "They call this Sepulchre Street chapel; what a place to bury strangers in!" When, therefore, steps were taken to erect the Bar Church, in the western part of the town, Mr. Salt gave it his liberal support; but in the course of a few years; this church became insufficient to accommodate the summer visitors, so that a public hall had also to be provided, as a chapel of ease, during four successive seasons. It seemed an imperative duty to erect a permanent edifice, to meet the necessities of the case. A site was therefore selected on the South Cliff, at a cost of £1,250, which was soon afterwards increased to £1,500, on which it was resolved to build a church as early as practicable.

Mr. Salt, from his frequent visits to Scarborough, had become familiar with the above facts. What was our surprise, one day, when meeting him casually in the street, he said, "I hear you have purchased a site for a new church. That's right." Then putting his arm in ours, and walking a few yards, he quietly said, "I should like to have the honour of paying for that site."[244]

This generous offer was so unexpected, that though the time for further action seemed yet uncertain, it came as a voice from heaven, saying "Arise and build." When a building committee was formed, Mr. Salt was asked to become its

---

[244] This is a further example of Salt supporting the building of a quite grand Congregational landmark – and another example of a major church building project of the kind that had been embarked upon in the preceding decade, as described in a footnote in Chapter XI. We judge the Scarborough venture to be the last in which Salt himself was directly engaged. For an account of the Congregational church building in Scarborough, see Appendix 1.

chairman, but instead of giving an immediate answer, he said "I'll think about it." Little did we know at the time what to him the acceptance of the post meant, or even what his "thinking about it" involved; for, when on the following day, he returned an answer in the affirmative, it was in these words :—" Your proposal has cost me a night's sleep, but I think I must obey the call of duty." Does not this circumstance reveal another feature of his character? Not *feeling* but *duty* was the rule of all his actions. Would not some men have contented themselves with a handsome subscription, and regarded it as their proxy in such a work? It was not so with him; he held his personal influence as a trust as well as his wealth; his time as well as his property; and all these gifts he was willing to consecrate to God. That his heart was in the erection of this church is abundantly evident. His part as chairman of the committee was one, not only of honour, but hard work, of which the minutes (carefully kept by Mr. G. B. Dobson,) testify. Frequently he made a special journey to Scarborough to attend the committee meetings, returning by the last train to Methley, which he could not reach till midnight. The foundation stone was laid on his 61st birthday, by Mrs. Salt, and in the following summer the church was opened for divine worship, when the Revs. Dr. Mellor[245] and Newman Hall[246] preached. The cost

[245] Rev. Enoch Mellor (1823–1881) was for many years minister of the Square Congregational Church, Halifax, and a close friend of Balgarnie. Born at Salendine Nook, near Huddersfield, Mellor was educated at Huddersfield College and Edinburgh University, before receiving his training as a minister at Lancashire Independent College. A politically outspoken and occasionally controversial character, Mellor's first pastorate was at the Square Church, Halifax, where he established a long and successful association with the Crossley family. Mellor's abilities attracted a large congregational following, and the Old Square Church was, in time, and with support of the Crossleys, replaced by the magnificent New Square Church. In 1861 he was prevailed upon to take up a ministry in Liverpool, and during his time there Mellor was elected, in 1863, chairman of the Congregational Union of England and Wales. However, he returned to Halifax and the Square Church in 1867, and remained in that ministry until his death (Refs: HalG, 29th October, 1881, p7; Balg1). Two years prior to his death, on 13th April, 1879, Mellor took part in a novel and successful experiment. On that day the telegraph service between Halifax and Manchester was temporarily disconnected to allow the substitution of the highly novel "telephone apparatus". The transmitter was fixed in the pulpit of Square Church, and the preacher's words from Halifax were listened to in awe by those gathered in Manchester (Ref: Bret3, Part V, pp100-101).
[246] Rev. Dr. Christopher Newman Hall (1816–1902) was a much-celebrated figure in the Congregational Church. A graduate of London University, from 1842 to 1854 he was minister of Albion Church, Hull, from where he moved to be minister of first Surrey Chapel and then its successor, Christ Church, Westminster. A successful writer of hymns and scriptural

was about £16,000, towards which Mr. Salt gave, inclusive of the site, £2,500. The committee desired that the large stained window, in the western transept, should be a memorial of the chairman; but he, with characteristic modesty, declined the honour.

The Congregational churches of Scarborough were not the only recipients of his liberality. The Baptists and Primitive Methodists shared it. To the Royal Sea-Bathing Infirmary, the Dispensary, the Mechanics' Institute, the Cottage Hospital, he was a generous benefactor. When disaster befell the sea-faring portion of the community he was prompt to aid them. It was in connection with them that a touching incident once occurred at Methley, of which we were cognizant. The *Leeds Mercury* of one morning contained an account of the upsetting of a boat on the previous day at Scarborough, when two fishermen were drowned. At family prayer the widows and orphans were specially commended to God. When we rose from our knees he seemed much affected, and, taking a ten-pound note from his pocket-book, he said "Give them that." The gift following the prayer reminded us of one of old, to whom the angel said, "Cornelius, thy prayer is heard, and thy alms are had in remembrance before God." It was frequently our privilege to be one of his many almoners, though we cannot recall a single instance where pecuniary aid was directly solicited of him.

It was the spontaneity of his gifts, that invested them with peculiar value. He had only to be informed of any case of real distress, or a worthy institution struggling with difficulties, then his heart was moved, and his purse opened. Those who have seen his pocket-book so often brought out, when his bounty

---

publications (his Come to Jesus sold over four million copies and was circulated in forty different languages), he was an active worker for temperance reform. He was to become chairman of the Congregational Union of England and Wales in 1866. Newman Hall had close links with Balgarnie - he had baptized Balgarnie's first child, the daughter Florence, on 19th August, 1856 in Scarborough (P. McNaughton, pers. comm.) and he and Balgarnie were to travel together, in 1867, to America. While in America, he preached before the two Houses of Congress in the Hall of Representatives – a rare honour for an Englishman. Reknown in America, he even has a geographical feature (Newman's Ledge) in the Catskill Mountains named after him (S. McGrath, pers. comm.). In his autobiography of 1898, he was to pay warm tribute to both Balganie and Salt. Newman Hall died at Vine House, Hampstead, England, and is buried in the same London Nonconformist cemetery (Abney Park) as Balgarnie. (Refs: DNB; ConYB, 1903, pp178-180; NewH, pp106-108; ScarF, p106; also see Appendix 1).

was to be dispensed, might almost wish it had a voice, for it would reveal the heart of the owner, by deeds, which in words cannot be expressed. The supply of bank notes which it contained, we sometimes called his "tracts," and which, in their distribution, carried blessings both to the bodies and souls of men. May we not add, the "tract depository" always seemed like the oil cruse at Zarephath, never exhausted?[247]

But let us glance at his domestic and social life, at Methley. The younger children were then about him, and in their pastimes he found relaxation and delight. When little children were sojourning there, he loved to become young again, and to take part in their childish sports. On one occasion, we remember him heading a juvenile procession in the hall and marching to the unmelodious sound of the fire-irons, he being chief musician and leader. When Christmas came, and both children and grandchildren met under the parental roof, his domestic felicity was complete. And when the yule log blazed and crackled on the capacious hearth, (which seemed to have been originally constructed for the purpose,) and the old baronial hall became familiar, once more, with scenes of festive mirth, the echoes of olden times were revived. Methley, at that time, was seldom without guests, and its hospitalities were dispensed with characteristic generosity. The late Earl of Mexborough, who then resided on the estate, was occasionally invited to join the social circle, which he enlivened by his personal reminiscences of the home where his own life had been passed. Among the guests there once happened to be a distinguished group, consisting of Owen Jones, Digby Wyatt, and Sir Charles Pasley.[248] In the course of the evening the

---

[247] A biblical reference (1 Kings Chapter 17 Verse 16).
[248] The group was not only distinguished, as BALG states, but it also constituted an interesting collection of three generations of leading artisans. BALG is unspecific about the date of the gathering, but clearly it predates the death of Pasley in 1861, and occurs after Salt's move to Methley in 1858. Sir Charles Pasley had been born in 1780 and, following active service in the Royal Artillery and the Royal Engineers, spent much of his later life on developing the art and science of military engineering. In 1841 he had been made inspector-general of railways. Owen Jones (1809-1874) and the somewhat younger Matthew Digby Wyatt (1820-1877) had worked together on the Great Exhibition in 1851, the former as Superintendent of Works, the latter as Secretary of the Exhibition Committee. Three years later, when the "Crystal Palace" was re-erected in Sydenham as a permanent exhibition hall, Jones and Wyatt used the hall to build within it ambitious, full-scale models of historical and foreign architectural styles. In 1856 Jones had published *Grammar of Ornament*, a monumental and magnificent documentation and reproduction of over 2,000

conversation turned upon art and literature, in which several of the guests took part. The host was a silent, but not uninterested listener. The "flashes" of his silence were sometimes equivalent to an articulate speech in conversation. The last-named gentleman, turning to the host, said "Mr. Salt, what books have you been reading lately?" "Alpaca," was the quiet reply; then, after a short pause, he added, "If you had four or five thousand people to provide for every day you would not have much time left for reading." The late Sir William Fairbairn and other old friends were once invited to dine with him; unfortunately, he was laid up in bed by a severe attack of gout. What was to be done in the circumstances? He would not permit the invitations to be recalled, nor be entirely deprived of the society of his guests; he, therefore, held a levee in his bedroom, and, though suffering considerable pain, his original intentions were carried out as far as practicable.

It is not unworthy of note, that about this period Mr. Salt abandoned the habit of smoking, to which he had been accustomed for many years. He was known to keep choice cigars, so that his guests addicted to smoking were fortunately situated for the gratification of their tastes; but they found that a sudden and an unexpected change had come over their host. We mention the circumstance as shewing the self-mastery of Mr. Salt. Perhaps some persons would have gradually emancipated themselves from a longstanding habit; but he acted with decision. Does he not, in this, present an example worthy of imitation? We know not the motives that induced him to take this sudden resolution, but of this we are confident, he kept it throughout his subsequent life. He was not, however, intolerant to smokers, though he had a characteristic way of conveying a broad hint on the subject. When the cigar box was handed to them, a few tracts on anti-smoking were usually placed on the top. Sometimes he offered his

ornamental designs and patterns from a great many cultures and periods. The book became one of the most influential works on ornamental design ever published. Even in the present day, almost 150 years later, it remains a source of reference for craftsmen and designers, and can be purchased in electronic form. Jones was also well known as an interior and pattern designer, and in later life designed home interiors for wealthy patrons. Digby Wyatt went on to be knighted in 1867 (Ref: DNB). When the meeting took place, Pasley was clearly in his late seventies, if not older; Jones and Salt would be in their fifties; and Digby Wyatt would be approx. 40. Not surprising, perhaps, that it was the elder statesman of the group who had the forthrightness to enquire about Salt's reading preferences.

friends a bundle of what seemed to them, fine Havannahs, when, lo! on closer examination, it proved to be a box of chocolate!

Thus the "random tricks" of the schoolboy would sometimes re-appear in the man. Another instance of a similar kind may be mentioned. He had brought a party of friends to Saltaire on a fair day, and as he passed with them along the Street, a gipsy, not knowing who he was, offered him for sale her brooms. Imagine her bewilderment when he bought the whole stock! To each of his friends he presented one, and distributed the remainder amongst the children who were wonderingly looking on. Why do we mention these trifling incidents? Just that the man may be seen in his true character. How few saw him on all sides!

> Tender as a woman. Manliness and meekness
> In him were so allied,
> That they who judged him by his strength or weakness,
> Saw but a single side.

What were his out-door pursuits at Methley? He was not a great horseman, nor a sportsman; occasionally he would ride out with his children. His chief delight was in the cultivation of fruits and flowers.[249] On his coming to Methley, the vineries and green-houses were rebuilt, and supplied with the most modern means of heating and ventilation. With the botanical names of various plants he had but a slight acquaintance; but their form and colour filled him with exquisite pleasure. The grape and pineapple were his favourite fruits, until after his return to Crow Nest, where the cultivation of the banana, or "bread fruit," took precedence; yet all these were cultivated not alone, for his personal gratification, but for that of friends —and especially invalids, to whom a basket of beautiful flowers or fruits from Methley was always a welcome boon.

> For his bounty
> There was no winter in't; an autumn 'twas,
> That grew the more by reaping.[250]

---

[249] Salt's interests in horticulture were shared by his sons George, Edward and Titus Jr. (see Appendix 3).
[250] Shakespeare's Antony and Cleopatra, Act 5, Scene 2.

CHAPTER XV.

"His daily life, far better understood

In deeds than words, was simply doing good;

So calm, so constant, was his rectitude,

That by his loss alone we know his worth,

And feel how good a man has walked with us on earth."

—WHITTIER[251]

HIS PARTNERS IN BUSINESS—HIS RESOLUTION CHANGED—PARIS EXHIBITION OF
1867 —CORRESPONDENCE ABOUT SALTAIRE—RECEIVES THE LEGION OF
HONOUR—NO PUBLIC HOUSE IN SALTAIRE—ERECTION OF THE CLUB AND
INSTITUTE—DESCRIPTION OF IT—ADDRESS AT THE OPENING—CHANGED INTO A
HIGH SCHOOL—OTHER INSTITUTIONS AT SALTAIRE.

AFTER Mr. Salt's retirement from Parliament,[252] he resumed his former duties
at Saltaire and Bradford; but his frequent attacks of gout prevented him taking
that prominent part in business which he had done in former years. He was,
however, fortunate in having associated with him in the firm those whose
practical knowledge was invaluable, and who, by a division of labour and
cordial co-operation amongst themselves, were well able to carry on
successfully the work of the establishment.[253] Still, the head of the firm was
always consulted, and received at their hands that respectful deference to which
he was justly entitled. True, he was often slow in forming a judgment on matters
submitted to his decision, and their patience had sometimes to be exercised; but

---

[251] John Greenleaf Whittier (1807–1892) was born of Quaker parents at Haverhill,
Massachusetts. He was a strong advocate of, and writer on, the abolition of slavery (Ref:
DicLB). Whittier may have met Balgarnie during the latter's travels in the USA.
[252] This event occurred in January 1861, see Appendix 6.
[253] The associates in the firm in 1861 to whom BALG refers are judged to include William
Henry, George and Edward Salt; Charles Stead and William Evans Glyde – all being
named in the 1859 Articles of Partnership of Titus Salt Sons and Co. (Ref: Part).

if the working of his mind was slow, he was always prompt in execution.

It has been said that when his mind was made up to any given course, it was impossible to turn him from it. This was true as a rule, but it had its exceptions; some of these have already been mentioned, and one other instance may here be recorded. It happened at the time when several large manufactories were converted into Joint Stock Companies, Limited, and employés were permitted to invest their savings and to share in the profits.[254] Mr. Salt was at first enamoured of such a scheme, as one likely to promote sympathy and goodwill between master and workman; he therefore cherished the resolution of adopting it at Saltaire, but the other members of the firm offered strong objections to the scheme. Happily, a middle course was ultimately taken, which was mutually satisfactory. The employés were placed on piecework, which gave them a direct interest in the produce of their labour, without any pecuniary risk. Thus, while Mr. Salt's resolution was abandoned, the principle in question was retained, and the works that bear his name remained under the sole control of the firm.

At the great Exhibition of 1851, the manufacturers of Bradford stood preeminent among the exhibitors of worsted textures; but it was not until the Exhibition of 1862 that a collective display of local products took place. Then Bradford was declared by the jurors to stand unrivalled, especially in alpaca and mohair, for which a medal of the highest class was awarded to the Saltaire firm. When the Paris Exhibition of 1867 was in course of construction, the Imperial Commissioners established a new order of reward, for establishments erected with a view to the welfare of the persons engaged in them. The money value of the prize amounted to 100,000 francs. As Saltaire had become known throughout the country as a model town, the firm was urged to enter into competition, and the chances of success were said to be decidedly in their favour; but Mr. Salt declined the proposal. As the correspondence on the subject serves to throw light on his character, we therefore present it here :—

---

[254] Among the enterprises so converted were the Halifax companies of James Akroyd and Sons and of the Crossleys. Both companies offered shares to their workers in their Halifax enterprises (Refs: Bret1, pp93-94; Bret3, Part II, p80).

Copy of Correspondence with Henry Cole,[255] Esq., C.B., Secretary and Executive Commissioner, of the Paris Industrial Exhibition, &c., submitted to a Friend, by Mr. Salt.

Dear Sir,—What has been attempted at Saltaire arose from my own private feeling and judgment, without the most remote idea that it would become a subject of public interest and enquiry. A sense of duty and responsibility has alone actuated me, and I would have avoided publicity, but for the representations made in the following correspondence :—

31st December, 1866.

Sir,—The Imperial Commissioners for the Paris Exhibition have established a new order of reward for establishments promoting the welfare of the persons engaged in them, and it has been suggested by the National Association for the Promotion of Social Science, that your establishment could afford, in a high degree, the information which the Imperial Commissioners desire to elicit. I have the honour to send to you the documents relating to this new order, and to express a hope that you may see fit to fill up the questions and return them to me. And I desire to remark, that, under any circumstances, the collection of this information and its publication, seem calculated to be of general public benefit.

I have the honour to be, Sir,

Your obedient servant,

To Titus Salt, Esq.,

Saltaire.

HENRY COLE,

Secretary and Executive Commissioner.

———————

Saltaire, Bradford, January22,

---

[255] In addition to his role in the 1867 Paris Industrial Exhibition, Henry Cole (1808–1882) had many other credits to his name. A gifted administrator, his career had started as a civil servant in the Records Office. He came to national prominence through his successful organization of the Great Exhibition of 1851. He was responsible for the building of the Royal Albert Hall, which occurred around the time of this correspondence. Salt was a supporter of the Royal Albert Hall project, and had in fact just months earlier (in May 1866) offered a substantial contribution to the venture (see Chapter XVII). Cole became the first Director of what is now known as the Victoria and Albert Museum, just a few hundred yards from the Royal Albert Hall. It seems likely, from the correspondence reproduced in BALG and their involvements in the Royal Albert Hall venture, that Salt and Cole knew each other. Mindful of the months spent by Salt in London as M.P. in the early 1860s, as well as other visits to London, it is possible that Salt and Cole met on occasions over a period of several years.

1867.

To Henry Cole, Esq., C. B.

Dear Sir,—It would afford me much pleasure to place in the hands of the Imperial Commissioners the results that have attended the establishment of Saltaire. I cannot, however, do so as a competitor for any prize, or be subject to the arbitrament of a jury.

The memoranda of the necessary illustrations can be readily furnished, if in these terms you think the information I could supply would be of service to the Imperial Commissioners, or benefit the public.

I have the honour to be, dear Sir,

Yours truly,

TITUS SALT.

———

23rd January, 1867.

Dear Sir,—I cannot doubt that the information about Saltaire would be useful to the public, and I hope you will send it, coupled with the conditions you mention about not being a competitor.

Yours faithfully,

Titus Salt, Esq.   HENRY COLE.

If the answers given to the questions of the Imperial Commissioners, or if any of the facts, which experiment or experience has elicited, prove of benefit to the public, and should lead others to adopt, and enable them to surpass the result of my effort, I shall be thankful.

For myself, I can enter into no competitive rivalry for well-doing, and the particulars and illustrations furnished of the establishment of Saltaire, are placed at the service of His Imperial Majesty's Commissioners on the distinct understanding that they are not given in competition for any prize, nor subject to the arbitrament of a jury.

I have the honour to be, dear Sir,

Very truly yours,

TITUS SALT.

In the above correspondence will be seen the high moral principle that influenced Mr. Salt in declining to become a competitor on this occasion. To some, the prize of £4,000 might have been a strong inducement to enter the lists, especially when the chances of success were in his favour; but was he not right in affirming that "competitive rivalry for well-doing" towards his fellow creatures, was not a matter for human tribunals to touch? Was not the spirit thus manifested worthy both of the man and the Christian? Surely, when any one acts from such high motives as the glory of God and the love of men, he can afford to wait, in the assurance of a higher verdict and reward, even this—"Well done, thou good and faithful servant, enter thou into the joy of thy Lord."[256]

The questions contained in the schedule sent were carefully answered and forwarded to Paris. For the most part they relate to the arrangements for the material, moral, and intellectual well-being of the work-man, the substance of which has already been given to the reader. We shall therefore only present the medical report, appended to the schedules, and forwarded at the same time to the Imperial Commission :—

High-class work and good wages have brought together a large number of first-class workpeople and mechanics, whilst the comfortable homes and houses provided for them have awakened, in the minds of the people, that home feeling which has led them to tastefully and neatly decorate their dwellings—a very sure sign of social happiness. Every medical man and visitor amongst the poor, very well knows how such things combine to prevent vice and disease, and how much they renovate and cheer the sick, give a higher tone, and tend to develop the mental stature of the people themselves. This is a most important point. A man in a dirty house is like a beggar in miserable clothing: he soon ceases to have self-respect, and when that is gone there is but little hope.

In almost every house at Saltaire some form of musical instrument is found; and, indeed, the choral and glee societies, together with the bands, have become household names. A large number of the skilled workmen devote their leisure hours to scientific amusements such as Natural History, Taxidermy, the making of philosophical instruments, such as air pumps, models of working machinery, steam engines, and articles of domestic comfort, whilst some have even manufactured organs and other musical instruments.

There is no public-house in Saltaire! Thus, with comfortable houses and every inducement to stay at home—with literary and social institutions in their very midst, with high-class tastes, and, to crown all, a beautiful temple to the worship of God—it would be strange indeed had Saltaire not a

---

[256] A second use of the biblical quotation first found in Chapter XII.

reputation and a name.

The erection of baths and wash-houses has been a great advance. Cleanliness is the great condition of health; whilst the removal of whole masses of damp clothes from the streets, and of the steam of washing-tubs from the houses, greatly conduces to the health and comfort of the inhabitants. Indoor washing is most pernicious, and a fruitful source of disease, especially to the young.

The diseases peculiar to poverty are almost unknown in Saltaire, namely, typhus fever, rheumatic fever, and cutaneous affections.

An accident infirmary and dispensary is erected, so that patients will be spared that great source of danger to life, hemorrhage, during the transit to a distant hospital. Hitherto there has not been a single death from this cause.

The writer, from his medical duties, has been constantly in the town, day and night, and can bear testimony to the great absence of drunkenness; whilst in many of the houses no spirits are kept, except on the approach of a confinement. There is a remarkable absence of certain diseases.

During the visitation of cholera to this country, a system of disinfecting and deodorising by means of the application of carbolic acid and chloride of lime to the drains, ashpits, privies, and sinks, was carried out. The carbolic acid was given to any one who would mix it with lime for the purpose of whitewashing. The result was remarkable; no case of cholera occurred, and even an immunity from typhoid fever and other autumnal diseases was experienced.

Having thus drawn attention to the general moral and physical condition of the people, it will be well to look at the other side of the question, and mark the direction in which progress has still to be made. The prevalent diseases in manufacturing districts are typhus fever and phthisis; these are, therefore, the most common forms of serious ailment at Saltaire. To get rid of consumption from the disease list is almost, if not quite, impossible. Where persons of different temperament, constitutional vigour, and age, often carelessly clothed, leave home early in the morning, generally without partaking of food, and this in all kinds of weather and seasons, and that, too, in our irregular and often inclement northern climate, consumption must and will result. The question involved is rather one that rests upon the people themselves, than one in which masters can interfere. The workpeople can only be taught that warm clothing instead of finery, good food and regular hours, combined with home sanitary regulations, are necessary to keep down this terrible malady. Much is accomplished at Saltaire to prevent the disease by having the works erected close to the town, so that there is really no excuse for the workpeople going to their work in wet clothes; and, further, by the mills and sheds being thoroughly well lighted, warmed, and ventilated.

With regard to typhoid fever, it is otherwise, although from this cause very few deaths have occurred. This is a disease which can be kept down by sanitary regulations. What precautions, then, are necessary?

(1) An absolute restriction to prevent overcrowding by lodgers in any one house. Let a proper number of cubic feet be allowed to each inmate, and on no pretence whatever ought this rule to be evaded.

(2) A system of ventilation with which the inmates cannot interfere. Instances have occurred in which it has been purposely obstructed.

(3) The system of drainage at Saltaire is thorough and complete. Bell-traps to sinks, if fixed, become choked; and if unfixed, are removed, and often lost. Syphons in the drains do not always prevent the back current from them. Where the nightsoil is preserved in ashpits, as at Saltaire, for agricultural purposes, a system is required for removing it without annoyance to the people. Recently an admirable plan has been adopted by which the inhabitants are compelled to empty their dust and ashes into the closets, so that the ordure is constantly mixed with that best of disinfectants, finely divided carbon and dry earthy matter. This ought everywhere to be done. Provision is made for the adoption of every sanitary improvement.

A few of the lessons to be learned at Saltaire have been briefly pointed out, and, though others might be given, these will probably suffice.

(Signed)   SAMUEL RHIND,[257]

L.R.C.P., Edin., M.R.C.S., Lond., Scholar in

Anatomy and Physiology.

Such was the medical report forwarded to Paris, which we have given at length, because it will enable the reader to see what pains Mr. Salt had taken for the welfare of his workpeople; also the success that followed. But, let it not be forgotten, that at the time Saltaire was erected, sanitary science was comparatively in its infancy, so that his views were then far in advance of the age, and even now, are not a whit behind it. According to the express condition on which the information was sent, no reward was expected, but the Emperor of the French signified his high appreciation of the superiority of this "model

---

[257] Rhind was a young surgeon from Chelsea, living in 1861 in Shipley (Ref: PRO, Census 1861, Shipley).

town," by conferring on its founder the Legion of Honour.[258]

Among many facts contained in the above report, not the least interesting is that which relates to the absolute prohibition of public-houses on the estate. Mr. Salt had strong reasons for the adoption of such a course. During the year of his mayoralty of Bradford, he had been deeply affected by the large number of cases brought before him in his magisterial capacity, as the palpable results of intemperance; and when cholera raged in the borough, he had seen that many of the poor who had fallen victims to the malady, were also the victims of strong drink. We remember him returning from the assizes at Leeds, where he had sat on the grand jury, and expressing his horror at the fearful catalogue of crime there brought before his notice, and the emphasis with which he said "Drink and lust are at the bottom of it all." He would, therefore, have been unfaithful to his own moral convictions, had he not passed this "prohibitory bill" on his own property, when the decision rested solely with himself, and no Act of Parliament was needed to enforce it. It was with paternal solicitude for the moral and physical health of his people, he resolved that no public-house should be planted in their midst. That the course he adopted was wise and beneficial to the town, is amply confirmed by the foregoing report. It is true, that on the confines of Saltaire, public-houses have since been erected, but for these he was not responsible; indeed, to prevent them was beyond his power.[259] Still, we hold that the course he adopted and continued, is worthy of the highest commendation,— shall we not also say, worthy of imitation on the part of proprietors placed in similar circumstances? At all events, the above fact may be regarded as his emphatic protest against the greatest evil that afflicts the nation.

Having thus prohibited public-houses in Saltaire, he felt that it was an incumbent duty to provide every facility in his power for the moral and physical welfare of the community. The Saltaire Club and Institute was, therefore, established, at an expense of £25,000. As this building is, perhaps, the most

---

[258] The Legion of Honour is the highest award given by the French Republic for outstanding service to France, regardless of the social status or the nationality of the recipients. Originally created in 1802 by Napoleon Bonaparte, the award recognizes achievements in both civil and military fields, its members being appointed for life.

[259] BALG is writing these words in 1877. By that time the Rosse Hotel and the Victoria Hotel had both been erected on their present day sites in Bingley Road and Saltaire Road respectively (Ref: PRO, Census 1871, Shipley).

unique of its kind in the country, a description of it will be interesting to our readers. It is situated on the east side of Victoria Road, and, like the schools,— immediately opposite,—stands back forty feet from the line of the street. The space in front is tastefully laid out in flower beds, with a broad walk leading up to the entrance. At the north and south angles of the enclosure, two massive sculptured lions present a striking feature. It will be remembered, that in front of the schools, and occupying a corresponding position, other two lions are placed, representing "Vigilance" and "Determination." The two in front of the Institute represent "War" and "Peace," the whole of the figures being the work of Mr. T. Milnes. Approaching the main entrance, the appearance of the building is that of a university college. It consists of three floors; the basement being built of stone and in the Italian style of architecture. Over the entrance, figures are placed, representing "Art" and "Science," thus indicating the purpose to which the building is devoted. A tower rises in the centre, and terminates in the form of an angular cone. Let us enter the vestibule. The reading-room opens on the left; the dimensions of which are 53 ft. by 35 ft. This apartment is fitted up with every convenience, and supplied with the daily papers and current literature. The library is situated on the right hand, with a classroom adjoining. Further on, to the left, are a large cloak-room, lavatory, etc., and at the end of the vestibule, fronting the main entrance, is the splendid lecture-hall, measuring 90ft. by 60ft., and 40ft. high, with sitting accommodation for 800 persons. The platform is 35ft. wide. The hall is decorated with a refinement of taste such as is seldom seen in a public building. It is known as the Victoria Hall.[260]

Here, first-class concerts are frequently held, and lectures and entertainments given. In the upper storey, the front part is occupied on the left by two rooms, as the "School of Art," one being elementary, and the other more advanced. These rooms are supplied with models, drawings, and every appliance and means necessary for the cultivation of art. Parallel with the art department, on the right, is a handsome billiard-room, 53ft. by 35ft., furnished with four tables. On the same storey there is also the committee-room. In the basement is a lecture-room, 40 ft. by 35 ft., with accommodation for 200 persons, and which is used for

---

[260] BALG's account of the Club and Institute is drawing heavily on the earlier account of Hol1, pp50-62. A more recent account is available (Ref: SHR, pp14-15).

scientific purposes. Connected with this is a laboratory, supplied with all the instruments and apparatus requisite in scientific demonstrations. A complete set of instruments is provided for each student in attendance. A valuable clock, constructed by Mr. George Salt, was presented by him to the institute.[261] These two schools of art and science are in connection with the South Kensington Science and Art Department.[262] On the left side of the corridor is a class-room measuring 31ft. by 26ft., with curator's house adjoining. Passing onwards, the room on the left is allotted to bagatelle; that on the right is used as a lavatory. Further on to the right is the classroom; to the left the armoury, where the arms of the Saltaire corps[263] are kept. Adjoining the armoury is the gymnasium and drill-room, 57ft. by 60ft., and 18ft. high. The hall is fitted up in the most complete style with trapeze, horizontal bars, hurdles; in fact, with everything necessary for muscular development. The fees for membership are almost nominal, ranging from 2s. to 6d. per quarter. The constitution of the Institute, is, of course, disassociated from any religious or political party, and is open to all who choose to avail themselves of the benefits which it offers. The aims and objects sought by the founder of this magnificent building will be gathered from the following address by Mr. Titus Salt, jun., delivered when it was opened :—

The Saltaire Club and Institute, as the name indicates, is to be, in the first place, a social club; and secondly, an educational institute. It is intended to supply the advantages of a public-house, without its evils; it will be a place to which you can resort for conversation, business, recreation, and refreshment, as well as for education—elementary, technical, and scientific. After careful enquiry into the constitution of various Mechanics' Institutes, the conclusion has been arrived at that they do

---

[261] The clock still stands, in working order, in Victoria Hall.
[262] The Science and Art Department in South Kensington was another of the institutions established in that area of London in the mid 19th century. (The Saltaire schools of art and science were not alone in having "a connection with" the Science and Art Department. The latter had a series of such links, including ones with appropriate bodies in Wakefield and Sheffield). The functions of the Science and Education Department were to be eventually taken over in 1899 by the newly formed Board of Education, and subsequent evolution is closely linked to the present day Science Museum, again sited in close proximity to the present day Victoria and Albert Museum, as well to the Royal Albert Hall (Ref: SciM).
[263] BALG may be referring to the Thirty Ninth West Riding Rifle Volunteers, which were based in the village (Ref: Trail, p19). The armoury held Snider rifles (Ref: Hol1, p57), a weapon of the time that was issued to a wide variety of troops in many countries.

not meet the wants of the working-classes during the hours of leisure, namely, from the fact of their being almost purely educational societies, and of their presenting to only a very limited extent means of social intercourse and healthy relaxation. In the belief that "it is gude to be merrie and wise," provision is made in the constitution of the Saltaire Club and Institute for innocent and intelligent recreation, which it is intended should occupy a place almost as prominent as that accorded to the means of mental culture. The accommodation provided in the building is as follows :— 1, reading-room; 2, library; 3, laboratory ; 4, class and draught-rooms; 5, smoking-room; 6, billiard-room (four tables); 7, bagatelle-room (three tables); 8, lecture-hall; 9, lecture-theatre; 10, school of art; 11, various class-rooms; 12, curator's house; 13, gymnasium and rifle-room, lavatories, &c. It is intended that agencies and appliances of various kinds, both for recreation and instruction, shall be brought into operation, with the view of making the institution both attractive and useful. The building will, in the first instance, be furnished at my father's expense, and will be occupied by the committee at a nominal rent. The charges for membership are fixed as low as possible, so that all who wish may be able to avail themselves of the advantages of the new institution. The committee of management will consist of eight members appointed by the firm, and an equal number appointed by the present members of the Saltaire Literary Institute. Of the committee thus formed eight will retire at the end of the first half-year, four from each class. The institution will be purely unsectarian, and free from any political bias: its ruling principle should be the broadest charity amongst its members; the object to be aimed at is the greatest good to the greatest number, and no one should seek membership with the selfish object of promoting alone his own pleasure or advantage, without due regard to the wishes of others. In conclusion, I would express my father's earnest desire that the Saltaire Club and Institute may long supply rational relaxation to those whose honest labour has best fitted them for its enjoyment, and that it may, for very many years, furnish means of advancement in what is good, noble, and virtuous to the inhabitants of the town which he has built, and which is so closely associated with his fortunes and his name.

"The minde of man is the world's true dimension.

And knowledge is the measure of the minde."[264]

It will, therefore, be seen with what generosity of heart Mr. Salt endeavoured to compensate his people for the absence of public houses, and to promote their best welfare. We have said that the sanitary condition of Saltaire at the time of

---

[264] The quoting of Fulke Greville (1554-1628) (Ref: ILGS) by Titus Salt Jr. suggests both a literary mind, and perhaps, a differing body of literary interests to that of Balgarnie.

its erection, was in advance of the age; what shall be said of the educational institutions in connection with it? They, too, were in advance, so that when board schools were erected for the district, the Saltaire schools were unnecessary. But what then? Mr. Salt, foreseeing the rapid strides education was likely to take in the future, resolved to convert his own day schools, together with the Club and Institute, into higher grade schools, for the promotion and encouragement of education in its advanced branches. These premises have been left in the hands of a board of governors, chosen by the ratepayers of Shipley, and henceforth will be known as "The Salt Schools, Shipley." Provision has also been made for several exhibitions, to be designated "The Salt Scholarships," and which are to be awarded according to merit, as the result of competitive examination. The value of the property thus bequeathed for educational purposes is not less than £40,000. With regard to religious instruction and moral training, it is provided that the teachers shall not endeavour to inculcate or controvert the doctrines of any sectarian religious creed, but shall strive to instil into the minds of the scholars such views and principles as will improve their habits, elevate their moral tone, and give them a true appreciation of those mutual obligations in all human relations, on which the welfare of mankind is based; it being intended that the duty of providing distinctively theological instruction shall be left to the parents or guardians.

Of other institutions that have sprung up at Saltaire since its erection, we must notice the dining-hall, which is situated opposite "the works." It was started on the Glasgow penny dinner system; a fixed tariff is published, of which the following is a specimen :— A good plate of meat, 2d.; a cup of tea or coffee, ½d; a bowl of soup, 1d. The workpeople who prefer to bring their own food, may have it cooked, and dining accommodation free of charge. The manager of the establishment has a fixed salary, independently of the profits, so that all temptations to stint the allowance is avoided. The "crumbs" that fall from the table are sold to the feeders of pigs, by which the sum of £50 a year is realised, towards the funds of the dining-hall. There are also the following, —a fire brigade; a horticultural society, which has its annual show; a cricket club, well known in Yorkshire; a brass band, which in several musical contests has been successful; a string and reed band; a glee and madrigal society; an angling association; a co-operative and industrial society; a coal society; a funeral society; and men's and women's societies for the relief of the sick.

> Honours be thine, whose active mind
> This earthly paradise designed;
> Far double conquests kings may war,
> Thine is a nobler conquest far.
> As rivers soon return in rain,
> So, good deeds shall come back again;
> And thou shalt know within thy breast,
> Who blesses, shall himself be blessed.

CROW NEST, LIGHTCLIFFE.

THE RESIDENCE OF SIR TITUS SALT, BART.

CHAPTER XVI

Whoe'er amidst the sons
Of reason, valour, liberty, and virtue,
Displays distinguished merit, is a noble
Of nature's own creating. Such have risen,
Sprung from the dust; or where had been our honours?

—THOMSON.[265]

How vain are all hereditary honours
Those poor possessions of another's deeds,
Unless our own just virtues form our title,
And give a sanction to our good assumptions.

—SHIRLEY.[266]

CROW NEST BOUGHT—RETURNS "HOME"—DESCRIPTION OF HOUSE AND GROUNDS—MR. SALT'S DAILY DUTIES—SOME OF HIS CHARITIES—HIS GIFTS CONDITIONED—£10,000 TO LANCASTER ASYLUM AND BRADFORD INFIRMARY—LIVINGSTONE AND MOFFAT AT CROW NEST—BARONETCY CONFERRED—CONGRATULATIONS—RETROSPECT OF CAREER—OPENING OF CHURCH AT LIGHTCLIFFE—GUTHRIE AND BINNEY, AS GUESTS—SERVICE FOR CHILDREN.

IN a former Chapter reference was made to the circumstances that rendered removal from Crow Nest necessary. We have now to advert to the return of Mr. Salt and his family to their old home. The mansion at Methley, notwithstanding its internal beauty and surrounding attractions, had certain drawbacks. It was

---

[265] Coriolanus (Act 3, Scene 3) by James Thomson, Scottish poet (1700-1748).
[266] James Shirley, English dramatist (1596-1666).
Both quotations allude to Salt's receipt of his baronetcy, which is reported in this chapter. BALG dwells on the significance of this event, and seems anxious that the reader appreciates both the merits of the recipient and the implications that the process has for society as a whole.

twenty miles from Saltaire, and therefore inconveniently distant from business. It was isolated from those means of social and intellectual enjoyment to be found in proximity to a large town.[267] Moreover, several members of his family now possessed houses of their own, so that such a large establishment as Methley seemed unnecessary.[268] When, therefore, it was ascertained that Crow Nest was to be sold, no time was lost in effecting its purchase. Great was the joy of the family, when he returned one day,[269] with the news that Crow Nest was now his own; for around that spot their affections had lingered, and to go back to it, was, to them, like "going home." Happily, no difficulty was experienced in relinquishing the lease of Methley, inasmuch as the present Lord Mexborough had succeeded his father, and was fortunately in a position to occupy the seat of his ancestors. Such was the mutual desire to meet each other's wishes, and his lordship's personal gratitude to Mr. Salt, for the improvements on his estate, that when the valuers appointed had finished their task, both parties were fully satisfied with the result. Farewell, then, to Methley, where so many interesting events had occurred, some of which have been already woven into this memoir. But when the time of departure came, shadows of regret seemed to flit across the mind of the outgoing tenant, and at the last social party within its walls, he remarked to a friend, "What a pity to leave it all!"

The return to Crow Nest took place in December, 1867, and henceforth it is associated with Mr. Salt's declining years, and with the final scene of all, when his remains were borne to their last resting-place.[270]

It is superfluous to say that the name "Crow Nest" must have been originally derived from the fact that crows once built in the neighbouring trees. But

---

[267] Methley is approx. 6 miles from the centre of Leeds – a not dissimilar distance to that between Crow Nest and Bradford (5miles). However Crow Nest is within approx. 3 miles of Halifax, and other smaller conurbations. Methley was, and remains today, the more remote of the two sites.

[268] By this time (1867) the three sons William Henry, Edward and Titus had all married. Herbert in 1861 was still at the family home, but was "a farmer of 316 acres, employing others" (Ref: PRO Census 1861) and so may not have joined the move back to Crow Nest. George (aged approx. 33) was yet to marry, but may not have remained at the family home. The deaths had occurred of Fanny, and of course of Whitlam and Mary. It seems likely that, of the Salts' children, only the three sisters Amelia (aged 32), Helen (15) and Ada (14) were still attached to the family home when it moved back to Crow Nest.

[269] 5th April, 1867 (Ref: HtoT, p477).

[270] By December, 1867, Salt was 64, his wife 55.

strange to add, no evidence of it had existed for many years previously. The old trees still stood near the mansion, but their black-feathered visitors had long since disappeared. Surely they must have had a secret grudge against some former owner, and, after their own fashion, had handed down, from one generation to another, a warning to "avoid the place." The new proprietor regretted this exceedingly, and was evidently desirous to allure them back, for he caused decoy nests to be placed, and when, the birds at last condescended to come near, they found not only a welcome on the trees, but also on the ground, where food had been abundantly scattered. The device was successful; a large colony of crows soon settled there, so that the propriety of the name has become once more self-evident. The pleasure Mr. Salt derived from watching their industrious habits, and from hearing their noisy "palavers" was ample compensation for his pains.

Perhaps a stranger visiting Crow Nest for the first time, would say the second part of the name must have been derived from its position. It is built in a hollow, and, when seen from the principal approach, has the cosy appearance of a nest. The mansion is of hewn stone, and consists of the centre portion, with a large wing on either side, connected by a *suite* of smaller buildings, in the form of a curve. It is the front, or north side, that is given in the illustration; but this is not, by any means, the most striking; the south side presents a landscape of secluded beauty, in which wood and lake, lawns and terraces, flower gardens and statuary, delight the eye. The conservatories are also situated on the south side, in a line with the mansion, and are so lofty and extensive as almost to dwarf its appearance. The central conservatory is more spacious than the others, and contains, in a recess, an elaborate rockery and cascade, of French workmanship, which were objects of great attraction at the Paris Exhibition. The lake was constructed after Mr. Salt's return, and affords another illustration of his fine eye for the beautiful and picturesque in nature. It is of uniform depth, well stocked with fish and aquatic birds, the latter finding shelter on the island in the middle. The vineries, pineries, and banana house are situated at a considerable distance from the mansion. We have previously stated that Mr. Salt took great delight in the cultivation of fruits and flowers, but the banana was his special favourite at Crow Nest, and it attained dimensions rarely met with in this country. Its luxuriant foliage, immense height, and gigantic clusters of bread-fruit more resemble those of a tropical than of a temperate clime.

Let us enter the mansion itself. On the right hand of the entrance-hall stands the colossal bust[271] presented by the workpeople in 1856, close to which is the business-room, so called, because it was used for the reception of visitors who called upon him for the transaction of business, or deputations for the presentation of appeals, &c. On the left hand is the morning-room, where he usually sat with his family, and from which a door opens into the spacious library, which is the largest and handsomest room of all. In the library is a beautiful bust of Mr. Salt, sculptured in white marble. This is the last delineation of his features, which have been well brought out by the artist, Mr. Adams-Acton. The dining, drawing, and billiard-rooms are furnished with exquisite taste. And this is the scene to which Mr. Salt retired to spend the evening of his life!

As the removal of the family in 1858 caused much regret in the neighbourhood, so their return in 1867 created unwonted joy, which was expressed in an address of "Welcome back." It took a considerable time ere Crow Nest assumed its present aspect. The whole estate required much expenditure, both of thought and money; but it was now in the hands of a proprietor whose delight was to plant and to build not only for the sake of necessity and comfort, but in the gratification of a refinement of taste peculiarly his own. His time was henceforth spent between private occupations at home and occasional business engagements at Saltaire, which were broken at intervals by visits to his married children, the seaside, or the metropolis. Let us take one day's occupation at Crow Nest, as a specimen of many. The hour of breakfast is eight o'clock, but before that time he has made his first appearance in the dining-room, where the lion's share of the post-bag awaits him, containing, for the most part, applications from various parts of the country, and from all "sorts and conditions of men," for pecuniary aid. Perhaps, one half of them are appeals for building churches or schools, or for the liquidation of debts upon them; the other half has a variety of wants to make known. One institution is restricted in its usefulness by want of funds, and much needs a helping hand; a widow is

---

[271] The bust now stands in Saltaire United Reformed Church.

destitute, and the family cast upon the world; a young man wishes to go to college; a literary man is bringing out a book and wants it circulated; a deputation hopes to be allowed to present a "pressing case!" All these letters he briefly scans; but they are afterwards to be carefully perused and respectively answered. After breakfast the household assembles for morning prayer; the head of the house slowly reads a portion of Sacred Scripture with much impressiveness, then prayer is solemnly read from the "Altar of the household." Thus, the day is begun with God, and when evening comes it is closed in the same manner. Now the family separate to their respective duties. His occupation to-day is to answer the numerous letters that have arrived. In this important business his eldest daughter[272] is his confidential secretary, which post she ably filled until the time of her marriage. That the office was not an easy one we can testify from the experience of a single day. It happened at Scarborough, when he was there alone, and in order to relieve him from the burden, we undertook the duty of scribe; but we never had a wish to do so again. If the letters written at his dictation were illegible, slightly blotted, or loosely expressed, this was fatal to their acceptance, and the workmanship, which we had imagined worthy of commendation, had to be improved. The experience thus gained enabled us to understand the nature of the work that had often to be done at Crow Nest by his sympathising and willing amanuensis, who often expressed her father's wishes and intentions in such a felicitous and kindly manner, as to enhance greatly the value of the gift she conveyed. Every letter received was judged on its own merits; the shorter and more concise the epistle, the greater were its chances of a favourable answer. Of the majority of applications sent he knew personally nothing, but he had a shrewd insight which enabled him to measure men, whether they expressed themselves in speech or writing; and though he was occasionally deceived, he would still give the applicant the benefit of a doubt, and himself the "luxury" of rendering help, rather than return an absolute refusal. Many of these letters received answers with cheques for various amounts, but frequently with conditional promises: as for example, if the debt of a church were extinguished in a year, he would give the last £100; or if a church

---

[272] Amelia.

were commenced in a given locality, his donation would be the first. In this way he sought to stimulate effort in others, and seldom did the condition he imposed remain unfulfilled. Sometimes, when he wanted further information in connection with an application, he wrote to some well-known person in the neighbourhood; or it was reserved for the opinion of some friend who was likely to know the facts of the case. Thus, his gifts were not scattered indiscriminately, but care was taken to bestow them on worthy recipients. Persons unacquainted with Mr. Salt sometimes erred in asking the aid of a mediator to recommend their ease, which, when done, was generally of little avail, for in doing good he preferred being influenced rather by the facts of the case than by any personal recommendations. Was not such benevolence governed by commendable motives?

But, as we have said, most of the objects of his generosity must remain a secret. Yet there are some instances that could not well be hid, even when done in a corner. When the Lunatic Asylum for the Northern Counties was established at Lancaster, he gave a donation of £5,000.[273] The charities of Bradford had a large share of his sympathy. One instance stands out from the rest in connection with the local infirmary. He had been asked to contribute towards a temporary building as a fever hospital, but to the surprise of the committee, a letter was received from him offering to give £5,000. It is said the letter was handed from one to another, accompanied by the remark, "there must be some mistake here; he cannot mean to give such a sum for this temporary hospital." But when it was put into the hands of Mr. Charles Semon,[274] he replied "there is no mistake about it: this means a new building, and not a

---

[273] Founded in 1868, and situated in Ashton Road, Lancaster, the asylum was built to accommodate 500 inmates from the six northern counties of England at a cost of £42,900 (Ref: BLDR, Vol. XXVI 27th June, 1868, p477). The building later became the Royal Albert Hospital; it still stands in the present day, and now serves as a school.

[274] Charles Semon was mayor of Bradford from November, 1864 to November, 1865. A native of Dantzig, Germany, he had become a naturalized Englishman while in early manhood, and engaged in Bradford's worsted trade. He was notably philanthropic, and was active in the establishment of several medical facilities in Bradford, including the Infirmary, the Fever Hospital, and the Eye and Ear Hospital. He was to die a few months after Salt, in July, 1877, aged 63, in Switzerland (Ref: Cud3, pp160-161). His remains are interred in an imposing monument in the Jewish Cemetery within Bradford's Scholemore Cemetery.

temporary one." Mr. Semon's own generous heart rightly interpreted that of the donor, and the Convalescent Home recently erected at Ilkley remains a memorial of his own liberality. A friend thus writes :—" Mr. J. K. was killed by the upsetting of the Grassington coach, leaving a widow and three children. I wrote to Mr. Salt about it, and received a kind letter, requesting me to call at his warehouse in Bradford. To my astonishment, he handed me a cheque for £100. In answer to another application from me on behalf of a village church, I received the following note from Miss Salt :—" My father wishes me to acknowledge your letter of yesterday, and to say he will be glad to give £100 towards a school-room at Brown Royd." Thus, from his home at Crow Nest, he was the centre of influence and usefulness which were felt far and wide.

But what shall be said of the hospitality which he shewed to ministers and missionaries who were privileged to sojourn under his roof? Among these, the names of David Livingstone and Robert Moffatt[275] may be mentioned. In connection with the latter, an interesting circumstance occurred. During a missionary tour in the neighbourhood, Crow Nest was his home.[276] On the evening of his departure a dinner took place, at which Mr. Samuel Morley,[277] M.P., was present. The conversation turned on the honoured guest who had left that very day, and the noble life he had consecrated to the work of God in Africa. A subscription to buy him a house was proposed around the dinner table, which amounted to £750. When the act of this generous company became

[275] Robert Moffat (1795-1883) was the father-in-law of David Livingstone (1813-1873), and was himself a leading missionary in Africa, though his fame is not as great as that of his son-in-law. Having been accepted by the London Missionary Society (as, later, was Livingstone himself), Moffat had first embarked on missionary services at the age of 21, travelling to Capetown, South Africa (Ref: DNB). Balgarnie himself also originally aspired to missionary work, and in 1842, at the age of only 16, he offered his services in an interview with Moffat. Moffat advised him to wait a few years before giving his decision (Ref: ScarF, p105). Balgarnie never realized his original ambition, see Appendix 1. The London Missionary Society is a recurring and common focus of benevolent activity for Salt, his family and his associates.
[276] David Livingstone was entertained at Crow Nest on 24th November, 1857, when the missionary and explorer spoke at St. George's Hall (Ref: Rob3).
[277] Samuel Morley (1809-1886) was himself an eminent textile manufacturer, temperance worker and a campaigner for Nonconformist emancipation. An M.P. for Nottingham and for Bristol, he endowed Morley College, London, which still exists in the present day as a centre for adult education in Westminster Bridge Road, London. He is buried in the same London cemetery (Abney Park) as the author Balgarnie.

known, the subscription was taken up and enlarged by other friends of missions, and ultimately reached the sum of £3,000. Thus, the veteran missionary was placed in a position of independency during his remaining days. Dr. Moffat cherished an affectionate gratitude for his generous host, which was touchingly exemplified shortly before the latter died. We had written to say that we had been drawing him up and down the terrace in an invalid's chair; to which he replied, "I envy you the honour, and wish I had the privilege of performing such an office for him whom I respect and love."

It was while thus busily engaged in benefiting his fellow-men that Mr. Salt received the offer of a baronetcy[278] from the Queen, by the hands of the Prime Minister. The following is a copy of the letter conveying the honour :—

Raby Castle, Darlington, Sept. 9,1869.

Dear Sir,—I have received authority from Her Majesty to propose that by her favour, you should receive a baronetcy, and I trust it may be agreeable to you to accept such a distinction. Though we have not been so fortunate as to keep you within the precincts, perhaps, I ought to say, the troubled precincts of Parliamentary life, you have not failed by your station, character, and services, to establish an ample title to the honourable distinction which it is now my gratifying duty to place at your disposal.

I beg to remain, dear Sir,

Your very faithful and obedient, servant,

Titus Salt, Esq.   W. E. GLADSTONE.

This honour was so unexpected, and, coming as it did, through the hands of one, whom he regarded as the greatest living statesman, he hardly knew what answer to return. The advice of several friends was unfavourable to its acceptance; some thought that a higher distinction than a baronetcy was his due; others, that as the name of "Titus Salt" was that around which the affections of the community gathered, the proposed title would not enhance that name, but rather break its spell. Amid this diversity of opinion, how could he do otherwise than act upon his own judgment, which finally led him to accept the proffered

---

[278] A baronetcy is a hereditary title descending through the male line, bestowing a knighthood on the recipient.

honour? Henceforth, the subject of this memoir is designated "Sir Titus Salt."

Among numerous letters of congratulation addressed to him on the occasion, the one from the residents of the neighbourhood may be transcribed :—

TO SIR TITUS SALT, BARONET.

We, the undersigned, desire to present our sincere and hearty congratulations on the distinguished mark of Royal favour bestowed by our Sovereign in conferring upon you the dignity of a Baronetcy of the United Kingdom.

We cannot but regard this gracious act of Her Majesty as an honour to the district in which you reside, and as a proof of her deep interest in the commercial prosperity of her kingdom; a prosperity which has been materially promoted by your persevering and successful labours in connection with the manufactories of this locality. As a citizen and a public benefactor, the honourable distinction so graciously conferred, has been most deservedly earned. While your sympathy with every good cause, and your unbounded liberality, have gained for you the respect and esteem of all classes.

As friends and neighbours, we hail with gladness your return to your former residence amongst us, and would respectfully convey to Lady Salt and yourself, the expression of our sincere esteem, and our earnest hope that you may be spared many years to enjoy the honours of your exalted station, and the still higher satisfaction of continuing to do good.

December, 1869.

[Signatures.]

But his elevation to the rank of baronet, could not raise him higher in public opinion, nor did it in any way affect the simplicity of his character. The title changed nothing in the man.

> "The rank is but the guinea-stamp,
> The man's the gowd for a' that."

From this point in his history, may we not look back, and mark the several steps that have led up to it? Think of him as the child, riding the wooden horse on the pavement, at Morley; as the schoolboy, trudging to Batley; or jogging on a donkey from Crofton to Wakefield; as the youth, not remarkable for ability, but rather regarded as "dull"; as the young man, coming to Bradford, and beginning wool-sorting at the Rouse's works; as the wool-stapler, pushing his way in business; as the manufacturer, striking out new paths of commercial enterprise; as the founder of a town, which, for its beauty of situation, and its moral and educational advantages, stands unrivalled; as the chief magistrate of the borough of Bradford, and its representative in the Senate; as the philanthropist, who sympathized with humanity in all its sufferings and conflicts; as the generous benefactor, whose helping hand was not restricted by religion, politics, or nationality, but extended to the most deserving; as the possessor of great wealth and influence, seeking retirement for the rest of his days; and now, the baronet, raised to the dignity by his Sovereign.

Is not such a career worthy to be studied, and, as far as possible, imitated by young men generally? He dreamt not of fame, yet he acquired it; he sought not honours, yet they came; he was unswerving in his religious and political principles, and hence he was respected by his fellow-men; he lived not for himself, but for others, and hence the reverence attached to his name. His commercial enterprise brought wealth and honour to the nation, which was recognised by the Sovereign, and endorsed by the Prime Minister. He honoured God, and to him was fulfilled the promise of old, " Them that honour me I will honour."[279]

It has sometimes been the case, in the history of Nonconformity, that persons attaining to wealth and social position, have waxed either cold in their attachment, or turned away from the church of their fathers.[280] It was not so with Sir Titus Salt. His principles were too deeply rooted to wither in the sunshine of worldly prosperity. He regarded the Nonconformity of England as that which had done much to promote evangelical religion, both at home and abroad; to advance social and religious liberty; and to give bone and muscle to the national

---

[279] 1st Samuel Chapter 2 Verse 30.

[280] This assertion by Balgarnie concerns not only a person's change of religious affiliation, but more particularly the motives for that change. Leaving aside the issue of motives, it is noted that Balgarnie, writing in 1877, was probably not to know that some of Salt's own children were to "turn away from the church of their father". William Henry and Edward both appear to have embraced the Anglican Church; both are buried in Anglican Church graveyards (see Appendix 3). We know of no evidence to suggest their motives were financial; we suspect the reasons for such changes were probably other than financial.

character. To turn away from it, would, therefore, have done violence to his deepest convictions.

Sir Titus Salt, with his family, regularly attended the Congregational Church at Lightcliffe. The history of this church is connected with the times of 1694, when service was conducted in a private house, and when Nonconformity was associated, in the minds of many, with disloyalty and revolution; yet, even then, several of the leading families in the neighbourhood were in hearty sympathy with its principles and aims. The place of worship at Lightcliffe was a very humble one, and had rather the appearance of a conventicle; yet even the walls were dear to the congregation, for when they resolved to erect a new church, the old sanctuary was converted into school-rooms. In the erection of this church, Sir Titus Salt and his family took the warmest interest. The corner-stones of the edifice were laid by two of his daughters.[281] He was the chairman of the building committee, and the principal contributor to the fund.[282] The church is a prominent object in the village, conspicuous from a distance, and its spire an object of beauty from the windows of Crow Nest. Its style is Gothic; it has a public clock, a peal of bells, and a manse. The Rev. J. Thomson[283] has been, for thirteen years, the esteemed pastor. The opening of the church, in 1871,[284] was a memorable event at Crow Nest. On that occasion, the Revs. Thomas Binney, Thomas Guthrie, D.D., Newman Hall, LL.B., and others, were invited to take part in the opening services, and to be the guests of Sir Titus.[285] With such a

---

[281] The ceremony took place on 22nd August, 1870, the two daughters being Helen and Ada, the youngest of Salt's surviving children (Ref: HtoT, p499).

[282] Salt contributed £2,000 (Ref: Bret2, p45).

[283] Rev. Thomson was later to be one of the ministers to officiate at Salt's funeral – see Chapter XX.

[284] The exact date was 18th October (Ref: HtoT, p499).

[285] The three named reverends were substantial and well-known figures of the Congregational church. (For discussion of Newman Hall, see Chapter XIV). Binney (1798-1874) was for a great many years the minister of King's Weigh-House Chapel, Eastcheap, London. A forceful opponent of the concept of an established church, he was elected chairman of the Congregational Union in 1848. In the mid 19th century, there was a process of change occurring in the structure of Congregational gatherings, and Binney was an influential voice in the introduction of a more structured liturgy, with an emphasis on musical content (Ref: Peel, pp89-90). Guthrie (1803-1873) was a Scottish preacher and philanthropist, perhaps best known for his advocacy of free education for working class children. A promoter of Ragged Schools, he supported the movement which led to the Scottish Education Act of 1872. He retired from active ministry in 1864, but remained in

group of distinguished men, the social circle could not fail to be interesting; though now, the remembrance of it is overshadowed by the thought, that the host and two of the principal guests are no more. Yet, the week spent then was a very bright one. Mr. Binney and Dr. Guthrie were full of wit and anecdote; while Sir Titus was all ear to listen. One day, at dinner, Binney having asked for boiled mutton, it was handed to him, with caper sauce, to which it appeared he had a great aversion. On sending it back, the host inquired what was the matter? "Oh, nothing," rejoined Guthrie, "it's only Binney cutting capers."[286]

At the public luncheon on the opening day, Dr. Guthrie vindicated the right of ministers to receive stipends adequate to their labour and position. "Some persons in Scotland," he said, "demur to this, because in primitive times, ministers had not even a house, but 'wandered about in sheepskins and goatskins, being destitute, afflicted, tormented.' I asked them how would they like to see Candlish and me walking along the streets of Edinburgh in sheepskins and goatskins, horns and all?"

On the following day, the guests went with their host to Saltaire, and it was arranged that they should be there at the dinner hour, when the people were leaving work. What a tide of human beings swept through the gates when the clock struck twelve! Dr. Guthrie stood watching them in amazement. He was particularly struck with their clean and cheerful appearance, but, most of all with the fact, that their attention, in passing, was not directed to the strangers, but to their master, who was there also looking on. Dr. Guthrie was deeply interested in everything he saw, and had a kind word to say to the workpeople whom he met. One of these was a boy, of about fifteen years of age. He questioned him on educational subjects, and then gave him five shillings to purchase a book. When the boy was afterwards told that the donor was Dr. Guthrie he was greatly delighted, "for," he exclaimed, "I take in the *Sunday Magazine.*" The church at Saltaire was a special object of admiration to all. On the south side is the entrance to the mausoleum. There stood Sir Titus, pointing

---

public life for several years before dying in St. Leonard's on 24th February, 1873. His funeral in Edinburgh attracted large crowds (Ref: DNB).

[286] The party did indeed stay a week at Crow Nest. Balgarnie elsewhere describes the dinner, including not only the anecdote of the capers, but also reporting on the playing of "Annie Laurie" by a lady pianist in the drawing room (Ref: Balg1).

his friends to the place where his children slept, and where too, he expected to be laid when his work was done. Little did he think that Guthrie, Binney, and himself, would, in a few short years, be "gathered to their fathers."[287] Another afternoon was spent at the Crossley Orphanage,[288] in Halifax, where Dr. Guthrie, with much tenderness, addressed the young people in reference to their future course, and commended them all in prayer, to the "Father of the fatherless."

But if there be any circumstance more hallowed than another in the retrospect of those few days passed at Crow Nest, it was the morning and evening worship in the family. Then the prayers of those saintly men seemed to lift us all near to God, so that the place was Bethel.

But the opening of the church did not end with the services for adults. Perhaps the most impressive of the series was the one arranged for the young. Sir Titus took his place amongst them, and was so deeply touched by the scene around him, that he wept like a child, especially when they sang the well known hymn, which concludes thus :—

> "Soon we'll reach the shining river,
>
> Soon our pilgrimage will cease,
>
> Soon our happy hearts will quiver
>
> With the melody of peace."[289]

---

[287] BALG's words contain a great irony. BALG describes the party inspecting the anticipated place of rest of Sir Titus, and goes on to comment on the subsequent and unforeseen passing of the party. Balgarnie wrote his words in 1877, presumably sitting in his Scarborough home. In fact Binney had died in 1874, in London, and had been buried in north London's Abney Park Cemetery, more than 200 miles from Balgarnie's home. Balgarnie could not possibly have anticipated at the time of his writing that he himself would eventually be laid to rest some 22 years later in a plot just feet from his friend Binney!

[288] The Crossley Orphanage had been founded in 1864, and was perhaps the greatest of the many benevolences bestowed on Halifax by the three Crossley brothers, John, Joseph and Francis, costing as it did over £55,000. The Crossleys are judged to have further provided a similarly large sum to support the annual endowment of £3,000 for the Orphanage (Ref: Bret3, Part IV, p6).

[289] The words quoted are from the still popular hymn "Shall we gather by the River", by the American Baptist clergyman Robert Lowry (1826-1899). The hymn had only been written in 1864, and so seems to have quickly established itself as a favourite

CHAPTER XVII.

In joys, in grief, in triumphs, in retreat,

Great always, without seeming to be great.

—ROSCOMMON.[290]

Generous as brave,

Affection, kindness, the sweet offices

Of love and duty, were to him as needful

As his daily bread.

—ROGERS.

"I'VE FINISHED NOW"—GIFT OF A PARK TO SALTAIRE—DESCRIPTION OF SAME—PRESENTATION OF HIS PORTRAIT—SIR TITUS'S ACKNOWLEDGMENT—THE CHILDREN'S GIFT—ILLUSTRIOUS VISITORS TO SALTAIRE—THE ROYAL ALBERT HALL—VISITS LONDON AND SCARBOROUGH—SIR TITUS AND THE FISHWOMAN—MARRIAGE OF HIS ELDEST DAUGHTER—GIFT TO LONDON CITY MISSION—HAWKE'S BIBLE STAND—HIS INTEREST IN BIBLE-WOMEN—PASTORS' RETIRING FUND—£11,000 TO BRADFORD GRAMMAR SCHOOL—VIEWS ON CHURCH AND STATE—LOCAL POLITICS—SUNDRY CHARITIES.

IN the last chapter, the reader has been made acquainted with Sir Titus Salt's private occupations at Crow Nest; but as building operations were always claiming his attention at Saltaire, let us see what improvements are going forward there.[291] The town still continued to grow; though, when each new addition was completed, he would say, "I've finished now"; yet, soon afterwards, some other local want was perceived, which he proceeded to

---

[290] Wentworth Dillon (Earl of Roscommon), 17th century writer and poet.

[291] The events described in this chapter relate mainly to the period 1870 onwards, but some of the benevolences referred to predate this period, as does the reported visit of Lord Palmerston.

supply.[292] One of these was a recreation-ground for the workpeople. We have already seen the provision made in various ways for their welfare; but open air amusements being an essential condition of health, he, therefore, resolved to provide the Saltaire Park.[293] It is situated on the north side of the Aire, and within five minutes' walk of the town. The area enclosed for the purpose contains 14 acres, and the tastes of old and young have been thoughtfully considered in the plan of its arrangement. One half of the ground is beautifully laid out in walks and flower-beds, and separated from the other half by a broad gravelled terrace, in the centre of which is a music pavilion for the band. The largest portion of the park is devoted to cricket, croquet, and archery. The river, as it approaches the park, has been widened, so that boating, bathing, and swimming, may be enjoyed with safety. There is no charge for admission. No person is allowed to enter or remain there, in a state of intoxication. No intoxicating drinks are to be consumed there. No profane or indecent language, gambling, or pitch and toss, are allowed; nor any meeting for the purpose of making religious or political demonstrations, without special permission.

The ceremony of formally declaring the park open took place on the 25th of July, 1871, in the presence of a large concourse of spectators. The works at Saltaire were stopped a little earlier to give the workpeople an opportunity of being present at the ceremony. When the Volunteers, with their brass band, had entered the park, the gates were thrown open to the public, Sir Titus, accompanied by several members of his family, occupying a place on the pavilion. Mr. Edward Salt, on behalf of his father, said that the park was bequeathed to them and their successors, and it was hoped they would long enjoy it for the purposes of recreation and amusement. He called their attention to the regulations of the park, and hoped that each would see it to be their duty to observe them. Sir Titus said that he was very sorry that Lady Salt was unable to be present to declare the park open, but her eldest daughter[294] would do so in her stead. Miss Salt then declared the park duly open to the public.

---

[292] This account suggests that the development of Saltaire was unplanned. As already discussed in Chapter IX, this was not the case. Although the development occurred over a period of approx. 20 years, there is the evidence referred to previously that as early as 1854 a plan existed for comprehensive development. It was perhaps more in the execution than the strategic planning that development was piecemeal.

[293] Saltaire Park is known in the present day as Roberts Park. The change of name came about in January 1920, when Sir James Roberts (who had previously acquired the mill business and associated properties, including the park) gave the park to Bradford Corporation.

[294] Amelia.

A *feu-.de-joie* was then fired by the Volunteers, amid loud and prolonged cheers; the bells in the church rung out a merry peal, and the band struck up the National Anthem. Sir Titus and the party then walked round the park and the memorable proceedings ended. (See "Saltaire and its Founder,"[295] p. 68.)

But while Sir Titus was thus manifesting his warm attachment to the workpeople and his solicitude for their welfare, they, on the other hand, sought opportunity to express their gratitude to him by the presentation of his portrait. That portrait, painted by J. P. Knight, R.A., now hangs in the Institute,[296] and represents him standing in an easy attitude by the side of a table on which he is leaning with his left hand. At the foot of the frame there is the following inscription :—

Presented to Sir Titus Salt, Bart., of Crow Nest, by 2296 subscribers, 1871.

The presentation took place in the large hall of the Institute, in the presence of Sir Titus and Lady Salt, with the other members of the family. The following address was read on the occasion:—

To Sir Titus Salt, Bart., of Crow Nest and Saltaire, on
presenting him with his Portrait.

DEAR SIR TITUS,—It gives unfeigned pleasure to your employés and other inhabitants of Saltaire and neighbourhood, to be able to give effect to their long-cherished purpose to present you with a full length portrait of yourself.

The subscribers, however, are deeply sensible that no such testimonial is necessary to perpetuate your memory or enhance your fame. Your public spirit, commercial enterprise, deeds of charity, and great Christian benevolence, have already erected to your honour, in many parts—monuments more lasting than marble tablets or granite pillars.

And the noble institutions by which we are here surrounded—the splendid club and institute, that will be graced by this portrait; the almshouses and infirmary; the baths and schools; the comfortable

---

[295] See Hol1. The words quoted by BALG are a précis, rather than a verbatim copy, of those found in Hol1.The latter gives a fuller record of attendees, and also a fuller account of the park's design and rules (Ref: Hol1, pp62–70).
[296] The portrait still hangs in Victoria Hall, on the wall of the first floor landing.

homes; the beautiful church; the park—will all proclaim to posterity, in language which cannot be mistaken, the true greatness and philanthropy of the noble founder of Saltaire.

But, while all this is true, we feel persuaded that this testimonial will occupy a place peculiarly its own. For when you, Sir Titus, shall have passed away—a time we trust far in the distance—this portrait will present to succeeding generations, and keep ever before them, in so far as art can do so, the appearance of him whom so many delighted to honour both as master and friend.

We beg your acceptance, Sir Titus, of this testimonial, as an expression of the esteem and regard of the subscribers. The spirit in which the proposal was at first made, the liberal response it has received, and the thoroughness with which it has been carried out, cannot fail to be gratifying to your feelings.

In the volume which accompanies this address, you will find the names of no less than 2296 subscribers, and it is their earnest desire and prayer that you may be long spared to your family and the world, and that when you are gathered to your fathers, this likeness may represent your features to generations yet unborn, and point to many lessons which may be learned from your interesting history.

(Signed on behalf of the Subscribers.)

Saltaire, August 16th,[297] 1871.

The screen was then drawn from the picture amid the cheers of the assembly. Sir Titus, who was very much affected, said:

My Dear Friends,—You need not expect any speech from me. I shall ever remember this day, as the greatest of my life. This testimonial of your friendship and kindness, I accept with the greatest gratitude, I assure you; and I hope it will find a place here, to be viewed for generations yet to come, as an emblem of your kindness. I may now congratulate you and myself on the completion of Saltaire. I have been twenty years at work, and now it is complete; and I hope it will be a satisfaction and a joy, and will minister to the happiness of all my people residing here. If I was eloquent, or able to make a long speech, I should try to do so, but my feelings would not allow me. I thank you most cordially.

A pleasing testimonial was also presented by the children of Saltaire,

---

[297] We believe the specification of the date to be incorrect. Other sources (Ref: Hol1, p73; AofY3, p416) identify the date as 26th August (a Saturday).

consisting of two silver-plated breakfast dishes.[298] The reason for the selection of these articles was "that they might be a memento daily before his eyes." The wishes of the subscribers were complied with, for their kind present has ever since been in daily use.

Among many visitors attracted to Saltaire at this period,[299] from various parts of the world, two or three may be specially mentioned. The first was Lord Palmerston, when Premier, who included Saltaire in his visit to Bradford, when the foundation-stone of the New Exchange was laid. Sir Titus received his lordship, and conducted him to the church, the schools, and the various departments of the mill, making use of the hoist as a means of transit from one storey to another. On his arriving in the centre of the weaving-shed, the engines were stopped, and about 2,000 of the hands had thus an opportunity of seeing him. After luncheon in the private dining-room,[300] his lordship left in the Scotch express, which had been detained for him.[301]

The second illustrious visitors were the Burmese ambassadors, who were attired in their eastern official dress, and were conducted over the town and "works" by Mr. Titus Salt[302] and Mr. Charles Stead.

The third were the Japanese ambassadors, accompanied by a numerous suite.[303] All these foreign visitors had been attracted to Saltaire by the fame of it,

---

[298] This presentation occurred on 17th September, 1870 (Ref: Hol1, p72) (also a Saturday).

[299] The term "at this period" is inaccurate. The second and third visits which BALG proceeds to describe did indeed occur in 1872 (Ref1: Hol1, p79). However the first of the visits occurred at a much earlier date, in 1864. In the account of the three visits, BALG can be seen to be drawing on the account found in Ref: Hol1, pp78–79, which does not in fact identify the year date of the visit by Lord Palmerston.

[300] Entry to the private dining room of the mill was gained via the steps and external entrance still seen today immediately to the north of the mill's main Victoria Road entrance.

[301] A much fuller account of Lord Palmerston's visit to Bradford and Saltaire can be found in Ref: AofY2, pp272–288. Lord Palmerston arrived on the evening of Monday 8th August, and departed on 10th August. He stayed at the home of Mr. H. W. Ripley in Lightcliffe, just a short distance from Salt's Crow Nest home. Ripley at the time was chairman of the Exchange Company, which was responsible for the development of the planned new Wool Exchange in Market Street, Bradford (Ref: GtPat, p211). Somewhat in contrast, Salt had at one stage given financial support to a plan which would have left the newly cleared site in Market Street as an open space, but the plan was under subscribed and failed to materialize (Ref: Cud3, pp155-156). The invitation to Palmerston was a source of controversy, and led to some protests (Ref: GtPat, p211).

[302] Titus Jr.

[303] An account of the visit of the Japanese delegation is given in Ref: Hol1, pp79-80.

that had gone forth; but, such was their wonder at the vastness of the establishment, and the completeness of the arrangements, that it was evident "the half had not been told them." The hospitality shewn to these oriental guests was marked by the thoughtful arrangements of the firm. The dining-room was decorated for the occasion with a variety of plants, indigenous to the native country of the visitors; and, instead of wine, (to which they are unaccustomed,) they were regaled with the choicest fruits.

One of the metropolitan institutions, in which Sir Titus took much interest, was the Royal Albert Hall, Kensington. Towards its erection he very largely contributed; and, he also purchased one of the largest and best boxes, at a cost of £1,000.[304]

Sir Titus was a frequent visitor to the hall, when any special concert was given. Not that he, himself, had much taste for music, but the brilliancy of the scene delighted him, and his own pleasure was much enhanced, when he had friends around him to share it. Seldom was his box unoccupied, for when unable to he present himself, it was generously placed at the disposal of others.

After the dignity of baronet was conferred upon him, he was presented at Court, and went in the attire of a deputy-lieutenant; but after the ceremony, his

---

[304] Salt was indeed a major contributor to the building of the Royal Albert Hall. However this statement in BALG implies that Salt's purchase of a box was in addition to another contribution which he made. A search of RAH archives has failed to reveal any record of a contribution other than the purchasing of ten seats at £1,000, which is recorded in a list of subscribers dated 1st May, 1866. In this list Salt is identified as one of many vice presidents, the president being HRH The Prince of Wales. Acquisition of Grand Tier Box 23, containing the ten seats, was certificated on 31st March, 1870. A good account of the history of the RAH, particularly of its financing, is available. In this account, Salt is identified as an "irrepressible optimist" for his support of the project (Ref: RAH, p20). One of the ways in which the building of the RAH was financed was through a unique arrangement whereby purchasers of the boxes were to be "entitled" to retain their seats throughout the Hall's 999 year lease (or until they sold their interest in the meantime). The destiny of Grand Tier Box 23 can be traced through RAH archives. Following Salt's death in 1876, ownership of the lease passed to his son-in-law Henry Wright (who lived in Kensington, within a few hundred yards of RAH); following Wright's death in 1893 ownership of the box passed to the latter's widow Amelia (Salt's eldest daughter). The box eventually passed out of the family's possession in 1895, around the time that Amelia moved from the Kensington home to live in Tunbridge Wells (see Appendix 3). The box contained ten seats, and Salt had originally put his name down for these ten seats "to be endowed for the use of his firm, and persons employed at Saltaire when they come to London" (Ref: RAH, p20). Salt's will is silent on the issue.

court-dress and sword were never assumed again.

When in London, he stayed at Thomas's Hotel,[305] where, on one occasion, he had a severe attack of illness. Happening to be in town, we visited him, and spent some time with him alone; on rising to leave he said, "Let us have prayer before you go." On Sundays he generally attended Westminster Chapel, (the Rev. Samuel Martin's); occasionally he went to Surrey Chapel,[306] of which the Rev. Newman Hall was then the minister, and whose noble efforts in the erection of Christ Church received his liberal support. Once he worshipped at the Metropolitan Tabernacle, and was much impressed with a sermon by the Rev. C. H. Spurgeon; but as his hearing had become impaired, it was a strain to listen to a discourse throughout, yet he eagerly watched the countenance of the preacher with manifest sympathy.[307]

During his autumnal visits to Scarborough he was seldom absent from the services of the South Cliff Church, both on weekdays and Sundays; once only was he late, and then from no fault of his own. He joined heartily in the singing, and his attitude was ever that of profound reverence. Once a prayer-meeting was held at the close of an evening service, at which he was unable to remain. On proceeding to his hotel afterwards, we found him with his Bible open before him, and as he closed it when we entered, he said "I could not remain at the prayer-meeting, but I have remembered you here." From frequent attacks of gout, his walking powers became considerably impaired, so that a drive or a stroll on the Esplanade was as much as his strength would allow; but there were many incidents in his daily life there which are interesting to recall, and which

---

[305] Thomas's Hotel stood in Berkeley Square, Murray's *Handbook to London As It Is, 1879* describing it as "well managed".

[306] Surrey Chapel, now demolished, stood in Blackfriars Road at its junction with Charlotte Street, on the south side of the river.

[307] The Metropolitan Tabernacle is at the Elephant and Castle, Newington Butts, London. At the time BALG was written, the Tabernacle had been recently built (1859–1861) to accommodate the huge congregations drawn by the charismatic Baptist minister Spurgeon. The main hall accommodated 6,000, with a lecture hall and schoolroom accommodating a further 900 and 1,000 respectively. Contemporary reports of gatherings describe scenes in which throngs of worshippers packed not only the Tabernacle but also the areas around the building to catch his words (DNB). The chapel was rebuilt following a fire in 1892, and then destroyed through enemy action in 1941. The present day chapel results from a rebuild in 1959, but the magnificent portico remains a truly impressive reminder of the Tabernacle's heyday.

illustrate his character and disposition. It was a diversion to him to visit the fish-market, and there purchase the necessary supplies for the table. On one occasion he was accosted by a fishwoman and asked to buy a fine cod, but having forgotten his spectacles, he made this the excuse for declining to purchase it. The woman, not willing to lose a good customer, offered to lend her own, which offer was readily accepted, and a bargain followed; but he forgot to return the borrowed spectacles, and quietly walked away. Imagine the sequel! The fishwoman hurrying after him, and claiming her property, which he was unconsciously carrying off on his nose! Another of his characteristics by the seaside was the interest he took in the children. A certain confectioner's shop in the town was frequently visited, and such "good things" as would please the young people, were purchased in considerable quantities. These he would not only send to those he knew, but even the children of strangers had a share in his kindness! He always remembered "The Fifth of November," and regularly sent a donation to certain boys in whose pyrotechnic demonstrations he was particularly interested. But, perhaps, his chief enjoyment at Scarborough was the quiet evenings spent with his family, and a few intimate friends around him; then he would freely join in conversation, or take part in any social games that were introduced. As the time for evening prayer approached, the present writer was generally expected, and when the usual hour arrived, pastime was suspended or terminated for the evening, and all gathered around the family altar.

In the autumn of 1872, an event occurred that affected not only his own heart, but, still more so, the heart of his eldest daughter, who became engaged to Henry Wright,[308] Esq., J.P., of London. Miss Salt had been, for several years, brought into closest intercourse with her father, not only as his confidential secretary, but by her loving ministrations in his times of sickness, so that the prospect of losing her presence and valuable help, seemed like parting with his "right hand." We question whether on any other occasion his character stands out more nobly than it did in this. When he had satisfied himself that her suitor was, in all respects, worthy of the affections of his daughter, he cordially

---

[308] Henry Wright played a significant role in Salt's story, and an account of his life and role is included in Appendix 3.

welcomed him into the family, and readily sacrificed all personal considerations, that their happiness might be promoted. When the time of their marriage approached, he took a journey to London, to visit her future home,[309] and to see that nothing was wanting for her comfort. After an inspection of the interior arrangements, he entered the dining-room to rest; at that moment a favourite canary struck up a song, as if in the secret of the visit. Turning towards the songster, he playfully said, "Well, you seem to be saying, 'What do you think of it all?'" The marriage, which was celebrated shortly after, was the answer to the imaginary question. The happy event took place at Lightcliffe Congregational Church, on the 2nd of April, 1873, when the Rev. Thomas Binney and the Rev. J. Thomson performed the ceremony. An incident occurred in connection with it which revealed the heart of the father, on an occasion so trying to himself. To the question "Who giveth this woman," Sir Titus replied, "I do, with all my heart" So the days of rejoicing and parting came, and she, who had been her father's helper, went forth leaning on the arm of a husband, to whom she was united, not only by the bond of marriage, but by another, that even death cannot sever.[310]

Henceforth, a visit to London, by Sir Titus, was invested with an interest it had not possessed before. Instead of sojourning at Thomas's Hotel, there was a home at Kensington, to which two hearts were ever glad to bid him welcome;

---

[309] The home was at 22, Upper Phillimore Gardens, Kensington (Ref: KenN, 12th August, 1893). This fashionable part of west London had recently been developed, and in a particularly attractive way, immediately adjacent to Holland Park. The house still stands, in a still fashionable part of the city. It remained the home of Mr. and Mrs. Wright until the death of the former in 1893.

[310] It is noteworthy that this is the only account given in BALG of the marriages of the children of Sir Titus. Even the 1866 marriage of Titus Jr. to Catherine Crossley – a union between two of the most distinguished families in mid Victorian West Yorkshire, and with both families being very committed supporters of the Congregational church – is not mentioned in BALG. Balgarnie's decision to provide an account of Amelia's marriage may be partly due to its relatively recent occurrence when Balgarnie was writing the biography, and to Amelia's special role as her father's confidential secretary, but it is probably in part also a reflection of Balgarnie's own satisfaction at the match. Henry Wright's standing in the Congregational movement was very high. Balgarnie and Wright worked together on London based enterprises such as the London Missionary Society, and, particularly at the time of Balgarnie's writing the biography, on the Memorial Hall project in Farringdon Street (see Appendix 5). Wright was also a frequent visitor to Scarborough, and he presided over the semi-jubilee celebrations of Balgarnie's ministry there (Ref: Balg1).

and of whose hospitality he once facetiously remarked, "I prefer 'Henry's Hotel' to any other." Under the guidance of his son-in-law, he became acquainted with various localities of interest in the metropolis unknown to him before, and of religious and benevolent institutions with whose names he had long been familiar, and which had often been the recipients of his generous help. Among these was the Memorial Hall, Farringdon Street, in which he was much interested. One Sunday morning, when unable to attend public worship, he spent the time in reading the *London City Mission Magazine,* which Mrs. Wright had placed on the table. The nature of the work carried on among the poor of the metropolis, as therein described, deeply affected him. In the course of the day, he said to Mr. Wright, holding up the magazine, "Do you know anything about this work? I should like to send a cheque for £100 to it tomorrow, if you will take it for me." A similar incident took place in the Paris Exhibition of 1867, where Mr. Hawke had a stand for the distribution of the Scriptures in various languages. Sir Titus was much interested in witnessing the eagerness of foreigners to possess a portion of God's Word. He went up to the proprietor and said, "I am just going to the hotel to pay my bill; when that is settled, I should like to give whatever money I have over, to this good work." He soon returned, and handed £50 to Mr. Hawke, although only a few months previously he had forwarded £100 for the same object.

Perhaps no religious work in his own neighbourhood enlisted his sympathies more than the Bradford Town Mission,[311] and the Bible-women. The latter movement was originated seventeen years ago, by Miss Helen Taylor, well-

---

[311] Bradford Town Mission was instituted in January 1850, with Salt as its founding treasurer, a post he held until March 1853, when he stood down, being replaced by Samuel Smith. From the outset, Salt subscribed £50 annually, and also made incidental donations to the organization. The object of the Mission was "to extend the knowledge of the Gospel, irrespective of peculiar tenets in regard to church government, among the inhabitants of Bradford and its vicinity (especially the poor) by domiciliary visits for religious conversation and reading the Scriptures; etc, etc.....". The town was divided into districts, within which paid agents, under the direction of a superintendent, would carry out the work of the mission. Agents had to be of suitable evangelical character, with evidence of personal piety. By 1859, missionaries were deployed in six districts, with a further 11 districts designated, awaiting funds. The six districts were Otley Road, George Street, Broomfields, Manchester Road, Silsbridge Lane and White Abbey. Twenty five years after its founding, Salt was still supporting the venture, as were many other familiar civic figures. From 1869 onwards the three sons George, Titus Jr. and Edward were also subscribers (Ref: BfdTM).

known for her benevolent exertions on behalf of the poor. But her good work seemed, at one time, paralysed for want of funds. Happening to meet Sir Titus, she told him her dilemma. But, as he had never heard of "Bible-women" before, he begged her to come to his house, and give him more information about them. As the best method of shewing the nature of the work, she read to him a few extracts from the journal of one of the "Bible-women," known as "Ruth." As he listened, tears were in his eyes, and at the close, he said to Miss Taylor, "That's a good work, go on, I'll help you." And he was as good as his word; for not only did he pay all the expenses of the first year's domestic mission, but, from first to last, he manifested, in various ways, a peculiar interest in this simple, humble agency. He believed in the power of Christian sympathy, and rejoiced to hear from year to year, of the increase of these messengers of mercy, to the homes of sadness and sorrow. Once, every year, the Biblewomen were most heartily welcomed to Crow Nest, and most hospitably entertained at his table; and those who have been present, will never forget his thoughtful kindness on these occasions; making every arrangement for their enjoyment, and doing everything in his power to make their visit a happy and refreshing one. He always sent his carriage to the station to meet them, and, on their arrival, they were as warmly welcomed by himself and family, as if they had been the most distinguished visitors. He has frequently entertained at his table noble guests, but never did he look happier than when surrounded by his ten humble friends. When the day's pleasure was over, and his carriage was waiting at the door to take them to the Station, he shook hands with each, giving them a large bouquet of flowers to cheer them in their own homes. "Ruth" was his special Bible-woman. She was supported entirely by him, and greatly valued for her faithful service. Almost the last money given by him was sent to her. Having heard that she had overworked herself, and gone to the seaside for rest and change of air, he sent her a five-pound note to defray the expenses of her journey. There are many instances of his attachment to Christian ministers, and his sympathy with them in their work. A fund having been opened for aged ministers, called "The Pastors' Retiring Fund,"[312] he forwarded to the treasurer the sum of £1,800.

---

[312] The Pastors' Retiring Fund was a fund maintained within the Congregational movement. Typical yearly payments to recipients would be approx. £20, so Salt's donation was quite

It may truly be said that as the close of life drew nearer, he seemed more desirous to compress into it a greater amount of work for God and man; for he well knew that "the night cometh when no man can work." Hence his liberality still more abounded; as being the only way left by which he could work. He was determined that what property he had at his disposal, should not be bequeathed, but given; not taken, after death, from his cold grasp, but that his own heart and hand, stirred with the warmth of life and love, should present it while living. One of his latest benefactions was the promise of £11,000 to provide two scholarships for boys, of £120 each, at the Bradford Grammar School, and two of £100 each available for girls.

Having long held the opinion that the support of religion should be entirely voluntary,—that the patronage and control of the State militated against its spiritual power,—that for any particular church to be established by law was equivalent to a monopoly, which was unjust in itself, and inimical to religious liberty,—that the appointment of bishops by a political minister, and their sitting in Parliament, were foreign to the genius of Christianity; he was, therefore, heartily in favour of every legitimate means to bring the union between Church and State to an end. He had helped in his day to abolish monopoly in trade; he had lived to see a mighty impulse given to the commercial life of the country, when trade was left to itself; and he confidently believed that were the Church of England also free, it would give new impulse to her usefulness, and to the spiritual life of the nation. It was, therefore, not merely on religious grounds, but as a man of business, that he supported the Liberation Society,[313] and latterly gave to it the sum of £5,000.

We have had ample evidence of his sympathy with seafaring men. Another instance may be mentioned. Hearing of disastrous shipwrecks on the east coast, he offered a lifeboat, but as each station was at that time supplied, it was sent to

---

appreciable.
[313] The Liberation Society had been founded in 1844 and operated alongside the great evangelical societies of the 19th century such as the London Missionary Society, the Bible Society and the Anti-Slavery Society.

Stornoway,[314] where it is still in use and known as the "Saltaire Lifeboat."

During the last few years of his life, he was unable, from physical infirmities, to take that prominent part in local politics to which he had been accustomed. Yet, his attachment to his former principles never wavered. The Liberal party ever regarded him as a tower of strength, when those principles had to be vindicated. In 1869, a vacancy occurred in the representation of the borough, by the decision of Baron Martin, touching one of the recently-elected members.[315] The election that ensued found Sir Titus at his post; he was chairman of Mr. Miall's committee, and the triumphant return of that gentleman to Parliament was, to him, a matter of great satisfaction, from the similarity of their views on ecclesiastical questions. At the general election in 1874, his physical strength was so much impaired, that all public excitement had to be avoided, but he watched the issue of it with intense interest. His old political friend, Mr. Forster, seemed to him, by his great Education Bill, to be putting fresh facilities into the hands of the State Church clergy for controlling popular education.[316] This opinion was shared by a large portion of the Liberal party in Bradford, and throughout the country generally, and produced a spirit of antagonism among political friends, who had hitherto acted in concert. It also evoked strenuous

---

[314] BALG identifies Stornoway as the site of the lifeboat. However, in the present day, a plaque on the wall of Stromness lifeboat station states that at that site the Saltaire Lifeboat was first launched on 6th October, 1868. A model of the lifeboat remains on display in Victoria Hall; its accompanying plaque also quotes the site to be Stromness.

[315] BALG's euphemism hides a real drama. The "decision of Baron Martin" refers to the unseating of H.W. Ripley as M.P. following the successful petitioning against the result of the election which had seen Ripley appointed, on the grounds of unfair practices (bribery). Mr. Baron Martin presided in the Court-house in Hall Ings, Bradford, when the petition was heard. What is of particular note in the context of BALG, and which may help explain the author's diplomacy, is that one of the petitioners against Ripley was Titus Salt Jr. Ripley had recently moved his religious affiliation from Congregationalism to Anglicanism and had stood in the election as an independent Liberal against the Liberal Electoral Association candidates supported by Salt. As BALG goes on to explain, the unseating of Ripley at this stage led to a further election in which Miall, the Liberal Electoral Association candidate, was elected. (Refs: GtPat, pp329–332; BO, 30th April, 1881). Relationships between Salt and Ripley must have been severely strained by these events, but it is reported that personal friendships seem to have survived (Ref: GtPat, p68). As BALG goes on to explain, Ripley's political fortunes were subsequently revived, and in 1874 we find Ripley, as M.P., speaking in praise of Salt at the unveiling of a statue erected in his honour – see Chapter XVIII.

[316] There was in fact an exchange of correspondence on the subject between Salt and Forster in the *Bradford Observer*, the tone of which is sharp.

opposition to the return of Mr. Forster and Mr. Ripley, whose views on this question were considered identical. Notwithstanding the opposition, both these gentlemen were successful. We refer to these incidents, as illustrative of the character of Sir Titus; whatever were his principles in politics or religion, he stood up for them at any personal sacrifice; but when the strife was over, he was too generous to cherish other than feelings of respect for those who conscientiously differed from himself.

His large subscriptions and donations to public charities placed in his hands a considerable amount of patronage, in the way of voting. At the election of applicants for admission into the Hull Orphanage or the Lancaster Idiot Asylum, his interest in any particular case generally secured its election. In view of the occasion, he was frequently inundated with letters, but the applications that received his sympathy and help were the most deserving, whom he selected after careful deliberation. As a liberal subscriber to the *British Workman*,[317] he received 400 copies monthly of that publication, which were sent to the Bradford Town Mission, for distribution. From the Tract Society he received a large monthly supply of tracts, which willing hands circulated for him. As for books and pamphlets, the variety and number which he gave away were remarkable; for when he invested in literature, it was not on the scale of ordinary purchasers, but with a liberality that testified his gratitude to the authors, and his desire to benefit others by the promulgation of their opinions.

Thus, the evening of his life was spent in doing good, and by his deeds we know his life.

> He liveth long, who liveth well,
> All other life is thrown away;
> He liveth longest who can tell
> Of true deeds truly done each day.[318]

---

[317] The publication sought to educate and improve the lot of "the British workman".
[318] Thought to be the words of Horatius Bonar (1808–1889). A Scottish preacher and hymn writer, Bonar had, in the controversy known as the "Great Disruption" in May 1843, left the Church of Scotland's General Assembly and helped form the new Free Church of Scotland.

CHAPTER XVIII.

How wise, a short retreat to steal,

The vanity of life to feel,

And from its cares to fly;

To act one calm, domestic scene,

Earth's bustle and the grave between,

Retire, and learn to die!

—HANNAH MORE.[319]

BIRTHDAY FETE AT CROW NEST—DESCRIPTION OF IT—SPEECH OF SIR TITUS SALT—ERECTION OF THE SALT STATUE—INAUGURATION BY THE DUKE OF DEVONSHIRE—TESTIMONY BY S. MORLEY, M.P., LORD F. CAVENDISH, M.P., JOHN CROSSLEY, M.P., AND H. W. RIPLEY, M.P.—MEDAL STRUCK—ERECTION AND OPENING OF SALTAIRE SUNDAY SCHOOLS.

IN this chapter, three events in the life of Sir Titus Salt will be noticed, as, perhaps, the most important of his closing years.[320] These were, the celebration of his seventieth birthday; the erection of his statue; and the opening of the new Sunday-schools at Saltaire. The birthday anniversary had often been celebrated in the bosom of his family; but on this occasion he had a desire, once more to gather his workpeople around him, that they might share his joy, and partake of his hospitality. Such a desire seemed all the more natural, inasmuch as this period was also the twentieth anniversary of the opening of Saltaire. Festivities had frequently been held since the memorable banquet of 1853; numerous gala days and excursions had been given to the workpeople, amongst which was one

---

[319] Hannah More (1745-1835) was a playwright and educator, and a member of the Clapham Sect. The latter campaigned on several social issues including slavery, prison reform and poverty. Her publications included *Cheap Repository Tracts*.

[320] The events described in this chapter relate to the period mid 1873 through to mid 1876.

to the Manchester Art Treasure Exhibition;[321] but the one that took place on the 20th of September, 1873, far exceeded in magnitude that of 1856, and was emphatically the climax of all. The number of guests on this occasion amounted to 4,200; three special trains being chartered to convey them from Saltaire to Crow Nest. It was in the higher part of the grounds that the *fete* was held. Three bands of music occupied the stands, around which crowds were gathered. But there were other attractions provided. A portion of the park was set apart for the well-known exhibition of "Punch and Judy," which, though intended for children, drew around it others of a "larger growth". Another enclosure was devoted to athletic sports, which consisted of high jump, hurdle, and sack races, etc. All kinds of gala games were indulged in, and now and then an extemporised dancing party was got up, so provokingly merry was the music. There were present, managers, clerks, weavers, woolsorters, spinners, engine-tenters,[322] and messengers; but they all had such a respectable appearance, that it was impossible to say to what particular occupation anyone belonged. At two o'clock dinner took place, in an immense tent, formed in the shape of the letter T, (like "the works" of Saltaire), and which covered 4,200 square yards. The tables were 1,188 yards in length, and the sitting accommodation double that length, or, nearly a mile-and-a half. Joints of beef, weighing in all 2,600lbs., were placed at equal distances, the intervening spaces being filled with cakes and fruit in rich profusion; while tea-urns and crockery were there in sufficient quantities to stock a dozen ordinary shops. Sir Titus and his family took their seats at the central table, and the whole assembly rose at the preconcerted sound of a bugle, and sang grace with a fervour which was thrilling.

When the meal was concluded, one of the workmen stood up and said they were celebrating two most important events: one being the twentieth anniversary of the opening of Saltaire. When it was commenced it was thought that works of such magnitude went beyond all bounds of prudence and

---

[321] The Manchester Art Treasures Exhibition (formally the Art Treasures of the United Kingdom) opened in a custom-built pavilion at the Botanical Gardens, Old Trafford, Manchester in 1857. Opened on 5th May by Prince Albert, the exhibition was a great popular hit, and Salt was by no means the only textiles employer to have his workers visit it (Refs: GU, AofM). Salt's workers outing took place on 19th September (Ref: GtPat, p315).
[322] An engine-tenter in this context is judged to refer to the operator of a machine which stretches cloth whilst drying.

moderation. From the commencement to the present time, Saltaire had gradually increased, and now it was one of the most complete industrial establishments in the world—there was only one Saltaire! The other event was the seventieth anniversary of their worthy employer, Sir Titus Salt, Baronet. "In the name of your employés, then," (addressing Sir Titus,) "I wish you may be long spared to live amongst us, and that you may see the return of this day many and many times. On behalf of your workpeople, let me return you their most sincere thanks for the kind, hospitable, and courteous manner in which you have entertained us this day." An eye-witness thus describes the sequel :—"When Royalty and loyalty occasionally meet together in the streets of large cities, there may be something in the way of cheering that will correspond in loudness with the cheering of those workpeople; but, for downright heartiness, commend us before all to such manifestations as those which startled the birds at Crow Nest on this occasion. Well might the united bands, at this moment, chime in with the feelings of the people, and play 'The Fine Old English Gentleman'; only, instead of thinking of the founder of the feast of 'the olden time' as the song has it, they were enabled to claim him as essentially of the *present* time."

Struggling to control the emotion so natural at such a moment, Sir Titus replied :—"I am exceedingly glad to see all my workpeople here to-day. I like to see you about me and to look upon your pleasant and cheerful faces. I hope you will all enjoy yourselves this day, and all get safely home again without accident after your day's pleasure. I hope to see you many times yet, if I am spared; and I wish health, happiness, and prosperity to you all.

"If I am spared!" The infirmities of age were then coming upon him, and though the warmth of his heart was as strong as ever, he knew that it did not become him to speak confidently of the coming years.

My birthday! What a different sound,
That word had in my youthful ears;
And now each time the day comes round,
Less and less white its mark appears.[323]

---

[323] The words are those of Thomas Moore, Irish poet (1779-1852).

The second event of this period, was the erection, in Bradford, of a public statue. It was the custom of the ancients, not to sacrifice to the gods until after sunset; and it has not been the custom to erect statues to men, until their sun has set. But to this, there are, in our day, a few well-known exceptions, and chiefly of men renowned for their military achievements. It was as a great captain of industry, a leader in commercial enterprise, a distinguished citizen, and a benefactor of his fellow-men, that this honour was paid to Sir Titus Salt during his lifetime. The project was conceived two or three years before it was brought to a consummation; and, the shape it took, from the first, rendered perfect concealment from him, whom it was thus intended to honour, almost impossible.

A circular, headed "The Salt Statue," had been sent to all his friends, which, at last, came under his own notice. He read it attentively and then returning it, quietly added, "So they wish to make me into a pillar of Salt!"

But, before the committee could proceed further, it was necessary to communicate their intention to Sir Titus, himself, and a personal interview with him was solicited. That interview will never be forgotten by those who were present. Great as their admiration for him had hitherto been, they felt they had only begun to learn his true worth. His modesty and genuineness were so transparent, that they felt constrained to exert themselves all the more, to give effect to their wishes. But we prefer to give the words of the chairman, (Mr. Vickerman,)[324] in reference to that interview :—

---

[324] We judge this to be John Vickerman (1816?–1888), and his appointment as chairman of the "statue committee" is of interest. Vickerman was a Bradford yarn merchant, having come to Bradford from his native Chickenley, near Dewsbury, as a young man. Early in his career he had worked as a junior clerk at the Bradford Post Office, at a time when the main postal business of the town was still conducted through a sliding panel of a window in Union Passage (a passage which led from the town's Kirkgate into the Post Office Yard of the time). Vickerman subsequently became first cashier and then buyer for Messrs. Semon, Siltzer and Co. (stuff merchants), prior to his involvement with John Vickerman and Co. (yarn merchants). A Liberal, he was noted for his philanthropic and social activities, and also had a long association with the Bradford Festival Choral Society. His obituary records that although "in no sense a prominent townsman" his pleasant, cheery character "attached to him many friends" (Ref: BO, 6th March, 1881, p7); such status and characteristics would probably have marked him well as an appropriate person to chair the committee in question.

THE SALT STATUE,

BRADFORD

One of our number was deputed to introduce the subject, and was instructed to let it be clearly understood that our purpose was taken, and that the intention *would* be proceeded with. Sir Titus, while displaying considerable emotion, resolutely refused to sanction the movement, and pleaded most earnestly that we would abandon our plan. We assured him that we had taken our resolution; and were well aware, that to erect a statue during the lifetime of a man, was somewhat unprecedented. But, that we had the feeling, that it was not without its disadvantages to the people generally, when men of sterling worth and principle were first allowed to pass away, without any recognition by those with whose interest and welfare they had been associated. Our efforts to induce Sir Titus to sanction the movement were, however, altogether useless; and when, at length, we said that our resolution was determinedly fixed, he then implored us, to permit him to die before our plans were made known. To this request, we felt constrained to offer what resistance was possible. And, ultimately, Sir Titus, at our urgent request, engaged to remain quiet, and not publicly announce that the movement had not his sympathy.

The sculptor selected for the work was Mr. John Adams-Acton, who, on receiving the commission, proceeded to Cararra, in order to obtain a piece of marble, similar in quality to that out of which he had previously carved the statue of Mr. Gladstone, in his robes as Chancellor of the Exchequer. The block secured weighed fourteen tons, and required sixteen horses to convey it from the wharf to the studio.

After many sittings given by Sir Titus to the artist, there came forth from his hand the colossal statue now standing in front of the Town Hall. It represents him in a characteristic attitude; the right arm resting on the chair in which he is sitting, and holding in his left a scroll, on which some lines are drawn, representing the plans of Saltaire. The features of Sir Titus are well brought out; the largeness of his forehead, and amplitude of beard, giving force and dignity to the countenance. The canopy was designed by Messrs. Lockwood and Mawson, and is not only in harmony with the character of the statue, but with the architecture of the Town Hall, to which it appears a suitable adjunct. The base of the canopy is 17ft. square, and upon it rests the base of the statue, 5ft. high. From the four corners of the base, rise grouped shafts of granite, supporting the arches. Over each of the shafts is a crocketted pinnacle, with angular shafts. The canopy itself is composed of four large stones, which form a groined roof, with moulded ribs, and a large pendant cross in the centre. The arches contain statuettes, each with its symbol, representing "Justice," "Prudence," "Temperance," and "Charity"; the whole is surmounted by a spire, 40ft. high. The canopy is enclosed behind with tracery-work, the other three sides being open. The cost of the statue, canopy, &c., was about £3,000, which was raised by subscriptions varying from the child's penny to the maximum, £5.[325]

The unveiling of the statue took place on the 3rd[326] August, 1874, which was a red-letter day in Bradford, being kept as a general holiday throughout the borough. In the procession from the railway station to the statue were His Grace the Duke of Devonshire,[327] attended on one side by the Mayor of Bradford,[328] and on the other by the Lord Mayor of York, preceded by the Saltaire Band. Then followed members of Parliament, mayors of neighbouring towns, ex-mayors of Bradford, the Town Council, private friends &c. Those parts of the speeches delivered on the occasion,
and bearing on the subject before us, we briefly present to the reader.

The Chairman of the Committee said :—

They were met to do honour to one of Bradford's worthiest citizens, and to proclaim that, in the midst of their intensely busy life, which was apt to generate selfishness, they could admire those in their midst whose career had been a long one of unsullied honour—whose wealth had been spent in high and worthy objects— whose modesty of disposition and strength of character are worthy of imitation by the rising business men of the town, and whose faithfulness to the principles which have guided them have been most unswerving. It was to witness the unveiling of the statue of a man pre-eminently distinguished in these respects that they were now assembled.

---

[325] Presumably in setting this maximum, the committee was seeking to ensure that the statue would be, and would be seen to be, the result of popular subscription, and not the result of largess by a small number of wealthy supporters. The committee must have been confident of the outcome – a reflection of Salt's standing in the community.

[326] This date is incorrect; the correct date was 1st August, 1874 (a Saturday). Not only is this earlier date quoted in other publications, it is confirmed by newspaper reports. An extensive biographical account of Salt appeared in the Saturday edition of the *Bradford Observer* and its Monday edition carried an account of the unveiling (Refs, respectively: BO, 1st August, 1874, p7; BO, 3rd August, 1874, p3).

[327] William Cavendish, 7th Duke of Devonshire.

[328] The mayor of Bradford at this time was Manoah Rhodes (Ref: Cud3, p200).

After giving an account of the rise and progress of the movement, the Duke of Devonshire was requested to unveil the statue. His Grace, having withdrawn the covering, said :—

He had gladly undertaken to unveil the statue of their distinguished fellow-townsman; distinguished by his enterprise as a manufacturer, and more distinguished by his enlightened regard and solicitude for the welfare of those employed by him. But he could not consider that the noble example of Sir Titus Salt was a matter that concerned Bradford only; or, even Yorkshire only. It was a matter of national and of general interest. Englishmen were sometimes spoken of, as if they were so immersed in matters of business, or so engrossed in the pursuit of wealth, as to be insensible, in a great degree, to claims of a higher and nobler kind. But such an assertion was a great calumny against the national character. Very much had been done, both by public and private enterprise, to elevate the moral and physical condition of the entire community. But it would be impossible to name any more remarkable instance of plans wisely and systematically devised, and successfully and energetically carried into execution, for the well-being, the happiness, and the moral advancement of the population, than was to be found in what may be truly called the model town of Saltaire. They would not find there any dark or noisome alleys, or any of those abominations that disgrace the civilisation of the present century. As for the factory, its construction was very different from other buildings of that description. It afforded a most favourable example, of what could be done in the way of combining architectural grace with purposes of utility. Beauty is, in itself, and in its indirect consequences, to be preferred to ugliness; and a debt of gratitude was due to those who gave an example of the former, rather than of the latter. The people of Saltaire have had ample provision made for their comfort and well-being in their dwellings, gardens, baths and washhouses, park, almshouses, infirmary, schools, and institute. He would congratulate the people of Bradford, on having shewn in so marked a way, their appreciation of the great services of Sir Titus Salt. They had taken the best means in their power to guard against the possibility of those great services being hereafter forgotten, by erecting a statue to his honour. No doubt there were other forms of memorial which have their recommendation; but, after all, it appeared to him, that this, which is the oldest, is also the most proper form in which distinguished and eminent men, and the good they have done in their day and generation, can be handed down to posterity.

Mr. Morley, MP., said

It might be asked why he, connected all his life with London, and having no direct communication with Bradford, should be present on this occasion; but he represented this feeling,— that the honour they were doing that day to Sir Titus Salt was shared by thousands of persons not connected with the town. During the last forty years, in all those great conflicts during which great principles had been established, which had promoted liberty of person, liberty of opinion, greater domestic comfort,—in all these undertakings there was not a man in England who had taken a more earnest, more continuous, or more liberal part than Sir Titus Salt. He was here to thank him for the stimulus of a noble example, and to express his thankfulness for this—that there is not a home in Great Britain that is not happier, more pure, with more comforts in it, owing to the continuous and earnest efforts made by enlightened and earnest men, amongst whom Sir Titus Salt had always held a prominent position. There had never been an object presented to him that could tell in any way upon the well-being either of his neighbours or fellow-countrymen, which had not found in him a readiness to give either personal service or pecuniary help to the fullest extent required; and, therefore, he was entitled to the fullest expression of public gratitude, and their desire was, even while he is living, to show him that they were not unmindful of the services he had bestowed. In this money-loving and wealth-acquiring age, it was refreshing to find a man possessed of means, and glad of opportunities—almost thinking it a favour when opportunities were put before him—for dispensing the wealth which in so large a measure God had given him, as the result of his own intelligent efforts. He might add that, as by conviction, and in obedience to conscience, Sir Titus Salt was a Nonconformist, he had never confined his princely liberality within the narrow limits of a mere sect, but had been ready, with a liberality of spirit which had always done him honour, to promote the erection of churches and schools, and the promotion of any organisation whatever which, by God's blessing, might tell upon the material, social, and, above all, the religious well-being of the people among whom he has lived. There were thousands now before him, each one of whom might take a lesson from the life of this distinguished man. They might depend upon it that, when the history of England came to be written, a very substantial chapter would be given to the class of men of whom Sir Titus Salt was a distinguished ornament, and who, by personal sympathy and continuous earnest effort, have contributed so largely to the good work that has been done during the last forty years. There was need when such men were advancing in years, or passing away, for an accession of fresh men to come forward, to carry on the work that had been so nobly begun. He commended, with all his heart, the example of Sir Titus Salt's life to the imitation of every inhabitant of the town.

Lord F. Cavendish,[329] M.P., said :—

If they looked around in that prosperous town, and asked who were the men who had made it so prosperous, the answer would be, that to none was it more due, than to Sir Titus Salt, who had first introduced the great trade of alpaca. They honoured the man who had founded a community, which, he ventured to say, was, unequalled, not only in England, but throughout the world; and, whose influence was felt, wherever great industrial enterprises existed. He believed that nothing had been more marked in recent history, than the increased care and solicitude for the welfare of the employed, which had been shewn by the great employers; and one potent cause of this, had been the example of men like Sir Titus Salt. He could but hope, that when that noble site, close to the Exchange and Town Hall, was thronged, as it was every market-day, by busy merchants and manufacturers, they, as they passed by that statue, would remember the example to be learnt from Sir Titus Salt, and would see that their own welfare and good name would be best obtained, by following that example which he had so nobly set.

Mr. John Crossley, M.P., said :—

It had been his privilege, for many years, to be intimately acquainted with Sir Titus Salt, and the more he had known him, the more he had esteemed his high character.

Mr. Ripley, M.P., said :—

He had watched the way in which Sir Titus Salt had conducted first a small business, and then a large one, advancing from one thing to another, until his name became almost of world-wide renown. And, all this had been done by straightforward honesty, probity, and perseverance. These qualities had been an example to many a man standing before him, to persevere in the midst of difficulties. His wealth had been freely used and distributed to promote the comforts and relieve the wants of many thousands of homes.

A gala in Peel Park followed, which was attended by several thousands of

---

[329] Lord Frederick Cavendish was M.P. for North Yorkshire and Brighouse. He was subsequently murdered in Phoenix Park, Dublin in May 1882.

people. The whole was concluded by a display of fireworks, the finest that had ever been seen in Bradford, the finale consisting of a piece of illuminated workmanship shewing the words "Bradford's Gratitude to Sir Titus Salt."

Such is an epitome of the events of that memorable day; and, surely, Bradford, in thus honouring her most distinguished townsman, did honour to herself.[330] As for him to whom this high mark of respect was paid, and concerning whom these eulogiums were spoken, he was at the time quietly pursuing his wonted avocations at Crow Nest, undisturbed by the exciting scenes then transpiring in Bradford. To him the event could not be otherwise than gratifying; but we doubt not that a shadow sometimes crossed his mind, when he remembered that his life-work was well-nigh ended, and the time drawing near "When he should return no more to his house, neither should his place know him any more."

In commemoration of the event a medal was struck, on which was represented the statue, thousands of which were bought by the general public, to be preserved as a memento of him whom the community delighted to honour.

The erection of the Sunday-schools at Saltaire was the last great undertaking[331] of Sir Titus Salt's life. As we have seen in a former chapter, he had been, in his younger days, a Sunday-school teacher; and ever since, his interest in this department of Christian effort was unabated. The Sunday-school anniversary at Saltaire usually brought him from Crow Nest, and in the afternoon service for the scholars, he took special delight. On one of these

---

[330] Perhaps Bradford did less honour to itself in subsequent years. A generation later, the statue was moved from its designated location to its present day location in a north corner of Lister Park. The unveiling ceremony was held on 17th August, 1896, the move being justified on the grounds of the statue in its original position being an obstruction to traffic (Ref: Rob1). The subsequent pedestrianization of the area in the late 20th century did not lead to a return of the statue to its original site. By 1896 the Salt family's fortunes had changed. The ownership of the mill had passed out of the family's hands, Sir Titus and Lady Salt had died, and the surviving sons and daughters of the family had left the area. Only Catherine Salt, widow of Titus Salt Jr., remained (see Appendix 3).
[331] Sadly the Sunday-schools, although the last of the major buildings undertaken in Saltaire by Salt, were to be an early casualty of redevelopment. In 1972 the building was demolished (Ref: SHR, p23). The site is, in the present day, a car park.

occasions he came from Scarborough, and, though at the time, suffering acutely from gout, he would not be persuaded to stay away. It had been represented to him that the premises occupied by the Sunday scholars were inconvenient, he therefore resolved to supply the deficiency. Well he knew, from experience, the great importance of commodious school-rooms, and how much the voluntary service of teachers had a claim on the sympathy and co-operation of Christian men. It is possible, also, that, believing secular education was the more immediate duty of the State, and religious instruction that of the Church, he was anxious that the church at Saltaire should have all needful appliances for the spiritual training of the young. In the erection of these schools Mr. Titus Salt took a leading part; and it afforded the father no small joy to see, not only his son, but his grandsons associated in this good work. The corner-stones were laid on the 1st of May, 1875, by Gordon and Harold Salt,[332] who were presented on the occasion with silver trowels and mallets. Sir Chas. Reed, chairman of the London School Board, presided. The schools stand upon a portion of the allotment gardens, near "the works," having a frontage of 75ft. to Victoria Road, and a considerable depth to Caroline Street. The principal front is of chaste character, and contains two entrances, for boys and girls respectively, with eight circular-headed windows, surmounted by a handsome cornice. On the ground floor there is an assembly-hall, 85ft., by 40ft., from which open ten class-rooms, five on each side, with a vestry and lecture-room in the rear. Running round the assembly-hall is a large gallery, from which open twelve other class-rooms, five on each side, (as on the ground floor), and two of larger size, above the lecture-room. As the scholars assemble, they proceed to their places, either on the ground floor, or the gallery, and in this collective position, they join in the opening and closing services. Accommodation is made for 800 scholars.

It will thus be seen, that the leading idea in the arrangements is, that the teaching shall be carried on in separate rooms; not in one large building, as in most Sunday-schools. The library is placed between the two front entrances, and can thus be reached without disturbing the teachers in their duties. Each class-room is furnished with a small table and chair for the teacher; and the entire

---

[332] The eldest sons of Titus Jr. and Catherine (nee Crossley) Salt, who at this time were aged eight and six respectively.

suite is carpeted with Brussels carpet, which was provided by a special fund, originated by the teachers; in fact, no expense has been spared to render these premises as complete as possible, and they may be justly regarded "The Model Sunday-schools" of the country." Suspended over the eastern gallery, is a life-size portrait of Sir Titus Salt, which was publicly presented by the teachers at the opening ceremony. A magnificent organ-harmonium was also presented by Mr. George Salt. The entire cost of the structure, exclusive of site, was about £10,000. The opening ceremony took place on the 30th May,[333] 1876, in the presence of Sir Titus, Lady Salt, and family; Mr. and Mrs. Wright, Mr. John Crossley, M.P.; Mr. E. Crossley, Mayor of Halifax; Mr. Henry Lee, of Manchester, president of the Sunday-school Union; Alderman Law, &c.

Mr. Titus Salt said :—

It was exactly twelve months since the memorial stones of that building were laid. He was almost tired of hearing about the completion of Saltaire. Six years ago, that consummation was supposed to have been reached, and still it was unfinished. Since that time, however, there had been an educational revolution. School Boards were extending, and the general inclination of elementary education was towards what was the proper condition of things, namely, under the control of the ratepayers. At Saltaire, they had handed over their day-schools to the School Board. But while this was so, it became all the more incumbent upon them, to see to the religious instruction of the young; and, therefore, his father had erected that building, which he thought would be second to none in the kingdom for its own especial purpose. He hoped and believed that the intention of his father, in the erection of that edifice, would be fully realized.

Sir Titus Salt was present, and at his request, his grandchild, Harold Crossley Salt, declared the building open, amid several rounds of cheering. This was the last public ceremony at which Sir Titus was present; indeed, the enfeebled state of his health prevented him remaining until the close of the proceedings. Thus, his work at Saltaire was finished, and as he retired from the scene in which his

---

[333] The date quoted (a Tuesday) is incorrect. The ceremony actually took place on Saturday 29th April, 1876, as reported in a subsequent newspaper account (Ref: BO, 1st May, 1876, p4).

children and grandchildren had taken a prominent part, it seemed almost the fulfilment of a Scripture promise—"Instead of thy fathers shall be thy children: * * I will make thy name to be remembered in all generations."[334]

---

[334] Psalm 45 Verse 16.

CHAPTER XIX.

The death of those distinguished by their station

But by their virtues more, awakes the mind

To solemn dread, and strikes a saddening awe:

Not that we grieve for them, but for ourselves

Left to the toil of life.

—THOMSON.[335]

DECLINE OF HEALTH—PERSONAL APPEARANCE NOW—"THE FATHER OF THE COMMUNITY"—HIS INCREASING GENEROSITY—CHEERING LETTERS—LAST VISIT TO LONDON—INCREASING WEAKNESS—CONVERSATION WITH THE WRITER— ROWLAND HILL'S SOLILOQUY—AS "A WEANED CHILD"—LAST VISIT TO SCARBOROUGH—RETURNS HOME TO DIE—HIS STATE OF MIND IN VIEW OF DEATH—HE PASSES AWAY—NOTES OF THE END.

FROM the beginning of 1876, the health of Sir Titus perceptibly declined. Each attack of illness left him less able to cope with the one that succeeded. Walking exercise became irksome, and was now chiefly confined to the library or garden terrace. Yet occasionally, when he felt a little stronger, he would set out for Saltaire, where an hour or two was quietly spent, after which, he returned home, wearied with the effort. How familiar to the people of Bradford was his well-known figure, clad in the characteristic attire, which for many years had consisted of trousers of Scotch plaid, waistcoat of the same material, with gilt buttons, and a frock coat of black cloth. They might still have recognised in him the same "remarkably intelligent eye" as of old, the calm demeanour, and that somewhat cold exterior, which so often misinterpreted the warmth within. All these features were much the same; but, alas! his bent frame, silvery locks, feeble gait, with hand leaning heavily on a staff, were unmistakable signs that his earthly pilgrimage was drawing to a close. The respect and reverence paid to

---

[335] We presume the writer again to be James Thomson (see Chapter XVI).

him in the streets, was very remarkable. It was as though "the father of the community" was passing by. What rendered this circumstance more worthy of notice was, that he to whom this homage was thus silently paid, seemed perfectly unconscious of it. Perhaps the language of Job, (with some allowance for its oriental imagery,) might appropriately have been put into those lips now sealed in death: "When I went out to the gate, through the city; when I prepared my seat in the street; the young men saw me, and hid themselves, and the aged rose and stood up. The princes refrained talking, and laid their hand on their mouth; unto me they gave ear and waited, and kept silence at my counsel. And they waited for me as for the rain, and they opened their mouth as for the latter rain."[336]

The days at Crow Nest were, sometimes, to him rather monotonous; with his mind still active and alive to all that was transpiring in the busy world, no wonder that he felt the restraints which his bodily infirmities imposed. "The spirit indeed was willing, but the flesh was weak" Still, the numerous letters he received furnished him, during the forenoon, with congenial occupation, in answering which he was assisted by his second daughter.[337] The generosity that had hitherto been so remarkable in him was not in way diminished. Some men in old age have become hard, grasping, and penurious even when in possession of plenty. It was the opposite with Sir Titus Salt; at the close of life his hand was more bountiful than ever, and his heart more enlarged. Nor was this because his mental faculties were weakened. No; but because the light of an Eternal World had fallen upon his spirit, and his sense of responsibility was quickened. He felt that his day was closing, and he must needs work in the lingering light of the setting sun. The last considerable act of generosity, of which we were cognizant, was in the month of April. The annual session of the Yorkshire Congregational Union was then being held at Halifax.[338] A fund was there commenced for the extinction of debts on village churches. When Sir Titus was informed of the

---

[336] Job Chapter 29 Verse 7.

[337] Helen, who had in fact succeeded Amelia as her father's private secretary following the latter's marriage to Henry Wright in 1873 (Ref: Bret2, p45).

[338] Balgarnie himself was actively involved in the session, and also delivered the vote of thanks at the civic reception which took place to mark the occasion (Ref: HalC, 8th April, 1876, p6).

scheme he immediately said, "I should like to help it," and taking out his notebook, he wrote the name of the society, and opposite to it £600. Many such promises payable in two or three years were recorded, amounting to many thousands of pounds, but which he did not live to fulfil. After his decease, it was found that no provision had been made in his will[339] to meet such promises, but the family have generously taken the responsibility upon themselves.

During this time of enforced seclusion, his heart was often cheered by the receipt of various letters expressive of gratitude, from persons whom he had helped in time of need. These letters he highly prized, and many that have come to hand since he passed away, would still more have gladdened him. One writer says :—" For the last fourteen years I had in Sir Titus Salt the best of earthly friends; a friend through whose generous aid I have been enabled to educate myself, and to gain the position I now hold in connection with the public press. It was once my lot to beg my bread as a starving village lad: but Sir Titus Salt, becoming aware of my anxiety to raise myself in the social scale, took the liveliest interest in my progress, and, by God's help, never let go my hand, but was ever ready to help me on my journey."

In the advancement of the sons of widows, of young men studying for the Christian ministry, or starting in business, he always took a deep interest. Many were the letters that came from such during his life and after his decease. A minister thus wrote :—" He is blessed by thousands, and not the least by students and ministers whom he has helped. I am not the only one from Airedale College who is thankful for the help he rendered and the kind way in which it was done."

Yet, it was all the while painfully evident that his physical infirmities were increasing, and the sands in the glass were running out—the more rapidly because they were fewer. In the month of April, he went with Lady Salt and his daughters to Harrogate for change of air, which was the means of reviving him for a while; indeed, so much was he invigorated by it that he was able, in the

---

[339] In July 1876 Salt issued a second codicil to his will, when he made various revisions to provisions relating to his family and his designation of trustees, but he did not use the opportunity to make any provision at that time for the benevolences referred to. In fact Salt's will and its codicils are notably devoid of benevolences to the charities and church bodies he supported so much in his life – see Appendix 5.

following month, to pay a visit to his eldest son[340] at Maplewell, in Leicestershire. Thence he proceeded to London, to spend a few weeks with Mr. and Mrs. Wright. It was to them a cause of rejoicing to have the domestic circle of Crow Nest once more transferred to Kensington; yet this joy was overcast by the feeble appearance of Sir Titus, and especially with his loss of appetite. No wonder, then, that in the midst of their social gathering, fears were awakened, if not expressed, that perhaps this might be his last visit to them. That there were grave reasons for this foreboding soon became evident by symptoms of irregular action of the heart, and the recurrence of fainting attacks, to which he had recently been subject. He had always been averse to medical treatment, except by his own rules, but, in deference to the wishes of the family, an eminent physician was consulted. The opinion then given was so unfavourable, that the journey home was undertaken with much solicitude.

Let us return with him to his Yorkshire home, to see how the few remaining months are passed, and watch the lamp of life as it burns in the socket. Throughout the whole of those months, he was, more or less, an invalid, though it was not always easy for him to be treated as such. Once he ventured with his family to church, but the effort was so exhausting, that henceforth there was no more worship for him in the earthly sanctuary. The church was now to be "in the house". There he had frequent communion with God alone; or, when his pastor visited him, and the family were gathered, a short devotional service was sometimes held. It was our privilege, also, occasionally to see him during those trying months, and to speak words of comfort in his ear. The memory of those visits is precious, and, though almost sacred, we would recall a few incidents connected with them, which indicate the state of his mind in the prospect of death. One evening, when the hour of family prayer arrived, we gave him an arm to the dining-room, and, when expressing a hope that he was a little stronger, he pointed to his shrunken frame and said, "You see I am only now a bag of bones." His chair was so placed in the room that he might hear every word that was read. Sometimes, with his inverted hand behind his ear, his whole countenance evinced intense earnestness; the ejaculatory utterances of his heart were often audible, and his emphatic "Amen" at the close of the prayer, left the

---

[340] William Henry.

impression that he had himself been speaking with God. On another occasion we asked him if his faith in Christ Jesus were firm, his hopes clear, and prospects bright? "No," he said, "not so much as I should like them to be; but all my trust is in Him. He is the only foundation on which I rest. Nothing else! Nothing else!" We encouraged him by saying that his salvation was not dependent upon his feelings; that with his depressing physical weakness, these might fluctuate and change; but "Jesus Christ, the same yesterday, and to-day, and for ever". "*That* is what I want to realise," he said. The answer given was "Cling simply to the Cross, and leave health, life, soul, all, in the Saviour's hand, and this will yield perfect peace"; on which he said, with much calmness, "I can do no more, but leave myself there!" We then repeated the well-known soliloquy of Rowland Hill, shortly before his death,—

> "And when I'm to die,
>
> Receive me, I'll cry,
>
> For Jesus has loved me, I cannot tell why;
>
> But this I do find,
>
> We two are so joined,
>
> He'll not be in glory, and leave me behind."

With these lines he was greatly comforted and cheered. "Are they in print?" he said; "Where can I find them?" If ever mortal man had merited heaven by "good works" it was Sir Titus Salt. But, no! he never referred to anything he had done, or made it a ground of boasting. In the presence of God, and in the prospect of eternity, he appeared as a man stripped of all self-righteousness, and clothed with the righteousness of Christ as his only raiment. Some might regard this as a sign of failing nature. Nay; it was rather the evidence of grace abounding. And when we contrast this humility and self-abasement with the position he had occupied, which was like that of "a king among men," the words of another king seem appropriate, "I have behaved and quieted myself as a child that is weaned of his mother: my soul is even as a weaned child."

But while these spiritual fruits were comforting to those who discerned them, the symptoms of increasing bodily weakness were painfully evident to all. His nights were often sleepless, and as he tossed to and fro, longing for the dawn, he would sometimes sink into a brief slumber. For awhile he was unable to leave his bed till noon, but one morning when we were there, he made an effort to be up early. It was a matter of surprise that he should wish to rise so soon, but the reason was at once apparent. It was to be present at family worship, which now seemed to be his chief pleasure. As he was unable to walk up stairs, he was carried in an invalid's chair by two men-servants: but even in this, his characteristic punctuality was manifest. When the hour of retiring had struck, the order was given to his attendants, and having said "Good night" to his family circle, he was borne away, waving his hand as he disappeared into the hall and up the staircase to his bed-chamber. The remark was once made by a member of the family that no express train could have been started with more regularity and precision than were observed on these occasions.

During the day, when the sun was bright, he was occasionally drawn, along the garden terrace, in a spring carriage, by his beloved daughters, with his devoted wife always by his side. But here, too, another habit would unconsciously assert itself, namely, that of "Commander-in-chief"; for even the control of the vehicle, the spots to be visited, the time to return, were never entrusted to others, but kept under his supreme command.

The month of October was the usual time for the family to visit Scarborough, but owing to the state of the invalid's health, little reference had been made to the subject. What was our surprise, one day, when he seriously said, "Can you find room for us this year at Scarborough?" At first, the proposal was considered by his family as fanciful; but when it appeared as a fixed purpose, his regular medical attendant, (Mr. Charteris,[341]) unwilling to take upon himself the responsibility of such a journey, took the opinion of his former medical adviser and friend (Mr. Scattergood,[342] of Leeds). Their united consent was given to the proposal. In support of this there were two reasons: one being that the sea air might probably give an impetus to the patient's rallying force: the

---

[341] We judge this to be William Charteris, a young surgeon of Hipperholme, a village adjoining Lightcliffe. Born in Dumfriesshire, Scotland he was approx. 37 years old at the time in question. He remained in Hipperholme beyond the turn of the century (Ref: PRO, 1901 Census). Charteris was to be in attendance when Salt died, see Chapter XX.
[342] We judge this to be Thomas Scattergood, who in later years was to became the first Dean of the Leeds Medical School, a post he held until his death in 1900.

other was, that the change was absolutely necessary for Lady Salt, whose long and unwearied vigils had well nigh exhausted her strength; and thus it came to pass that Sir Titus, even in his enfeebled condition, once more visited his favourite watering-place. For many years we had welcomed him on his arrival at the station, but never before in such affecting circumstances as the present. What a change! The strong man had become weak as a child, so that a carriage had to be drawn up close to the train to receive him. In taking this journey his medical attendant accompanied him, which circumstance, together with other particulars connected with his health, were recorded in the daily press; but such was his dislike to read bulletins about himself, that, in deference to his wishes, the reporters abstained from sending them.

The change of scene and air at Scarborough had for a while a beneficial influence, and as his appetite improved, his spirits revived, and when he could be drawn into the sunshine on the Esplanade, a faint hope was awakened that his life might yet be prolonged. Indeed, his local medical adviser at first encouraged that hope, for there was no sign of organic disease, but only of physical exhaustion; alas! the hope was only temporary. What human skill could keep the wheels in motion that had revolved so long? What change of temperature or locality could renovate the frame that had borne such a strain, and was now worn out? One night a terrible storm raged, which violently shook the windows of his apartment, and greatly alarmed the invalid; the cold also chilled him, so that the little strength he had previously gained was soon lost. Then returned those fainting attacks, which again caused great anxiety and indicated to all that a return home was now most desirable. Yet, in the midst of all these anxieties, his mind was calm and his heart kind, he still thought how he might do good. Unable to attend church on "Dispensary Sunday,"[343] he sent £5 to the collection; too weak to visit in person the Cottage Hospital, he forwarded £100 to its funds. Thus closed his last visit to Scarborough. When he left the station, many friends stood at a distance to witness his departure, knowing full well that they "should see his face no more." The arrangements made by the station-master for the comfort of the invalid, in his homeward journey were gratefully appreciated; but

---

[343] Dispensary Sunday was the annual occasion when prayers were particularly given for the sick, and monies collected for local hospitals.

- 232 -

when he entered Crow Nest, he never again crossed its threshold. He had returned to die, and to exchange his earthly abode for "an house not made with hands, eternal in the heavens."

It was well for him that he had nothing to do but to die. As a man of business, he had long before set his house in order, so that no earthly thoughts distracted his mind now. He had no arrears of duties to wipe off; these had received his attention at the right time. He had committed the "keeping of his soul to Him in well-doing, as unto a faithful creator," and now he calmly waited to be gathered to his rest. The season of Christmas was approaching, when the family circle was wont to assemble under the parental roof; but this year how different! On Sunday, the 17th December, 1876, Sir Titus became much worse, and the telegraph summoned his absent children to "'come at once". It was a long "Sabbath-day's journey"[344] to some of them; but one by one they arrived, and, what does not often happen in a large family, none were absent when their father was dying. Yet still he lingered by the margin of the river. We were privileged to see him there. But the stream was not "dark" or "cold", as some have pictured it: and he seemed just waiting for the signal to pass over. We repeated the lines so oft whispered in the ear of the dying :—

> Hide me, O, my Saviour, hide,
>
> Till the storm of life be past;
>
> Safe into the haven guide,
>
> O, receive my soul at last![345]

With his hands clasped in prayer, he said with emphasis, "How kind He is to me". And so we left him! to meet no more on earth. Still he lingered! Sometimes, when unconscious, his thoughts seemed to be running back to early days, and to the companions of his boyhood. A brief note from Crow Nest, dated 24th December, says, "He is still with us, and it may be hours before he joins the host above. Nothing can be taken but the smallest quantities of water. Consciousness remains; weakness increases, but no pain. The earth here wears a white mantle; snow is about four inches deep. A holy calm now reigns within and without" Yet the lagging wheels of nature were slowly moving; the spark of

---

[344] BALG's phraseology is biblical (Acts Chapter 1 Verse 12).
[345] From the hymn *Jesu, Lover of my soul*, by Charles Wesley (Ref: ConCH, p222).

life was flickering in the socket, and loved ones kept fanning it, and watching lest any rude blast should hasten its extinction. But on Friday afternoon, the 29th December, 1876, at twenty minutes to one o'clock, he passed away.[346]

When all was over, a note, written by a member of the family, contained the following :—" He has gone away, from the land of the dying to that of the living. I quoted to him again and again 'I will never leave thee, nor forsake thee'. 'I give unto them eternal life'. 'No man is able to pluck them out of my Father's hands'. 'The Lord is my shepherd, I shall not want'. It was my lot to be almost constantly with him during his last days. I was with him to the last, and when the end had come, I could not help touching his hand and saying, 'Farewell, happy spirit !' with the joyous belief that we shall meet again. Happily, for those who remain, there was no physical suffering, and his breath died away like a soft summer breeze."

> How blest the righteous, when he dies!
> When sinks a weary soul to rest;
> How mildly beam the closing eyes!
> How gently heaves the expiring breast!
>
> So fades a summer cloud away;
> So sinks the gale when storms are o'er;
> So gently shuts the eye of day;
> So dies a wave along the shore.
>
> Life's labour done, as sinks the clay,
> Light from its load the spirit flies;
> While heaven and earth combine to say,
> "How blest the righteous when he dies."[347]

---

[346] The death was registered on 1st January, 1877. The death certificate records the death as occurring in the district of Brighouse, the informant being "W. Charteris, Surgeon" who is recorded as being present at the death. The cause of death is recorded as "Senile Decay Exhaustion", this cause being certified by the same W. Charteris.

[347] Composed in 1844 by William Bradbury (1816-1868). Contained in J. Funk's *Harmonia Sacra,* 12th edition 1867.

CHAPTER XX.

Go to the grave; though, like a fallen tree,
    At once with verdure, flowers, and fruitage crown'd;
Thy form may perish and thine honours lie,
    Lost in the mouldering bosom of the ground; -

Go to the grave; for there thy Saviour lay
    In death's embraces, ere he rose on high;
And all the ransomed, by that narrow way,
    Pass to the eternal life beyond the sky.

               —MONTGOMERY.[348]

PROPOSAL OF A PUBLIC FUNERAL—CORTEGE LEAVING CROW NEST—ITS PROGRESS THROUGH BRADFORD—PUBLIC BODIES REPRESENTED—APPROACHING SALTAIRE—ARRIVAL AT THE CHURCH GATES—BURIAL SERVICE—EXTRACT FROM DR. CAMPBELL'S ADDRESS—FUNERAL SERMONS AT LIGHTCLIFFE AND SALTAIRE—"OUT!"

THE death of Sir Titus Salt was soon flashed throughout the kingdom, and produced deep regret among all ranks and classes. This was strikingly exhibited in various articles that appeared in the daily press. From the London *Times*,[349] to the remotest provincial newspaper, there was hardly one that did not announce his death, and give a brief outline of his marvellous career. As for the town of Bradford, the mournful event cast over it a dark shadow, for the inhabitants felt, that upon them especially, the stroke fell heavily, since their foremost citizen and greatest benefactor was now no more. The great bell of the Town Hall, tolling at intervals, was the voice that expressed the sorrow of the community.

---

[348]Judged to be J. Montgomery (1771–1854), hymn writer.
[349]See issue of 30th December, 1876, p10.

But this was not all. When the news became known that Sir Titus Salt was dead, the Mayor[350] received communications from all quarters, suggesting that a public funeral was due to him who was gone. True, they had conferred upon him, in life, all the honours within their power, but now they would add one tribute more to his Worth. His worship at once addressed a letter of condolence to Lady Salt, by the hands of the Town Clerk, who at the same time conveyed an official request, that the family would kindly permit the public to shew their respect for the deceased in the way that their feelings prompted. It would, no doubt, have been more congenial to the wishes of the family, had all outward pomp been avoided, and that they could have carried their dead to the sepulchre, in the way other mourners have done. But in deference to the general wish, the arrangements, so far as the passing of the cortege through Bradford was concerned, were left in the hands of the Mayor; one proviso only being made, namely, that, as far as possible, everything should be of an unostentatious character.

On Friday, the fifth of January, 1877, the funeral took place, amid such a concourse of people as Yorkshire, or even England, has seldom witnessed. The weather during the week had been unusually severe; the hills and dales in the neighbourhood were covered with snow, which on the previous Wednesday was increased by a heavier downfall that impeded the traffic of the streets, and threatened to mar the well-laid plans for the mournful ceremony. On the Thursday it was necessary to employ hundreds of men to clear the main thoroughfare for three miles, in anticipation of the morrow. But when Friday came, with a magnificent sunrise and a soft breeze, it seemed as if the elements smiled on the bier of him who had often carried sunshine into many a home, and whose life had been signalised by many noble deeds of charity. It was a quarter-past nine in the morning when the funeral left Crow Nest. His attached servants carried the coffin of their late master to the hearse, which, though very handsome, had no funereal plumes and was preceded by a detachment of the West Riding Mounted Constabulary. No mourning coaches were provided; the relatives of the deceased followed the hearse in their own private carriages, seven in number. Outside the grounds of Crow Nest groups of villagers had

---

[350] George Motley Waud (Ref: Cud3, pp209-211).

assembled to pay the last tribute to him whose living presence had been a blessing to them. On reaching the outskirts of Bradford, the great respect in which the deceased was held was at once observable. Shops were closed; window blinds drawn, and even busy manufactories were silent for a while. Manchester Road, on both sides, was thickly lined with people, the crowd becoming more dense as the centre of the town was approached; but it was at the Town Hall where the public bodies assembled, and the procession commenced. The wood pavement in front of the hall had been swept and sanded, and the entire area was kept free of people except for those who had to take part in the ceremony. Policemen bearing printed cards on black staffs, indicated where each of the public bodies had to fall in. The Salt Statue was tastefully draped with black cloth, and on each side were placed immortelles and festoons of laurel leaves, while, inside the railings, evergreen plants were grouped at the base. As eleven o'clock approached, the crowd swelled in volume, and every place from which a sight of the procession could be obtained was occupied; yet the quietness of the scene was broken only by the great bell which boomed out muffled peals at intervals. It seemed as if the well-known punctuality of the deceased was to receive recognition in the arrangements for his funeral, for just as the clock struck eleven, the hearse passed the Town Hall, halting for a moment in front of the statue; then the procession moved off in the following order, preceded by the bands of the Artillery and Rifle Volunteers, alternately playing the Dead March in *Saul* :—Detachment of Police; Second West York Artillery Volunteers; Third West York Rifle Volunteers; Members of the Oddfellows' Society; the Temperance Societies; the United Kingdom Alliance; Band of Hope Union; the Independent Order of Good Templars; the Working Men's Teetotal Association; the Scientific Association; Boards of Health of neighbouring districts; Board of Guardians; Clergy and other Ministers of Religion; Licensed Victuallers; deputations representing the following institutions and public bodies, viz., the Congregational Union of England and Wales, Bradford Ragged Schools, Industrial Schools, Eye and Ear Hospital, Fever Hospital, Nurses' Training Institution, Infirmary, Grammar Schools, Mechanics' Institute, merchants, manufacturers, tradesmen, and shopkeepers, Liberal Club, Hull Sailors' Orphanage, Lancaster Royal Albert

Asylum, Mayors of other towns, and gentlemen representing other bodies than the above, Mayor and Members of the Town Council, Members of Parliament, and, last of all, one hundred and twenty-six private carriages. We give these details as an index of the deep and universal respect of the community for him whose name had long been a household word amongst them.

Such was the *cortege* that passed along the streets on the funeral day! But the long crowd of spectators through which it moved, was, perhaps, a still more impressive tribute of affectionate respect. It seemed as if the entire population had assembled as mourners. Amongst them might be seen old men reverently uncovering as the hearse passed by. Perhaps some of them might be recalling the time when the deceased entered Bradford, unnoticed and unknown. What a contrast! A stranger might have thought a prince had fallen, and the people had come to witness the funeral pageant on its way to the tomb of his royal ancestors. There, too, were men of middle age, who, as they gazed on the spectacle, and remembered the successful career now ended, must have received an incentive in prosecuting their own life work; while mothers might be seen holding up their little children, who were to tell to another generation something of this great sight.

When the boundary of the borough was passed, the Bradford procession officially ended, and that of Shipley and Saltaire began; but many connected with the former proceeded to the destination by another route, and there awaited the arrival of the remains. In the morning of that day, a Sabbath stillness prevailed throughout Saltaire. For once, on a weekday, the powerful engines were motionless, the looms were still, the tide of human life that had daily ebbed and flowed through the gates, was arrested. A greater business was in hand. From the roof of the vast establishment, two flags floated half-mast high, as the symbol of the mournful event that called away the workers from their wonted toils. A like symbol was hoisted from the Park, and the whole aspect of the town conveyed the impression that in every house there was one dead. As for the rows of almshouses. erected by the late baronet, their window curtains had never been raised since the day he died.

Released from their ordinary duties, the inhabitants of Saltaire, attired in the garb of mourning, went forth in a body to meet the *cortege*. The scene from

Shipley to the gates of the church was most touching. Here the more personal character of the loss was apparent, and the expression of sorrow more heartfelt; two streams of mourners now met and commingled, the one, commencing at Crow Nest, the other at Saltaire; the difference being, that while the former mourned for the deceased as the father of their family, the latter sorrowed for him as the father of the community. But there were others in that procession, sharing that sorrow, who represented institutions that had shared his generosity. Amongst these were two groups of orphans that attracted much attention: the one came from the Sailors' Orphanage at Hull, the other from the Crossley Orphanage at Halifax. It was not until one o'clock that the hearse drew up at the church gates, where about 40,000 persons were assembled. Twelve of the workmen who had been longest in the service of the firm carried the coffin up the avenue to the church, preceded by the Rev. D. R. Cowan, the resident minister. Within the edifice were gathered only those whom an official card from the Mayor of Bradford permitted to enter. It was an assembly of representative men, such as are not often brought together. In addition to the mayor and corporation, there were senators and magistrates, merchants and manufacturers, artists and scientists, politicians of different views, and clergy of all denominations; among the latter one figure stood out from the rest worthy of special mention, inasmuch, as while these lines are being penned, his own funeral obsequies are about to be observed at York—one who was not only a personal friend of the deceased baronet, but the unmitred archbishop of Congregationalism in Yorkshire—we refer to the late Rev. James Parsons. All these were gathered on this mournful occasion. When the coffin had been placed in front of the communion-table, the Rev. J. Thomson read a portion of the Burial Service; the present writer led the congregation in prayer; and the Rev. Dr. Campbell[351] delivered the funeral address.

The following is an extract :—

The grave is open, and waiting to receive all that remains to us of the most marked man amongst us; one who has not had his equal in our community; one of the fathers of our people, whose life

---

[351] Rev. Dr. James Robert Campbell was the minister of Horton Lane Chapel, see Appendix 4.

was not hid from us in the mist of distance, either of time or place; who grew with our great growth, of which he was both the symbol and demonstration; was with us and of us, in the industry and ambition of his youth; and has passed from the midst of us in the fruitful plenitude and power of a ripe age. He was our pride and our boast. We are here to bury him. And we all and severally feel, as if by his removal we had this day sunk into the commonplace and mediocrity of a secondary epoch. His life, his influence, his acts of patriotism and benevolence, stretched far and wide; but they never enfeebled, in the least, his attachment to this homestead of his fortunes. Holding a position of wealth and rank, which detaches many from their early connections, his personal interest in his old neighbours was as true, and their claims as binding upon him, in his retirement, as when he was in the thick of the struggle. The inscription on Wren's monument, *Circumspice*,[352] might be fitly borrowed here, where every step of our foot, or glance of our eye, shews some feature of the force and compass of his life. To him, human life to be of any account, meant work, good work, work well-wrought, so as to be sure that it would come to something. I cannot remember his doing anything whatever slightingly. In commercial, social, and political questions, this was his guiding idea—good thorough work. It is a great and worthy thing to have raised a family to wealth and rank; but the house which bears his name, and the town which will long remember him as its pride, will only inherit a shred of the legacy this good and great man has conveyed to them, if they do not find, as he did, that the real fruit and reward of wealth is, to make it work out the happiness of our neighbours. As for his beneficence, it is impossible ever to know it fully. The more conspicuous gifts are but the peaks and higher elevations, bearing but a small proportion to the whole mountain mass. The main part of it is recorded in no register, but is breathed in the still gentle voice of grateful love, which has no chance of being heard amid the thunders of applause. We are mourning a common loss, and it is irreparable. We shall not soon 'look upon his like again.' It is fit that the Worshipful Mayor and Honourable Corporation, and all the leaders of the people, should render honour to one who, in office and out of office, was a wise and gracious ruler of men; that all forms of charity should bear their flambeaux in the vast procession that carries the tried friend of all into the dark tomb; that religion in every form should acknowledge this man, who, with his own special faith, had reverent respect for the sincerity of others; that the poor, the lame, the halt, and the blind should lend their plaintive strains to the common lament. It is now many years since I gathered from himself, a comfortable assurance that his soul rested in that ever-blessed and divine hope of sinful

---

[352] In St. Paul's Cathedral, London, adjacent to the tomb of Sir Christopher Wren (1632-1723) is a tablet inscribed with his epitaph, which ends with the words: "Si monumentum requiris, circumspice" (If you seek his monument, look about you).

and suffering man, the Lord and Saviour Jesus Christ. And but a few days ago, when the dying invalid, with a look of attenuating purity and youthfulness, was visibly passing into the light, he answered me, with that marvellous force of sincerity which marked all his speech, that his full and entire hope was in Christ. We trust in infinite mercy that he now rests with Him. Dear friend! farewell! Go, carry him to his rest. He has done his work grandly! Let him sleep! And let us all and every one pray that when the great reckoning comes, he and we shall have the eager longings of our soul answered by the Lord's approval, "Well done, good and faithful servant, enter thou into the joy of thy Lord."

When the service was over, wreaths of flowers, which loving hands had prepared, were placed on the coffin, which was not removed to the mausoleum until the evening; but even then it was not out of sight. Such was the eagerness of the public to pay their last tribute, to his memory, that the vault was allowed to remain open for several days, during which thousands of persons beheld where they had laid him, and where the remains of three of his children and a daughter-in-law had previously been placed. The annexed illustration gives the interior of the mausoleum, which is a chamber of chaste design, with tinted light, falling from the roof. Underneath this is the vault. A white marble figure represents the Angel of the Resurrection, pointing to a scroll on which is inscribed part of I Cor., XV. Beneath the figure is the memorial tablet of dark granite, which now bears the words, "Sir Titus Salt, Baronet: born September the 20th, 1803; died December the 29th, 1876," while above is the text, "Blessed are the dead who die in the Lord."

On the following Sunday, funeral sermons were preached, in memory of the late beloved baronet, in various churches, both in the neighbourhood and at a distance, irrespective of denomination. At Lightciffe, where the family attended, the Rev. J. Thomson chose as his text Matthew XXV., 21: "His Lord said unto him, Well done, thou good and faithful servant: thou hast been faithful over a few things, I will make thee ruler over many things. Enter thou into the joy of thy Lord." An extract from the discourse will shew the pastor's estimate of the deceased :—

His greatness was the greatness of a great nature rather than of any separate, or showy faculty. There was no meanness or littleness about anything he did. He lifted, by the sheer force of his own greatness, any matter in which he became vitally interested, out of the realm of commonplace, and carried it irresistibly forward to final success. He moved without effort among great undertakings, liberal enterprises, and bountiful benefactions. What he did and gave was from the level in which he lived, and to which other men rise with effort, and only for a time. He could not be said to be a great reader, a great thinker, a great talker, a great expositor. He was better. He was a great man, having in him something responsive to all these forms of greatness; and standing among men, he was seen from afar; his very immobility, for it was the repose of strength, affording that support in trying times, that gave a staying power to the undertakings with which he was identified, and which made them ultimately successful. Men knew always where to find him, and came also to trust that the cause to which he lent his name and influence had some just claims to consideration, and would finally succeed. In his personal friendships, where he trusted, he trusted wholly, and would not soon forsake one to whom he had given his confidence. The rising from one position to another, in the social scale, had no effect on his friendships. The friends of his youth were with him to the close; or, if not, it was they who had fallen asleep, or fallen away from him, and from those noble enterprises to which he had consecrated his strength and resources. He was a pioneer, a creator of the new era. He shewed how the graces of the old feudalism that was being supplanted, could be grafted on and exemplified by the men who brought forth and moulded the better age. No feudal lord could have set open his doors and offered his resources to the retainers of generations, in the way he provided for those that laboured under his directions. The new era had, as it were, from the first, a grace and benevolence that other social forms have never known, or known only in decay; and it owed and owes it to the personal characters of the men who laid its foundations, and not least to him whose removal we deplore. He was always seen to advantage among the people, surrounded by them, making his way among them, and through the path that they, with native courtesy, made for him. He treated them more at last as a benevolent and large-hearted father treats his children, than as an employer treats his servants, or a leader his followers. The grand old chief of the Liberal party, he was never visited by that illumination, that leads backward, nor did he spend one-half of life in undoing and unsaying what the other half had been spent in promoting. No! he went steadily on and forward, and feared not. Good as these things are that have been realised, he believed in a better future yet to be. While a decided and consistent Nonconformist, he was not such by accident, nor with any latent misgiving of purpose. Nonconformity to him meant freedom, breadth, the right of religious life to manifold and various expression, without let or hindrance. He was ready to take his

THE MAUSOLEUM.

full share in the work and the responsibility that the fight for freedom and self rule and religious autonomy involved. He was one of the great givers of the age; and it is no small part of the glory of Congregationalism that it has trained men within its fold whose names as benefactors and princely givers to every good cause are well known. The names of the Salts, Crossleys, and Morleys, are sufficient to shed a lustre on any denomination, and the catholicity of their benefactions is a sufficient reply to charges of illiberality or sectarian narrowness. He found in the pleasure of doing good a reward and a satisfaction all the rarer that it was known only to God, to the recipient himself, and to none besides. He lived his religion. His life was better in its devotion to duty, in its simplicity, in its uniformity, in its devout reverence, than any speech. Like all who have been of any worth in the world, he had an abiding reverence for duty, for the written Word, for the Supreme Master. His friends among the ministers were not the restless heralds of change and novelty, but men who told simply with great plainness of speech and directness of personal appeal the old, old story of the Cross, of man's need and God's love. As his pastor, I have to say that, during these years of intercourse, no shadow ever fell from his lip or life upon my mind to make me troubled, or cause me to doubt, or make my hands weak or my work a burden. He troubled me with no suggestions of superior methods; he had no pet plans to which he was committed. And now he is gone from us, we shall miss him. The poor will miss a benefactor, and the rich will lose the benefit and the stimulus of his example. He will be missed in his own home,—the home that he had made most beautiful, and a synonym for all that is large-hearted, open-handed, unostentatious, and good. He will be missed abroad in this great country among all men of all parties and all creeds. He will be missed by the nation at large. True, loyal, and liberal, he will be missed in the day of conflict, and on the day of calamity. He leaves a name that he has surrounded with an imperishable lustre, and he leaves with it a great responsibility to those who succeed to his honours and his place. Men will not easily be reconciled to the word "failure" in the future, in regard to anything that he planned or purposed. He nests amid the industrial homes and palaces and schools that he created, and the people whom he loved. In the ages to come the founder of Saltaire cannot be forgotten, and when men read the record of this in another age they will again and again tell the story of his life whose princely industry and whose wise philanthropy and simple faith shone and shines in works of his hands. During the whole of the agitated and trying week that came to such a fitting climax on Friday last, the people of this great nation, by the various organs of public expression, and with little or no distinction of creed on party, have said— "Well done!" The echo comes back from other lands— "Well done!" May we not accept the augury, and believe that the voice of the people is the voice of God; that a voice from the Divine Throne, from the midst of the excellent glory, has said— "Well done!" And that again, on a greater day, and before an assembled universe, it will repeat the benediction— "Well done, good and faithful servant."

The service at Saltaire church on the same day was conducted by the writer, and was of a most impressive character. How could it be otherwise in the presence of a bereft and mourning community, in the sanctuary associated with the name of the deceased, and at the very threshold of his tomb? The church proved quite inadequate to accommodate the immense number of persons who desired to gain admission; many being unable to proceed further than the porch. The choir sang the opening anthem, "Cast thy burden on the Lord, and He will sustain thee." The hymns sung at the funeral, "Friend after friend departs," and "Jesus lives!" were sung during the service. The text was selected from John XI. 34, "Where have ye laid him?" The following is an extract

Dear brethren,—Let us try to realise what we ourselves are when assembled by this unclosed grave. Love and skill have prepared it, but sin hath rendered it necessary. The manly form we have been wont to look upon with reverence and affection, must be buried out of our sight. Sin and death have done their worst upon him, but after this they have no more that they can do. Read there, that the earthly house of this tabernacle must be dissolved; that this earth is not our permanent home, and all it can yield us at last is a grave. Read there, the emptiness of wealth, and rank, and fame, and human glory; for to this narrow house we must come at last. Read there, that "Blessed are the dead which die in the Lord; they rest from their labours, and their works do follow them." Read there, that though earth hath claimed his dust, heaven hath claimed his spirit; and it was not because his noble virtues, and princely gifts, and large-hearted benevolence unlocked the heavenly gate, and secured him an entrance; ah, no! but he entered as a little child, trusting only in the merits of the Lord Jesus Christ. Read there, that heaven is gathering into its bosom our friends on earth that are ripest; calling home her children whose education is completed, that they may possess the inheritance purchased for them by the blood of Jesus; and though to us earth now is poorer, heaven is richer, because they are there. Yes! sorrow we must, "but not as others that have no hope." Weep we must, for they have vanished from our sight, but "they have gone to the mountains of myrrh and the hills of frankincense, until the day break and the shadows flee away." But the "day-break" anticipated, is not for them, but for ourselves. Upon them the sun shall no more go down, nor night spread her sable wing, nor death cast its gloomy shadow. No!

Dreams cannot picture a world so fair,

Sorrow and death may not enter there;

Time doth not breathe on its fadeless bloom,

For beyond the clouds and beyond the tomb,

It is there; it is there.[353]

But in the arrangements for the memorial services of the Sunday, the children of Saltaire were not forgotten. They had ever occupied a large place in the heart of the deceased, and an opportunity was given on this mournful occasion, of manifesting their love for his memory. A special service was held in the Assembly Room of the new Sunday-schools, which will long be remembered by the crowd of young people who there were gathered. Special hymns were sung; and the sermon, preached by the writer, was taken from Jer. III. 4, "Wilt not thou from this time cry unto me, my Father, thou art the guide of my youth?"

Thus he was honoured in his burial!

Since that day several memorials of him have appeared, but the most recent are two beautiful windows of stained glass, placed in the Congregational Church, Lightcliffe; the one being a tribute of love from his surviving children; and the other of respect by his friends.[354]

The visitor, entering "the works" of Saltaire by the western gates, will observe a board, on which the names of the gentlemen constituting the firm are inscribed. Opposite each name is inserted a movable slide, indicating which members of the firm are, at the time, out or in. The name of the late baronet is the first on that board; but opposite it will be seen the word "Out." How suggestive of the question, Where is he? He has gone "out," to return no more. Out! for the toils of business are over, and he has gone home to rest. Out! for he hath passed from time into eternity; from the land of shadows into the regions of

[353] Mrs. Felicia D. Hemans, English poet (1794-1835).
[354] The stained glass windows are still in place in the present day, but the building no longer serves as a church; it has been sympathetically converted to business premises.

endless day. Thus may it be with the reader, when his work on earth is done: not cast upon the shores of another world without any definite hope, beyond the present; but like him, whose career we have traced, may his faith rest on the "Rock of Ages," then shall life be serene and useful, death peaceful, and Heaven secure!

FINIS.

PRINTED BY S. W. THEAKSTON AND CO., SCARBOROUGH.[355]

---

[355] S.W. Theakston and Co. was a long established printing company in Scarborough. As early as 1834 Theakston was in business in 5 & 6 Long Room Street, Scarborough (Ref: Pig2).

APPENDICES

APPENDIX 1

REV. ROBERT BALGARNIE
(1826 - 1899)

Patricia M. McNaughton

Robert Balgarnie, Sir Titus Salt's friend and biographer, came from a humble background, but like many Victorians displayed immense vitality, boundless energy, an interest in people around him, and a conviction that he had to do his best for his fellow man. The early history of both Bar Congregational Church and South Cliff Congregational Church in Scarborough are a catalogue of Robert Balgarnie's achievements between 1851 and 1887.

Most of what we know about Balgarnie's early life comes from newspaper articles written about him during the 37 years he lived in Scarborough, and others published in Dalkeith, Scotland, which he wrote himself.[356] Of his private and family life little appears to be on record.

Born in the farmhouse of Whitehaugh, Peeblesshire on 1st January, 1826, Robert was the son of a farm-worker. His father was employed by Sir Adam Hay who owned large estates in the area. There were several other children in the family: a child called Jean born in 1818 appears to have died in infancy, as does Robert born in 1820. Then came Elizabeth, born in 1823, then Isabella (1825), Robert himself, Jane (1828), James (1829), Marion (1831) and John (1833).

Robert's early education was at Peebles Grammar School, under the tutelage of a Mr. Sloane. When he was about nine years old the family moved to Newbattle, approx. seven miles SE of Edinburgh, where his father worked on the Marquis of Lothian's estate, and the boy attended Brown's Academy in Dalkeith, then Lasswade Parish School. At the latter establishment everybody studied together, rich and poor.

---

[356] Refs: ScarM, 6th May, 1887; ScarP, 28th July, 1887; DalkA, 21st November, 1895 and 21st January, 1897.

Contemporaries of Robert were the family of Robert de Quincy, famous as the author of *Confessions of an Opium Eater* and Charles Aitchison, who became lieutenant-governor of the Punjab.

By the time Balgarnie was 15 years old, he was already organising various religious and temperance societies in the area, as well as Sunday Schools, mission services and libraries. His parents attended the Congregational Church in Dalkeith, and biblical readings and teachings were at the forefront of family life. There were also meetings in houses in the village at which the Bible was read, religious discussions took place, and prayers were said. Even as a teenager Robert was sometimes asked to say the closing prayers.

He left home to start work in Edinburgh in 1842, at the age of sixteen, a post having been found for him in the Scottish National Insurance Office. He held this job for five years, staying in Edinburgh during the week, and returning home at weekends, because he enjoyed those precious hours spent with his family.

During his five years in the capital, he became more and more involved in religious works. It was a time of great upheaval and controversy in the Scottish Church, resulting in the Great Disruption and the formation of the Free Church. He actually witnessed the walk-out of seceding ministers at the General Assembly of 18th May, 1843.

At the same time, Robert Moffat, missionary, and later father-in-law to David Livingstone, was touring the country describing his life as a missionary in Africa. Young Robert was so moved by Moffat's accounts, that he immediately arranged an interview with the good doctor, and offered himself as a trainee missionary. Tactfully, Moffat suggested that he was somewhat young and inexperienced for such a course of action.

Not to be deterred, Balgarnie spent his time in Edinburgh wisely. He joined the Edinburgh Young Men's Society, eventually becoming honorary secretary. He also attended various classes and lectures, studying Hebrew under Rev. Dr. Lindsay Alexander at the Congregational Academy, and when time allowed being tutored in Greek and Latin by his own pastor, Rev. Dr. Gowan of Dalkeith.

Still determined to be a missionary, when he reached the age of 20, Balgarnie applied to the London Missionary Society to be accepted as a missionary student. After a personal interview with the Board, and a theological examination by Rev. Dr. Wardlaw of Glasgow, he was accepted. At the beginning of 1847 he proceeded to Bedford, where Rev. John Jukes of Bunyan Chapel gave him extra tuition, before he entered Cheshunt College, Hertfordshire, the following September. The college was then under the direction of a Rev. Dr. Harris, well-known author of a book entitled *Mammon*. The College being affiliated to London University, Balgarnie first matriculated at the university, taking up a college course embracing classics, mathematics, mental and moral philosophy, Hebrew, Chaldee and theology.

It was the policy at Cheshunt to give the students plenty of opportunities to exercise their talents by employing them to preach in surrounding villages and occasionally even in London. In the College chapel, as in all the Countess of Huntingdon's[357] chapels, the prayers of the Established Church (the Church of England) were read, and the pulpit was occupied by the students in turn.

Scarborough newspapers recount the outcome of Balgarnie's first sermon. In the congregation that day was a notoriously miserly old man, who was so impressed with the vigour and directness of the sermon, which urged the duty of self-sacrifice for Christ, appealing for an open heart and an open hand, that without delay he made his way to London. There he called upon the Secretary of the London Missionary Society, before whom he proceeded to take off one of his boots, and presented the startled man with a bundle of bank notes, saying "Thank a young man at Cheshunt for that."

He then proceeded to the Home Missionary Society, where in the other boot he had a similar gift, which he presented with the same

---

[357] Selina Hastings, Countess of Huntingdon (1707 – 1791) was a prominent aristocratic non-conformist, who built a number of chapels, all registered as dissenting places of worship, and who founded a seminary for training ministers at Trevecca House, Talgarth, North Wales. Despite all this she never entirely severed her connection with the Anglican church (Ref: DNB).

message.

One writer says that some people in Scarborough did not find Mr. Balgarnie's preaching style at all attractive, whilst others found him fascinating and impressive, but it cannot be denied that he was a popular and successful preacher. That particular writer felt there was no deep insight or original thought in either Balgarnie's preaching or writing, but did acknowledge the vigour and sincerity of his words, and praised him for being an "indefatigable and consistent worker."[358]

During his time at Cheshunt, Balgarnie became a popular and highly esteemed preacher, who was much in demand. He frequently assisted well-known preachers of the day such as Rev. Dr. Collyer, George Clayton, James Sherman, Dr. George Smith, and J. Baldwin Brown in and around London. It was through assisting the last named that Balgarnie arrived in Scarborough, and reached a turning point in his life.

The original Independent Chapel in what was then Merchants' Row, which the Salt family attended when on holiday, was no longer large enough to accommodate summer congregations. It was over a century old, had become dilapidated, and as the centre of the town moved northward due to expansion, the area nearer the foreshore became less fashionable and less salubrious. It was plain to see, according to some of the congregation, that a new church, in a more accessible area, and with better accommodation, was required. Moves towards building this church began in 1848.

Rev. Baldwin Brown, who had heard Balgarnie preach, was visiting Scarborough when he was asked by a gentleman called Sir William Lowthorpe, Chairman of the New Church's Building Committee if he knew of anyone who might be suitable to take up the post of pastor in the new church. He would have to be energetic, enthusiastic, able to build up a congregation, and able to raise money to pay for the building's completion. Baldwin Brown gave the Committee a favourable description of a young missionary student he had heard, saying that he (Balgarnie) had preached for him (Baldwin Brown) recently and had left a deep

---

[358] ScarP, 28th July, 1887.

impression on the congregation. Unfortunately this young man was a missionary student and not likely to settle in England.

However, the College was requested to permit Balgarnie to come to the town to preach one Sunday. He proved so popular that he was invited to stay for a week and preach for a second Sunday. That was enough for the Building Committee: he was promptly invited to become the first pastor of the church on its completion. This offer was too serious to be accepted or rejected without being given a great deal of consideration, and Balgarnie realised he would need sound advice before making a decision. As a missionary student he was not his own master, but when he took his problem to the College board, it said he had to make up his mind for himself. He had another year of study before his college course was finished, and the Building Committee was willing to wait until then. However, though Balgarnie thought he had set his feet on the missionary path, things had already begun to change radically. In December, 1847, the year he began his training, his beloved father died, leaving a widow and two dependent children still at home. James, 17 at the time, would eventually become a chartered accountant, but would then be earning very little, if anything, as an articled clerk; John, aged 13, would be still at school, though he later became a banker. This meant that Robert would have to consider staying in Britain, supporting his mother and these younger siblings, and any unmarried sisters still at home and not in employment. (The 1851 census shows Isabella still at home, apparently helping her widowed mother look after the house).

So, Balgarnie accepted the invitation to be the first pastor of the new church, which, being situated outside the Newborough Bar, or Gate, came to be called the Bar Congregational Church. The fledgling congregation consisted of 19 people detached from the Old Independent Meeting House (originally a Presbyterian foundation). In November 1851 the Rev. Robert Balgarnie took up his post, at the age of 25. He brought with him "all the qualifications of a young and promising Christian pastor." He travelled from York in a third-class railway carriage without seats or covering, the carriage being known as a "tub."[359]

Between the railway station and his new church the aspect was positively rural. The members of the congregation who lived in the neighbouring village of Falsgrave carried lanterns with them, to light the way through fields and hedges, there being no street lights.

His public ordination took place the following February, and being a novelty at the time drew a large congregation. After answering a series of questions about his young life, and the reasons for believing he was a Christian, the doctrinal views he held and his plans for the future of his ministry, the ordination prayer was said, with the laying on of hands, by Rev. J. C. Potter of Whitby. The Rev. Dr. Smith of Poplar, London, delivered the charge to the minister, and the Rev. Newman Hall, who was to become a great friend of Balgarnie, preached to the congregation.

The new church, and the financial debt he felt he owed the London Missionary Society, would require all Balgarnie's "magnificent constitution", and "unquenchable zeal in the service of God." In a very short time he managed to raise the money to pay off the £3000 debt the church owed, then set about raising even more money for Sunday School accommodation, for which he laid the foundation stone in 1852. His persuasive powers, resourcefulness and sagacity were lost to the missionary sphere, but were put to very good use in his new home. Within a short time he had also repaid to the London Missionary Society the cost of his tuition at Cheshunt.

During his early years in Scarborough, he met Mr. Thomas Birks, a Sheffield brewer, with whom he stayed both in Sheffield and at Birks' retreat in Bolsover. It was whilst preaching at the Wicker Church in Sheffield that Balgarnie first met the woman who was to become his wife.

On 27th December, 1854, at East Parade Chapel, Leeds, Robert Balgarnie married Martha, the only surviving daughter of Mr. Thomas Rooke, a linen draper of Minster Gates, York. They were to have four

---

[359] Ref: HisSc.

daughters: Florence (1856), Mary Rooke (1858), Jessie Marion (1860) and Ada (1865), the last dying in infancy; and three sons: Robert Edward (1862), Wilfred (1863) and Harold (1867).

As Sunday School classes increased in size and number, further accommodation was needed, and when the bi-centenary of non-Conformity was celebrated in 1862 a lecture room behind the church was built, the foundation stone for this being laid by Dr. Peter Murray M.D., who would also become one of Balgarnie's friends and supporters. This building alone cost £2,000.

In the meantime, Balgarnie found time to visit Newbattle occasionally. He also officiated at the wedding of his brother James to Louisa Lovell in Bedford in 1858, and was a witness when James, tragically widowed, married for the second time in 1864. Later he officiated at the marriage of his brother John in Glasgow in 1872.

As time passed and Balgarnie's popularity grew, people actually arranged their holidays in Scarborough so that they could go to Bar Church and hear him and other celebrated preachers declaiming from the pulpit there. In summer the congregation became so large that the church was often crowded an hour before the service, and many people could not even get in. This led to extra services being arranged at the Town Hall, or the Mechanics' Hall, the latter becoming a chapel of ease for the Bar Church during some summers. These services were by no means "second class"; the most eminent preachers of the day occasionally took part in them: Revs. Dr. Vaughan, Halley, Spence, Alexander Raleigh, Alexander, George Smith, Enoch Mellor, and Newman Hall.

By 1863, realising that another new church was required, the congregation of Bar Church purchased land at the top of St. Thomas Street; but as the population of the town began to drift towards the south side, the plan was abandoned and the site sold.

In 1866, after 15 years as Pastor at the Bar Church, Balgarnie produced a booklet, a summary of the work and achievements of the congregation during his pastorate up to that point. He observed that he had arrived 15 years before, fresh out of college, "inexperienced, untried, unknown", and that he was now the oldest Protestant minister in the town - at the ripe old age of 40! Every place of worship, except Bar Church, has changed its ministry in this period, three ministers having died, and another retired in advanced years. His own record, he believed, spoke for itself: only once in that 15 years had he been unable to preach because he was ill, and once he could not due to "domestic anxiety"; he had never been absent from "the ordinary celebration of the Lord's Supper." During his pastorate to date, he estimated, he had preached over 2,000 sermons from the pulpit and over 120 in the open air. Of course, he admitted, it was impossible to know how much influence he had had over people's lives, and only the Lord would know the results of Balgarnie's seed-sowing.

The church's record during this part of his pastorate is impressive, largely due to his untiring hard work and enthusiasm. From a small beginning with a mere 19 members, the membership roll of the church had reached 601. Bar Church had seen 300 baptisms, though some of those babies, including one of his own, would never reach adulthood. Though Nonconformists were by then permitted to marry in their own churches only 55 couples had so far married at Bar Church, many still preferring to use the Parish Church. He showed his feelings about this by saying "(It is as if) their own Church were respectable enough for the worship of God, but not for their marriage service! As if their own minister were eligible to teach religion, to visit their sick, to baptize [sic] their children, to bury their dead, but not to unite them in marriage. Brethren, your minister needs all the moral support you can render him, and it ought not to be that in times of sorrow you send for him, but in times of joy you pass him by." It is quite clear that this issue rankled.

Obviously some of his words did fall on receptive ears and hearts, as six young men went from Bar Church to the ministry, and though unfortunately he names no names, two ministers are mentioned in later newspaper reports. Their ministries were somewhat widespread: including Australia, the South Seas, the South of England, London (Rev.

J. Morley Wright) and St. Helens (Rev. R. I. Ward). He cites the number of Bible Classes held at the church as "nurseries" for the work of the church. In 1866 there were five classes, with an average total attendance of 100 students.

The Sunday School commenced in 1851 with about 20 scholars. In the intervening years 2,000 scholars had featured on its register, the total in 1866 being 400, with 40 teachers. A branch school had commenced in Cambridge Street, with around 90 pupils. Also in the realm of education, Bar Church had been instrumental in setting up a Ragged School in Quay Street, offering a rudimentary education to children who attended no other school. It was only open in the winter months, perhaps because in summer these children would be employed in various capacities in local "industries", e.g. fishing, working in boarding houses and shops, running errands, etc. All the teachers were volunteers, and at least 120 children were taught every year.

The Band of Hope was founded in 1853, and there was also support work for the Home and Foreign Missions. Apart from being one of the originators and first secretary of the Scarborough Town Mission, he was also secretary of the British and Foreign Bible Society, a post he would hold for over 30 years.

The work of the church was not confined to Sundays and other times of organised worship at Bar Church itself. There were Cottage Meetings, where members of the congregation held gospel meetings in people's own homes, seven "brethren" being thus occupied in the winter. One wonders whether any ladies took part. These were similar to the fireside meetings which Balgarnie describes himself and his father attending in Newbattle.[360] He obviously felt that it was part of his job at Bar Church to be a kind of Home Missionary, taking the gospel to those who might otherwise never have come to church, and so never receive the "Good News."

One section of Scarborough society had been particularly neglected, indeed almost vilified from time to time - the Cabmen. They seem to

---

[360] Ref: DalkA, 21st January, 1897.

have been generally perceived as the very lowest class of society. Balgarnie set out to bring the cabmen and their wives together "for the promotion of their social and religious improvement."

Cabmen's Prayer Meetings were held during the winter and were well attended, though whether they came for the sermon or the warmth and shelter may be debated. Balgarnie, together with his friends, especially Dr. Peter Murray, and his congregation, organised Christmas Lunches and Suppers for the cabmen and their wives, which were held, over the years, in a number of local hotels. Full details of these can be found in newspapers of the time. When he left the town in 1887 these suppers had been taking place for 30 years. What had begun with 30 cabmen had become an event which in 1886 was attended by 300 people, as widows and postilions were also included. Over the years money was raised to build cabmen's shelters, a fund started to support an ailing cabman until he died, and another, who was badly injured, was helped to set himself up as a shopkeeper.[361]

Balgarnie was justifiably proud of the speed with which the congregation of Bar Church paid off the sums borrowed to build the church itself and the other buildings which were added from time to time, apparently taking no credit to himself. They also raised a substantial amount towards the building of South Cliff Congregational Church - of which more later. Most of the money raised came in the form of "Free Will Offerings", either the collections taken at services, or raised at special fund-raising events. Various societies also received donations: the London Missionary Society in particular, as well as the Ragged Schools, the North Riding Home Missions, Moravian Missions, the Town Dispensary, and the Hull Sailors' Orphans' Home.

Perhaps, looking back on his 15 years' hard work, Balgarnie was entitled to feel a little self-satisfied, but says he feels he "could do more"! One thing which did give him satisfaction was the fact that the Congregational Church, particularly the Bar Congregational Church, welcomed anyone and everyone: all ranks and classes, all religious

---

[361] Refs: ScarG, 15th July, 1875; ScarM, 6th May, 1887.

denominations - and those with perhaps none - having entered the building and worshipped there. Without altar, priest, vestments or "gorgeous ceremonies" worship had been successfully carried on in Bar Church.[362]

At this point he also explained something which the congregation may not have considered. Some may have felt that during the season he gave his own flock less attention than the visitors. But, he said, visitors had a claim on his attention because many of them came to Scarborough as invalids, and to them a pastor's ministrations were particularly welcome. Even those who came purely for recreation and pleasure needed a minister here as much as they did at home. And - perhaps most important of all, even if he does not *quite* say so - it must be remembered that visitors contributed largely to the funds for the running of the church, and liberally supported fund-raising efforts, so service to them should be given gladly. Clearly he knew his flock well, knew what they felt and thought, and how to win them round!

The Ragged School, which Balgarnie mentioned in his list of achievements associated with the Bar Church, is worth a special mention. Mrs. Ann Wright was for many years the superintendent of the Ragged School, and when visiting the homes of pupils who had been absent through illness saw for herself the terrible conditions in which poor, sick people were struggling to recover, conditions which made the illness longer, or recovery impossible. She decided that a Cottage Hospital was required, so she bought a cottage which was adapted to take a handful of patients, whose treatment and board were financed from donations. Another cottage was added, and the location changed a few times, until eventually it became quite a large institution which was generously supported by Bar Church's congregation. Mrs. Wright became known as "The Florence Nightingale of Scarborough", and continued as superintendent of the hospital until the age of 87, dying at the age of 91. When the present Scarborough General Hospital was built in the 1930s one ward was named "The Ann Wright Ward", as it is to this

---

[362] Ref: BarCM.

day. Mrs. Wright was the widow of a doctor who had practised in Birmingham. Mrs. Wright, a member of Balgarnie's flock, was a Scotswoman who, after her husband's death, had come to Scarborough to retire![363]

Balgarnie was also twice president of the Scarborough Hospital and Dispensary, during his first presidency having the honour, as he put it, to raise the money to free it from debt. For several years he was the honorary secretary, and drew up its annual report for over 30 years.

When Balgarnie wrote his report on his 15 years in the town, he was actually looking after two churches, Bar Church and South Cliff Congregational Church. The latter, as he was obviously pleased to record in its first minute book, "is the child of the Bar Church and was born, not of strife and division, but of Christian love, unity and peace animated with a supreme desire to extend the Kingdom of Christ in Scarborough."

As has been mentioned, in the summer season Bar Church was not large enough for all the people who wished to worship there and other premises had to be hired. The scheme to open another church in town had foundered because the population was moving from the older parts of town to the newly developing areas, especially the South Cliff.

Consequently, a Building Committee was set up, which met in a Leeds hotel early in 1864. Salt was chairman of the Committee, and Balgarnie was the secretary. Balgarnie told them "an eminently suitable site" near the Esplanade had already been chosen and would cost about £1,200. It was anticipated that the total cost of the land, building, fixtures and fittings would be about £9,000, much of which had already been promised. Lockwood and Mawson were chosen as the architects, their plans showing a Gothic church capable of seating 1,000 people, or 1,200 if galleries were included.[364]

Salt offered to pay for the site, John Barry of Scarborough was awarded the building contract, and work began in May 1864. Though

[363] Refs: ScarM, 6th May, 1887; ScarE, 19th January, 1950.
[364] Ref: ScarG, 11th February, 1864.

there was a stoppage when the workmen demanded better pay, the magnificent building would be completed in the remarkably short time of 14 months.

Everything was to be the most modern, the most up-to-date, the best. Wailes of Newcastle made the stained glass windows, Seldmans of Coventry installed a gas lighting system. There were to be vestries for the minister, the deacons and the ladies. Circular letters distributed to visitors and other congregational churches brought donations from all over England, and some from Scotland; but the West Riding in particular was extremely generous, members of Salt's family, his partners and associates being among the subscribers mentioned in a list pasted into the Church Minute Book.

On 20th September, 1864, her husband's 61st birthday, Mrs. Salt laid the corner stone of the new church. Fittingly the procession started at the Bar Church, and proceeded to the new church. There were members of other congregational churches there, as well as a large number of the general public. After various hymns and speeches, Mrs. Salt watched the stone being lowered into place. Beneath it was a large bottle containing silver and bronze coins of the realm, *cartes de visite* of both the Salt and Balgarnie families, a list of the subscribers, a history of the church, the order of the day's service, a copy of the declaration of faith and various other documents, including copies of several national and local newspapers. As Mrs. Salt performed her task with a silver trowel, Henry Lockwood reminded her that exactly 11 years before the engines at Saltaire had made their first turn. She spread the mortar and gave the stone the customary three blows, saying "I declare this corner stone of the South Cliff Congregational Church well and truly laid, in the name of the Father, and of the Son and of the Holy Ghost."[365]

Before the church was finished, Salt would contribute more money, buying the rest of the site on which the church was built so that it could not be overlooked by future development.

Balgarnie now had oversight of the proceedings at South Cliff as well

---

[365] Ref: ScarG, 22nd September, 1864.

as his duties as minister at Bar Church and all that that post entailed. He must have been a proud but weary man when on Wednesday 26th July, 1865 the church finally opened.[366] Here is not the place to go into all the details of this magnificent building, but its nickname "The Cathedral of Yorkshire Congregationalism" or, perhaps meant disparagingly, but maybe in grudging admiration, "Balgarnie's Cathedral", gives some idea of its size and magnificence. Even today some people still refer to the building as, quite simply, "Balgarnie's."

The first Divine Service was held on the morning of Wednesday 26th July, after a preliminary prayer meeting at seven o'clock. Rev. Enoch Mellor, at that time a minister in Liverpool, preached to "a most respectable congregation", and the collection raised £69 5s.

Salt presided over the proceedings, which took the form of a public luncheon in the Bar Church schoolroom, followed by toasts and speeches. Rev. Mellor seems to have been particularly amused by a publication which warns Anglicans not to be deluded by the appearance of the new building, as it has no claim to be called a church, being only a "Congregational Chapel." He said that in his opinion Dissenters had as much right to call their places of worship "churches" as had anybody else, and lightheartedly suggested the writer was a deluded person in need of special care. In the evening Rev. Newman Hall preached to an overflowing congregation and the collection totalled £39.

For a time Balgarnie continued as pastor of Bar Church, overseeing events at the South Cliff Church, whilst visiting preachers filled the pulpit there. Then, in 1868, it was decided the church could now stand on its own feet, and Balgarnie was asked to become its first pastor.

The *Scarborough Gazette* of 6th December, 1868, describes how anxiously everyone waited for his decision, and the Bar Church Minute Book contains a full report of the Building Committee's meeting at which it was decided to ask him to be the pastor of the new church, together with his own account of the heart-searching which making the decision entailed. Finally, he decided to move to the South Cliff Church with 55

---

[366] Ref: ScarG, 27thJuly, 1865.

Bar Church members to form a nucleus of the new congregation.

Meantime, and deserving a well-earned break, in August, 1867, Balgarnie went on a trip to America with his friend Rev. Newman Hall. During this time he wrote to his congregation at least twice, and to the deacons, but he said nothing very personal, just, in the last-mentioned letter, which is pasted into the Church Record Book, that he might not be back in time to take the communion service on the first Sunday in November, so perhaps they might like to delay it till the following week. However, in the November he was given a very public welcome home, after which he told the assembled company all about his trip to America. The account was serialised in the *Scarborough Gazette* over a number of weeks.[367]

They sailed from Liverpool, on board the *Cuba,* calling at Halifax, Nova Scotia, before continuing to Boston. Their extensive tour took in Newport, Rhode Island, New York, the Catskill Mountains, Utica, and Niagara Falls. After Niagara they went to Hamilton, Ontario, where Balgarnie met, for the first time in 16 years, his sister Elizabeth, whom he scarcely recognised. He was much taken with the names of the towns round about Hamilton - places called Scarborough, Whitby, Malton and Pickering!

Newman Hall returned to Niagara, but Balgarnie remained in Hamilton, taking the opportunity to visit an Indian settlement, which he found interesting, but he does not seem to have approved of the way the women had to do all the work. After touring Hamilton, he joined Newman Hall again for a trip to London where they saw oil wells, then they travelled to Windsor.

By mid-September they were in Chicago, where they visited churches of various denominations, including a "negro church" where Balgarnie and Newman Hall were the only two white people present. They met Robert Lincoln, son of the late President. Next stop Springfield, Illinois, where Newman Hall was to give a lecture in the Presbyterian church

---

[367] Refs: ScarG, 21st and 28th November, 5th and 19th December, 1867, 16th January, 20th February, 12th and 19th March, 1868.

which Lincoln himself used to attend. They visited Lincoln's tomb, and his house which, though lived in by a family called Fulton, had become a kind of museum. From Springfield their trip took them to St. Louis, where it was so hot, says Balgarnie, that one night in the city was enough. They were glad to leave for Buffalo, where they parted company for a few days; Balgarnie returned to Hamilton via Niagara, joining Newman Hall in Buffalo, whence they travelled together to Toronto, and preached in turn at the Presbyterian and Methodist churches.

From Toronto they went by steam-boat to Montreal, which they reached on Sunday 29th September. Here both Newman Hall and Balgarnie fulfilled a number of preaching engagements, and had their photographs taken in a studio. Then they moved on to Quebec, from where they visited the Montmorenci Falls. After sightseeing in the White Mountains they went to Portland, Maine, where Newman Hall was to deliver a lecture, and Balgarnie met an old school fellow from Dalkeith, a Mr. Porteous.

They returned to Boston, where both preached, Balgarnie taking a trip to Plymouth and other places associated with the Pilgrim Fathers. He then left for New York, as Newman Hall had elected to remain to preach and lecture. Balgarnie's journey to New York, which he reached on 14th October, took him via New Haven and Hartford, Connecticut. After an overnight stop he went to Washington, travelling by train through New Jersey and Philadelphia. In Washington he visited a number of schools and addressed the pupils; Ford's Theatre which was by then a museum of Civil War photographs and memorabilia; and various other "tourist attractions."

Balgarnie went by way of Baltimore to Gettysburg, where he visited the battlefield which had seen so much bloodshed a mere four years previously in 1863, and the Cemetery where the dead from both sides were buried. From here he returned to New York, making his way to Boston to join the *Cuba*. En route he met up with Newman Hall again at Newport, where they made the acquaintance of Harriet Beecher Stowe and her daughter. Newman Hall returned to New York, whilst Balgarnie travelled via Providence to board the *Cuba*. He describes his voyage home and his arrival in Liverpool, where he stayed with friends overnight before returning "to the bosom of my family, and of my flock, with renewed health and a grateful heart."

Some of Newman Hall's letters describing their journey were published in the *Christian World*, and re-printed in the Scarborough newspapers.[368]

By 1869 Balgarnie was inviting subscriptions for a clock to be added to the tower of South Cliff Church.[369] In March 1871 it was installed and ready to be handed over to the Borough Council to become a municipal clock. This meant that the council, not the church, became responsible for its upkeep. Once again it was a case of "biggest and best'" with Gillet and Bland of Croydon supplying a clock with full Westminster Chimes which could, apparently, be heard all over town! The hours were struck on a 13 cwt tenor bell, and the mechanism was the most up-to-date which could be procured.[370] It is little wonder that before long the residents of the South Cliff were complaining about the noise. The bells were silenced, and sold, together with the striking mechanism, to a Leeds clock-maker after the Second World War.[371]

In 1875 a lecture room and classrooms were added at the northern end of the South Cliff Church, though the ceremony of laying the corner stone and various memorial stones was somewhat marred when the scaffolding on which some of the dignitaries were standing collapsed, they fell 15 feet and had to be treated for minor injuries and shock.[372]

In 1876 Balgarnie celebrated 25 years of ministry, and a mark of the esteem in which he was held by townspeople whatever their denomination is evinced by the testimonial he received. The names upon the subscription list belonged to people from all classes, 600 guineas being raised. The presentation was made at a public meeting at the South Cliff Church, where nearly 400 people sat down to tea in the

---

[368] Refs: ScarG, 26th September and 24th October, 1867.
[369] Ref: ScarG, 19th August, 1869.
[370] Ref: ScarG, 9th March, 1871.
[371] Ref: ScarE, 27th January, 1945.
[372] Ref: ScarG, 5th August, 1875.

school-room, before adjourning to the church where others joined them, for various speeches and presentations. The chair was taken by Henry Wright, Esq., J.P., of London who was Salt's son-in-law, and Salt himself is mentioned as being one of the people supplying flowers to decorate the church. Various speeches were made, including one by the Mayor. Balgarnie was presented with a silver salver, for which the ladies of the church had subscribed, with the purse containing 600 guineas on top of it. He also received a testimonial of esteem from the cabmen. After Balgarnie's speech of thanks, full of reminiscences, Newman Hall had a few words to say. Votes of thanks followed and the proceedings closed.[373]

It was only fitting that the January 1877 Monthly Meeting of the South Cliff Church should be cancelled, Balgarnie being required in Saltaire to attend and preach at the funeral of his great friend Sir Titus Salt. The congregation sent Lady Salt and her family a letter of condolence, to which her son-in-law, Henry Wright, subsequently replied. Both letters have been written into the Minutes of the Church Record Book.

In April 1882 Balgarnie visited Rome, writing a letter to his congregation back at South Cliff to tell them about his journey. It is obvious from his writing that St. Paul was a great influence on his life, and he clearly relished following in the saint's footsteps, visiting the places where he had been and imagining what Paul must have felt. Whilst in Rome he also visited the college set up by Fr. Gavazzi,[374] who had visited Scarborough at Balgarnie's invitation, and spoke to the students.

Ever the evangelist and missionary he had originally intended to be, Balgarnie sought to take the Word to the smaller places on the outskirts of Scarborough, where no Congregational mission rooms or Sunday Schools as yet existed. Deciding in 1867 there was a requirement for a Sunday School in Seamer Road, he found a cottage which could be

---

[373] Ref: ScarG, 26th October, 1876.

[374] Father Alessandro Gavazzi, (1809 – 1899) was an associate of Garibaldi and founder of the (Protestant) Free Church of Italy (Ref: NEB).

used for this purpose, and when this became too small, they used the kitchen at the mill house, until a small building was erected - red brick and homely, "premises very suitable for a working-class locality" as the newspaper put it. There evangelist George Walker oversaw the work, which consisted of Sunday services and communion, a Sunday School, Band of Hope, mothers' meetings, even a savings bank and a night school.[375]

Wheatcroft, on the Filey road, was similarly lacking in Congregational facilities, with the Sunday School being held in a cottage, with occasional Sunday services, until a mission room was built in 1879. This was also under George Walker's direction.[376]

One of the most unique and successful parts of Balgarnie's work was his open-air services. These were first held on the Sands, but after Foreshore Road was built, the crowds used to gather in front of the Sea Bathing Infirmary (later St. Thomas' Hospital) to listen to an hour's service. These services continued for 31 years without a break. At first Balgarnie's "pulpit" was a boat or a plank, with the congregation gathered round him. Then he acquired a pulpit on carriage wheels. Tracts in a number of languages were distributed at the end of every service. They were mainly in English, German, French and Dutch, which says something about the number of foreign visitors to the town. It was estimated that several thousand people must have heard him preach on the sands over the years.[377]

Balgarnie's first book *Going Home*, the touching narrative of the death of Miss Annie Winn, a young lady from Scarborough, sold 23,000 copies and was translated into Danish. He also had success with *The Wreck off the Spa*, a sermon based on the disastrous events of 2nd November, 1861 when Lord Charles Beauclerk, Mr. Tindall and several lifeboatmen lost their lives; *That Night of Storm*, covering the same event; *The Burning of the Spa Salon*; and *Fishing For Men*, which all achieved large

---

[375] Ref: ScarM 6th May, 1887.
[376] Ref: ScarM 6th May, 1887.
[377] Ref: ScarM 6th May, 1887.

circulations; but perhaps one of the most successful of his booklets was *Harvest-time*, the annual missionary sermon to young men, delivered in London at the request of the London Missionary Society, which ran to 12 editions. Besides the Salt biography, his largest work, Balgarnie commemorated the life of his friend Dr. Peter Murray in *The Beloved Physician: the Life of Peter Murray, M.D.* Both biographies reached their third edition.[378]

At this point it is appropriate to comment that it is particularly noticeable in the Salt biography that Balgarnie uses the editorial "we" which both conveys inclusion of the reader in events, and reinforces the idea that the Salt family and others close to them were providing information and encouragement during the writing of this work. In his other writings Balgarnie has been happy to refer to himself as "I", perhaps because he was more intimately involved in the events he was writing about. Or perhaps he wished, in the biography, to demonstrate a degree of reverence towards his influential, innovative and charitable friend, and to show his respect for Salt by subsuming his own personality in the editorial "we".

It was noted that Mr Balgarnie's work was not confined to members of his own church, he had been a minister to the town without distinction of class or denomination. "The sick and the sorrowful, the poor and the needy have sent for him in the time of trouble, and invalid visitors from all parts have found in him a sympathetic friend."

In his early years in Scarborough, Balgarnie wanted to do something to help the widows and orphans of fishermen, so he set up a special fund, the money from which was invested in the Savings Bank. The recipients drew their weekly allowances from the Bank. For some reason this was later discontinued. He continued this work by becoming a friend and supporter of the Port of Hull Orphanage, for which he raised money in various ways, including organising an annual visit of the orphaned children to Scarborough, where they had a special tea, and paraded through the streets collecting for the Orphanage. He also arranged,

---

[378] Ref: ScarM, 6th May, 1887.

where necessary, for the orphans of Scarborough fishermen, to be taken to the Orphanage, where, it was hoped, they would be well cared for and taught a trade. Salt was the major financial supporter of the Orphanage at this time.

As if all the foregoing were not enough, when he left town and the newspaper summarised his activities over the years, they noted his involvement in the Yorkshire Congregational Union, (second secretary, elected in 1873), the Temperance Society, the Cambridge Extension Lectures, Cambridge Local Examinations, the Charity Organization Society, the Royal Seabathing Infirmary (where at one point the overseer and matron were members of Bar Church) and the Society for Prevention of Cruelty to Animals. He was also for some time a member of the Scarborough School Board, with his daughter Florence having the distinction of being the first woman on that Board.

He invited or encouraged several eminent people to come to Scarborough among them Dr. Moffat, the Jubilee Singers, Dr. Joseph Parker, and Rev. Henry Ward Beecher. He also originated the Annual Flower Service for London Hospitals, which continued for many years. In 1886, for example, he took to London over 3,000 bunches of flowers, though unfortunately it is not reported whether he took them over a period of time, or all at once! He also inaugurated, to keep people entertained and uplifted in the winter months, the South Cliff Winter Lectures, the first of their type in the area, and persuaded high-class lecturers to come along to speak.

In May 1887 the *Scarborough Gazette* published an article on the Congregational Churches, which largely featured Balgarnie and his works. It noted that he was now the senior minister in the town, looked upon by other Nonconformist clergymen as their representative on public occasions. It was, however, also noted that he was not a narrow sectarian, and that he lived on terms of goodwill with his Anglican counterparts, his Nonconformity not being a barrier to friendship.

At the close of the thirty-fifth year of his ministry, in 1887, Balgarnie shocked his friends and congregation by announcing that he intended to devote the rest of his life to evangelistic work throughout England.

On 28th July a Conversazione was held at South Cliff Church to mark his departure. There was a large attendance, all three Congregational Churches in the town joining together for the event. Those present included Revs. Bryan Dale, M. A. of Halifax, S. G. Jowett of Bradford, James Hart from Leckhampton near Cheltenham, and the Chairman of the Yorkshire Congregational Union, R. Fletcher.

Again there were speeches, testimonials and presentations, and when the churchmen had finished, the Cabmen's representative, George Hall, stepped forward to hand over a travelling timepiece and a barometer, and a small cruet stand for Mrs. Balgarnie. The reverend gentleman gave a gracious speech of thanks, reviewed his years in Scarborough and noted that the £120 debt which was the last owing on the church had finally been paid off. However, Mr. Birdsall revealed that Balgarnie himself had paid it off, as he wished to leave the church unfettered by debt. However, the church members would be giving their pastor a present when he returned in September to receive a gift from the town.

This is one of the few occasions when we hear anything of the other members of the Balgarnie family. Jessie Balgarnie had been a Kindergarten teacher for eleven years and was presented with a travelling bag and album on behalf of the scholars and her fellow teachers.[379]

Balgarnie preached his final sermon on 31st July, 1887 at the South Cliff Church, but the town had not finished with him yet. On 29th September, 1887 during a meeting held at the Scarborough Savings Bank, testimonials were presented to him in recognition of the many public services he had performed for the community in the thirty-six years he had lived here. One was from the townspeople in general, an illuminated address and a cheque for £160, presented by the Vicar of Scarborough, the Ven. Archdeacon Blunt. All classes of people were represented, the Mayor (J. W. Woodall, Esq) chaired the meeting, various leading citizens and dignitaries gave speeches wishing him

---

[379] Ref: ScarM, 29th July, 1887.

health, happiness and success, whilst regretting his departure. Another testimonial came from the Board of Governors of the Scarborough Hospital and Dispensary. That evening the church members and congregation at South Cliff assembled to bid him a grateful and affectionate farewell. Again, there were speeches and reviews of his work, and a cheque for £140 10s was handed over. Balgarnie himself remarked on the irony of Newman Hall being present at both his ordination and his departure. Once again the work done by Mrs. Balgarnie and her daughters was publicly acknowledged.[380]

However, even though he moved on to become an evangelical preacher, he apparently visited Dalkeith where his family lived, preaching there often, and he returned to Scarborough almost every year.

For ten years he travelled all over England, from the family home at Crouch End. Working as an evangelist among the churches, he obviously enjoying fulfilling in some measure his original ambition to be a missionary, though his boundaries were somewhat narrower than those he must have envisaged when he attended Cheshunt College. He continued to be closely associated with the London Missionary Society, being a director of its Board, and was an inspirational speaker wherever he went. His friendship with the Salt family appears to have continued after he moved to London, as he was one of the officiating ministers at the Dowager Lady Salt's funeral in 1893.

In the obituary published in the *Congregational Yearbook, 1900* Balgarnie's phenomenal record of service in Scarborough is once again quoted, and it is noted that he brought into social and municipal affairs the standard of the religion he preached.[381]

We know very little about his family life, but he must have relied a great deal on his wife, Martha who provided a happy home, we are told, for his children, and was a helper in his church activities and in all the good works he undertook. Florence continued her interest in education, the temperance and the welfare movements, whilst Jessie worked as a

---

[380] Ref: ScarM, 30th September, 1887 (two reports).
[381] Ref: ConYB, 1900.

secretary for the London Missionary Society. Neither of them married, and they were still living at the family home in 1901.

Balgarnie travelled and preached until the January before his death. His health began to deteriorate, and he spent a little time at Bournemouth, returning home only a short time before he died on Sunday morning 28th May, 1899, at his home at Crouch End.

Obituaries and reports on the funeral were published in the local, Scarborough and Dalkeith newspapers.

The number of mourners who attended from far and wide testified to the esteem in which he was held, and the obituaries published in London, Scarborough and Dalkeith attest to the honour and affection of his many friends.[382] Rev. Newman Hall, ever-present when anything important happened in his friend's life, was, sadly, unable to attend his funeral. The Rev. Alfred Rowland read out a letter from him, testifying to the respect he (Newman Hall) and others had had for Balgarnie.

Representatives from both the Bar Church (Mr. R. Foster), and South Cliff Church (Mr. W. Birdsall) attended, together with other eminent Scarborians, including Mrs. Dobson, from the South Cliff Church, Mr. Joshua Rowntree and Mr. J. H. Rowntree. The combined Bar and South Cliff Congregations sent a wreath, as did Mrs. Titus Salt (Saltaire, near Bradford), Mr. and Mrs. Stevenson, the latter being Salt's youngest daughter, and various other institutions with which he had been connected.

The *Dalkeith Advertiser* recorded his passing and that his funeral was attended by Mr. T. Kemp of Dalkeith, who may have been a relation by marriage.

The eulogy spoken by Rev. Alfred Rowland ended "He will be missed, but he leaves behind sweet memories and a Christ-like example."

Rev. Robert Balgarnie was buried at Abney Park Cemetery, where Rev. Rowland conducted the grave side service. At exactly the same time, a memorial service was held at the South Cliff Congregational Church, which was attended by representatives of various churches and

---

[382] Ref: ScarM, 30th September, 1887.

denominations, J.P.s and aldermen, doctors and eminent laymen, all of whom had known the deceased and been involved in his life and work. Ten girls and ten boys from the Hull Sailors' Orphan Homes attended, as did Mr. Poole, the East Coast Missionary and resident agent at Scarborough. Balgarnie's favourite hymns were sung, his achievements acknowledged by an impressive congregation, and his loss felt by those who had known him as a pastor, supporter and friend.[383]

© Appendix 1 text Patricia M. McNaughton 2003.

---

[383] Refs: IslnA, 3rd June, 1899; ScarP, 29th May and 1st June, 1899; DalkA, 1st June, 1899.

SCARBOROUGH CONGREGATIONAL CHURCH

APPENDIX 2

CHRONOLOGY OF EVENTS

This chronology is intended to help the reader when reflecting on the sequence of events associated with the lives of Titus Salt, his family and his associates, and with events that followed his death. A limited number of other events have been included in the chronology where we felt it would be of interest to the reader. The chronology is inevitably limited, and we have chosen to terminate it in 1935, with the passing of Salt's last surviving child. The information in this Appendix is not referenced here; such information is provided, in the majority of the events, elsewhere in the book.

YEAR	DATE	EVENT
1773		Bradford Piece Hall opened
1774		Branch canal from Bradford to Shipley opened
1777		Bingley to Leeds section of Leeds-Liverpool canal opened
1778		Bowling Iron Works opened
1779	Mar 15	Grace Smithies (mother of Titus) born
1781	Jun 5	Daniel Salt (father of Titus) born
1786	Oct 10	Robert Milligan born at Dunnance, Balmaghie.
1789	Feb 19	William Fairbairn born in Kelso
1801		Population of Bradford: 13,262; number of spinning mills: 1
1802	Jul 5	Daniel Salt marries Grace Smithies
1802		Daniel Salt's mother dies
1803	Jun	Act of Parliament leads to establishment of Lighting & Watching Commissioners
1803	Sep 20	Titus Salt born in Old Manor House, Morley
1803	Nov 9	Salt's first baptism, in Nonconformist church, Morley
1804	Mar 7	Daniel Salt's father dies
1804	Dec 2	Sarah Salt (sister of Titus) born
1805	Feb 27	Salt's second baptism, in Parish church, Batley
1806	Jul 13	Hannah Maria Salt (sister of Titus) born
1807	Apr 26	Hannah Maria Salt (sister of Titus) dies
1807	Nov 14	Anne Salt (sister of Titus) born
1808		Robert Milligan moves to Bradford
1810	Jul 11	Isaac Smithies Salt (brother of Titus) born
1811		Henry Francis Lockwood born in Doncaster
1812	Apr 17	Caroline Whitlam born
1812	Sep 9	Grace Salt (sister of Titus) born

YEAR	DATE	EVENT
1813		Salt family move from Morley to Crofton
1814	Feb 9	Edward (brother of Titus) born
1814		Henry William Ripley born
1816	Jun 16	William Fairbairn marries; living in Manchester
1816		Completion of Leeds - Liverpool canal
1818	Jul 11	William Edward Forster born, in Bradpole
1819	Sep 19	Isaac Smithies Salt (brother of Titus) dies
1819	Oct 18	Henry Wright born
1820		Salt placed with Jackson's of Wakefield, to learn woolstapling
1821	Oct 14	Hannah Salt (sister of Titus) born
1822	Feb 13	Hannah Salt (sister of Titus) dies
1822		Salt moves to Bradford with parents
1822		Salt starts two year period of work at Rouse's
1823		Charles Stead born
1824		Woolcombers & weavers form union
1825	Feb 3	Last Bishop Blaize festival held in Bradford
1825	Jun	Woolcombers & weavers start six month strike
1825	Sep	Daniel Salt elected Lighting & Watching Commissioner
1826	Jan 1	Robert Balgarnie born at Whitehaugh, Peebles
1826	Apr 27	Salt enlisted as Special Constable
1826		First power looms in Bradford set up at Horsfall's mill
1826	May 1-3	Riots at Horsfall's mill. Two killed. Salt, William Rand active in dispersing rioters
1830	Aug 21	Salt marries Caroline Whitlam, in Grimsby
1830		Outram of Greetland processes alpaca wool
1831	Dec 5	William Henry Salt born (1st son, 1st child)
1832	Jun 6	Reform Bill passed, leading to parliamentary representation for Bradford
1832	Dec	Cunliffe Lister & John Hardy (Reformers) elected as M.P.s
1832		Messrs. Hegan, Hall & Co. of Liverpool receive first consignment of alpaca wool
1833	Apr 22	George Salt born (2nd son, 2nd child)
1833	Dec	William Byles comes to Bradford to manage *Bradford Observer*
1834	Feb 6	*Bradford Observer* first published, price 7d
1835	Oct	Rev.ThomasTaylor (Horton Lane Chapel) dies
1835	Nov 29	Amelia Salt born (1st daughter, 3rd child)
1835		Bradford Reform Society instituted; Salt a founding member
1836	Jan 29	Salem Chapel, Manor Row, Bradford opened
1836		Salt makes first purchase of alpaca wool from Messrs Hegan, Hall & Co.
1836		Salt family move from North Parade home to Thornton Rd home.
1836		Henry William Ripley marries Susan, adopted daughter of Robert Milligan
1837	Apr 3	Edward Salt born (3rd son, 4th child)
1837	Nov 20	Confrontation outside Court House, Bradford, where meeting of Guardians taking place; soldiers clear protesters
1838		Branch of Northern Union of Chartists established in Bradford

YEAR	DATE	EVENT
1839	Jul	William Scoresby becomes Vicar of Bradford
1839		Alpaca prices rise from 16$ to 30$ per quintal (100lbs.)
1839		Salt combines alpaca with cotton warp
1840	Jan	First public disturbance in Bradford by Chartists, in Rawson Place
1840	Apr 17	Herbert Salt born (4th son, 5th child)
1841	Aug 7	Fanny Salt born (2nd daughter, 6th child)
1841		Edward Ripley & son Henry William buy Home House, Lightcliffe
1841		W. E. Forster, aged 23, arrives in Bradford
1842	Aug	Widespread Chartist riots in West Riding
1843		Salt appointed Chief Constable of Bradford
1843	Aug 28	Titus Salt Jr. born (5th son, 7th child)
1843	Dec 28	Daniel Salt dies, aged 62; buried in Salem Chapel burial ground
1844	Mid	Salt family moves to Crow Nest, Lightcliffe
1844		Queen Victoria sends two alpaca fleeces to Salt to be made into dress goods
1845		Bradford Amicable Book Society meet at Salt's Crow Nest home
1846	Jan 4	Catherine Crossley born
1846	Oct 20	Whitlam Salt born (6th son, 8th child) *(exact date unconfirmed)*
1847	Mar	Leeds-Bradford railway extended through Saltaire to Keighley
1847	Apr 24	Charter granted for establishing Bradford Corporation
1847	Aug 18	First meeting of Bradford Town Council. Salt elected alderman (South Ward). Robert Milligan elected first mayor of Bradford
1847	Sep 23	Salt granted family Coat of Arms
1847	Oct 18	Coat of Arms acquired by Salt for newly incorporated Bradford
1847	Dec 29	Transfer of responsibility from Bradford Commissioners to Bradford Corporation
1848	Early	W. E. Forster draws up petition supporting Chartists' aims
1848	May	Confrontation in Manchester Rd, Bradford between Chartists & police, soldiers & cavalry
1848	Jul	Salt appointed as one of Bradford's 11 magistrates
1848	Oct	Council announce plan to control smoke emissions from mills. Salt already had one in operation
1848	Nov	Salt elected 2nd mayor of Bradford
1848		Salt appointed Deputy Lieutenant of Yorkshire
1848	Sep 30	James Roberts born in Howarth
1849	Apr 30	Mary Salt born (9th child, 3rd daughter)
1849	Jun 25	'Moral Survey Report' commissioned by Salt
1849	Jun	Salt elected 1st President of Freehold Land Society
1849	Summer	2000 of Salt's workforce given outing to Bell Busk
1849	Jun/ Oct	420 people die in Bradford cholera outbreak
1849	Nov	Henry Forbes elected 3rd mayor of Bradford
1850	Jan	Bradford Town Mission instituted; Salt is first treasurer
1850	Mar 7	'Moral Survey Report' conclusions printed in *Bradford Observer*
1850	Jul 20	Parliament passes Bradford Improvement Act
1850	Aug	Public meeting held re memorial to Sir Robert Peel
1850	Aug	Bar Congregational Church opened in Scarborough
1850	Sep 25	Bradford Improvement Act made effective

YEAR	DATE	EVENT
1850	Nov	Salt meets with architects Lockwood & Mawson regarding possible building of mill at 'Saltaire'
1850	Dec 31	Salt buys Dixon's Mill & surrounding land
1851	Feb	Salt & Forbes buy Girlington Estate
1851	Apr 5	Whitlam Salt (1st child to die) dies, aged 4 *(exact date unconfirmed)*. Buried at Lightcliffe, later re-interred in family mausoleum
1851	May 14	Mary Salt (2nd child to die) dies, aged 2. Buried at Lightcliffe, later re-interred in family mausoleum
1851	Jul 11	Salt & 12 other Bradford businessmen acquire Undercliffe Cemetery site
1851	Aug 7	Railway station opened at Lightcliffe
1851	Autumn	Construction work commences on Salt's Mill at Saltaire
1851	Nov	Foundation stone of Salt's Mill laid
1851	Nov	Balgarnie moves to Scarborough
1851		Salt exhibits goods at Great Exhibition, Hyde Park, London
1851		Bradford Chamber of Commerce established; William Rand elected first president
1851		Population of Bradford: 103,778; number of spinning mills: 129
1852	Feb	Balgarnie ordained 1st Pastor of Bar Church, Scarborough
1852	Jun 19	Helen Salt born (10th child, 4th daughter)
1852		Salt resigns aldermanic office
1853	Mar 21	Samuel Smith (mayor of Bradford) succeeds Salt as treasurer of Bradford Town Mission
1853	Aug 30	St.George's Hall, Bradford opens
1853	Sep 20	Salt's Mill opens, marking Salt's 50th birthday
1853	Nov 18	Ada Salt born (11th & last child, 5th daughter)
1854	Nov 10	Grace Salt dies, aged 76; buried in Salem Chapel burial ground
1854	Dec 7	William Henry Salt marries Emma Dove Octaviana Harris
1854	Dec	Balgarnie marries Martha Rooke in Leeds
1854	Dec	Rev. Jonathan Glyde (Horton Lane Chapel) dies, aged 48. Buried in Undercliffe Cemetery
1854		Saltaire Literary Institute founded in Albert Terrace
1854		Building regulations introduced in Bradford
1855	Nov 6	Sir Robert Peel statue unveiled at Peel Place (formerly Spice Corner), Bradford
1855		Samuel Smith elected president of Bradford Chamber of Commerce
1856	Sep 20	Salt's workers outing to Crow Nest, marking Salt's 53rd birthday
1856	Sep 20	Salt presented with bust by workers at St. George's Hall
1856	Sep 27	Foundation stone of Saltaire Congregational Church laid by Mrs. Salt
1856		Salt elected president of Bradford Chamber of Commerce
1857	Sep 19	Salt's workers outing to Manchester Art Treasures Exhibition
1857	Nov 24	Salt entertains David Livingstone at Crow Nest
1857		Robert Milligan retires from Parliament on account of his age
1857		Salt re-elected president of the Bradford Chamber of Commerce

YEAR	DATE	EVENT
1858		Salt family move to Methley Park, near Leeds
1858		H.W. Ripley elected president of Bradford Chamber of Commerce (continuing in post for 10 years)
1858		Charles Stead submits plans for building 'The Knoll' to newly formed Baildon Local Board
1859	Apr 13	Saltaire Congregational Church opened
1859	Apr 30	Salt & Henry Wickham Wickham elected M.P.s for Bradford
1859	May 31	Salt attends 17th parliamentary session, ending Aug 13
1859	Sep 20	Salt's workers outing to Methley Hall, marking Salt's 56th birthday
1859		Salt welcomes John Bright at public meeting in St. George's Hall; Reform Conference held on following day
1860	Jan 1	New 7 year partnership agreement implemented at Salt's Mill. In addition to Salt, other partners are: sons William Henry, George & Edward; & William Evans Glyde, Charles Stead
1860	Jan 24	Salt attends 18th parliamentary session, ending Aug 28
1860		Mausoleum erected at Saltaire Congregational Church by Messrs. Beanland of Bradford (reportedly not completed until after death of Fanny Salt, which occurred in August, 1861)
1861	Jan	Salt resigns as M.P.
1861	Feb 11	W. E. Forster elected M.P. (unopposed)
1861	Jul 10	Edward Salt marries Mary Jane Susan Elgood
1861	Aug 4	Fanny Salt (3rd child to die) dies, aged 19, at Methley Hall. Eventually interred in family mausoleum
1861	Sep 9	New Horton Lane Chapel foundation stone laid by H.W. Ripley
1862	Jul 1	Robert Milligan dies, aged 75
1862	Jul 5	Robert Milligan buried in Undercliffe Cemetery
1862	Jul 8	Salt lays foundation stone of Castleford Congregational Church
1862		West Park Congregational Church, Harrogate, opened
1862		Salt conveys land on north side of River Aire to Edward (3rd son) for the building of 'Ferniehurst'
1863	Mar 29	Salt lays foundation stone of Bradford Eye & Ear infirmary
1863	Jul 6	Saltaire baths & wash-houses opened
1863	Jul 29	Castleford Congregational Church opened
1863	Sep 30	New Horton Lane Chapel opened
1863		Peel Park presented to Bradford Corporation
1864	Early	South Cliff Congregational Church (Scarborough) Building Committee convened in Leeds
1864	May	Construction work starts on South Cliff Congregational Church, by builder John Barry of Scarborough
1864	Aug 8	P. M., Lord Palmerston, stays at Lightcliffe home of H. W. Ripley
1864	Aug 9	Palmerston lays foundation stone of New Exchange, Bradford
1864	Aug 10	Palmerston visits Saltaire
1864	Sep 17	Salt's workers outing to Scarborough, where Salt was in residence, and son George's yacht *Oithona* was on display
1864	Sep 20	Mrs. Salt lays foundation stone, South Cliff Congregational Church, Scarborough
1865	Jul 26	South Cliff Congregational Church, Scarborough, opened

YEAR	DATE	EVENT
1865		*Bradford Times* first published
1866	Mar 15	Titus Jr. marries Catherine Crossley
1866	May 1	Salt subscribes £1000 for grand tier theatre box at Royal Albert Hall, London
1866	Oct 6	Saltaire Wesleyan Chapel foundation stone laid
1867	Mar 12	Bradford Exchange opening ceremony
1867	Apr 5	Crow Nest sold privately to Salt by Mr. Sutherland Walker for £28,000
1867	Aug 7	Inauguration of Sailors' Orphanage Home, Park St, Hull
1867	Aug	Balgarnie & Newman Hall visit North America, returning in Nov
1867	Sep 23	H. W. Wickham, M.P. dies
1867	Sep	Salt lays foundation stone for Tradesmen's Homes, Lilycroft, Bradford.
1867	Dec	Salt family returns to Crow Nest
1867		Salt attends Paris Exhibition, receives Legion of Honour
1868	Jan	Salt distributes 100 tons of coal to poor of Shipley
1868	Feb 7	Saltaire Wesleyan Chapel opened
1868	Mar 19	Brief strike at Salt's Mill
1868	Jun 2	Saltaire School, Victoria Rd opened
1868	Sep 23	45 almshouses & infirmary in Saltaire completed
1868	Oct 5	*Bradford Observer* becomes daily newspaper, price 1d
1868	Oct 6	'Saltaire' lifeboat launched, Stromness
1868	Nov 16	H. W. Ripley & W. E. Forster elected M. P.s for Bradford
1868		*Bradford Daily Telegraph* first published
1868		Balgarnie ordained 1st pastor, South Cliff Church, Scarborough
1868		Salt's New Mill built, to north of original mill
1869	Mar 9	Founding of Lunatic Asylum for the Northern Counties, Lancaster
1869	Mar 12	H. W. Ripley unseated as M. P., on petition; Miall (Liberal Party) subsequently elected
1869	May 15	Richard Oastler statue unveiled at the end of Market St, Bradford
1869	Jul 3	Official opening of enlarged Sailors' Orphanage Home, Park St, Hull
1869	Jul	Building contract for Saltaire Club & Institute let to John Barry of Scarborough
1869	Jul 30	Saltaire almshouse residents present Salt with gold spectacles & silver-mounted staff
1869	Sep	Queen Victoria confers baronetcies on Salt & William Fairbairn
1870	Mar 31	Salt becomes proprietor of Box 23, Royal Albert Hall (cost £1000)
1870	Jun 21	Saltaire Almshouses Chapel opened
1870	Aug 22	Misses Helen & Ada Salt lay memorial stone of Lightcliffe Chapel
1870	Sep 17	Children of Saltaire present Salt with silver plated dishes
1870	Oct 9	Mary Jane Salt, 1st wife of Edward, dies
1870	Oct 14	Mary Jane Salt interred in Salt's mausoleum
1870	Oct 16	Henry Forbes dies in Harrogate
1870		W. E. Forster, Minister of Education, introduces Education Act
1870		Salt, as chairman of building committee, gives £2000 towards building of Lightcliffe Chapel

YEAR	DATE	EVENT
1871	Jan 18	Salt signs his final will
1871	Jun	Saltaire Club & Institute completed
1871	Jul 25	Saltaire Park opened
1871	Aug 26	Portrait presented to Salt by people of Saltaire
1871	Oct 18	Lightcliffe Congregational Chapel opens
1871	Nov 1	Edward Salt marries Sarah Amelia Rouse, elder (adopted) daughter of late William Rouse
1871		Salt becomes vice-president of Yorkshire Penny Bank
1872	Apr	Saltaire Primitive Methodist Church foundation stone laid
1872	Jul 30	Bradford Trades Council (New Movement) established
1872	Sep 2	Burmese ambassadors visit Saltaire
1872	Oct 25	Japanese ambassadors visit Saltaire
1872	Nov 21	Saltaire Club & Institute Main Hall opened
1873	Jan 4	Salt signs 1st codicil to his will
1873	Apr 2	Amelia Salt marries Henry Wright at Lightcliffe. They move to his London home; Helen Salt succeeds her sister Amelia as Salt's confidential secretary
1873	Sep 9	New Bradford Town Hall opened
1873	Sep 20	Salt celebrates 70th birthday by entertaining 3000 workers & 1200 guests at Crow Nest
1873		Balgarnie elected president of Yorkshire Congregational Union
1873		Pullman, railway coach manufacturer, visits Saltaire
1874	Feb 4	H. W. Ripley & W. E. Forster elected M.P.s for Bradford
1874	Aug 1	Salt statue unveiled in front of Bradford Town Hall
1874	Aug 18	Sir William Fairbain dies
1875	May 1	Gordon & Harold Salt lay foundation stone Saltaire Sunday School
1876		Celebrations held to mark Balgarnie's 25 years of ministry in Scarborough
1876	Apr 29	Salt makes last public appearance, at opening of Saltaire Sunday School
1876	Jun 23	Start of two week strike & lockout at Salt's Mill
1876	Jul 28	Salt signs 2nd codicil to his will
1876	Dec 29	Sir Titus Salt dies, aged 73, at Crow Nest
1877	Jan 5	Sir Titus Salt's funeral; 120,000 line route
1877	Nov	Balgarnie's biography *Sir Titus Salt, His Life and It's Lessons* published
1877		Two stained glass windows, in memory of Sir Titus Salt, installed in Lightcliffe Chapel
1877		Salt Trust created
1878	Jan 14	Ownership of Box 23, Royal Albert Hall, transferred to Salt's son-in-law Henry Wright
1878	Jul 21	Henry Lockwood dies, aged 66, at Richmond, London; buried in Kensal Green Cemetery, London
1878		Lady Caroline Salt, & two unmarried daughters Helen & Ada, leave Crow Nest, for new home of Broadoak, Clapham
1878		Richard Kershaw (silk spinner of Brighouse) buys Crow Nest

YEAR	DATE	EVENT
1880		Queen Victoria confers baronetcy on H. W. Ripley
1881	Jul	Firm of Sir Titus Salt Bart. Sons & Co. Ltd. is incorporated
1882	Jun 23	Prince of Wales (later King Edward VII) opens Bradford Technical College; royal couple stay at Milner Field as guests of Titus Jr.
1882	Nov 10	Sir H. W. Ripley dies
1882		Charles Stead mortgages 'The Knoll' as security for the mill company
1883	Jul 11	Ada Salt marries Edmund Herbert Stevenson at Grafton Square Congregational Church, Clapham
1884	Dec	Rev. J. R. Campbell (Horton Lane Chapel) dies
1886	Apr 5	W. E. Forster dies
1886	Apr 10	W. E. Forster buried in Burley-in-Wharfedale
1887	May 6	Royal Yorkshire Jubilee Exhibition and new Schools of Art and Science opened in Exhibition Rd by HRH Princess Beatrice
1887	Jul 31	Balgarnie preaches farewell sermon at South Cliff Church, Scarborough
1887	Oct	Royal Yorkshire Jubilee Exhibition ends
1887	Nov 19	Titus Jr. (4th child to die) dies suddenly, aged 44 at Milner Field; buried in family mausoleum
1889	Apr 25	William Mawson dies, aged 61. Buried in Undercliffe Cemetery
1889		Saltaire (Moorhead Lane) steam car shed opens
1890	May 31	Mrs. Titus Salt opens Crowghyll Park, Shipley
1890		Organ in Saltaire Congregational Church enlarged, under supervision of Gordon Salt
1890		U.S.A.'s President McKinley imposes heavy duties on plush fabrics
1890		Sir Titus Salt, Bart. Sons & Co. Ltd. establishes a plush factory at Bridgeport, USA
1892	Jul 7	Sir William Henry Salt (5th child to die) dies, aged 60, at his home in Maplewell, Leicestershire; buried in church yard of parish church of St Paul's, Woodhouse Eaves, Maplewell
1892	Sep 3	Sir Titus Salt Bart. Sons & Co. Ltd. goes into liquidation
1892		Gordon Salt (with others) lays memorial stone of Lightcliffe Chapel School
1893	Apr 20	Lady Caroline Salt dies, aged 81, at St. Leonard's
1893	Apr 25	Lady Caroline Salt interred in family mausoleum, Saltaire
1893	Jun	Salt's company bought by four Bradford business men (John Maddock, John Rhodes, James Roberts, Isaac Smith)
1893	Aug 3	Henry Wright dies at Harrogate, aged 73
1893	Aug 9	Henry Wright buried in Grove Rd Cemetery, Harrogate
1893	Nov 3	Ownership of Box 23, Royal Albert Hall transferred to Amelia Wright
1893		Charles Stead looses 'The Knoll' when bank forecloses on the mortgage; moves to Freshfield, near Southport, Lancs
1893		Edward Salt looses 'Ferniehurst', which had also been previously mortgaged as security for the firm. Edward leaves the area, moving first to London & then Bathampton
1895	Jun 6	Ownership of Box 23, Royal Albert Hall, passes out of Salt family

YEAR	DATE	EVENT
1896	May 1	Opening of orphanage villa 'Sir Titus Salt', Newland, Hull
1896	Aug 15	Statue of Sir Titus Salt, now relocated to Lister park, unveiled
1896		Isaac Smith, John Maddock retire
1899	May 28	Balgarnie dies, aged 73, at 51, Crouch Hill Rd, London
1899	May 31	Balgarnie buried at Abney Park Cemetery, London
1901		*Bradford Observer* continued as *Yorkshire Daily Observer*
1901		Joseph Wright made president of the Salt Schools
1902		John Rhodes retires, leaving James Roberts fully in charge of company
1902		Charles Stead dies in Southport; buried in Nab Wood Cemetery
1903	Oct 24	Edward Salt (6th child to die) dies in Bathampton, aged 66
1903	Oct 29	Edward Salt buried in graveyard of parish church of Bathampton (St. Nicholas's)
1903		James Roberts purchases 'Milner Field' from Mrs. Catherine Salt
1903		Statue of Sir Titus Salt erected in Saltaire Park (Centenary of Birth)
1904	Jul 2	Lady Emma Dove Octaviana Salt, widow of Sir William Henry Salt, dies, aged 72
1904	Aug	Tramcar sheds in Keighley Rd, Saltaire, opened
1904		James Roberts sells the Mill Gas Works to Shipley Urban District Council
1904		Tramshed in Exhibition Rd, Saltaire, demolished
1909		Baronetcy conferred on James Roberts
1912	Jul 21	Herbert Salt (7th child to die) dies, aged 72
1912	Jul 26	Herbert Salt buried in Norwood Cemetery, London
1913	May 8	George Salt (8th child to die) dies, aged 80, in London
1914	Jun 21	Amelia Wright (nee Salt, 9th child to die) dies, aged 78, in Tunbridge Wells
1914	Jun 25	Amelia Wright cremated at Golders Green Crematorium, London; ashes interred in the grave of her late husband Henry in Grove Rd Cemetery, Harrogate
1916	Sep	Grand Duchess George of Russia visits Saltaire Mills
1918	Feb 1	Sir James Roberts retires. Village & goodwill sold to Sir James Hill (£2M)
1918	Jul 18	Edmund Herbert Stevenson dies, aged 65
1918	Jul 20	Edmund Herbert Stevenson cremated at Golders Green Crematorium, London; ashes dispersed in Garden of Rest
1920	Jan	Sir James Roberts presents Saltaire Park to Bradford Corporation; park renamed "Roberts Park"
1921		Coal strike causing temporary closure of the mill (2000 workers laid off)
1923	Jul 23	Salts (Saltaire) Ltd. formed
1924	Jun 11	Helen Salt (10th child to die) dies, aged 71, at Eastbourne
1924	Jun 16	Helen Salt cremated at Golders Green Crematorium, London; ashes dispersed in Garden of Rest
1926		General Strike; short time working & lack of coal leads Salts (Saltaire) Ltd to suffer trading loss

YEAR	DATE	EVENT
1929		Saltaire village sold to Bradford estate agent Mr. Fred Gresswell
1929	Jul 31	Sarah Amelia Salt, widow of Edward, dies, aged approx. 83
1929	Aug 2	Sarah Amelia Salt cremated at Golders Green Crematorium, London; ashes dispersed in Garden of Rest
1930	Jan 22	Catherine Salt, widow of Titus Jr., dies, aged 84, in Harrogate. Cremated; ashes interred in family mausoleum
1930		Milner Field put up for sale; no buyer found
1931		Two-Shift working came into operation at The Mill
1933	Oct 6	Village (dwellings & shops) sold to Bradford Property Trust Ltd
1933	Late	Largest Turbo-Alternator in Textile history Installed at The Mill
1935	Nov 22	Ada Stevenson (nee Salt), last surviving child of Salt dies, aged 82, in London
1935	Nov 25	Ada Stevenson (nee Salt) cremated at Golders Green Crematorium, London; ashes dispersed in Garden of Rest

APPENDIX 3

THE SALT FAMILY

During their marriage of more than 46 years, 11 children were born to Sir Titus and Lady Caroline Salt, in the period 1831-1853. Balgarnie's biography provides an account of events up to the death of Sir Titus, but it helps the historical account to trace and record, as far as possible, the later life of the Dowager Lady Salt, and also the lives of the Salt children.

Salt, as we see in Balgarnie's biography, had the ambition that his sons should follow him in his undertakings, and to a considerable extent that ambition was realized. Several of the children were, in due course, to be directly engaged in the family business, both before and after the death of Sir Titus; and his philanthropic traditions were also, to a degree, continued. Inevitably as the years went by, circumstances changed. Apart from the consequences of Sir Titus' death in 1876, the events of 1892, when the company went into liquidation, proved to be a watershed for those directly involved. The Dowager Lady Salt outlived this later event, as did most of the children, one of who was to live on for a further 43 years.

This Appendix seeks to add to the historical record of the family, mindful that there is much remaining to be discovered and recorded. Information in this Appendix has been gained partly from Registry certificates and wills; from Directories available for relevant areas (particularly London and Tunbridge Wells); from the various census records now available, and to a limited extent from existing publications on the subject.[384] However, many other sources have also been used. References are quoted where judged helpful or necessary.

Before turning to the events following the death of Sir Titus in 1876, it is worth adding to the account given by Balgarnie of the family's circumstances up to that time.The seven eldest children (William Henry,

---

[384] E.g. Ref: GtPat.

George, Amelia, Edward, Herbert, Fanny and Titus Jr.[385]) had all been born during the time that the family was living in Bradford, first at a house in North Parade (a continuation of Manor Row) and subsequently, from 1836, at a house at the junction of Thornton Road and Little Horton Lane. The family moved to Crow Nest in 1844, and that is where we take up the story.

Salt's fortunes in 1844 were good in every sense. His Bradford based mills were thriving; his standing in Bradford society was high; his status within the influential Congregational community in particular was secure; and he was the head of a young and growing family. Crow Nest, with its elegant drive, landscaped acres and imposing mansion must have been a welcome retreat from the chaos of nearby Bradford. Salt, in his early 40s, was already deeply concerned about the social problems resulting from industrialization. However his major acts of paternalism and benevolence were to come later.

William Henry and George, the two eldest sons, attended Huddersfield College for a time, receiving an education judged suitable for those whose future lay in business, but in 1847, William Henry (then 16), George (14) and Edward (10) were sent to Mill Hill School in London. As was the case with Huddersfield College, this latter school was deemed appropriate for the children of well-to-do Dissenters, but unlike the College, its curriculum corresponded to the conventions of education thought necessary for the sons of gentlemen. The two daughters, Amelia (then 11) and Fanny (6), were to receive private educations, not uncommon in the circumstances of the time. By this time Whitlam, destined to be the last of the Salt sons, had been born.

Thus visitors to Crow Nest in the late 1840s would find the elder sons away at boarding school, and the daughters and younger children at home with the family, being raised in the privileged setting of a country estate. The scene at festive times, with the sons no doubt returning from boarding school, is easily visualised.

---

[385] In order to distinguish between father and son, we refer, throughout our commentary in this book, to the son as "Titus Jr.". His correct name was simply "Titus".

Around 1848, William Henry returned after a year at Mill Hill School, and probably entered directly into the family business, being followed by George a year later. Herbert (9) also entered the school around this latter time, and was to continue at the school for several years, as was Edward. Mary Salt, the third daughter, was born in the same year, 1849.

A Christmas gathering in December 1850 would have found the two parents with 9 of their 11 children now born – William Henry (19), George (17), Amelia (15), Edward (13), Herbert (10), Fanny (9), Titus (7), Whitlam (4), and Mary (1). Since first arriving at Crow Nest, Salt's success and standing had much increased. He had served his term as Mayor of (recently incorporated) Bradford, the *Moral Survey* he had instigated had been produced, business was thriving, his elder sons were by now in the family business, and his thoughts of a new industrial community were beginning to take shape – the architects Lockwood and Mawson had had their first meeting with Salt in the November, and on 31st December, 1850, Salt purchased the land required for the new site.

Tragically, in the spring of 1851, the youngest children Whitlam and Mary died in successive months of scarlet fever. The family must have come under great strain, losing the two children born at Crow Nest. Salt was no doubt heavily committed in the running of his five Bradford mills; by now plans for the gigantic new mill were well advanced; and the company was involved in the prestigious Great Exhibition in London. Infant mortality was no respecter of status. Both Whitlam and Mary were laid to rest in the burial ground of the nearby Bramley Lane Congregational Chapel at Lightcliffe.

Better family fortune lay ahead. On 19th June, 1852 Helen was born, to be followed on 18th November, 1853 by Ada.[386] In fact at the opening ceremony of the mill on 20th September, 1853, Mrs. Salt would have been seven months pregnant with Ada. Helen and Ada were almost a decade younger than the other siblings, and with an age difference of a mere 17 months are likely to have been particularly close. It is interesting to reflect on the likely relationship between the two young sisters and

---

[386] These dates have been confirmed from official Registry records.

their elder sister Amelia (18 years older than Ada). As we shall see in the later lives of the three sisters, Amelia may have been a leader to whom the younger sisters were apt to turn.

In 1854, Titus Jr. (11) joined Herbert (14) at Mill Hill School, but their schooling was interrupted the following year, when an outbreak of scarlet fever at the school prompted their evacuation. They were not to return, their educations being completed elsewhere. None of the sons excelled academically, but later accounts reveal significant abilities that they put to good use. It is thought that all of the sons, with the possible exception of Herbert, at some stage worked in the family company.

There was an age difference of almost 22 years between the eldest and youngest of the Salt children, and so it was that in 1854 when William Henry married, the youngest Salt child (Ada) was only one year old. William Henry (23) married Emma Dove Octaviana Harris, only child of John Dove Harris of Leicester – a part of the country to which the couple would, in later life, move. Their first residence was at Ashgrove, near Halifax, sufficiently close to the (by now well established) Saltaire works for William Henry to continue in the family business. The young family moved subsequently to Summer Hill, Rawdon.[387]

It was in 1854, in fact, that William Henry and George, the two eldest sons, were made junior partners in the family business, along with two non-family stalwarts, Charles Stead and William Glyde. William Henry appears to have had more than a mere professional interest in the Saltaire area. That same year he helped finance Saltaire's budding new library, at a time when it was housed in one of the newly built Albert Terrace boarding-houses. He was granted a game certificate in 1856, at which time he was described as being "of Saltaire", but such location may simply be reflecting his place of work. Also granted a certificate in the same session was the young Edward (19) who was still at the family home in Lightcliffe.[388]

Meanwhile at Crow Nest, the other members of the family no doubt

---

[387] Ref: BO, 8th July, 1892, p7.
[388] Ref: BO, 9th October, 1856, p6.

helped Mr. and Mrs. Salt host the visit, on their father's 53rd birthday in 1856, of the 3,000 strong workforce of Saltaire mill. The elder children were present also at the evening celebrations in St. George's Hall, Bradford, at which Salt was honoured by his workers.[389]

1858 brought the move from Crow Nest to Methley Park, near Leeds, and the following nine years there saw the family maturing, with the number of family members under the one roof decreasing. By 1859 it seems likely that, in addition to William Henry and George, Edward (22) had also entered the family business. Perhaps it was this situation, together with the continued presence of partners Stead and Glyde, that informed Salt's decision to stand for Parliament in 1859. Election was bound to take him away from the business for lengthy periods, but no doubt he had confidence in their abilities.

During his time as an M.P., and when Parliament was sitting, the family occupied apartments at Fenton's Hotel, just a few minutes carriage-ride from Westminster. We do not know which members of the family accompanied the parents to London; it may have been only the four daughters - Titus Jr. (approx. 16) was still studying; Herbert (20) may have remained at Methley Hall. The eldest daughter Amelia by this time would have been in her mid-twenties, and had probably taken up her role as her father's confidential secretary.

The 1861 census return for Methley Hall shows Mr. and Mrs. Salt in residence, together with Herbert (20) and Titus Jr. (17). Herbert is recorded as being a "farmer of 316 acres, employing others"; if Herbert ever worked in the family business it could only have been for a very brief period. Titus Jr. is recorded as a "scholar". Interestingly there is no record of any of the daughters, or of George, at the family home. During his involvement with the mill at Saltaire, George is reported to have lived for many years "at the mill house".[390] Edward was to marry in July 1861, and indeed appears in the Baildon census. Methley Hall is recorded as having 10 domestic staff. Clearly the Salt family lived in considerable

---

[389] Ref: BO, 25th September, 1856, p6.
[390] Ref: BfdWT, 16th May, 1913, p2.

style.

Edward's marriage to Mary Jane Susan Elgood of Leicestershire strengthened an earlier link between the two families – Mary was the cousin of William Henry's wife Emma. The home that Edward and Mary established at Ferniehurst, in Baildon, on the north side of the River Aire, was to be the first Salt residence in the immediate environs of Saltaire. The mansion house was newly built by Edward, and lavishly fitted and furnished. The interior boasted 12 bedrooms, a library, and a billiard room. Elsewhere on the estate there were tennis courts, numerous greenhouses, a farm, a dairy, a carriage-house large enough for six carriages, and several other buildings. Here Edward was to live for the next three decades, engaging not only in the mill's business but also in his other interests. He enjoyed riding to hounds, angling and shooting. He also followed in his father's footsteps with his horticultural interests, and became a renowned grower of orchids. In due course he would be appointed a Justice of the Peace for the West Riding, and a Deputy Lieutenant of the county.

Salt by this time was successfully engaged in both the building of Saltaire and his philanthropic enterprises. Even so, life had its tribulations. The second eldest daughter Fanny had been certified in 1859 as suffering from "tubercular phthisis". Visits to spa towns such as St. Leonard's and Pau (France) may have eased her symptoms, but on 4th August, 1861, just a few days before her 20th birthday, Fanny died of the condition at Methley Hall. Balgarnie speaks movingly of the circumstances (see Chapter XIII), and one senses that the relationship between the families of Salt and Balgarnie was quite close. An example, of less import, of the relationship between the Salt children and the Balgarnie family is found in the May 1863 issue of the *Evangelical Magazine and Missionary Chronicle* (the *Missionary Magazine*), which reveals the young daughters Helen and Ada contributing to Mrs. Balgarnie's collections for missionaries in Madagascar and elsewhere.

The next marriage of a Salt son occurred in March, 1866, when Titus Jr. (22) married Catherine Crossley (20), second daughter of Joseph

Crossley of Halifax. It was also around this time that Titus Jr. entered the family business.[391] The Salt and Crossley families had much in common. Salt's sister Anne had married John Smith of Jersey, whose sister Hannah had married Joseph Crossley. Both families had developed major, successful textile enterprises; both families were Congregationalists, and were at this time heavily engaged in philanthropic ventures and civic duties. Titus Jr. and Catherine were to follow in the families' ways, adhering to the Congregational Church and to the traditions of civic duty and paternalism. They were also to become leading socialites in the area, acting as hosts of royalty on two separate occasions. Their home, Milner Field, was the second of the large estates to be developed across the river from Saltaire by Salt's sons. Covering approximately 300 acres, the estate was truly grand. Unlike Ferniehurst, of which no photographs are known to have survived, there are many photographs of Milner Field available, some of which have recently been published.[392] (On the subject of photographic records, we know of no such evidence for the Salt children other than Titus Jr.).

Thus it was that, in the late 1860s, several of Salt's sons were engaged in the family business, and three of the sons – William Henry, Edward and Titus Jr. – were married. George and Herbert were to remain bachelors for several more years. George is known to have been involved in the family business, and had developed an interest in yachting that seems to have been sustained throughout his subsequent life; his yacht *Oithona* was kept moored at Scarborough.[393] Herbert is reported to have established himself by this time as a gentleman farmer of Bell Busk, west of Skipton.[394]

The family's move back to Crow Nest in December, 1867, would have found Mr. and Mrs. Salt, aged 64 and 55 respectively, with probably just the three daughters remaining in the family home - Amelia (32); Helen

---

[391] Ref: BfdDT, 21st November, 1887.
[392] Ref: Firth.
[393] Ref: BO, 22nd September, 1864, p5.
[394] Ref: GtPat, p86.

(15); and Ada (14). As Balgarnie states, the coming period was to mark Salt's declining years, and the now reduced size of the family group at Crow Nest reflected, perhaps, the passing of Salt's prime. However, recognition of Salt's contribution still lay ahead, with the award of his baronetcy in 1869, and his commitment to social causes being in no way diminished. Also in 1873, Crow Nest was to see the hosting of another feast for his 3,000 workers, to celebrate his 70th birthday in September of that year.

Sadly Edward's wife Mary Jane Susan was to die young, at the age of 29 in October, 1870. Her remains were interred in the family mausoleum adjoining Saltaire Congregational Church, but interestingly the main memorial to her can be found in the Anglican Church of St. John's, Baildon. The memorial takes the form of a beautiful stained glass window. The following year, on 1st November, 1871, Edward remarried, to Sarah Amelia Rouse, the elder (adopted) daughter of William Rouse (deceased). It was, of course, with the Rouse family business that Salt had first worked when arriving in Bradford almost 50 years earlier, and with whom he acquired his textile trade skills. Rev. Saville, who the Salt family had known since its time at Methley Hall, assisted at this second marriage of Edward, which took place at St. Mary's Church in Burley-in-Wharfedale. Edward, with his second wife, continued to live at Ferniehurst.

William Henry, having started in the family business before it consolidated at Saltaire, and after approx. 25 years of service, retired relatively early.[395] Still in his 40s, he and his family moved to Leicester, the birthplace of his wife Emma. The three sons remaining in the business – George, Edward and Titus Jr. – are seen to have been a considerable force in pursuing the company's interests. Salt opposed the statutory limitation on hours of work for his employees, and the three sons helped to pursue this policy in the early 1870s when the Nine Hour Bill was presented in Parliament. The Bill sought to limit the working hours of women and children in factories to nine hours per day. The

---

[395] William Henry's name does not feature in the 1873 Articles of Partnership (Ref: Part).

majority of employers in the region opposed the Bill. George Salt chaired a meeting of Bradford employers which considered the issue; Titus Jr. seconded the meeting's motion of opposition to the Bill; and Edward led the delegation which presented their protest to the Home Office. The Bill, when presented, failed to pass into law; a more modest Ten Hour Bill was passed by the Disraeli government.[396]

In 1873, Amelia (37) married a leading lay Congregationalist of the time, Henry Wright (53) of Kensington. Henry Wright operated a successful railway wagon manufacturing company, the Metropolitan Railway Carriage and Wagon Works, which his father had started in Saltley, Birmingham. Wright was also the first to introduce a system of hiring coal-wagons, and by this and other means was regarded as a leading figure in the development of the country's burgeoning railway industry. An example of the company's products dating from 1854 – initially used as a first class carriage for the Swedish railway – has been preserved.[397] Beyond his business successes, Wright was a distinguished lay member of the Congregational Church, being for more than 30 years Deacon of Kensington Chapel, and the first lay member to be Presidential Chairman of the London Congregational Union. For many years Henry Wright was a prominent activist in the London Missionary Society, and other activities such as the founding of the Memorial Hall in London. Salt gave financial support to both enterprises and there can be no doubt that Wright had been well known within the family for some considerable time before the formal engagement in 1872. Amelia and Henry married at Lightcliffe Congregational Church on 2nd April, 1873, at which time they moved to his London home at 22, Upper Phillimore Gardens, Kensington. Helen (20) succeeded her sister as Salt's confidential secretary.

The last of the Salt children to marry before the death of Sir Titus may have been George, who – according to Burke's Peerage – was married, in 1875, at the age of approximately 42, to Jennie Louise Fresco.

---

[396] Ref: GtPat, p320, 338-339.
[397] Ref: Rail, p222.

However there is some confusion about the date of their marriage (see later).

Unsurprisingly, the death of Sir Titus in late 1876 was to bring about a major upheaval in the social and domestic arrangements of the family. Quite apart from the changed circumstances at Crow Nest, Salt's will made substantial provisions for the several family members, which no doubt changed the individual circumstances of some of the recipients. Lady Salt inherited the Crow Nest estate, and an annuity of £5,000. Legacies of £100,000 were awarded to each of William Henry and Herbert (being the two sons at this time lacking involvement with the family business), and £80,000 (in trust) to each of the daughters. The other sons (George, Edward and Titus Jr.) were partners in the company; the will made provision whereby any such son leaving the company or dying within twenty years of Sir Titus' death was to receive payments reflecting the value of their share in the company, payable in annual installments over a twenty year period. Additionally, a legacy of £100,000 was given to trustees to provide for those succeeding to the baronetcy. The will made various other provisions, but the foregoing gives a good indication of the main provisions insofar as they affected the family members.

The Dowager Lady Salt would have found herself now with just her two unmarried daughters Helen (24) and Ada (23) in the family home of Crow Nest. She resolved to leave the West Riding, and move south, to Clapham, with her two daughters.

Shortly after the funeral of Sir Titus, Lady Salt spent time at the Kensington home of her eldest daughter – this is recorded in a letter dated 26th February, 1877, written on her behalf by son-in-law Henry Wright to the Church Members of South Cliff Congregational Church, Scarborough, acknowledging their condolences. Lady Salt was presumably familiar with London to some extent, through time spent there with her husband during Salt's time as M.P., and no doubt more recently, through visits to the Kensington home of her daughter Amelia. However the full circumstances prompting her decision to move permanently to Clapham remain unclear. Probably the large estate of Crow Nest was no longer suitable to the needs of the now much reduced family group. Perhaps her motives were financial. It may have been a wish to be closer to Amelia, although Kensington and Clapham were a four-mile carriage-ride apart. Perhaps one or more of her many siblings had settled in the area, although that possibility is unsupported by our limited search through census returns. She may also have been looking to the futures of Helen and Ada. Finally there is also the possibility mentioned in the footnotes of Balgarnie's biography, Chapter XIII that Salt had had at some stage a property in Clapham.[398] Whatever the reason, in 1878 the Dowager Lady Salt moved to Broadoak, Clapham. At this time the area was still a fashionable rural idyll in the Surrey countryside, and had yet to be engulfed by London's suburban expansion. Broadoak was an impressive mansion standing in grounds overlooking the south side of Clapham Common. This was to be the home of Lady Salt for the remainder of her life.

A 1929 description of Broadoak describes it as "one of the best of the later Georgian mansions remaining (…having) a frontage of brick with four Ionic pilasters and the name 'Broadoak' carved upon it." The description goes on to speak of the interior being decorated in the Adam style, and makes specific reference to the presence of the Salt coat of arms in the entrance hall.[399] However, a more authoritative account of the building's history indicates that it was built for Lady Salt circa 1877.[400] Adjacent buildings include what was probably originally a stable; there is also a Roman Catholic chapel, introduced at a later date, in Italian renaissance style, which serves the needs of the present day occupants (see below).

Broadoak still stands today, within the grounds of St. Francis Xavier College, west of the very nearby underground station of Clapham South. Inspection of both the interior and exterior in 2002 found that all evidence

---

[398] Ref: ClapO, 2nd June, 1883. (There is no reference to such a property in Salt's will).
[399] Ref: Clap1, p59.
[400] Ref: Clap2, p41.

of the Salts' period of occupancy, including the coat of arms, had disappeared.[401] The building judged to have originally been the stable is, in the present day, a children's nursery.

Lady Salt and her daughters remained true to their Congregational roots and it is clear from subsequent events that they attended the nearby Grafton Square Congregational Church, an imposing building near the NE corner of Clapham Common, and destined to be demolished following serious war damage. The Church's Minister from 1865 until 1895 was Dr. James Guinness Rogers, an outstanding activist who served as an adviser to Gladstone. His autobiography speaks at some length on the issue of education, where he refers to "Mr. Forster's rudeness."[402] Guinness Rogers was a near contemporary of Balgarnie, being born in 1822, in Enniskillen, and the two Ministers were later, in the 1890s, to work together on the Executive Committee of the Memorial Hall, Farringdon Street.

The 1881 census provides an interesting snapshot of the dispersed Salt family a little more than four years after the death of Sir Titus. The female side of the family was settled in London – Lady Salt and the unmarried daughters Helen and Ada (now in their late twenties) in Clapham, and Amelia with her (now retired) husband Henry Wright in Kensington. Perhaps characteristically, the Wrights had two missionaries visiting them at the time of the census.

The relocation of the Dowager Lady Salt and the three daughters to London could be seen as drawing a line under their associations with Saltaire, apart perhaps from occasional later visits. There is no evidence, from their subsequent actions of which we are aware, that indicates any affiliation to the village. In the case of the three daughters, Saltaire was an early part of their lives, the majorities of which would be spent in the south of England.

Whereas the female members of the family were to be geographically

---

[401] The inspection of Broadoak was made possible by kind permission of the College, and under the very helpful guidance of Alan Collins.
[402] Refs: Guinn; Peel, p123.

close in London, by 1881 some of the Salt sons had gone their separate ways. Having inherited the baronetcy on the death of his father, the eldest son Sir William Henry Salt was living in some style with his wife Emma Dove Octaviana at Maplewell Grange, Woodhouse, Leicester, where he was farming 400 acres. The mansion had a staff of nine servants, and his farm employed 10 men. Their son Shirley Harris (23), had already married and was living at 96, Regent's Park Road, London, studying at the Inner Temple. Their daughter Constance Dove Salt (25), unmarried, was living with her brother. Edward (44) and his second wife Sarah Amelia (34) were living at Ferniehurst, where, although without children of their own, they were hosting several young nieces and nephews and their mother Edith Gordon, younger sister of Sarah Amelia. The 1881 census records Herbert Salt living at Carla Beck House in Carlton in Craven, one mile SW of Skipton. It may be that it was from this address that he had been farming land at Bell Busk (approximately 7 miles from Carlton) as reported earlier, but by 1881 his occupation is recorded simply as "annuitant" – suggesting he was living on the yearly allowance inherited through his father's will. George Salt is recorded in the 1881 census as a visitor at Radleys Hotel in Southampton St. Mary, Hampshire. The census records him as being unmarried, which may be simply an error. However, a search of the census also fails to reveal Jennie Louise Salt, who he reportedly married in 1875 (later records relating to George's wife often spell her first name "Jenny", a spelling that we have adopted in our account). The issue merits further research than we have been able to pursue.

At the time of the 1881 census, most of the growing family of Titus Jr. were not actually at home at Milner Field. Titus Jr. was visiting his brother-in-law Henry Crossley at Aldburgh Hall, Burton on Ure, and his wife Catherine was visiting her step-mother Elizabeth Crossley in Hornsey, Middlesex. (There may have been serious illness in the Hornsey home, where a hospital nursing sister is recorded as a visitor). Their four children were also dispersed – Gordon (14) at Winchester College, Harold (12) at Temple Grove Grammar School, Mortlake,

Surrey; only the younger children Lawrence (6) and Isabel (4) were actually at Milner Field, apparently in the care of seven servants, with the six year old son ambiguously identified as head of household.

The 1880s were to bring more changes in the fortunes of the Salt family. On 11th July, 1883, Ada (29) married Edmund Herbert Stevenson (30), a civil engineer living in Streatham, Surrey. The marriage, at Grafton Square Congregational Church, is recorded in a very modest announcement in the local newspaper.[403] There is evidence that Stevenson, like the other son-in-law Henry Wright, was held in a position of regard and trust within the Salt family – in due course it would be Edmund Stevenson who would be granted probate in the wills of Lady Salt, Edward and Amelia. Ada and Edmund were to have one child, Monica Helen, who was born in Clapham in 1886 (or possibly 1885).

In Saltaire the mill was continuing production, and adapting to the changing circumstances of the times. Although the move had been resisted during the life of Sir Titus, the younger generation of partners, in July 1881, had the firm incorporated as a joint stock company, with the title Sir Titus Salt, Bart., Sons and Co. Shares were not offered to the public, but were made available to the partners and certain members of their families. All of Salt's family became shareholders. The first directors of the new company were Edward, Titus Jr., Charles Stead and William Stead, Titus Jr. taking on the role of Company Secretary. He had, in addition to his role at the Saltaire works, commitments in the USA. The Saltaire company had acquired an extensive ironworks at Dayton, Tennessee. Titus Jr. frequently visited the Dayton concern, which became very profitable.[404] He inherited the mantle of paternalism which his father had carried - it was Titus Jr. who was particularly active in the issues of the educational needs of the village's workers and their children. An interesting instance of the Radical edge to the thinking of Titus Jr. is seen in his hosting a dinner at his Milner Field home on 17th April, 1880, to "commemorate the overthrow of Lord Beaconsfield, and of

[403] Ref: SLP, 21st July, 1883.
[404] Ref: BfdDT, 21st November, 1887.

Imperialism in England, at the General Election, 1880;" an original invitation to the dinner is held in the Saltaire Studies Centre, Shipley College.

He and his wife Catherine played their social role in the local community, and hosted royalty on two occasions during the decade. In June 1882, they received the Prince and Princess of Wales (later King Edward VII and Queen Alexandra) at Milner Field. The royal couple opened Bradford's new Technical College. In 1887 Titus Jr. led an ambitious project, the Royal Yorkshire Jubilee Exhibition, designed to raise funds for new accommodation for the Saltaire Schools of Science and Art. The Schools had proved so successful in their original Saltaire Club and Institute location that additional space was required to house their expansion, and that space was to be provided through the building of a new College to the east of the Institute. Titus Jr. planned the project as a testimony to his father. Falling as it did in Queen Victoria's jubilee year, the Exhibition took on a double role, centred on the newly constructed College in the appropriately named Exhibition Road. This was perhaps the most important public building development in Saltaire in the "post- Sir Titus" period, and stands today as a tribute to its leading advocate, Titus Jr. The Exhibition covered 12 acres, extending eastwards from Exhibition Road across the area now covered by Maddocks Street, Rhodes Street and Baker Street. To the north of the College was a Concert Hall that could seat 3000, behind which lay a large park with bandstand, café and photographic studio. The Exhibition itself was on a grand scale, and included its own Police Station manned by 20 officers. Visitors, paying an entry fee of 1s, could enjoy such diverse entertainments as a toboggan run, musical performances and - not without some irony - demonstrations of the rustic art of wool combing by hand. Opened by HRH Princess Beatrice on 6th May, 1887, the Exhibition ran until October of that year. Tragedy was shortly to follow. In the following month, on 19th November, Titus Jr. died suddenly, aged 44, at Milner Field. Having previously been diagnosed as having a heart weakness, his death was not entirely unexpected, and was perhaps partly a consequence of the hectic life he had probably had to lead over the preceding months. Titus Jr. was buried in the family mausoleum. (Although he had been an advocate of cremation,[405] the practice in 1887 was still highly novel, and the only facilities existing in the country were at Woking Crematorium, Surrey, where in 1886 the total number of cremations was ten). Obituaries testify to the regard in which Titus Jr. was held.[406]

The loss of Titus Jr. was widely felt. His brother George (approx. 53) had retired from the company, after more than 30 years service, in 1886, and so the death of Titus Jr. left only one family member actively involved in running the mill – Edward. Catherine Salt continued to live at Milner Field until 1903, and remained active in the affairs of the community during that time. She was a life governor of Saltaire Hospital, and a governor of the Salt Schools until such time as they were taken over by the local Education Authority. Actively involved in Saltaire Congregational Church, Catherine was also the leader of the Saltaire Conversazione, initially set up to popularize the dress fabrics of local manufacture. Crowghyll Park, in Shipley, was formally opened by her in 1890. After leaving Milner Field, Catherine moved to Denton Hall, Ben Rhydding, where she remained until 1911, going then to live at the Old Rectory, Thorp Arch. The last four years of her life were spent in Harrogate. Her death, at the age of 84, on 22nd January, 1930 was followed by cremation. Catherine's ashes were placed in the family mausoleum in Saltaire, the last interment to take place there.[407]

The Dowager Lady Salt and the daughters Helen and Ada were not the only members of the family to move to Clapham. From census and burial records, it is seen that Herbert also moved there, and for many years lived at 50, South Side, Clapham, overlooking the same Common as his mother and sisters in Broadoak, the two properties being just a little way apart. (Renumbering of properties on Clapham South Side may

---

[405] Ref: BfdDT, 21st November, 1887.
[406] Refs: BfdDT, 21st November, 1887; BO, 29th November, 1887.
[407] Refs: BfdTA, 23rd January, 1930; BfdTA, 27th January, 1930; HarrH, 29th January, 1930.

have occurred during the period in question, perhaps accounting for a change in Herbert's address at some time from No. 50 to No. 49). Frustratingly, we have not yet firmly established Herbert's date of first residing in Clapham, but there is reason to believe that Herbert was living in the area as early as 1889 (see later).

The early 1890s were ill-fated for the Salt family. In July, 1892, Sir William Henry died at the age of 60. William Henry was the fifth of the Salts' 11 children to die, and it is sad to realize that Lady Salt was to see so many of her children predecease her. He is buried in a modest grave in the graveyard of the Parish Church of St. Paul's, Woodhouse Eaves, Leicestershire – one, but not the only of the Salt sons to turn from the Dissenters' beliefs of his parents. His widow, the Dowager Lady Emma, lived on until 1904, when she too died, being buried in a grave alongside that of her husband (her gravestone bears a date of 1905, for reasons that are unclear).

Less than two months after the death of Sir William Henry, Sir Titus Salt Bart. Sons & Co. Ltd. went into liquidation. Edward, being the one family member remaining in the business, was probably most affected by the event. Having mortgaged his property of Ferniehurst as security for the company in the 1880s, he now found that the bank called in the loan, and he lost his home of more than 30 years. The predicament worsened when the Ferniehurst house and estate were put up for auction, by order of the bank, in October 1893. It had been estimated that Edward had spent no less than £35,000 on the property – a very large sum of money – but failure to attract any bids beyond £12,500 caused the property to be withdrawn from sale. The property was sold three years later, in 1896. Edward's changed circumstances were followed by his leaving not only the company but also the area. He was to settle in Bathampton, two mile east of Bath. The sad circumstances surrounding Edward's departure met with the sympathy of his former employees and the residents of Saltaire, 1400 of who subsequently subscribed to a testimonial to him. In what must have been a moving ceremony at St. Pancras Hotel, London, in November 1893, a delegation from the village presented to Edward a silver casket, surmounted by a model of an alpaca, and an illuminated address of appreciation. The casket had been thoughtfully designed, the side panels being decorated with orchids and lapagerias, both species apparently favoured by the recipient. Edward, in his words of acceptance, explained that he would have found it too painful to have returned to Saltaire for the ceremony. His circumstances were obviously reduced to some extent since the heydays of Ferniehurst, but his days in Bathampton were spent in comfort and happy retirement, living first at Bathampton Lodge and then at Bathampton House, with a modestly sized domestic staff of three. The house at Bathampton unfortunately no longer exists, having been demolished to make way for housing development in the 1970s, but what photographic records remain show the house to have been a substantial property. It is known that Edward was able to continue his horticultural interests that had been renown at Ferniehurst. (It seems likely that the life style of Edward and his wife was sustained by Sarah's income; following his death in 1903, Edward's will revealed his effects to be valued at less than £500, far less than those of his siblings).

1893 was to see further deaths within what was becoming an aged family group. On 20th April, 1893, Lady Caroline Salt died, aged 81, at 25, Eversfield Place, St. Leonard's on Sea, a resort where it had been her habit, with her unmarried daughter Helen, to spend her summers. As might be expected, the death was well reported in the Bradford press, but with less grandness than had accompanied the passing of her husband 16 years previously. Lady Salt's body was brought by train from St. Leonard's to Saltaire on 24th April. On arrival, a procession of mourners escorted the coffin through the mill yard, across Victoria Road, and into the Congregational Church, the clock striking 6 pm as the mourners entered the Church. A short service was then held, in anticipation of the funeral the following day. At 11 am, Tuesday, the ceremony commenced, attended by a large and noteworthy gathering of mourners. Three Congregational Ministers officiated – Rev. J. A. Hamilton, pastor of the Church; Rev. J. Guinness Rogers, from Grafton

Square Church in Clapham; and Rev. R. Balgarnie, formerly of Scarborough but by this time of London. The body of Dowager Lady Salt was subsequently laid to rest in the family mausoleum.[408]

Notably absent from the list of funeral attendees recorded in the newspaper reports, although a wreath was sent by them, were eldest daughter Amelia and her husband Henry Wright.[409] This apparent absence may well have been associated with the latter's own declining health – Henry Wright died, aged 73, on 3rd August, 1893, at Harrogate. His death certificate records the cause of death as "General paralysis, 11 years, coma". Whatever incapacity Wright was suffering from 1882 onwards, it is not thought to have been total – he remained Chairman of the London Missionary Society's Finance Committee as late as 1886. Wright was buried in Grove Road Cemetery, Harrogate, in a grave that still stands in the present day. He was, at the time of his death, staying at nearby Spencer House, a small hotel in the fashionable district of High Harrogate, from where the funeral took place. It is a little surprising that he was buried in Harrogate, a town with which he had no known close affiliation (he was not attached to the Congregational Church in Victoria Road, Harrogate, for example), and one which would not have been immediately accessible to his widow Amelia, based as she was in Kensington.

The deaths of first the Dowager Lady Salt and then Henry Wright would have left the daughters Helen, at Clapham, and Amelia, at Kensington, with decisions to make about their futures, and both daughters moved on in the following year. Broadoak was vacated by Helen in 1894. It is not known where Helen went in the next few years, but Amelia's movements are more readily traceable. In 1894, and by now in her late 50s, Amelia disposed of her Kensington home and moved to Tunbridge Wells, to Little Court, 61, Frant Road (a rather grand house, by accounts, that was demolished to make way for the present day Birling Drive). Three years later, Helen (approx. 47) also arrived in

---

[408] Refs: BO, 22nd, 24th, 25th, 26th April, 1893.
[409] Ref: BO, 26th April, 1893.

the town, setting up home at Redroofs, in the attractive new area of Madeira Park, a few hundred yards down the hill from her elder sister. Remarkably, the Stevensons joined them in 1898, Ada and her small family moving into a house about a mile away, in Culverden Park Road, on the other side of the fashionable Victorian spa town's centre. Their only child, Monica, was approximately 12 when they arrived.

In the second half of the 19th century the Nonconformist movement was particularly active in Tunbridge Wells.[410] This may well have been a factor in Amelia's decision to move to the town in 1894; she clearly held dear the same values as first her parents and then her husband. In fact, all the adults were admitted to the Mount Pleasant Congregational Church and presumably kept in close contact with each other during their years together in Tunbridge Wells.

It is gratifying to imagine the three surviving daughters reunited in Tunbridge Wells, more than 20 years after their days together at Crow Nest. One senses that the two younger sisters had a strong allegiance to the elder sister Amelia. Unlike the sisters, the three surviving brothers of the family had by this time gone their separate ways to East Molesey (George), Bathampton (Edward), and Clapham (Herbert) (although it can be noted that Clapham and East Molesey are only a few miles apart).

The trio of sisters was together in Tunbridge Wells for seven years, but then in 1905 the Stevensons left Tunbridge Wells for Hampstead. The reason for this move is not clear; possibly it was work related – Edmund Stevenson being in his mid fifties at the time.

The census of 1901 shows that the eldest surviving son George (67) and his wife Jenny Louise (49) were living in a fashionable part of St. Marleybone, London, at No. 8, Welbeck Street, where George is described as being the head of household and a "Lodging House Keeper". However, this was their "London" address; their main home was The Hermitage, Palace Road, East Molesey[411], although we do not know when George acquired the latter property. Today East Molesey,

---

[410] Ref: NCTW.
[411] Ref: YO, 10th May, 1913, p8.

across the River Thames from Hampton Court, is commonly seen as part of Greater London, but in the early years of the 20th century it could readily have served as a country retreat from the madding crowd. Both Welbeck Street and East Moseley have retained their fashionable statuses in today's London. The census shows Herbert (60) at the Clapham address referred to earlier. By this time Herbert was married with a family, and the census records that, in addition to Herbert himself, the following members were in residence at 50, South Side: wife Margaret (46), sons Arthur (18) and Douglas (10), and daughters Eva (13) and Lorris (9). A step-daughter Rhoda de Lacy (22) and a step-son Albert de Lacy (18) were also resident. One gets a fuller picture of Herbert's family by going forward in time, to 1912, when Herbert (by then 72) died and was interred in Norwood Cemetery, London. The Burial Records Book at the Cemetery, and the relevant gravestone inscriptions, reveal that Herbert's first wife Elizabeth, had died, aged 37, on 2nd September, 1898. Also, sadly, an infant daughter, Dorothy Clarissa Salt, aged only 11 weeks, had predeceased Elizabeth, being interred on 8th February, 1889. Herbert's second wife, Margaret, was to die, aged 56, in 1910 (interred on 1st April), to be followed by Herbert himself in 1912. These four members of the family were buried in the same grave plot. Regrettably parts of the gravestone have been damaged and broken, but the epitaphs of Elizabeth and the infant Dorothy are seen in the granite headstone; markings on the stone suggest that plaques were later screwed onto the stone at some time, and these may have carried the epitaphs of Margaret and Herbert, but the plaques are no longer in place.

Returning to the very early years of the new century, Edward was to die on 24th October, 1903, having developed pneumonia following a stay in Weymouth earlier the same month.[412] His grave can be seen today, in the graveyard of St. Nicholas', the Parish Church of Bathampton, in a beautiful setting alongside the Kennet and Avon Canal. His widow Sarah Amelia was to live for a further 26 years. Her movements after the death of Edward can be traced through the "Court" section of Post Office

---

[412] Refs: YDO, 27th October, 1903; Bath, p4.

directories for London. In the period 1907–1918 Sarah lived at 61, Evelyn Gardens, London SW7. Subsequent to that she was first at 31, Kensington Court Mansions, London W8 (1919–1924), before moving to 92, Kensington Court, Kensington, London, her home when she died in 1929. On her death, she was cremated at Golders Green Crematorium – an event commemorated on the side of Edward's tombstone. Her ashes were dispersed in the Crematorium's Garden of Rest.

Following Edward's death, almost a decade would pass before another brother died. On 21st July, 1912, Herbert died a widower, still living in Clapham, being buried, as reported above, in Norwood Cemetery.

The surviving son George was to be the longest lived of the sons. However, following an illness of three months, he too died, aged 80, less than a year after his younger brother Herbert. He seems to have retained his interest in yachting since his days at Scarborough, being a member of the Royal Thames Yacht Club.[413] On his death on 8th May, 1913, the reported expectation was that the funeral and burial of George would take place in Saltaire.[414] The only place of burial in Saltaire was the family mausoleum. However, it is our understanding that there was insufficient space for the interment of a body in the mausoleum, and a later newspaper report alludes to this predicament. Whilst we have eliminated many of the possible outcomes, the final resting place of George is not known by us. It is also difficult to trace the arrangements for the disposal of George's estate. Unlike the other Salt children who grew to adulthood, it appears that George did not leave a will – no trace has been found in a search of the Principal Registry of the Family Division, London. It is possible that George, having no offspring, did not feel the need to make a will, being content that his widow Jenny would inherit his estate, but this does not seem likely to us; a common feature in the wills of the other children is the provision, as one might expect, for contingencies guarding against the unexpected predeceasing of

---

[413] Ref: YO, 10th May, 1913, p8.
[414] Ref: BfdDT, 9th May, 1913, p6.

potential beneficiaries. Further research is merited.

The death of George in 1913 marked the passing of the last of the Salt sons. The three daughters Amelia, Helen and Ada had outlived their brothers. Amelia and Helen had continued to live, for more than 15 years, in their respective houses in Tunbridge Wells, and it is known that Amelia remained active in the affairs of the town until her death, aged 78, in 1914. Her obituary in the local newspaper[415] records her work for, and support of, the Mount Pleasant Congregational Church, as does the author of a hundred year history of the church, written many years after her death.[416] The provisions in Amelia's will were comprehensive, no doubt reflecting what she held dear. In addition to her bequests to family members, Amelia's attachments to Congregationalism and bodies such as the London Missionary Society are evident. Funds were left to both the Mount Pleasant Congregational Church, Tunbridge Wells and, interestingly, to the South Cliff Church, Scarborough (which, almost 50 years previously, had been supported and used by her parents, her husband and - of course - Rev. R. Balgarnie). The bequests were made in such a way as to ensure that, were the churches to turn from Congregationalism, the monies were to be redirected to the Congregational Union.

Like her younger brother Titus Jr., Amelia seems to have believed in the practice of cremation, since arrangements were made for disposal of her own remains by such means. With a lack of facilities in the immediate vicinity of Tunbridge Wells, her body was taken to Golders Green Crematorium, London, from where her ashes were subsequently taken north, to Harrogate, where they were interred in the graveyard plot of her late husband Henry Wright, in Grove Road Cemetery. (A newspaper[417] reports an expectation that Amelia's ashes were to be interred in Highgate Cemetery, London, but that expectation, if it existed at all, was clearly not realized). Amelia, it would appear, was the first

---

[415] Ref: KentC, 26th June, 1914, p7.
[416] Ref: MPCC, p33.
[417] Ref: KentC, 26th June, 1914, p7.

family member to be cremated.

Helen stayed on in Tunbridge Wells after Amelia's death, remaining in the same house until at least 1918, possibly until as late as 1921, but by October of that later year she had settled in Eastbourne at 20, Southfields Road. She died at her home, aged 71, on 11th June, 1924. Helen had maintained her links with the Congregational Church to the end, and left £1,000 in her will to the nearby Upperton Congregational Church. Whilst Helen bequeathed most of her estate to members of the family, one non-family beneficiary of passing interest was Louisa Mellor, daughter of the late Rev. Enoch Mellor of Halifax – perhaps the bequest recognized a friendship dating back to the long-passed days at Crow Nest. Like her elder sister, Helen was cremated at Golders Green Crematorium, her ashes being dispersed in the Garden of Rest there.

The last of the Salt children to die was the youngest, Ada. After moving to Hampstead in 1905, the Stevenson family lived initially in Reddington Road (where their house number changed over the years, for whatever reasons); and later at 29, Platt Lane. Edmund was to die on 18 July, 1918, being cremated at Golders Green, where his ashes were dispersed. Ada subsequently moved, with her unmarried daughter Monica, to a more central, London address (Bickenhall Mansions in Portman Square). Ada was to live on until 22nd November, 1935, when she died, aged 82. Three days later her body was cremated, like those of her husband and elder sisters, at Golders Green Crematorium, and her ashes dispersed in the Garden of Rest.

This simple act could be seen as a closing of the book on Salt's immediate family. Ada, who was being carried by her pregnant mother Caroline at the opening of Salt's mill in 1853, had lived through a period of enormous change in English society. Her passing attracted very little attention in the press – a mere seven lines of small print on an inside page of Bradford's *Telegraph and Argus* of 26th November, 1935. The reader could understandably conclude that life in Saltaire had moved on, and that Salt's building of the mill and village was no more than history. But a turn of the page of that same newspaper forces a very different perspective. The page that followed the report of Ada's death summarized the Annual Report of Saltaire Hospital. Sixty seven years after its opening, the Hospital is seen to be financially secure, and to have provided, in the preceding year, 334 operations and 300 X-Ray examinations, dealing with 2,380 outpatients, and over 15,000 attendances - an impressive medical service provision to the community within and beyond Saltaire. Salt's immediate family had passed on, but his philanthropic legacy was still very much alive.

HORTON LANE CHAPEL AND CONGREGATION

PLAN OF THE CHAPEL

Yard						Yard	
		Pulpit					
		Singing Pew		Thompson			
Rev.Thos. Taylor	John Russell				Joshua Wood		
John Tordoff	Titus Salt				Thomas Greenlay	William Marten	
R. Pullan	William Byles				John McCroben	William Wyrill	
James Garnett	Daniel Salt				Benjamin Berry	George Haigh	
Robert Monies	James Rennie	James Hammond	Thomas Hammond			Richard Garnett	
		James Knapton					
Joshua Brigg	Samuel Smith	William McKay			George Rogers	Thomas Buck	
Robert Milligan		Henry Forbes	Mrs. Bacon		Jos. Hinchcliffe's Pupils		
		William + Joseph Hardcastle	Hargreaves	Clayton	Joshua Lupton		

A corner pew in the gallery was occupied by the Ripleys, of Bowling. In a front seat on the opposite side of the gallery Mr. Abraham Balme sat with his family.

Taken from ref: Cud5, p6.
Year of validity judged to be 1834.

APPENDIX 4

THE NONCONFORMIST MOVEMENT
AND
HORTON LANE CHAPEL

The histories of first Dissent and, later, Nonconformity have been documented extensively in many works on the subjects. A brief account is helpful in order to put into context the religious creed of Sir Titus Salt, which was to play such an important role in his life.

The 1534 Act of Supremacy ordered that "the King shall be taken, accepted, and reputed the only supreme head on earth of the Church of England."[418] Queen Elizabeth I, in her policy of compromise, dropped, in deference to the more Christian feeling in the country, the title of supreme head of the church, but the Act of Supremacy of her reign declared her to be "the only supreme governor of the church." The situation was felt unacceptable to many Christians for several reasons. Firstly, it granted the governor controlling rights, including, for example, the appointment of bishops – a power which allowed the Crown to control the Church. Secondly, the connection it brought about between Church and State was perceived to dishonour the Church – subjugating the Church to the will of the State, as expressed through the Sovereign, under guidance of the Sovereign's ministers. Thirdly, over time, and as a religious following developed outside of the structure of the Established Church, it was held that the situation was also a disservice to the nation, since Parliament spent time deliberating on the issues of the Established Church at the expense of other issues. For these reasons, Christian sects emerged outside the structure of the Established Church which, while having differing views on particular religious doctrines, were united

---

[418] Ref: ConPr. This book was commissioned by the Congregational Union of England and Wales, and published in 1894; from it the following account of Dissent and Nonconformity has been taken.

in opposition to the special status of the Established Church – they were "Dissenters".

The 1662 Act of Uniformity not only enforced the exclusive use of the Prayer Book in all public worship, but also stipulated "an unfeigned, consent and assent ..... from every minister of the church to all which was contained in it." The authoritarian rigidity of this Act met with such opposition that nearly 2,000 rectors and vicars refused to comply with it and were consequently expelled from the Established Church. These ministers would not conform to the requirements of the Act; they did not dissent from the idea of a State Church, but they refused to conform to the rubrics of the Prayer Book – they were "Nonconformists."

Within the Dissenting and Nonconformist sections of society there existed several sects, including Baptists, Congregationalists, Methodists, Presbyterians, Quakers and Unitarians. The distinguishing principles of the Congregationalists were that all church members had a right, indeed a duty, to take part in the government and welfare of the church; and that no body, civil or ecclesiastic, outside of a particular church had the right to revise the decisions of that church – the church was independent of external control. (In practice, some of the other sects had similar principles which differed from those of the Congregationalists only in specific issues of church doctrine, such as baptism).

Congregationalists were both Dissenters and Nonconformists.[419] Whilst insisting on the independence of individual churches, they did not preclude a loose fellowship of churches for purposes of mutual consultation and edification. To this end, in 1832, the Congregational Union of England and Wales was formed.

Salt was born into a Nonconformist family, in a town which itself was a notable centre of Nonconformity. Sharing his Nonconformist beliefs within and beyond his family, Salt no doubt relied on those beliefs to inform his social values and indeed his philosophy of life. However, he

---

[419] It is noteworthy that, in his biography of Salt, Balgarnie invariably uses the term "Nonconformist" in preference to "Dissenting." It is further noteworthy that, in describing Salt's early life in Morley, he does not use the term "Congregational;" it is only later, after the family has settled in Crofton, that the latter term begins to be used by the author.

went further than simply inheriting the family practice of chapel going – he positively embraced the religion, declaring in later life that he was a Nonconformist "from conviction",[420] and advocated application of its tenets in the practical circumstances in which he found himself.

In 1800, there were six places of worship in Bradford. With the single exception of the Parish Church of St. Peter's, these were all Dissenting chapels, belonging to the Baptists, Congregationalists, Quakers, Unitarians and Wesleyan Methodists.[421] The presence of the Dissenters in Bradford had increased in the second half of the 18th century. In the case of the Congregationalists, they had established, in the 1780s, a chapel in Little Horton Lane, then on the outskirts of the small town. Rev. Thomas Holdgate took up a ministry in 1784, shortly before the building of the chapel. In the 28 years of his ministry the congregation grew substantially. He died, aged 58, in 1806, to be succeeded by Rev. Thomas Taylor.

The new century was to see the enormous expansion of Bradford, and between 1800 and 1840 its population increased from 13,264 to 66,715. Surprisingly, throughout this period only three new Anglican churches were built in the town. In the first four decades of the 19th century, Methodism achieved rapid increases in its Bradford memberships; the Baptist and Congregationalist fellowships also grew, but at a more modest rate. A Census of Religious Worship was held in 1851, which showed that Bradford's population of 103,778 was being served by 54 places of worship, 12 of them being Church of England, 12 Methodist, and six Congregationalist. Nonconformity had an ascendancy over the Church of England in terms both of the number of places of worship and service attendance figures. The period could be seen, in retrospect, as a period of lost opportunity for the Established Church.

The increase in the number of Congregational chapels included the building of Salem Chapel in 1836, and College Chapel in 1839.

---

[420] Ref: BALG, p155.
[421] Ref: VicBd, p37. Many of the data quoted in this Appendix are taken from Jowitt's comprehensive account 'The Pattern of Religion in Victorian Bradford,' VicBd, pp37-61.

Additionally, the Horton Lane Chapel was extending its premises, under the successful ministries first of Rev. Taylor, who continued in post until 1835 (he was to live on until 3rd October, 1853, when he died, aged 86); and subsequently of Rev. Jonathan Glyde, who was to serve for 18 years, presiding over a golden period in the fortunes of this most important of Bradford's Congregational chapels. Jonathan was the elder brother of William Evans Glyde, who, having followed Jonathan to Bradford in 1837, was to become a partner in Salt's company in 1859. The two brothers were clearly talented in their respective callings, both being highly regarded in the town. William married the daughter of the former minister (Rev. Taylor).[422]

Several factors can be identified which account for the spectacular rises in the fortunes of Horton Lane Chapel and in the influence of its leading members. One factor was the arrival in a rapidly expanding Bradford of ambitious young men determined to make their way in the revolutionary new world of industry, and bringing with them their strongly Nonconformist beliefs. One such person was Robert Milligan (1786-1862); pre-eminent among this new generation, he was destined to become the first Mayor of Bradford on its incorporation in 1847. His business partner Henry Forbes (1794-1870) was a second example; and of course, the somewhat younger Salt was a third. As their business fortunes were made, they were each prepared to put their wealth to use in the service of their religious beliefs. A second factor was the exceptional talents of its ministers of the time, firstly Taylor (up to 1835) and more particularly Glyde (up to 1853).

There was a third factor that was to elevate the standing of Horton Lane Chapel Congregationalists. Relationships between the various Christian denominations in Bradford were largely harmonious – certainly Salt and others were not averse to supporting denominations other than their own, for example. However, there was one issue in the first part of

---

[422] The graves of the brothers, and those of several other Horton Lane Chapel stalwarts, are gathered in an area of Undercliffe Cemetery, next to the site of the (now demolished) Nonconformist Mortuary Chapel.

the 19th century that caused serious dispute – the compulsory levying of church rates, payable by followers and non-followers alike, to fund the upkeep of parish churches. Congregationalists such as Robert Milligan and Henry Forbes, who were in business partnership, had their goods seized for their refusal to pay this levy. Such refusal provided a rallying point for all those opposed to the levying of the rate. The poor handling of the issue locally cast the Congregationalists in a particularly good light, as being men prepared to stand by their beliefs.

A perspective of the Chapel's leading members can be gained from its seating plan,[423] which identifies who occupied which pews. The plan was published in 1893, and sought to show the composition of the congregation "sixty years ago." It is probably better ascribed to a slightly later date (perhaps 1834) since William Byles is shown as having a pew, and it is known that he did not move to Bradford until December 1833. A Singing Pew occupies a central position in front of the pulpit. There were few, if any, organs in Dissenting places of worship in the 1830s; an organ was installed in Horton Lane Chapel in 1845.[424]

The names recorded carry a strong resonance for students of Bradford's 19th century history. Rev. Thomas Taylor was still the minister at this time, not being replaced by Jonathan Glyde until 1835. Both Titus and his father Daniel have pews, Titus at this stage being married and living with his wife and two young sons in nearby Manor Row. William Byles (1807-1891) would have recently arrived from Henley-on-Thames, to launch the *Bradford Observer,* which, under his hand, would prove to be the mouthpiece of Liberalism in Bradford throughout the following 50 years. It is worth noting that Byles, who played such an important role in the affairs of the Horton Lane Radicals, and was undoubtedly a close associate of Salt, is never mentioned in Balgarnie's biography. Indeed, it is interesting to reflect that Byles would have been well placed to write a biography of Salt, given the association the two must have had over a period of 40 years. By the time of Salt's

---

[423] See illustration on p312.
[424] Ref: Cud5, p15.

death in 1876, Byles would have had access to, and awareness of, at least four decades of information relating to Salt. At the time of the unveiling of the Salt statue in 1874, the *Bradford Observer* provided a lengthy retrospective of Salt's achievements.[425] A comprehensive account of Byles and his stewardship of the *Bradford Observer* is available.[426] In 1877, Byles achieved the distinction of becoming the first layman to be elected Chairman of the Yorkshire Congregational Union.[427] James Garnett was one of the Chapel's Sunday School superintendents, and recruited the young Titus Salt to help in the work, as reported in Balgarnie's biography.[428] The name of James Garnett is set alongside that of Daniel Salt. The Garnetts were a well-known family of some generations standing. The James Garnett named was, perhaps, the grandson of the James Garnett who, in 1794, had set up the first spinning machine in Bradford, in the Old Paper Hall.

Samuel Smith (1804-1873) was a near contemporary of Titus Salt. Born in Halifax, Smith had moved to Bradford as a young man and, with his brothers, founded a successful dyeworks at Fieldhead, in Thornton Road. Smith was destined to become Mayor of Bradford, serving a three-year term starting in 1851.

Occupying the last pew in the left-hand aisle was Robert Milligan (1786-1862), whose name more than any other was to be synonymous with the growth of Bradford. Milligan came from farming stock in Dunnance, Balmaghie, Scotland. He first worked as a "travelling Scotch-man", with his elder brother, John, who had established a drapery business in Cross Hills, near Skipton. Milligan would literally carry the wares of the business, held in a wooden box containing two drawers each four feet long, from cottage to cottage across the moorland Pennines. In 1808[429] he settled in Bradford, setting up a retail business

[425] Ref: BO, 1st August, 1874, p7.
[426] Ref: VicBd, pp115-136.
[427] Ref: Rob3, p93.
[428] Ref: BALG, pp31-32.
[429] Other dates are quoted for Milligan's settling in Bradford, but it is recorded on his gravestone in Undercliffe Cemetery that he 'became resident in 1808'.

in premises in Westgate. Progressing first into wholesaling and then becoming a stuff merchant, he moved to premises in Piccadilly. In due course he came into contact with Henry Forbes (1794-1870), a traveller for a London firm. Forbes, also a Congregationalist, moved to Bradford, entered into partnership with Milligan, and can be seen to have had a pew just across the aisle from Milligan. The partnership prospered, developing into one of the leading merchant trading companies in Bradford. Both Milligan and Forbes would become Mayors of Bradford, Milligan having the honour of being the first Mayor following the town's incorporation. Milligan also served as M.P. for Bradford in the 1850s. Salt was a close friend not only of Milligan but also of Forbes, and the latter, as Balgarnie records, was to remain a close confidant of Salt until his death in 1870. Milligan's death at the age of 75, in 1862, was afforded the honour of a public funeral, at which Salt was one of the four pallbearers; his resting place in Undercliffe Cemetery is marked by a monumental gravestone of imposing height.

Two other notable presences deserve mention. Firstly, although not evident from the seating plan, the Ripley family occupied a corner pew in the upstairs gallery. More than one generation of the family left their mark on the town, to which Edward Ripley, the father of the more well-known Ripley, had come from Halifax, around the same time that Robert Milligan settled in the town (1808). Edward Ripley, together with his own father, had established the dyeworks Messrs. Ripley and Son, of Bowling. As the textile trade of Bradford grew, so did the success of the dyeworks, helped by the Ripleys' discovery of how to dye black wools. Edward Ripley was, like Salt, a respected philanthropist and when the town was incorporated he was appointed an Alderman. His son, Henry William, had an eventful life, as recorded in Balgarnie's biography, eventually serving not only as M.P. for Bradford, but also receiving a baronetcy late in life. It was to Henry William Ripley that the honour would fall of laying the foundation stone, in 1861, of the new Horton Lane Chapel. In addition to their extensive works in Bowling, the family also built houses for their workers (Ripleyville), but these, being close to

Bradford's expanding centre, have fallen victim, over the years, to redevelopment schemes. The other presence of note is the pew of "Jos. Hinchcliffe's Pupils." Hinchcliffe was the head of the Academy in Little Horton which, over time, included in its enrolments many individuals destined to become well known - Charles Stead, William Cunliffe Lister, Thomas Horsfall, Edward Akroyd and the aforementioned Henry William Ripley, to name but few. This then was the situation in the early 1830s, with Horton Lane Chapel having in its ranks a great many of the civic leaders of the future.

The next two decades saw their influence grow, and as the town moved to incorporation in the late 1840s, a succession of Mayors and Aldermen were being drawn from the Chapel's congregation. The enormous influence that the leaders of the Chapel had acquired was articulated in a memorable joke about the situation, made by a Councillor following events at the November 1850 meeting of Bradford Council. At the time the Corporation comprised a Mayor, 14 Aldermen, and 42 Councillors. The Council had elected Mr. William Rand as its Mayor for the coming year, in succession to Henry Forbes. Rand, while being a close friend of Salt, was a member of the Anglican Church, and the first Mayor to be elected who was not a member of Horton Lane Congregational Chapel. Councillor George Thompson Lister pointed out that of the 14 Aldermen, nine of them went to the same chapel and that among those "Nine Muses" there were three who had been mayor – the "Three Graces."

Lister's wit has become enshrined in the telling of the town's civic history, and it is an interesting exercise to try and identify, as far as we are able, to whom he was referring. The three ex-Mayors were, unambiguously, Robert Milligan, Titus Salt and Henry Forbes. As to the remaining six Aldermen (and from the accounts of the incident it does seem that Lister was using poetic license to include the Three Graces within the Nine Muses), one has to look at the composition of the Aldermanic bench at the time. The 14 Aldermen in office in November, 1850 were Robert Milligan, Henry Brown, Titus Salt, Henry Forbes,

Joseph Farrar, Thomas Beaumont, Joshua Lupton, William Murgatroyd, T. G. Clayton, Edward Ripley, William Rand, Samuel Smith, Joseph Smith and George Rogers.[430]

Informed by what we know of Horton Lane Chapel membership, we provisionally judge the six remaining Muses to be: Henry Brown (recorded as being an attached Congregationalist,[431] and as a "Horton Lane stalwart"[432]), T. G. Clayton (we have not established with certainty that the Clayton in the 1830s seating plan is the same Clayton who became Alderman; it was a very common name), Joshua Lupton, Edward Ripley, Samuel Smith and George Rogers. The 5 non "Horton Lane Chapel" Aldermen are provisionally judged to be: Rand (Anglican); Joseph Smith (of Quaker origin[433]), Beaumont (a Methodist[434]), Joseph Farrar (affiliation not known, but not active to our best knowledge in the Horton Lane Chapel), and William Murgatroyd (a member of the Bradford Reform Society and a Dissenter,[435] but perhaps not attached to Horton Lane). It may be that further research would give a different perspective of Lister's wit, and we would applaud those coming forward with a fuller, more definitive account.

Of the "Muses" we have identified, Henry Brown (1805-1878) merits further mention. Destined to become Mayor in 1856 for what became a three-year period of office, Brown was actually born near the premises in Market Street, Bradford from which he carried on his business as draper and clothier. Founded by his mother, the firm was the forerunner of the well-known department store of Brown, Muff and Co. Ltd. Brown left substantial legacies in his will for educational and charitable purposes.[436] His grave plot in Undercliffe Cemetery lies immediately adjacent to those of Robert Milligan and Samuel Smith.

Whatever the final interpretation of Lister's words, they reflect the

---

[430] Ref: Cud3, p227.
[431] Ref: Cud3, p145.
[432] Ref: Rob3, p92.
[433] Ref: Cud3, p142.
[434] Ref: GtPat, p27.
[435] Ref: GtPat, p92, p108.
[436] Ref: Cud3, p145.

dominance of Horton Lane Chapel's congregation in the affairs of mid 19th century Bradford. Other expressions of their role can be quoted: "A Powerhouse of Congregationalism," "The Pious Warehouse," "The Parent of all Congregational Chapels," "Chapel membership was the grease that turned many business wheels," "Bradford's Cathedral of Nonconformity," etc.[437]

The success of the Chapel was to continue for some time, and on 30th September, 1863, a new Chapel, two years in the building, was opened. Grandly designed by Lockwood and Mawson, the building provided improved facilities, and under the ministry of Rev. James Robertson Campbell, who had succeeded Rev. Glyde in 1855, the Chapel continued to prosper for many years. Campbell was an outstanding minister, leading to him being elected Chairman of the Congregational Union of England and Wales in 1867.[438]

However, an 1881 Religious Census carried out by the *Bradford Observer* revealed the beginnings of change, and indeed decline, in the fortunes of the Nonconformist Churches of Bradford.[439] The newly developing Salvation Army was attracting members at a considerable rate, having been introduced in the town in 1877. Like so many other religious movements, the Congregational Church would see a gradual decline in its appeal and influence. The end came in 1956, when the once glorious Horton Lane Chapel was demolished.[440]

Whilst some may dispute the motives of Salt and his fellow industrialists, there can be little doubt of the sincerity of his religious beliefs. Quite apart from his actions, the personal correspondence between Salt and the biographer Balgarnie highlights that sincerity very clearly. Nor can one dispute the enormous achievements of the leading members of the Congregational Church through the civic and other offices of 19th century Bradford.

---

[437] Refs: Rob3, p92; Rob3, p92; Cud4, p49; VicBd, p54, VicBd, p45, resp.
[438] Ref: Rob3, p92.
[439] Ref: VicBd, p48.
[440] Ref: Rob3, p94.

APPENDIX 5

SALT THE PHILANTHROPIST

One of the most celebrated traits of Sir Titus Salt was his philanthropy. The effusion in Balgarnie's accounts of Salt's acts of benevolence is understandable, and, in large measure, justified; other contemporary reports and commentaries on the subject are often similar in their tone. The scale of his charitable acts was exceptional, and of particular social significance when seen in the context of the newly created, urban society of the 19th century.

Mindful that it is one of the most important historical aspects of his life, it is of value to itemize Salt's known acts of philanthropy. Reynolds, in his 1983 book, provides a table of 'charitable and other contributions' that can be credited to Salt.[441] Here we augment that list, helped by information uncovered in the course of our researches. Additions have also come from the inclusion of firstly the major public facilities that were provided by Salt in Saltaire, which cost at least £57,000, and secondly his bequest of £30,000 for the sick and aged poor in the village.

Salt's will and its codicils are notably devoid of benevolences to the charities and church bodies he supported so much in his life. The will's contents relate primarily to the provisions for his large family, and in very modest measure for his servants. The only exception to this, and it is a major one, is his provision for the sick and aged poor of Saltaire. It had been Salt's intention during his lifetime to provide a perpetual endowment of £30,000 for this purpose. Realizing that he might not bring this about before his death, he made arrangements in his will to ensure its provision.

In compiling the table, which can be found at the end of this Appendix, there are some cases where it is debatable whether Salt's action was philanthropic. Salt's financial support of the Royal Albert Hall has not

---

[441] Ref: GtPat, p76.

been included in the table, pending better evidence that it was a benevolent gesture. The provision of the village's Infirmary has been excluded, since it was originally created to deal with accidents occurring in the mill. Later, the Infirmary certainly took on a more philanthropic role, meeting the more general medical needs of a larger community, but to quantify that requires further research. Similarly the almshouses are best assessed in a separate exercise. Where there are unspecific and unquantified references to Salt's philanthropy (e.g. to the several bodies in Scarborough (p163) and at Methley (p155)), further research would allow entries to be included in the list. Where information is lacking, the relevant entry in the table is left blank.

The total of Salt's identified benevolences in the table below is approx. £139,000. As expected, this is lower than the estimated £250,000 quoted by Balgarnie (see p154), but the table should not be regarded as complete. As further evidence comes to light in the future, the record can be extended.

Balgarnie's account obviates the need for further comment on many of the good causes listed in the table, but three do merit further words. The endowment of £30,000 for the sick and aged poor of Saltaire (or more precisely, as Salt's will specifies, those residing within three miles of the Saltaire Institute) was planned as a lasting provision for the needy. It would be interesting to research the use of the endowment. Some of the records of the Sir Titus Salt's Charity, Shipley, are held in West Yorkshire Archives and carry a wealth of interesting information, including cases of individual villager's needs in the 1890s.

It is surprising that Balgarnie makes no reference in the biography to the Bradford Tradesmen's Homes. The charity was inaugurated in 1865 with the object of erecting and maintaining at least 30 dwellings for elderly tradesmen and others who had at one time occupied a good position in society, but through financial reverses in life were no longer able to support themselves by their own resources. The houses to be provided were to be tenanted, free of rent, rates, taxes, by pensioners of the Tradesmen's Benevolent Society, and others. A site was purchased at Lily Croft, Manningham, two miles south of Saltaire, Salt laying the foundation stone in September, 1867. His financial support totalled £2,100, paid in three parts between September, 1866 and July, 1870. The 30 dwellings, built on the three sides of a square and incorporating a chapel, were completed and occupied by the early part of 1870. The interior of the chapel (used in the present day as a meeting room) retains beautiful stained glass windows to the memory of its founders, and a roll of honour recording the major benefactors of the enterprise, which includes other members of the Salt family. Outside the chapel stand two stone statues of alpacas, which it is thought may have adorned Methley Park at some time (Salt's laying of the foundation stone occurred shortly before the family left Methley Hall to return to Crow Nest). During 1877 and 1878, 13 more houses were to be added by Mrs. Eliza Wright in memory of her late husband and son. Bradford Tradesmen's Homes still stand today, serving their original purpose, and perhaps in the best-conserved state of all of Salt's many enterprises – a great credit to its current managers.[442] Its grounds are private.

The children of the Sailors' Orphanage in Hull became celebrated in the region. Their circumstance touched the hearts of many, and the first appearance of a group of them on tour seems to have created something of a sensation.[443] Large crowds turned out to see them in both Leeds and Bradford, where a police escort had to clear a way through a crowd of many thousands. On arrival in Saltaire, the streets again packed with people, they were received and dined in the Mill Dining Room by Sir Titus, before being shown round the village by Titus Jr. An evening appearance at St. George's Hall left thousands outside, unable to join those thronged inside the large concert hall. The common feeling of well-being that the orphans' presence clearly engendered is a fitting note on which to conclude a review of Salt's philanthropies.

---

[442] We would like to record our thanks to the Trustees of Bradford Tradesmen's Homes and Mr. and Mrs. C. L. Askew, for their kind help in our researches.
[443] Ref: LongW, p52.

SALT'S ACTS OF PHILANTHROPY

RECIPIENT	YEAR	REFERENCE	SUM (£)
Sick and aged poor of Saltaire	1876	Salt's will	30,000
Saltaire Club and Institute	1871	p42	25,000
Saltaire Congregational Church	1859	p59	15,000
Saltaire Sunday School	1876	p32	10,000
Saltaire Factory Schools	1868	p106	7,000
Bradford Boys' Grammar School		GtPat, p76	6,000
Bradford Girls' Grammar School		GtPat, p76	5,500
Memorial Hall Building Fund	1867	MemH	5,000
Hull Sailors' Orphanage	1867	p156	5,000
Bradford Fever Hospital		p186	5,000
Northern Counties Lunatic Asylum	1868	p186	5,000
Liberation Society		p206	5,000
Scarborough Congregational Church	1864	p163	2,500
Bradford Tradesmen's Homes	1870	BTH Accounts	2,100
Lightcliffe Congregational Church		HtoT, p499	2,000
Pastors' Retiring Fund		p205	1,800
Bradford Mechanics' Institute		GtPat, p76	1,200
Peel Park, Bradford		p85	1,000
Yorkshire College of Science		GtPat, p76	1,000
West Riding Congregational Union		GtPat, p76	1,000
Bradford Town Mission Subscriptions	1850-1876	BfdTM, Annual Reports.	800
Distress Relief Fund for Lancashire		GtPat, p76	500
Bradford Blind Institute		GtPat, p76	500

SALT'S ACTS OF PHILANTHROPY (cont'd)

RECIPIENT	YEAR	REFERENCE	SUM (£)
Sick & Wounded (both sides) Franco-Prussian War		GtPat, p76	250
Saltaire Wesleyan Methodist Chapel Building Fund	1866	ShCam, p35	100
Saltaire Primitive Methodist Church Building Fund	1872	ShCam, p35	100
Bradford Ladies' Educational Assoc.		GtPat, p76	100
Widow, Grassington Coach Crash		p187	100
School-room, Brown Royd		p187	100
Work of London City Mission		p204	100
Crossley Orphanage Home, Halifax		GtPat, p76	100
Scarborough Cottage Hospital	1876	p231	100
Turkish Atrocities Relief Fund		GtPat, p76	100
Parish Restoration Fund		GtPat, p76	50
Bingley Boiler Explosion		GtPat, p76	50
Saltaire Park	1871	p196	
Castleford Congregational Church	1862	p154	
Harrogate Congregational Church	1859	HisCH, p15	
Harrogate Congregational Church Manse	1870	HisCH, p20	
'Saltaire' Lifeboat	1868	p207	
Land, Saltaire Wesleyan Methodist Chapel	1866	ShCam, p35	
Land, Saltaire Primitive Methodist Church	1872	ShCam, p35	
Renovation, York Minster		p156	
Pulpit, Episcopalian Church, Lightcliffe		p156	

APPENDIX 6

SALT IN LONDON

Sir Titus Salt was well travelled within the country. Balgarnie's biography reveals how, as a young man, Salt was accustomed to attending public wool sales, buying from farmers, and holidaying away from the West Riding – activities involving journeys that took him not only to various parts of the provinces such as Liverpool, Norfolk and Lincolnshire, but also to the metropolis. As a young man he would have made his journeys to London by horse-drawn carriage – in 1821 it took 26 hours to travel by this means from Leeds to London.[444] Later in life, the coming of the railways would allow him to get to the capital in just a few hours. As one might expect, London was a centre where he was required to spend time, be it for business meetings, political duties during his time as M.P., or - in later years – on family visits to his daughter Amelia. His being a frequent visitor to the Royal Albert Hall suggests that he was accustomed to spending time in the city. His most prolonged stays in the capital were probably associated with his time as an M.P., when he presumably spent weeks, if not months, in residence in the capital.

A picture of some of his activities in the capital can be gained from the biography, from research of parliamentary records, London directories of the time, and from archives such as those of the Royal Albert Hall.

Three known venues for his stays in London are Thomas's Hotel in Berkeley Square (p201); the apartments he occupied at Fenton's Hotel, Saint James's Street (p146); and the home of his daughter and son-in-law in Kensington (p203). The Parliamentary Section of the *London Directory of 1860* gives a further address – that of the Reform Club, situated on the south side of Pall Mall. The club in Salt's time as an M.P. was a relatively new establishment, having been created by Liberal

---

[444] Ref: Coach, p172.

members of the two Houses of Parliament, around the time of the 1832 Reform Act.

For his religious needs, Salt usually attended Westminster Chapel, at the junction of Little James Street and Castle Lane (p146), occasionally crossing to the south side of the River Thames to visit Surrey Chapel in Blackfriars Road, or the Metropolitan Tabernacle at the Elephant and Castle, Newington Butts (p201). Trips to the Royal Albert Hall, if made from his daughter's Kensington home, would involve a journey of just a few hundred yards.

Most of the above venues are located in quite a small area of central London. One can visualize Salt in his parliamentary days, moving from his apartments at Fenton's Hotel, probably by carriage but on occasion perhaps on foot, to the imposing Palace of Westminster (in magnificent order following its rebuilding after a fire in 1834), and then on to the Reform Club or Westminster Chapel.

Salt had been returned to Parliament in the election of April 1859, winning a total of 1,727 votes, and having spent £1,238 on his election campaign.[445] The countrywide result was such that Lord Palmerston was able to form his second Cabinet, with a stable parliamentary majority (unlike many governments of the 19th century), which would keep him in office for a period of six years.[446] Regrettably Salt's parliamentary career lacked the mark of success that was stamped on his other endeavours. Having been elected in April, 1859, he resigned in January, 1861 due to failing health. This is quite a short parliamentary life, particularly noting that the House was only in session during part of that period:

      1859:   31st May – 13th Aug   ("17th Parliament")
      1860:   24th Jan – 28th Aug   ("18th parliament")

Sitting with Titus Salt during this period was the other Bradford MP, Henry Wickham Wickham. Inspection of archives[447] reveals no record of

---

[445] For an account of Salt's election and further commentary on his voting record, see Ref: GtPat, pp202-206.
[446] Ref: AgeR, p666.
[447] Ref: Hans, Vols. 154-161. The kind assistance of Ruth Best in pursuing this research is gratefully acknowledged.

either M.P. speaking in the House throughout the period in question – as has been noted elsewhere.[448] What is notable is that both Salt & Wickham were assiduous attendees at the House – all 17 recordings of Division voting traced show Salt[449] to have been present and voting, likewise Wickham except on one or two occasions. Salt's voting record is compatible with Balgarnie's account of his political beliefs (see p67).

SALT'S PARLIAMENTARY VOTING RECORD
(Year date of first two entries: 1859; remainder: 1860)

DATE	SALT'S VOTE	MAJORITY VOTE	ISSUE
Jul 6	AYE	AYE	Endowed Schools Bill
Jul 20	AYE	AYE	Edinburgh Annuity Tax Abolition Bill
Feb 2	AYE	AYE	Civil Service Expenditure: Appointment of Select Committee
Feb 8	AYE	AYE	Abolition of Church Rates Bill (2nd Reading)
Feb 9	AYE	NOE	Gloucester & Wakefield elections: Electors to give their votes by ballot
Feb 16	AYE	NOE	Flogging (Army & Navy)
Feb 20	AYE	AYE	Customs Act
Feb 27	NOE	NOE	Commercial Treaty with France: Budget
Mar 12	AYE	AYE	Paper Duty Repeal Bill
Mar 12	NOE	NOE	Commercial Treaty with France
Mar 20	AYE	NOE	Voting by Ballot
Mar 21	AYE	NOE	Endowed Schools Bill
Mar 23	NOE	NOE	Ways & Means Income Tax
Mar 28	AYE	AYE	Church Rates Abolition Bill
May 8	AYE	AYE	Paper Duty Repeal Bill
Jun 7	NOE	NOE	Representation of the Peoples Bill
Aug 6	AYE	AYE	Customs Act Paper Duty

---

[448] Ref: GtPat, p206. Salt's successor, Forster, who went on to have a notably long and distinguished parliamentary career, was to be very much in evidence in the recordings of parliamentary debates within weeks of his arrival at Westminster.
[449] In inspecting the voting records, one needs to be aware that there was another M.P. with the similar name of Thomas Salt. The latter Thomas Clutton Salt had been a Chartist activist in Birmingham as early as the 1830s.

Comment is merited on some of the issues involved. Major concern was felt in the mid 19th century about the country's provisions for education. The majority of children of working class parents were receiving a very rudimentary education, while the middle class frequently looked to endowed schools for better provision. Many of these endowed schools themselves lacked secure provisions, and the quality of the education was being questioned. The Bill was addressing these concerns. It was to be 1869 before the government of Gladstone carried through the Endowed Schools Act.

The Edinburgh Annuity Tax was a tax levied to provide for the city's church ministers. Not surprisingly, this evoked similar opposition to the levying elsewhere of Church Rates, and Salt's voting on both issues can be seen in the record. Opposition in the House of Lords prevented the Bill being passed; compulsory church rates were not to be abolished until 1868.

For the minority of adults entitled to a vote, there remained a serious obstacle to democracy, namely intimidation. In parliamentary elections, voters were required to openly declare their choice of candidate to a recording officer, who then took record of it. Some employers and others were not above intimidating electors voting against their wishes. Salt voted in favour of secret ballots, but the measure did not pass into law. It was not until 1872 that Gladstones' government passed the Ballot Act, which provided for votes to be cast in secret.

The Crimean War (1853-1856) had led to public outcry about the practice of summary floggings in the army and navy. Even before that time, the issue had given rise to strong objections for decades. The 1860 Bill to abolish the practice did not immediately pass into law. In 1868, and notwithstanding objections from military authorities, the British government imposed restrictions on the use of corporal punishment. Flogging could only be carried out following a court martial and was restricted to serious offences committed while on active service.

The Paper Duty Repeal Act, which finally gained assent in 1861, removed the last element of the so-called taxes on knowledge, namely the duty on the actual paper on which news was printed.

The Customs Act allowed duties to be lowered or removed on French imports such as wine and luxury goods. This freeing of trade with the continent was matched by France's reduction of tariffs especially for British textile products, a freeing of trade negotiated by Salt's friend Cobden, who was at the time President of the Board of Trade.

Whilst Salt's time in London as an undistinguished M.P. may be thought of as something of a low point in an otherwise illustrious life, the voting record shows him to have been true to his stated position on the issues of the day, and still ahead of the thinking in the Parliament.

APPENDIX 7

THE STREETS, BUILDINGS AND BUILDERS OF SALTAIRE

The lasting physical legacy that Sir Titus Salt bequeathed has proved to be the buildings that make up the village of Saltaire. The industrial heart of his enterprise was faltering as Britain's textile trade declined in the second half of the 20th century, and finally stopped beating in 1987 when the Mill ceased production. Following its closure, the Mill's machinery was removed. Today's visitors to Saltaire find no evidence of textile production, which was the original *raison d'etre* of the development, and which for generations united the community in a common cause. The demography of the village is rapidly changing, and within the foreseeable future the time will come when no-one remaining in the village will have ever witnessed the Mill's textile production. However, the original buildings of Saltaire remain remarkably intact. Very few of the 820 houses of the original development have been lost. With a two or three notable exceptions, the public buildings have also been preserved, as of course has the Mill itself. Thus today's visitors can look at the village and see, to a great extent, the same buildings and layout that Balgarnie describes in his account (pp102-107).

A site plan of the village can be found on the inside cover of this book, with an enlarged plan showing street names and individual dwellings at the end of the book. Much can be learnt from their study. The initial appeal of the site to Salt and his architects is evident. At the northern end of the site lie external resources essential for the Mill's functioning - a plentiful supply of water coming from the River Aire, together with good transport links to the outside world in the form of both canal and railway. These features lie in the valley bottom, with the ground rising from the riverbed in both north and south directions. The site was, in 1850, a (near) green-field site, well clear of the insufferable pollution and filth of industrialized Bradford, lying three miles to the south-east.

The positioning of the Mill was determined by the fundamental logistical needs for water and transport – the three had to be close together. The massive size of the Mill was dictated by the vision of Salt himself; its orientation was determined by the local terrain, the building's west/ east alignment following the contours of the hillside. Road access was to be via the pre-existing Dixon Mill Lane, which led from the long established Keighley/ Leeds road to the Mill, having served as an access to the earlier and much smaller Dixon Mill on the same riverside site (the lane in time would be improved and named Victoria Road, see site plan).

Having established the site of the Mill, what of Salt's vision for his workers and their families? It was Salt's aspiration, as he declared at the opening of the Mill, to establish a community "that would enjoy the beauties of the neighbourhood, and who would be a well fed, contented, and happy body of operatives.....nothing should be spared to render the dwellings of the operatives a pattern to the country" (see p100). By this time Salt had been fully exposed to the horrors of unplanned urban development brought about by the Industrial Revolution. He knew all too well the dire consequences of bad housing, poor sanitation, and inadequate social and welfare provision. He had, as Mayor of Bradford, agonized over the associated moral failings of society, and faced the cholera outbreak of 1848. The issue facing Salt and his young firm of architects[450] was how to design and build a practical and successful model industrial village for several thousand workers and their families. This was to be an exercise in social engineering that was unprecedented in its scale.

Saltaire was not the first model industrial village. A full 51 years before Salt had acquired the land for his venture, Robert Owen, on 1st January, 1800, had taken over the New Lanark Mill of his father-in-law David Dale. Here Owen was to start his revolutionary social developments in the early decades of the 19th century.[451] In those early decades, many

---

[450] In 1850, the architectural partners were surprisingly young. Lockwood was still in his thirties, and Mawson in his very early twenties.
[451] Ref: Owen.

thousands of visitors made the journey to New Lanark to learn of Owen's successes. At the instigation of its civic leaders, a delegation from Leeds (led by Edward Baines) visited New Lanark in 1819 and reported their findings, making recommendations on what work should be initiated in Leeds. Our inspection of the available New Lanark Visitors' Books[452] for the period reveal that, in the 13 years that followed, more than 50 visitors from that city also visited the Owenite community, anxious to learn its lessons. Furthermore, visitors from several other West Riding locations, including Bradford, are recorded. In the case of Bradford, the numbers are less - the town developed later than its near neighbour Leeds - but the few names recorded are familiar ones. Most notable is the visit by a Mr. and Mrs. Milligan, of Bradford, on 21st August, 1824. We cannot be sure at this stage that this was Robert Milligan and his wife, but it seems likely. Robert Milligan was not only a close associate and friend of Salt; the two were at the very forefront of civic activity in Bradford. (Unfortunately the most likely period during which Titus Salt himself might have visited New Lanark (between 1830 and 1850) is not a period included in the archive of Visitors' Books).

What is evident is that the planners of Saltaire in 1850 were well-informed by the experiences of other model industrial developments of the time. Nor were they alone in their plans. Others, notably Akroyd at Copley (8 mile SW of Saltaire), were in the process, in the late 1840s, of developing well-planned housing for their workers. None, however, were on the scale of the development being contemplated by Salt. If all the 3,000-4,000 workers, together with their families, were to be accommodated in the development, a grand, long-term strategy of development was required. Such total accommodation was never realized, but the building of over 820 dwellings and other premises, built over a period of approximately 20 years, was achieved.

The layout that architects Lockwood and Mawson settled on was a

---

[452] New Lanark Visitors Books are held in the Glasgow University Archives & Business Records Centre, Glasgow. The only period of the 19th century which is available is 1821 – 1832 (covered by two Visitors Books).

rigid grid of streets and housing, aligned with Dixon Mill Lane. The strict grid format can be seen on the site plans. The only interruption to the regularity of the rectangular layout is the pre-existing road (now named Saltaire Road) running through the southern part of the site.

With the Mill in production in September, 1853, no time was lost with the next development. The following month, tenders were let for the building of the first houses. By October 1854, 163 houses and boarding houses had been completed, 14 shops were ready for occupation and 1,000 people were in residence. The census of 1861 records that there were 447 occupied houses and a population of 2,510. In 1871, by which time the housing development had been completed, the figures had increased to 824 and 4,300 respectively, being served by 40 shops.

The bulk of the housing development can be seen to lie on the west side of Victoria Road. The broad sequence of development was such that the first houses to be built were at the northern end of the site, close to the Mill, thence southwards. The sequence of building can most readily be followed by reference to the street naming that Salt adopted, some words on which are merited. As can be seen from the enlarged site map, the majority of the street names are in homage to either members of the royal family or Salt's own family.

The main thoroughfare was named Victoria Street, before being renamed to the more dignified Victoria Road, after the Queen. A small group of houses in the Office and Stable Block are similarly named Victoria Terrace. The roads bounding the northern and western sides of the main development are named after Prince Albert. Following the completion of the 45 almshouses in the south of the site in 1868, the remaining member of the royal family seen to be honoured is HRH Princess Alexandra, who had married HRH Prince of Wales (later King Edward VII) in 1863.

Salt's wife Caroline is recognized by the naming of the long street running W-E. Their 11 children each have a street named after them. There is an order to these street names which follows that of the children's births, with one exception. Starting with the eldest child William

Henry, one can follow the naming through to the youngest child, Ada. The logical sequence is disrupted by the occurrence, in that street sequence, of Fanny Street before Herbert Street. It can also be noted that Titus Street has a different alignment to the other streets named after the children. The buildings in these streets were completed by 1857, although developments in Caroline Street and Titus Street, which extend across Victoria Road, continued until 1868. There are streets named after the four grandchildren who had been born before the end of the development of the village – Shirley, Constance, Gordon and Harold. There are also streets apparently named after the three daughters-in-law that existed at the time, although with some ambiguity in naming – the second names of Emma Dove and Mary Jane are used, as well as an alternative spelling of "Catherine."

It has been suggested that Myrtle, Daisy and Fern (names given to short streets completed in 1868) were the names of Lady Salt's personal maids,[453] but the idea is fanciful. We believe they are simply the names of flowers popular in the Victorian age. (We know of no evidence that any domestic staff of the Salts had such names, and the chances of three personal maids being named after flowers are remote). The naming of Lower and Upper School Street is unremarkable. Lockwood and Mawson Streets were named late in the development (around 1868) by which time the two architects had worked successfully for Salt for no less than 15 years and were no doubt judged worthy of the honour. Finally it can be noted that Exhibition Road was a later development, being named at the time of the event of 1887.

Like all the buildings in Saltaire, the houses are constructed of local stone, the great majority being two-storeyed. The enlarged site plan reveals variations in the sizes of the housing stock. The houses of Amelia, Edward, Fanny, Herbert, Whitlam, Mary, Helen and Ada Streets are similar in character – workmen's cottages consisting of living room, small kitchen, two bedrooms and a cellarette. William Henry Street and George Street have slightly bigger houses, intended for overlookers and

---

[453] Ref: SHR, p20.

their families. Each of these houses has a scullery, kitchen, sitting room, cellar, a third bedroom and a garden to the front of the houses. Properties facing onto Albert Terrace were originally lodging houses. The later part of the development, south of Titus Street, consists of "improved workmen's" cottages having a living room, kitchen and three bedrooms. The grandest properties are the 42 "executive/ improved overlooker" houses in Albert Road.

Many of the shops were (and remain) located along the northern part of Victoria Road. Forty-five almshouses were built for the sick and aged poor, around the three sides of Alexandra Square and across the road on the east side of Victoria Road. More detailed accounts of the housing stock are available.[454]

The quality of the housing stock was unusually good. Gas was supplied directly from the Mill (as was water in the early years, before being switched to the public supply). Each house had its own lavatory in the yard at the back of the house, with each pair of houses sharing an ash pit for the disposal of coal ashes (not all of these outbuildings have survived, but in the majority of cases they have, as shown on the enlarged site plan). All the properties were "through" houses – houses were not built "back to back," which was an unpleasant feature of much 19th century Bradford housing. Although the housing density was high and devoid of any relief in terms of landscaping along its terraces, the straightness of the streets ensured that pedestrians would always be aware of the scenic setting of the village, with the hills rising to both north and south, and open views along the Aire valley to the east and west. In addition, there were three allotment gardens, as shown on the site plan.

Public buildings were concentrated down the length of Victoria Road, their grand architecture giving a memorably attractive tone to the village, still to the present day. Outdoor recreational facilities were among the last to be provided, in the form of the well-landscaped Saltaire Park lying on the north side of the River Aire. (Victoria Road continued north across the river, providing access to the park and beyond, until its demolition in

---

[454] E.g. Ref: GtPat, pp266-273.

the 1950s, when a modern footbridge was provided.

The magnificently appointed public buildings - the Congregational Church, the Saltaire Club and Institute, the schools, the (now demolished) Sunday Schools - are well described by Balgarnie (pp109-115, pp175-179).

The architecture of Saltaire was not the only remarkable feature of the development. The enormous size of the Mill, with its 1,200 looms producing daily 18 miles of worsted cloth, was a wonder of the age. William Fairbairn, the civil engineer appointed to design and install the engineering facilities, had many skills that made him an ideal choice for the job. In addition to his Manchester iron-works producing the boilers for the steam engines that were to drive the machinery, Fairbairn was in the forefront of warehouse design. In 1844, he had produced a report on the fireproofing measures for warehousing, following serious fires in Liverpool, Manchester and other large towns. His report identified five criteria for safe design, all of which can be seen in the present day in the Mill in a walk through its interior rooms: the use of non-combustible materials such as iron, stone and brick in the construction of the building (no timber being used as structural components); every opening to the external atmosphere to be closable to prevent spread of fire; an isolated stone or iron staircase to be attached to every storey of the building; division of warehousing by the use of strong masonry partition walls; and all iron columns, beams and brick arches to be of sufficient strength to withstand not only continuous dynamic loading from machinery but additionally to resist extra impact from the falling of heavy goods.[455]

The motive power in the Mill came from the two condensing steam engines situated within the footprint of the Mill, at each side of the main entrance on the south side of the mill (the entrance can be identified on the site plan, between the West Mill and the East Mill). The steam was generated in 10 boilers positioned below ground level and some yards south of the Mill, between the engine houses and the railway line. The smoke from the coal-fired boilers was taken underground through pipes

---

[455] Ref: Fair, pp137-186.

to the base of the chimney, the design being such as to minimize pollution output.

Fairbairn's success in the structural and mechanical engineering of the works, together with the fireproofing of the Mill, was one of many in an illustrious career. A gifted intellectual as well as a practical designer, Fairbairn, like Salt, received a baronetcy in 1869. He died, aged 85, in 1874, and was buried in Manchester, where he had long lived.

Quite apart from the handsome overall design of the village, several of the buildings in Saltaire are, individually, outstanding pieces of architecture, and some words are appropriate about the lives and careers of Lockwood and Mawson. Henry Francis Lockwood, the elder of the two partners, was born in Doncaster in 1811. Having been articled to Peter Robinson in London, Lockwood, at the age of only 21, had superintended the rebuilding of York castle before starting in practice in Hull in 1834. He moved to Bradford in 1849, where he went into partnership with the young William Mawson (1828-1889). The latter had been born in Leeds, the son of William Mawson, a paper manufacturer. He too moved to Bradford around the time that the partnership was established, and for much of the next 25 years the two were to dominate Bradford's architectural scene. Quite apart from the design and building of Saltaire, the pair were responsible for the design and building of a great many of the town's outstanding landmarks: St. George's Hall (opened just three weeks before the Mill, on 30th August, 1853), St. Lukes Hospital (1852); Lumb Lane Mills (1861); the Eye and Ear Hospital (1861); Horton Lane Congregational Chapel (1863); the Wool Exchange (1867); Great Northern (Victoria) Hotel (1867); three separate developments in the Little Germany area of the town; the Town Hall (1873) and Kirkgate Market (1878). Beyond Bradford, they were closely involved in the building of Congregational churches in Harrogate, Lightcliffe and Scarborough. London designs included the Law Courts in the Strand (1867), the City Temple, on Holborn Viaduct (1873) and the Civil Service Stores, also in the Strand (1876). Lockwood was elected first president of the Bradford Society of Architects and Surveyors in

1874; that same year, he moved to London, setting up home at Heron's Court, Richmond, close by Richmond Bridge. He died on 21st July, 1878, and was buried in Kensal Green Cemetery, London. With that event, the firm was renamed as W. and R. Mawson, with Richard Mawson (1834-1904) as the second partner. William Mawson died, aged 61, on 25th April, 1889, and was buried in Undercliffe Cemetery. His imposing grave stands along the Cemetery's main terrace, a little distance from those of several of Bradford's civic leaders, with whom he and Lockwood had been so closely involved.

Salt, with his remarkable vision, and Lockwood and Mawson in their practical realization of that vision, created a truly exceptional development at Saltaire, made all the more remarkable by its extreme contrast with the prevailing squalor of the day in nearby Bradford. Recognition of their achievements came in December, 2001 when UNESCO inscribed Saltaire as a World Heritage Site. Its citation provides a fitting conclusion to this Appendix:

"Saltaire is an outstanding and well preserved example of a mid 19th century industrial town, the layout of which was to exert a major influence on the development of the 'garden city' movement.

The layout and architecture of Saltaire admirably reflect mid 19th century philanthropic paternalism, as well as the important role played by the textile industry in economic and social development".

THE MILL

APPENDIX 8

ILLUSTRATIONS

QUID · NON · DEO · JUVANTE

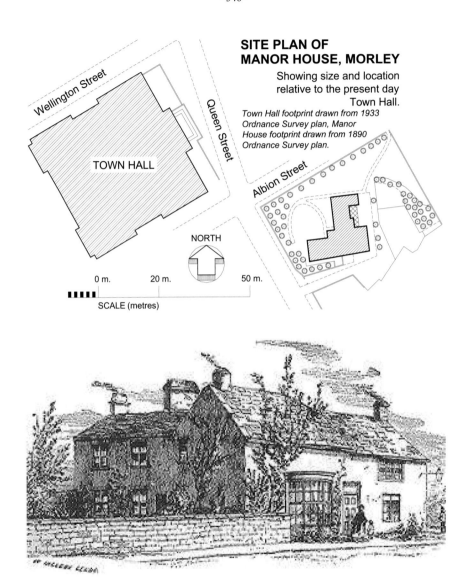

SITE PLAN OF MANOR HOUSE, MORLEY
Showing size and location relative to the present day Town Hall.
Town Hall footprint drawn from 1933 Ordnance Survey plan, Manor House footprint drawn from 1890 Ordnance Survey plan.

Wellington Street

Queen Street

TOWN HALL

Albion Street

NORTH

0 m. 20 m. 50 m.

SCALE (metres)

SOUTH VIEW OF MANOR HOUSE, MORLEY

Taken from ref: MAM, p205

**TITUS SALT'S RESIDENCE,
LITTLE HORTON LANE, BRADFORD**
(See p288)

METHLEY HALL, NEAR LEEDS

LADY CAROLINE SALT

SIR TITUS SALT, BART.

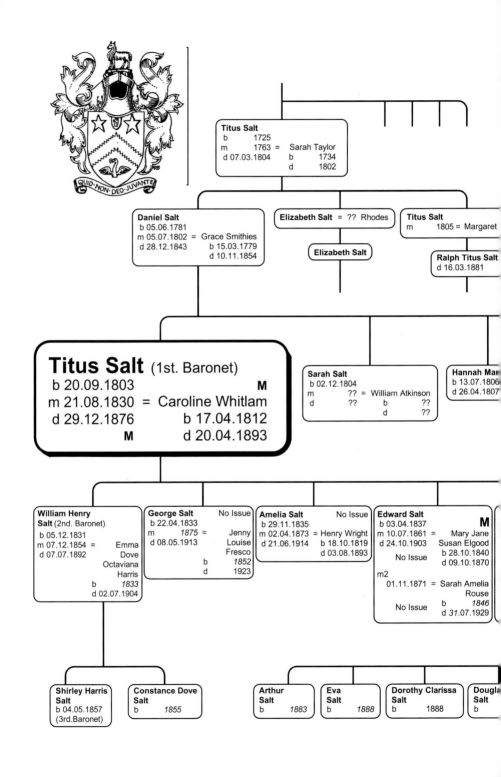

Titus Salt
b 1725
m 1763 = Sarah Taylor
d 07.03.1804 b 1734
d 1802

Daniel Salt
b 05.06.1781
m 05.07.1802 = Grace Smithies
d 28.12.1843 b 15.03.1779
d 10.11.1854

Elizabeth Salt = ?? Rhodes

Elizabeth Salt

Titus Salt
m 1805 = Margaret

Ralph Titus Salt
d 16.03.1881

Titus Salt (1st. Baronet)
b 20.09.1803 **M**
m 21.08.1830 = Caroline Whitlam
d 29.12.1876 b 17.04.1812
M d 20.04.1893

Sarah Salt
b 02.12.1804
m ?? = William Atkinson
d ?? b ??
d ??

Hannah Mar
b 13.07.1806
d 26.04.1807

William Henry Salt (2nd. Baronet)
b 05.12.1831
m 07.12.1854 = Emma Dove Octaviana Harris
d 07.07.1892 b 1833
d 02.07.1904

George Salt No Issue
b 22.04.1833
m 1875 = Jenny Louise Fresco
d 08.05.1913 b 1852
d 1923

Amelia Salt No Issue
b 29.11.1835
m 02.04.1873 = Henry Wright
d 21.06.1914 b 18.10.1819
d 03.08.1893

Edward Salt **M**
b 03.04.1837
m 10.07.1861 = Mary Jane Susan Elgood
d 24.10.1903 b 28.10.1840
No Issue d 09.10.1870
m2
01.11.1871 = Sarah Amelia Rouse
No Issue b 1846
d 31.07.1929

Shirley Harris Salt
b 04.05.1857
(3rd.Baronet)

Constance Dove Salt
b 1855

Arthur Salt
b 1883

Eva Salt
b 1888

Dorothy Clarissa Salt
b 1888

Dougla Salt
b

QUID·NON·DEO·JUVANTE

SALT FAMILY TREE

Compiled from a collection of available sources, including Registry
certificates, Probate Registry documents, burial and cremation records,
gravestones, censuses, newspaper reports and other publications.

Where judged appropiate, information has been taken,
if available, from official Registry certificates.
(A full availability is lacking, notably for the earlier events entered on the Tree).

Where confidence is lacking in the precision of a date, this is indicated by the
use of italics. Where information is lacking, this is indicated by '??'.

M = Interred in the
Mausoleum
at Saltaire.

*Entries in the Family Tree
have been terminated following
the births of Sir Titus Salt's
grandchildren.*

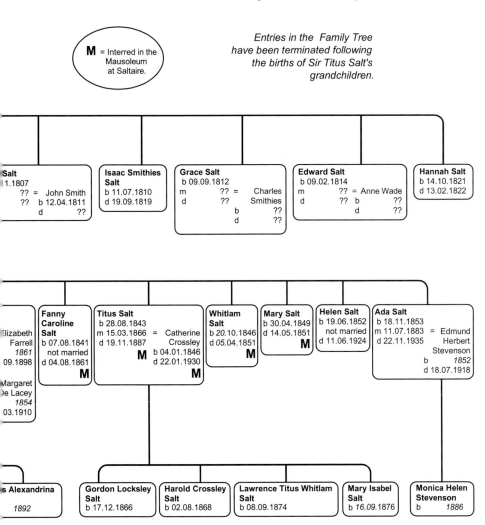

Salt
1.1807
?? = John Smith
?? b 12.04.1811
d ??

Isaac Smithies Salt
b 11.07.1810
d 19.09.1819

Grace Salt
b 09.09.1812
m ?? = Charles
d ?? Smithies
b ??
d ??

Edward Salt
b 09.02.1814
m ?? = Anne Wade
d ?? b ??
d ??

Hannah Salt
b 14.10.1821
d 13.02.1822

Elizabeth Farrell
b 07.08.1841
1861
09.1898
Margaret De Lacey
1854
03.1910

Fanny Caroline Salt
b 07.08.1841
not married
d 04.08.1861
M

Titus Salt
b 28.08.1843
m 15.03.1866 = Catherine Crossley
d 19.11.1887 b 04.01.1846
M d 22.01.1930
M

Whitlam Salt
b 20.10.1846
d 05.04.1851
M

Mary Salt
b 30.04.1849
d 14.05.1851
M

Helen Salt
b 19.06.1852
not married
d 11.06.1924

Ada Salt
b 18.11.1853
m 11.07.1883 = Edmund Herbert Stevenson
d 22.11.1935 b 1852
d 18.07.1918

s Alexandrina
1892

Gordon Locksley Salt
b 17.12.1866

Harold Crossley Salt
b 02.08.1868

Lawrence Titus Whitlam Salt
b 08.09.1874

Mary Isabel Salt
b 16.09.1876

Monica Helen Stevenson
b 1886

**ROBERT MILLIGAN,
FIRST MAYOR OF BRADFORD**

**WILLIAM RAND,
FOURTH MAYOR OF BRADFORD**

ARCHITECTS OF SALTAIRE

HENRY FRANCIS LOCKWOOD
courtesy Bradford Society of Architects and Surveyors

WILLIAM MAWSON

BROADOAK, DOWAGER LADY SALT'S CLAPHAM RESIDENCE

MOUNT PLEASANT CONGREGATIONAL CHURCH, TUNBRIDGE WELLS,
THE CHURCH ATTENDED BY THE SALT DAUGHTERS AMELIA, HELEN AND ADA

SALTAIRE CONGREGATIONAL CHURCH

LIST OF ABBREVIATIONS

AgeR   L. Woodward, *The Age of Reform*, 2nd Edition, The Oxford History of England, Clarendon Press, Oxford, 1962.

AHofL   J. Mayhall, *Annals and History of Leeds and other Places in the County of York,* Joseph Johnson, Rotation Office Yard, Kirkgate, Leeds, 1860. (The contents of this publication are identical to those of AofY1).

AofM   W. E. A. Axon, *Annals of Manchester*, John Heywood, Manchester, 1886.

AofY1   J. Mayhall, *Annals of Yorkshire. Vol.1. BC1021 to AD1859,* London: Simpkin, Marshall and Co., Leeds; C H Johnson, ND.

AofY2   J. Mayhall, *Annals of Yorkshire. Vol.2. 1860 to 1865,* London: Simpkin, Marshall and Co., Leeds;C H Johnson, ND.

AofY3   J. Mayhall, *Annals of Yorkshire. Vol.3. 1866 to 1874,* London: Simpkin, Marshall and Co., Leeds; C H Johnson, ND.

Bain   Baines, *Directory of Bradford*, 1822.

BALG   R. Balgarnie, *Sir Titus Salt, Baronet, His Life and its Lessons,* London, 1877.

Balg1   R. Balagarnie, *Some Worthies Whom I Have Known as Visitors to Scarborough*, Part III. ND.

BarCM   R. Balgarnie, *Bar Church Manual*, Scarborough, 1866.

Bath   Keene's *Bath Journal* No. 8311, 31st October, 1903.

BDA   *Bradford Daily Argus.*

BfdDT   *Bradford Daily Telegraph.*

BfdE1   *List of Bradford Borough Elections*, Squire Auty and Son, 1892.

BfdMp   *Bradford Local History Library Map Catalogue*, Bradford Central Library.

BfdOb   *Bradford Local History Library Obituary Catalogue*, Bradford Central Library.

BfdTA   *Bradford Telegraph and Argus.*

BfdTM   *Annual Reports of the Bradford Town Mission*, 1850–1875.

BfdWT   *Bradford Weekly Telegraph.*

BLDR   *The Builder.*

BO   *Bradford Observer.*

Bret1   R. Bretton, *Colonel Edward Akroyd,* Transactions of the Halifax Antiquarian Society,1948, pp61-100.

Bret2   R. Bretton, *Sir Titus Salt,* Transactions of the Halifax Antiquarian Society,1970, pp29-48.

Bret3   R. Bretton, *Crossleys of Dean Clough, Parts I - VI*, Transactions of the Halifax Antiquarian Society,1950–54.

Char   D. G. Wright, *The Chartist Risings in Bradford*, Bradford Libraries and Information Service, 1987.

ClapO   *Clapham Observer.*

Clap1   J. H. M. Burgess, *The Chronicles of Clapham*, Ramsden Press, London, 1929.

Clap2   A. Wilson (Editor), *The Buildings of Clapham*, Clapham Society, 2000.

Coach   T. Bradley, *Old Coaching Days in Yorkshire*, first published 1889; republished by S. R. Publishers Ltd., 1968.

ConCH   G. S. Barrett (editor) *Congregational Church Hymnal*, Congregational Union of England and Wales, Memorial Hall, Farringdon St, London, 1898.

ConPr   A. Goodrich, *A Primer of Congregationalism*, Congregational Union of England and Wales, Memorial Hall, Farringdon St, London, 1894.

ConYB   *Congregational Year Book.*

ConYk   J.G.Miall, *Congregationalism in Yorkshire*, John Snow and Co., London, 1868.

Cred   A. G. Credland, *Artists and Craftsmen of Hull and East Yorkshire,* Hull Museums and Art Gallery, 2000.

Cud1   W. Cudworth, *Round About Bradford*, Reprinted by Mountain Press, Queensbury, 1968.

Cud3   W. Cudworth, *Historical Notes on the Bradford Corporation*, Bradford, 1881.

Cud4   W. Cudworth, *Manningham, Heaton and Allerton,* Bradford, 1896.

Cud5   W. Cudworth, *Horton Lane Chapel, Old-time Reminiscences, a series of Articles in The Horton Lane Congregational Magazine,* 1893.

DalkA   *Dalkeith Advertiser.*

DicBR   *Chambers Dictionary of Beliefs and Religions,* Edinburgh, 1992.

DicEd   D. Rowntree, *A Dictionary of Education,* London, Harper and Row, 1981.

Dick   C. Dickens, *Household Words,* Vol. 6, No. 140, Sat 27th Nov, 1852.

DicLB   J. W. Cousin and D.C. Browning, *Everyman's Dictionary of Literary Biography English and American,* J. M. Dent and Sons Ltd., London, 1962.

DirRS   R. V. J. Butt, *The Directory of Railway Stations,* Patrick Stephens Ltd., 1995.

Dir56   *Lunds' Bradford Directory,* Bradford, 1856.

DNB   *Dictionary of National Biography.*

EPub   M. Jackson, *The English Pub,* Harper and Row, New York, 1976.

E19c   D. Thomson, *England in the Nineteenth Century (1815–1914),* Pelican, 1950.

Fair   W. Fairbairn, *On the Application of Cast and Wrought Iron to Building Purposes,* Longman et al, London, 1864.

FavHC *Favourite Hymns of the Church,* Eye Opener Publications, 1995.

Firth   G. Firth, *Salt & Saltaire,* Tempus Publishing Ltd., Stroud, Gloucestershire, 2001.

Forst   T. Wemyss Reid, *Life of the Rt. Hon. W. E. Forster,* Chapman and Hall Ltd, London 1888. Republished by Augustus M. Kelly, New York 1970.

GtPat   J. Reynolds, *The Great Paternalist,* Maurice Temple Smith, London, 1983.

GU   *Guardian Unlimited.*

Guinn   J. Guinness Rogers, *An Autobiography*, James Clarke and Co., 1903.

HalC   *Halifax Courier.*

HalG   *Halifax Guardian.*

Hall   M. Hall, *Leeds Statues Trail*, Walkabout Series, ND.

Hans   *Hansards Parliamentary Debates*

HarrH   *Harrogate Herald.*

HCon   A. Peel, *These Hundred Years: A History of the Congregational Union of England and Wales 1831–1931,* Congregational Union of England and Wales, Memorial Hall, EC4, London 1931.

HHarr   H. H. Walker, *History of Harrogate under the Improvement Commissioners 1841-1884*, Manor Place Press, Harrogate, 1986.

HisCH   W. Haythornthwaite, *A History of the Congregational Church in Harrogate*, 1962.

HisSc   A. Rowntree, *History of Scarborough*, J. M. Dent and Son, London, 1931.

Hol1   A.Holroyd, *Saltaire and its Founder,* Saltaire, 1873, 3rd edition. A facsimile based on the book was published in June 2000 by Piroisms Press in collaboration with Falcon Books.

Hopp   A. Hopper, *The Farnley Wood Plot and the Memory of the Civil Wars in Yorkshire*. The Historical Journal, 45, 2 (2002), pp28–303.

HtoT   J. Parker, *Illustrated History from Hipperholme to Tong*, Bradford, 1904.

HullT   *Hull and North Lincolnshire Times.*

HYCon   F. Wrigley, *The History of the Yorkshire Congregational Union. A Story of Fifty Years 1873–1923,* James Clark & Co Ltd, London, 1931.

Ibbet   Ibbetson, *Directory of the Borough of Bradford*, 1845.

ILGS   G. Dickins, *An Illustrated Literary Guide to Shropshire*, Shropshire Libraries, 1987.

IslnS   *Islington Standard.*

Jam1   J. James, *The History and Topography of Bradford*, 1841. Reprinted by Mountain Press Queensbury, 1967.

KenN   *Kensington News.*

KentC   *Kent and Sussex Courier.*

LADLP   J. Duloum, *Les Anglais dans Les Pyrénées et Les Debuts du Tourisme Pyrénéen,* Les Amis du Musée Pyrénéen, 1970.

LHWR   E. Waterson and P. Meadows, *Lost Houses of the West Riding*, Jill Raines, York, 1998.

LongW   C. Mitchell, *The Long Watch, a History of the Sailors' Children Society* 1821-1961, Sailors' Children Society, 1961.

MAM   W. Smith, *Morley Ancient and Modern,* London: Longmans, Green and Co., 1886.

MaMis   *Mechanization and Misery*, with Introduction by J. A. Jowitt, Ryburn Publishing, 1991.

Map1   Milnes and France, *Index map of a portion of the Town of Bradford, 1876, Bradford in the Nineteenth Century Shown in Maps*, City of Bradford Metropolitan Council - Libraries Division, Local Studies Dept, 1975.

Map2   J. Hart, *Block Plan of the Town of Bradford, 1861, Bradford in the Nineteenth Century Shown in Maps*, City of Bradford Metropolitan Council - Libraries Division, Local Studies Dept,1975.

Map3   J. Rapkin, *(Map of) Bradford, c1854, Bradford in the Nineteenth Century Shown in Maps*, City of Bradford Metropolitan Council - Libraries Division, Local Studies Dept, 1975.

MemH   *List of Subscribers to the Congregational Memorial Hall Building Fund; and the Minute Books of the Memorial Hall, Farringdon Street,* Dr Williams's Library, London.

ModEn   R.K. Webb, *Modern England from the 18th Century to the Present,* 2nd edition, London, George, Allen and Unwin, 1981.

MPCC   C. H. Strange, *Mount Pleasant Congregational Church, A Sketch of its History, 1830-1930*, A. J. Pelton, Tunbridge Wells, ND.

NCTW   C. H. Strange, *Nonconformity in Tunbridge Wells*, 1949.

NEB   *New Encyclopaedia Britannica.*

OED   *Oxford English Dictionary.*

Owen   I. Donnachie, *Robert Owen*, Tuckwell Press, Scotland, 2000.

Park   *Register of Parks and Gardens of Special Historic Interest*, Lister Park entry held by Bradford Council, December 1998, amended March 1999.

ParkS   *Park Street Centre, A Brief History of the Park Street Centre of Hull College,* Local History Unit, Hull College, Hull.

Part   *Articles of Partnership for Titus Salt, Sons and Company*, 1859 and 1873, West Yorkshire Archives, Bradford.

Peel   A. Peel, *One Hundred Eminent Congregationalists*, Independent Press Ltd., Memorial Hall, London, 1927.

PeelP   *1987 Guide to Peel Park.*

PEVSN N. Pevsner, *The Buildings of England – Yorkshire, West Riding*, Penguin Books, 1974.

Pig1   *Pigot's Commercial Directory,* Sowerby Bridge, Sowerby, Barkisland, Elland with Greetland, Ripponden, Stainland, Kings Cross and Neighbourhoods, 1834.

Pig2   *Pigot's Directory of Professions and Trades*, Scarborough, 1834.

Polc   G. Smith, *Bradford's Police*, Circa 1973.

PRO   *Public Record Office.*

RAH   R. W. Clark, *The Royal Albert Hall*, Hamish Hamilton, 1958.

Rail   H. Ellis, *The Pictorial Encyclopedia of Railways*, Hamlyn Publishing Group Ltd., London, 1968.

Rob1   A. H. Robinson, *Bradford's Public Statues*, Bradford Art Galleries and Museums, ND.

Rob2   A. H. Robinson, *Did Someone Twist the Lions Tale - A Saltaire Speculation*, Yorkshire Life, Vol. 22 No. 7, July, 1968.

Rob3   A. H. Robinson, *Horton Lane Chapel: "Pious Warehouse" or "Nonconformist Cathedral"?*, Bradford & Calderdale Chamber of Commerce Journal, February–March, 1980.

Rob4   A. H. Robinson, *William Rand,* Bradford & Halifax Chamber of Commerce Journal, Vol 2, No. 3, July–September, 1975.

ScarE *Scarborough Evening News.*

ScarF *Some Scarborough Faces (Past & Present),* published in book form by *Scarborough Gazette,* 1901.

ScarG *Scarborough Gazette.*

ScarM *Scarborough Mercury.*

ScarP *Scarborough Post.*

SciM *History of Collections,* Science Museum, London.

Scr1 W. Scrutton, *The Great Strike of 1825,* Journal of the Bradford Historical and Antiquarian Society, Vol. 1, p67, November, 1880.

Scr2 W. Scrutton, *The History of the Bradford Riot,* Journal of the Bradford Historical and Antiquarian Society, Vol. 1, p131, December, 1881.

ShCam M. Crabtree, *Shipley and District Through the Camera,* Hanson and Oak, Leeds, 1902.

SHR C. Woods, *Saltaire History and Regeneration,* 2000.

ShST *Shipley and Saltaire Times.*

SLP *South London Press.*

SMCH *Souvenir Centenary Handbook, 1868 – 1968,* Saltaire Methodist Church.

SofB M. C. D. Law, *The Story of Bradford,* Sir Isaac Pitman and Sons Ltd, Bath, 1917.

Spei1 H. Speight, *Upper Wharfedale,* London, 1900.

Trail *Saltaire Trail,* Bradford Metropolitan District Council, 3rd edition, 2002.

Trl2 J. Reynolds, *Saltaire City Trail No. 2,* Bradford Art Galleries and Museums, ND.

VicBd *Victorian Bradford,* edited by D.G.Wright and J.A.Jowitt, City of Bradford Metropolitan Council, 1981.

Ward J. T. Ward, *A Great Bradford Dispute,* Journal of the Bradford Textile Society, 1961–1962, pp117-131.

WkWak W. S. Banks, *Walks about Wakefield,* 1871. Republished by Wakefield Historical Publications, 1983.

WMofS Bill Hampshire, *Water Mills of Shipley*, Shipley Local History
Society, 2000.

WofSD *Works of Sewage Disposal*, City of Bradford, 3rd edition, 1931.

WorW *Woollen or Worsted? An Introduction to Wool Processing,*
Bradford Art Galleries and Museums, 1983.

YDO *Yorkshire Daily Observer.*

YO *Yorkshire Observer.*

YPBnk E. Ackroyd, M.P., *The Yorkshire Penny Bank. A Narrative,*
Longmans, Green and Co., London, 1872.

INDEX

ADAMS-ACTON, Mr. John,
sculptor, 184, 215.
AIREDALE COLLEGE, 227.
AKROYD, James & Son, Ltd.,
118,129.
ALDERSON, Christopher, Rev., 5.
ALPACA, 168,
environment, 51-52.
ALPACA WOOL, 50-57, 119.
AMERICA, 78, 265.
AMERICAN CIVIL WAR, effects on
cotton, 51.
ANGORA, 119.
ANGORA GOAT, 119, 123.
BAINES, Edward, M.P. for Leeds,
146, 337.
BALGARNIE, Robert., Rev.,
Correspond. with Salt, 149,
Salt funeral address, 246,
Biography, App. 1.
BANKS, George, candidate,
Bradford Election 1832, 67.
BAPTISTS, in Saltaire, 112.
BATLEY, 6, 189, Church, 10,
School, 14.
BELL BUSK, Herbert Salt, farming,
293,299.
BELL BUSK, Workers' outing, 78.
'BIBLE WOMEN', 204-205.
BINNEY, Thomas, Rev.,
191-193, 203.
BLAIZE, Bishop, Septennial
Festival of, 41-42.
BOLTON HOUSE ESTATE, 85.
BRADFORD,
Origin of word, 28.
BRADFORD,
British Assn. for Prom. of Social
Science congress 138.
Chamber of Commerce, 89.
Chartist Movement, 74.
Cholera,77.

Choral Society, 77.
Congregational Union assembly,
138-139, at Salt funeral, 237.
Exchange Buildings, 31, 74-76.
Grammar School, 206, history
and development of, 28-29.
Infirmary, 186.
Lister Park, 86.
Manor Row, 288.
Mayor, 69.
Parliament: candidates,
(1859) 131.
Peel Park, 85-86, 219.
Political history, 69-79.
Population, 29, 56, 76, 88, 257,
262.
Reform Bill, 66, 131, 132.
St. Georges Hall, 76, 98, 102,
124, 130.
Salt, elected M.P., 137.
Salt, work in Bfd., 25-35.
'Salt Statue', 212-220.
Town Hall, 215, 235, 237.
Town Mission, 204, 208.
Tradesmen's Homes, App. 5.
Unemployment, 74-76.
'BRADFORD OBSERVER',
comments on Salt's Mayoralty,
79.
Editor, *see* BYLES, William
BRICK LANE MILL, bought by
Salt, 46.
BROWN, Henry, App. 4.
BROWN ROYD, 187.
BYLES, William, 68, 69, 89, App. 4.
CAMPBELL, Rev., Dr., Salt funeral
address, 239-241.
CASTLEFORD, Congregational
Church, 154.
CAVENDISH, Lord Frederick,
(M.P.), and unveiling of Salt
Statue, 219.

SALT, Fanny, daughter, 59, ill-
health and death, 150-152, App.
3.
SALT, George, son, 59, 176, 222,
App. 3.
SALT, Gordon, son of Titus Jr.,
221.
SALT, Grace, mother of Salt,
6, 57, and Salem Chapel, 58,
ill-health, 13, dies, 58.
SALT, Hannah, sister of Salt,
13.
SALT, Harold Crossley, son of
Titus, Jr., 221, 222.
SALT, Helen, daughter, 83, App. 3.
SALT, Herbert, son, 59, App. 3.
SALT, Isaac Smithies, brother of
Salt, 13.
SALT, Mary, daughter, 83, App. 3.
SALT, Sarah, nee Taylor, grand-
mother of Salt, 6.
SALT, Sarah, Salt's sister, 13,
21.
SALT, Titus, uncle of Salt, 6.
SALT, Titus, Sir,
born, 7,
baptized, 10,
married, 47,
death, 233.
funeral, 236-247.
Alderman, 70,
Baronetcy, 188-189,
Deputy-lieutenant, 70,
Head Constable, 68,
Legion of Honour, 168-174,
Magistrate, 70,
Mayor of Bradford, 71,
Member of Parliament, 132-137,
Sunday School teacher, 32,
will, Apps. 3, 5.
SALT, Titus, (Jr.) son, 176,
222, and opening of Institute,
176-177, App. 3.
SALT, Whitlam, son, 83, App. 3.
SALT, William Henry, son, 59, 97,
App. 3.
SALT SCHOLARSHIPS, 178.

SALT SCHOOLS, 178.
SALT STATUE, 212-220.
SALTAIRE, Burmese visit, 199,
Japanese visit, 199.
SALTAIRE, Origin of name, 93.
'SALTAIRE AND ITS
FOUNDER', (Holroyd, A.), 3, 197.
SALTAIRE CLUB AND INSTI-
TUTE, 174-179, 197.
SALTAIRE ESTATE, 90, 142.
'SALTAIRE LIFEBOAT', 207.
SALTAIRE MILL, 91, 92,
description, 102-105.
SALTAIRE SUNDAY SCHOOL,
32, 220.
SCARBOROUGH, 51, 147, 150,
156-157, 160-163, 185, 221,
230, 231, 248, App. 1.
SEDGWICK, J., Rev., baptized and
taught Salt, 10, 14.
SHEFFIELD, original home of
Salt family in Yorkshire, 5.
SHIPLEY, 28, 89, 91, 112, 178,
238, 239.
'SHIPLEY AND SALTAIRE
TIMES', office in Victoria Road,
106.
SIMON, Henry, Rev., Minister of
Castleford Congregational
Church, 155.
SMITH, Samuel, App. 4.
SMITHIES, Robert, Salt's uncle, 25.
SOUTH CLIFF CHURCH, Scar-
borough, 201, 326, App. 1.
SOUTH KENSINGTON
SCIENCE AND ART
DEPARTMENT, connection with
Institute, Saltaire, 176.
STAFFORDSHIRE, Salt family
origins, 5.
STANSFIELD, W.C., original owner
of site on which Saltaire Mill
stands, 90.
STEAD, Charles, member of Salt's
firm, 89, 142, 199.
STEVENSON, E. H., marries Ada
Salt, App. 3.